AF528866

Thugs and Dacoits

The Imperial Archives

FROM DISCOVERY TO THE CIVILISATIONAL MISSION: ENGLISH WRITINGS ON INDIA

Volume 6

Thugs and Dacoits

Editor

Pramod K. Nayar

B L O O M S B U R Y

NEW DELHI • LONDON • OXFORD • NEW YORK • SYDNEY

BLOOMSBURY INDIA
Bloomsbury Publishing India Pvt. Ltd
Second Floor, LSC Building No. 4, DDA Complex, Pocket C – 6 & 7,
Vasant Kunj, New Delhi, 110070

BLOOMSBURY, BLOOMSBURY ACADEMIC INDIA and the Diana logo are trademarks of Bloomsbury Publishing Plc

First published in India 2023
This edition published 2023

Bloomsbury Academic
An imprint of Bloomsbury Publishing Plc

ISBN: HB: 978-93-94701-88-5; ePDF: 978-93-94701-97-7
2 4 6 8 10 9 7 5 3 1

Printed & bound in India by Replika Press Pvt. Ltd.

CONTENTS

PREFATORY NOTE

The archival texts have been retained in their original font, style and content in order to clearly show the environment of the time when these documents were produced. It is important to show in a book such as this the views held at that time and the profound effect they had on society. We acknowledge that several of the texts are derogatory about Indians, women and communities of different religious faiths like many hundreds of other colonial-era-based works. While these are clearly unacceptable to us today, we have not attempted to change any wording or redact the texts so that the contemporary reader may experience the rhetoric, attitude and ideologies that so clearly marked the Raj. In places, where the text had been smudged and rendered impossible to read, that specific segment has been deleted.

We would like to make clear that these are not the views held by the editor or Bloomsbury India and do not reflect our mission and values which are clearly stated on our website (https://www.bloomsbury.com/in/connect/about-us/missions-and-values/)

GENERAL INTRODUCTION: ARCHIVE AND EMPIRE

That the British writings on India occupy over several miles of shelf space in the British Library, London, is an apocryphal tale, but one which *may* have substance, given that there was no aspect of the subcontinent that did not pique the curiosity of the British or generate some document or the other.

In his *The Imperial Archive: Knowledge and the Fantasy of Empire* (1993), Thomas Richards demonstrated how the documentation (the subject of considerable work, notably in Bernard Cohn and others) and archivisation not only produced knowledge about the colonies but were also instrumental in generating the fantasy of absolute control. And yet, it is never easy to read these records produced by a diverse set of English, Irish and Scottish missionaries, administrators, men of leisure, nurses, teachers, wives and/or sisters of the men who occupied official posts in the colony, soldiers, mercenaries and others—many of whom, for many reasons, had their own dynamics and tensions with the *English*.

Several approaches to the imperial record exist, and this introductory chapter sets out some of them.[1] In the process, it also flags what the archive does in terms of the imperial structure and processes.[2]

The Power of the Archive

The archive is not a mere compilation of what John Malcolm (1823) advised his officers on the right approach to the native officers, or what Thomas Williamson (1808) described as the potential for the hunt in India. The archive is not a passive reflection of imperial power—it constitutes and constructs it. As diverse commentators—such as Cohn's work on the 'survey modality' (1997) and C.A. Bayly's *Empire and Information* (1999)—have pointed out, the Empire ran on information,

[1] I use the term 'imperial archive' throughout to refer to the corpus of published material across genres, as diverse as maps, geographical accounts, census reports, travelogues, administrative reports, ecclesiastical documents.

[2] These volumes work only with the print archive of British India, although a vast archive of visual material also exists, and has been the subject of significant studies. See, for example, Guégan (2011), Chaudhury (2012), Pinney (2014), Dohman (2017) on colonial photography, and Tobin (1999), De Silva (2011), Eaton (2013), among others, on colonial/imperial art and paintings.

and information-gathering constituted not just an act of power but was a *constituent* of the power structure. It classified, organised and legislated on the subject peoples, through the census, the geographies and anthropological studies. In the process, it defined who is counted as a subject/citizen. For instance, writing about the Todas or the Gonds, and then examining the numbers of Muslim students in schools, both the educationist and the statesman were constructing model imperial citizens who would benefit, resist or accept from 'modern' education. In other words, the imperial archive on education was not merely advocating 'modern' education: it was constructing *educate-able* citizens from among their colonial subjects while abandoning the others. Thus, archivisation and informatisation were ultimately about the power wielded over the identity-making and rights of the subjects.[3]

Relatedly, the archive and the documentation also made the subjects *visible to themselves*. With 'modern' education, for instance, the Indian colonial subject in school or college came to identify themselves in particular ways. They learnt what it means to be a good citizen, to be modern, to develop and demand certain skills, etc. They recognised their location on the civilisational scale in the books they read and assimilated (*primitive* and *non-modern* as opposed to the modern European). In an argument that resonates with my claims above, Antoinette Burton and Isabel Hofmeyr write about the power of the English book:

> The embodiment of English manly authority, the book was not simply 'a surrogate Englishman in his highest and most perfect state,' it was the very emblem of imperial sovereignty—with the rigorous spine a testimony to its singularity, its probity, its titular power ... books impressed themselves in the everyday lives of imperial subjects, manifesting the formal values of an elite or bourgeois self and modeling in their material form the coherence and commanding presence of British imperial power itself. (2014: 1–2)

The colonial subjects were told, through these English books, what kind of spiritual and moral training was required for them to 'improve'.

---

[3] It must be noted that it was not only the human subjects in the colony that became objects and subjects of the imperial archive. Fauna and flora, climate, landscape and topography—indeed the natural world in its entirety—were also archived. For studies, see Edney (1997) and Damodaran et al. (2015), among others.

As A.H. Benton of the Indian Civil Service wrote in *Indian Moral Instruction and Caste Problems*:

> [The Indian] People are on the whole kindly, docile, alert, keen-spirited, high and low, one of the best-mannered peoples in the world, and they would appear to offer a very promising field for right spiritual treatment. (1917: 92)

The education archive, and especially its insistence on moral training and moral apprenticeship of the subjects as a *preliminary* to training for political citizenship, was built on the

> founding assumption … that the native readership of English texts, and the recipients of English education, were amenable to their teachings, which led them to abandon their traditional manners and disciplines. This necessitated a solid moral training to make them good citizens. (Nayar 2020: 142)

The archive also, frequently, captures the rift and fracture within the colonial subject's responses to, say, Western/English education. See, for instance, Syed Mahmood's anguish about the Indian Muslim's refusal to accept this education:

> Such feelings of aversion towards English education entertained by the Mahomedans … stand in sharp contrast to the attitude of the Hindu community…. This difference in the sentiments of the two communities towards English education, is the real key to the reasons of the vast disparity of progress of English education which the two nationalities have respectively made. The effects of this disparity have been most baneful to the interests of British India in general, and to the Mahomedan community in particular. (1895: 23)

In time, the colonial subject, convinced of the 'truth' in the power of the Englishman's word or photographic record, not only accepted the arguments about their inferiority but also welcomed the interventions in the form of the civilisational mission of the Empire. The archive had, therefore, produced the *willing* colonial subject.

In particular cases, such as Thuggee, the archive enabled the colonial structures of law enforcement and the judiciary to enact legislation and, in the process, demonise specific cultural practices. Examining the Thuggee archive, Alexander Macfie writes:

> [W]hereas Sleeman and his colleagues tended to define the activities of the thugs in terms of wickedness, murder, deceit, cowardice and criminality, the thugs themselves tended to evaluate them in terms of courage, enterprise, bravery, daring, cunning, adventure and martial

> skill … in terms usually associated by both the British and the Indians with the heroic values of war. (2008: 396)

The Archive, the Coloniser, the Colonised and Cultural Exchanges

Shifting focus, Antoinette Burton has demonstrated how the imperial archive also fed into the coloniser's psyche, imagination and political imagination. A pithy summary of how the imperial corpus fuelled, inspired and controlled the social imaginary, policies, attitudes and responses of the Britons in the nineteenth century is available in Burton's *Empire in Question*. Victorian culture, writes Burton,

> as a racialized landscape shaped by decades, if not centuries, of colonial peoples, goods, and ideas coursing through its highways and byways … as always already imperial not just implicitly but as part of a pedagogical meta-narrative about the relationship of modernity to the world-historical phenomenon of colonialism in world history…. (2011: 2–3)

Burton proposes that English 'sensibility' was shaped by Britain's imperial role and character, and its concomitant racialised hierarchies—thus makes the production and consumption of texts (and commodities) about and from the colonised peripheries central to the making of Britain itself (also see Hall 2002).

The archive also instantiates, other than the racialised power binaries (white/black, coloniser/colonised), cross-cultural *influences* and *exchanges*. Contacts across races, ethnic groups and the coloniser–colonised divide were frequent through the colonial period.

The English language took into itself words from their colonial subjects. They also sought to document the grammars of the languages of the subcontinent for their own officers and staff. As a consequence, a vibrant field of cultural exchanges opened up in the languages, with Indian pandits and English philologists and grammarians collaborating. The imperial archive in this domain shows mutual influences of English on Indian languages and vice versa (including Sanskrit [Naregal 2001]) but also the *organisation* of knowledge around the latter (Lelyveld 1993; Rao 2004; Mir 2010; Auer 2014).[4] Scholars—the famous 'Orientalists'—translated texts from, say, Sanskrit into English. Organisations and societies, such as the Asiatic Society, the

[4] A detailed annotated bibliography on these and other aspects of English colonial discourse on India can be found in Nayar 2021.

Zoological Survey of India, the Archaeological Survey of India, were spaces through which the English statesman, *memsahib* and trader encountered Indian temples, art, food practices, superstitions, systems of healing, among others.

English literary texts, as numerous commentators have shown (Leask 1993; Teltscher 1997), began to introduce Indian 'themes' and motifs, whether the *sati* or the wealth of the country's landscape. This field of literary studies was one of contestation and adaptation (Vishwanathan 1990). Be that as it may, the circulation of the English novel in nineteenth-century India catered to the Indian audience attuned to the melodramatic and informed their own creative work (Joshi 2003). Other commentators like Harish Trivedi (1993) have noted how English literature was received in India and the transactional nature of this reception.

Local experts, *writers* and translators were an integral component of the East India Company and the British government. Even account and trade books were produced through a collaborative project (Ogborn 2007). In other domains, such as translations, Indian scholars like Kasinatha Bhattacharya enabled the work of Charles Wilkins (Davis 2015).

Manners, protocols of civic interaction and norms of social, interracial interaction were also sites where cultural exchange and mutual influence were visible. Even the idea of 'civility', as Anindyo Roy has argued, was treated by the native—and projected as such by *English* textbooks and teachers—as markers of 'modern progress and mobility' (Roy 2005: 11). Therefore, both English and Indian commentators (Webb 1915; El Edroos 1922) produced advice and courtesy books for Indians and Englishmen in India (Nayar 2016, 'Civil Modernity'). These contained suggestions like:

> Members of each class, without entering into political or official discussions and avoiding personal remarks, may have much pleasant intercourse by asking about and describing the manners and customs peculiar to each other's nationality, or about their art, music, poetry and literature.... Talk about sport is most suitable at club. (El Edroos: 89)

The Archive and the Global

Another approach to the imperial archive chooses to see the archive as instantiating not just the sensibilities, attitudes and modes of the British coloniser and the subcontinent's colonised, but as enabling *global and globalising imperial networks*. That is, the archive is seen as embodying not just the binary of an imperial 'centre' and 'periphery' (the colony), but a vast network of global connections. We see this interpretation in the work of John Darwin.

In *The Empire Project: The Rise and Fall of the British World-System, 1830–1970* (2009), Darwin shows how the 'interdependence' of various regions and colonies shaped the British Empire in four specific domains. First, there is the military interdependence of various geopolitical regions:

> the most obvious forms of such inter-dependence were naval and military.... British ability to provide naval protection or to send reinforcements to the scene of a conflict would have been very limited without the resources the imperial system supplied. It was strategic control of the Cape Colony (whose economic value was derisory before 1870) that secured the naval gateway to Asia from European waters. The prime function of Egypt, occupied by the British in 1882, was to preserve British use of the Suez Canal and protect the 'Clapham Junction' of imperial communications. Malta, Aden, Ceylon, Singapore, Hong Kong, Esquimalt (on Vancouver Island), the Falklands and Halifax, Nova Scotia, formed the network of bases from which the Royal Navy patrolled the world's sea-lanes. India played several roles in the British world-system, but perhaps its critical function was to be the main base from which British interests in Asia could be advanced and defended. Indian soldiers and a British garrison paid for by Indian revenues were the 'strategic reserve' of the British system in Asia. Because India played this role, other British possessions and spheres east and south of Suez were largely exempted from the costs of defence—a fact of crucial importance to their economic viability. (3–4)

Then there is the commercial interdependence and linkages:

> Both colonial territories and 'informal' colonies had to compete for investment and credits from London to expand their economies ... with the grand exception of the United States (which had received one-fifth of British foreign investment by 1913), British capital was shuttled by the City of London between the various sectors of its commercial empire (a vast global realm among whose key provinces were Canada, Argentina, India, Australia, Southern Africa, China and the Middle East), employing a calculus of prospective return and speculative gain. (4)

The third domain of such connections would be the demographic interdependence:

> Although two-thirds of British migrants went to the United States up until 1900, almost all the rest were distributed between the four main settlement zones of Canada, Australia, New Zealand and South Africa. Indeed, their economic development was usually seen as being closely dependent upon drawing labour and skills from the British supply.... Between 1834 and 1937, India exported some 30 million people to other British possessions as indentured labour, and perhaps one-fifth remained as permanent settlers. In the tropical empire (which British migrants avoided) they supplied much of the labour and business expertise to promote commercial expansion. (4–5)

Finally,

> the spheres of British expansion were progressively linked by a complex system of communication. From the 1840s onwards, this was provided by subsidised mail services, telegraph wires, undersea cables, an expanding rail network, fast passenger steamers and (in the twentieth century) imperial air routes. (5)

In consonance with the work of Darwin, other commentators have mapped these global connections and interdependencies of the British Empire. Thus, Tony Ballantyne, Jonathan Hyslop, among others, in their contributions to the *New Imperial Histories Reader*, map racial imaginings and knowledge formations, working-class presences across the Empire, from India to Australia and Southern Africa. The migration of people and goods in the 1850–1914 period, argue Gary Magee and Andrew Thompson in *Empire and Globalisation: Networks of People, Goods and Capital in the British World, c. 1850–1914* (2010), was instrumental in the making of an international economy. This, of course, put tremendous pressure on the colonised peoples but also made '"transnationalism"—living in and identifying with more than one country or place—a normal way of life for many British people in the half-century before 1914' (5); an argument that resonates with that of Antoinette Burton about Victorian England cited earlier.

Alan Lester's work in the field of imperial humanitarianism and the 'civilisational mission' has made similar connections to argue for a trans-imperial history. Through the late eighteenth and the nineteenth centuries, notes Alan Lester, we can discern the rise of a 'moral geography of the globe', where the Europeans felt responsible for 'distant strangers' (2000: 278). Thus, imperialism intersected with, fed into and drew from humanitarian ideologies and thought in *different* parts of the world/Empire. Subsequently, Lester et al.'s work focused on not 'national boundaries' (Britain's) but on 'transnational and trans-imperial connections' (2020: 2). They argue that 'the principles of freedom, civilisation and liberalism that motivated them were dissolved in a solution of violent racism through which British power was applied' in *various* colonies and geographical locations (2). Through a reading of three years—1838, 1857 and 1879—and the archive of Victorian imperialist statesmen and legal luminaries like James Stephen, Lester et al. demonstrate the linkage and common foundations (ideological, racism, etc.):

> [T]he ending of slavery and the rise of free trade doctrine, repeated Indian famines and the Uprising of 1857, the First and Second Afghan Wars, the First and Second Opium Wars, the Great Xhosa Cattle Killing and the Anglo-Zulu War, mass emigration from the British Isles, the self-governance of settler colonies in North America, Australasia and southern Africa and the devastation of Indigenous societies. (11)[5]

The Archive in 'New Imperial Histories'

The modes through which the archive has been read and employed have come in for criticism in the *new imperial history* turn. Nicholas Dirks summarises the problem with the slide between the production of the imperial archive and the production of the historical events within imperialism. Dirks writes:

> Begins the histories behind and beneath the production of the kinds of primary sources that have represented colonial knowledge even as they have been used to determine and justify colonial policy. The archive has enshrined, in [Michel] Foucault's sense, this raw material

---

[5] Philippa Levine and John Marriott in their Introduction to the massive *The Ashgate Research Companion to Modern Imperial Histories* (2012) argue that for many commentators, such as C.A. Bayly, 'modernity' in Europe itself is a consequence of its imperial actions—'The putative simultaneity of Europe's imperial ascent, globalisation and the birth of the modern world has led many to see an intimate interconnectedness.' (2)

However the trouble with this reading is, they note, 'that not only did Europe (or the west if we include the Americas) continue to display significant characteristics that might be regarded as pre-modern, but many of the features identified as modern were to be found equally in societies beyond and often unconnected to Europe.' (2)

> for subsequent historical representation. In the Indian case, the archive is both the precipitate of the history of conquest and rule and the basis on which that history has been written by colonial administrators. (2010: 95)

This 'colonial history' most notably in the 'Cambridge School' of historians, argues Dirks reading the archive of John Seeley and others, was in fact 'colonial fiction', which forwarded the idea that 'Indian politics emerged as a direct reflex of administrative initiatives set in motion by colonial rule' (95). Dirks continues:

> [such colonial histories argued] that local elites, the very groups that had been the collaborators for British rule, turned nationalist—in the context of participation in the progressively enlarged electoral arenas of provincial and municipal politics—when they realized that more of the pie could be obtained through autonomous political institutions than through colonial ones.... (95)

This meant

> [The Cambridge School] proved its arguments by using colonial sources—frequently police records and confidential files—that documented the spurious activities of nationalist figures in what was a large-scale colonial effort to track, contain, and debunk the very politics that sought to overthrow colonial rule. (96)

More recent readings have shown how colonial and imperial legacies and their discursive remains, even in the postcolonial era, turn to and retain its ideologies and representational modes. Nadine Attewell writes in *Better Britons*:

> [in] the afterlife of empire insofar as the projects of nation building with which it is concerned ... sexual reproduction [is the] key to, and a potent figure for, the (re)constitution of the national body after the 'end' of empire. (2014: 6)

This implies that the archive and the historical record—even as we debate what counts as the historical record—is very much an active constituent of the present postcolonial thought and actions as well.

*

The volumes here are only a small sample of the imperial archive. The range and depth of the archive are impossible to encapsulate in a few volumes. While I have made attempts elsewhere to capture some of this variety (Nayar 2007; 2009; 2013; 2016 [*Siege and Prison Writings*]; 2017; 2019), much more is required and possible. For example, the visual archive of the Empire, with its modalities and aesthetic grammars of 'composing' the subcontinent, whether in photography or painting (some of which may be found in Archer 1972), requires much more presence in the form of collections.

The present volumes focus on select aspects of the imperial archive: the accounts of 'discovery' and exploration—flora and fauna, geography, climate—the people of the subcontinent, English domesticity and social life in the subcontinent, the wars and skirmishes—including the *Mutiny* of 1857–1858—and the *civilisational mission*. It excludes legal documents and the many Acts and laws enacted by the British government.

Volume I consists of documents that deal with England's *discovery* of India, its exploration and mapping of the Indian land. This volume includes material as diverse as the letter from India of Thomas Stephens, often called 'the first Englishman in India', chorographic and cartographic accounts from geographical, meteorological, archaeological surveys that the various organisations and societies established for the purpose produced.

Volume II includes English studies of Indian languages and the social order. Ethnographic surveys of the subcontinent's people and cultural practices were published from the late eighteenth century. Practices like female infanticide, sati and thugee, seen as emblematic of the 'barbarous' Oriental, received special attention in the documentation. The characteristics of various tribes and ethnic group were also mapped in considerable detail.

Volume III shifts the focus entirely to the English home and social life. The documents include advice on gardening—an integral part of the English home—and on housekeeping. In the latter, the English were given instructions on how to monitor the domestic economy and manage the servants. Advice manuals on hunting and field sports were also published. Given the interracial dynamics at work, officers were issued manuals on etiquette and behaviour. Accounts of hill-stations and camps, and the social life in the Presidencies make up the rest of the volume.

Volume IV is a collection of accounts of a very different British life in India: as prisoners, under siege and in conditions of war. Starting with the notorious *Black Hole* of Calcutta to the 1857 *Mutiny*, the English wrote about being assailed, besieged and tormented in their war journals and prison accounts. These documented physical and emotional suffering, the losses of families and lives, even as they strove to depict British grit and determination.

Volume V documents England's *civilisational mission*. These documents offer a glimpse into British opinions and strategies on diverse subjects. It includes Macaulay's (in)famous Minute of 1835, accounts of medical missionary activities, views on establishing missionary activities and the British views on women's education.

Works Cited

Archer, Mildred. *Company Drawings in the India Office Library.* London: HMSO, 1972.

Attewell, Nadine. *Better Britons: Reproduction, National Identity, and the Afterlife of Empire*. Toronto: University of Toronto Press, 2014.

Auer, Blain. 'Early Modern Persian, Urdu, and English Historiography and the Imagination of Islamic India under British Rule', *Études de Lettres* 2–3 (2014): 199–206.

Bayly, C.A. *Empire and Information: Intelligence-Gathering and Social Communication in India*. Cambridge: Cambridge University Press, 1999.

Benton, A.H. *Indian Moral Instruction and Caste Problems: Solutions*. London: Longmans, Green and Co., 1917.

Burton, Antoinette and Isabel Hofmeyr. 'Introduction. The Spine of Empire? Books and the Making of an Imperial Commons'. In *Ten Books that Shaped the British Empire: Creating an Imperial Commons*, edited by Antoinette Burton and Isabel Hofmeyr. Durham and London: Duke University Press, 2014.

Burton, Antoinette. *Empire in Question: Reading, Writing, and Teaching British Imperialism*. Durham and London: Duke University Press, 2011.

Chaudhury, Zahid R. *Afterimage of Empire: Photography in Nineteenth-Century India*. Minneapolis: University of Minnesota Press, 2012.

Cohn, Bernard S. *Colonialism and Its Forms of Knowledge: The British in India*. New Delhi: Oxford University Press, 1997.

Damodaran, Vinita, Anna Winterbottom and Alan Lester, eds. *The East India Company and the Natural World*. London: Palgrave Macmillan, 2015.

Darwin, John. *The Empire Project: The Rise and Fall of the British World-System, 1830–1970*. Cambridge: Cambridge University Press, 2009.

Davis, Richard. 'Wilkins, Kasinatha, Hastings, and the First English *Bhagavad Gītā*', *International Journal of Hindu Studies* 19, no. 1–2 (2015): 39–57.

De Silva, Prasannajit. 'Representing Home Life Abroad: British Domestic Life in Early Nineteenth-Century India', *Visual Culture in Britain* 12, no. 3 (2011): 313–331.

Dirks, Nicholas B. 'Coda: The Burden of the Past.' In *The New Imperial Histories Reader*, edited by Stephen Howe, 92–105. Oxford: Routledge, 2010.

Dohman, Renata, ed. *Empire and Art: British India*. Manchester, UK: Manchester University Press, 2017.

Eaton, Natasha. *Colour, Art and Empire: Visual Culture and the Nomadism of Representation*. London: I.B. Tauris, 2013.

Edney, Matthew. *Mapping an Empire: The Geographical Construction of British India, 1753–1843*. Chicago: University of Chicago Press, 1997.

El Edroos, Aboobaker. *Modern Indian Etiquette: Of Mixed Society, Describing Ancient Social Usages and Important Indian Manners and Customs, Aiming at Social Amity Between Indians and Non-Indians*. Surat: H.R. Scott at the Mission Press, 1922.

Guégan, Xavier. 'Visualizing Alienation: Symbolism and Duality in Samuel Bourne's Photographs of British India', *Visual Culture in Britain* 12 no. 3 (2011): 349–365.

Hall, Catherine. *Civilising Subjects: Colony and Metropole in the English Imagination, 1830–1867*. Chicago: University of Chicago Press, 2002.

Joshi, Priya. *In Another Country: Colonialism, Culture, and the English Novel in India*. Oxford: Oxford University Press, 2003.

Leask, Nigel. *British Romantic Writers and the East: Anxieties of Empire*. Cambridge: Cambridge University Press, 1993.

Lelyveld, David. 'The Fate of Hindustani: Colonial Knowledge and the Project of a National Language'. In *Orientalism and the Postcolonial Predicament: Perspectives on South Asia*, edited by Carol Breckenridge and Peter van der Veer, 189–214. Philadelphia: University of Pennsylvania Press, 1993.

Lester, Alan, Kate Boehme and Peter Mitchell. *Ruling the World: Freedom, Civilisation and Liberalism in the Nineteenth-Century British Empire*. Cambridge: Cambridge University Press, 2021.

Lester, Alan. 'Obtaining the "due observance of justice": The geographies of colonial humanitarianism', *Environment and Planning D Society and Space* 20, no. 3 (2000): 277–293.

Levine, Philippa and John Marriott, eds. *The Ashgate Research Companion to Modern Imperial Histories*. London: Ashgate, 2016.

Macfie, Alexander Lyon. 'Thuggee: An Orientalist Construction?' *Rethinking History* 12, no. 3 (2008): 383–397.

Magee, Gary and Andrew Thompson. *Empire and Globalisation: Networks of People, Goods and Capital in the British World, c. 1850–1914*. Cambridge: Cambridge University Press, 2010.

Mahmood, Syed. *History of English Education in India, Its Rise, Development, Progress, Present Condition and Prospects. Being a Narrative of the Various Phases of Educational Policy and Measures Adopted under the British Rule from Its Beginning to the Present Period (1781 to 1893)*. Aligarh: M.A-O. College, 1895.

Malcolm, John. 'Notes of Instructions to Assistants and Officers Acting under the Orders of Major-General Sir John Malcolm, GCB.' In *A Memoir of*

Central India: Including Malwa, and Adjoining Provinces, Vol. 2, edited by John Malcolm. London: Kingsbury, Parbury and Allen, 1823.

Mir, Farina. *The Social Space of Language: Vernacular Culture in British Colonial Punjab*. Berkeley: University of California Press, 2010.

Naregal, Veena. *Language Politics, Elites, and the Public Sphere: Western India under Colonialism*. New Delhi: Permanent Black, 2001.

Nayar, Pramod K. 'English Discourse and India'. *Oxford Bibliographies Online*. New York: Oxford University Press, 2021, https://www.oxfordbibliographies.com/view/document/obo-9780190221911/obo-9780190221911-0114.xml.

______. 'Civil Modernity: The Management of Manners and Polite Imperial Relations in India, 1880–1930', *South Asia: Journal of South Asian Studies* 39, no. 4 (2016): 740–757.

______. 'Moral Readership and Political Apprenticeship: Commentaries on English Education in India, 1875–1930'. In *The Edinburgh History of Reading. Vol. IV. Subversive Readers*, edited by Jonathan Rose, 138–161. UK: Edinburgh University Press, 2020.

______. *Colonial Education and India*, 5 vols. London: Routledge, 2019.

______. *Days of the Raj: Life and Leisure in British India*. New Delhi: Penguin, 2009.

______. *English Siege and Prison Writings: From the 'Black Hole' to the 'Mutiny'*. London: Routledge, 2016.

______. *Indian Travel Writing, 1830–1947*. 1830–1947, 5 vols. London: Routledge, 2016

______. *The Penguin 1857 Reader*. New Delhi: Penguin, 2007.

______. *Women in Colonial India: Historical Documents and Sources*, 5 vols. London: Routledge, 2013.

Ogborn, Miles. *Indian Ink: Script and Print in the Making of the English East India Company*. Chicago and London: Chicago University Press, 2007.

Orsini, Francesca. *The Hindi Public Sphere: Language and Literature in the Age of Nationalism*. Oxford: Oxford University Press, 2010.

Pinney, Christopher. 'Sepia Mutiny: Colonial Photography and Its Others in India.' In *Feeling Photography*, edited by Elspeth Brown and Thy Phu, 71–92. Durham, NC: Duke University Press, 2014.

Rao, Velcheru Narayana. 'Print and Prose: Pundits, *Karanams*, and the East India Company in the Making of Modern Telugu'. In *India's Literary History: Essays on the Nineteenth Century*, edited by Stuart Blackburn and Vasudha Dalmia, 146–166. New Delhi: Permanent Black, 2004.

Richards, Thomas. *The Imperial Archive: Knowledge and the Fantasy of Empire*. London: Verso, 1993.

Roy, Anindyo. *Civility and Empire: Literature and Culture in British India, 1822–1922*. London: Routledge, 2005.

Teltscher, Kate. *India Inscribed: European and English Writing on India, 1600–1800*. Delhi: Oxford University Press, 1997.

Tobin, Beth Fowkes. *Picturing Imperial Power: Colonial Subjects in Eighteenth-Century British Painting*. Durham, NC: Duke University Press, 1999, 110–138.

Trivedi, Harish. *Colonial Transactions: English Literature and India*. Calcutta: Papyrus, 1993.

Viswanathan, Gauri. *Masks of Conquest: English Literary Studies and India*. London: Faber & Faber, 1990.

Webb, William Trego. *English Etiquette for Indian Gentlemen*. 5th ed. 1895. Calcutta: S.K. Lahiri, 1915.

Williamson, Thomas. *Oriental Field Sports*. London: W. Bulmer, 1808.

INTRODUCTION

Originally the word 'thug' or 'thag', in British India's best-known dictionary, *Hobson Jobson* (1885), meant a swindler or cheat. Indigenous sources have occasionally employed the term to describe highway robbers (Wagner 2009: 3–4).

Thuggee—the practice of killing wayfarers after befriending them—represented for the British all that was evil in Indian religion, particularly Hinduism. Texts on the practice argued that thuggee was a form of ritual murder, committed by groups of people who travelled with unsuspecting traders and others on the highways and, at an opportune moment, strangled them to death. Closely aligned with the thugs were the 'poisoners' who employed poisons such as *datura* to kill their victims, also during the course of a highway journey. For the British, these murders were committed under the auspices of Hindu gods such as Kali, for the thugs sought to propitiate the goddess.

Although the existence of thugs was known to the British from the early nineteenth century, it took the work of Sleeman and his cohort of anti-thuggee campaigners to transform the practice into a religion-based one through their writings. That is, the social reality of thuggee—banditry and highway robbery—was discursively transformed into an entirely different beast, of ritual stranglers, bloodthirsty conmen and violent criminals for whom the act of killing was more important than the pecuniary benefits to be obtained from the act. Kim Wagner has argued

> the thugs of the early nineteenth century as a kind of bandit-retainers, who were tied to local elites in a form of client-patron relationship. The thugs often lived on the land owned by the *zamindar*s or landowners, who took care of their families when the thugs went on expeditions and in return received a substantial share of the loot. (2008: 8)

There was a process by which the thugs became a community of robbers:

> To become a thug 'officially' one had to obtain the permission of the raja or zamindar, which reflected a certain degree of locally centralized power by which marauders and mercenaries could be lawfully integrated into the local authority. (9)

This aspect of thuggee, Wagner argues, was ignored by the British in favour of (re)presenting them as *ritual* stranglers. A social phenomenon based on economic relations and needs was transformed by the British into the 'religious Thuggee cult' (Wagner 2007: 19). In short, the thugs became the 'very epitome of the stereotypical image of religious fanatics, the thugs populated the same exotic realm as the Assassins, African leopard-men, witch doctors and cannibals' (Wagner 2007: 2). Wagner's point is that the thugs easily slid into the "orientalist" canon of exotica from the East, an exoticism tinged with the sentiments of danger, criminality and lawlessness, religious fanaticism and barbarism. Such a portrait enabled the 'rational' British statesman to invoke the grand presence of the law—which of course the Empire would project as its great boon to the colonized subject. A massive thuggee archive now exists (see Wagner 2007, 2009).

John Shakespeare published 'Observations Regarding Badheks and T'hegs' in the *Asiatic Researches* of 1820. Richard Sherwood (originally 1816), J.A.R. Stevenson, H.H. Spry and others published similar accounts in places like the *Journal of the Royal Asiatic Society* and the *Phrenological Journal and Miscellany*, besides book-length works studying the community of thugs and their depredations. Philip Meadows Taylor published his *Confessions of a Thug*, a novel, in 1839. But it was W.H. Sleeman, appointed the General Superintendent entrusted with the task of suppressing the thug gangs, who gave thuggee a celebrity status for the British back home. Much of the nineteenth-century and later perceptions of thuggee stem from the work and writings of Sleeman. He published *Ramaseeana*, a 'vocabulary' of the language of the thugs (1836). In 1839 he published a two-volume study of thugs, in which he added a section on the Pindaris (volume 1). His *Rambles and Recollections of an Indian Official* (1844) carried a chapter on the thugs and poisoners.

From the 1830s, a concerted campaign by Sleeman, Philip Meadows Taylor and specific departments set out to identify and arrest the thugs, often employing former gang members as informers. The Act XXX of 1836, by which time the anti-thuggee campaign was already under way, facilitated the conviction of individuals caught for poisoning and robbery. This Act, and the work of Sleeman and others, enabled the colonial state to construct thuggee as religious in origin and organised as a community's practice. Thugs were recast as 'dacoits' after 1840, and 'dacoits' became 'criminal tribes' after 1870. Eventually, entire communities and castes would be identified and labelled as 'Criminal Tribes' through the enactment of a law in 1871, which declared that the aim was 'to provide for the registration, surveillance and control of certain tribes', a process that began with Sleeman and the campaign against thuggee. This construction of entire communities of stranglers and bandits was an imperial biopolitical move because it consigned large groups of people to the attentions—often violent—of the legal system.

The campaign against thuggee was driven by the recognition that the thugs were beyond the imperial dominion and control and in order to ensure their continuous and cohesive power over the land, such pockets of vagrant, unidentifiable groups of resisters (violent at that) could not be allowed to exist. In short, the surveil-and-exterminate movement against thuggee was an instance of imperial expansion. The anti-thuggee campaigns were a part of the Company Raj's attempt to establish paramountcy, for which the robbers and dacoit gangs had to be broken up. The detailed accounts of identifying the religious and community affiliations of the thugs in Sleeman were thus an integral part of the surveillance and classificatory system of the Empire.

Sleeman refers to thuggee as a two-hundred-year-old practice and, in trying to attempt a genealogy, he paints a picture of an antiquarian movement. This enables Sleeman to suggest that nothing in India has changed. Ancient practices, even (or especially) barbaric ones, persist. Like Sleeman, other commentators too made the argument that thuggee is a natural consequence of the religious and idolatrous country that is the subcontinent. That is, thuggee is endemic in India because the culture is given to such barbaric activities.

Among the earliest accounts in colonial discourse are essays by Dr Sherwood and John Shakespeare, both dating back to 1820. Most of the commentators offered details of the thugs' modus operandi: their religious rituals and superstitions, their belief in omens and their festivities after a successful killing, family and community life, among others. Sleeman and the rest painted the thugs as remorseless, conscienceless criminals in works like *Thugs, or, Phansigars of India* (1839). Besides focusing on the religious 'roots' of the practice, they sought to establish thugs as driven by bloodlust alone. Their depredations proceeded from moral depravity, according to the British commentators, who implied that economic gain was only a secondary motive. Thus, F. Holick would declare: 'a singular people, who are thus made, by a peculiar education, to believe that Murder and Robbery, are MORAL and RELIGIOUS DUTIES, highly commendable, and partciularly grateful to the Divinity' (emphasis in original). Kaye would write in his *The Administration of the East India Company*: 'it is doubted whether any class of natives ever followed their peculiar avocations with a keener relish than these Thugs'. Others, like Sleeman and Holick, admit that the legislative processes of British India were not at first equipped to deal with the thugs, but over a period of time, had become rigorous and systematic enough to bring them to justice. The Thugi and Dacoity Department established for the campaign against thuggee would eventually evolve into the Criminal Investigation Department (CID). Other measures included the creation of units like the Irregular Horse, the extensive payrolling of spies and informers and a reward system.

Central India, extending as far as Etawah and Agra, and the kingdom of Golkonda in the Deccan, all saw massive campaigns against thuggee. Indeed, the officer John Malcolm treated the dispersal of thuggee into the region as an index of the collapse of all local (Indian) authority, so that the kingdoms were always at the mercy of the invading thugs and other marauders. Malcolm writes in 1823 (well before Sleeman):

> Amongst the most numerous of these bands are a tribe of Brahmins, from Bundelcund, who take the name of the sect of Canoje: they are at once mendicants, pilfering thieves, robbers, and murderers. A number of them are usually found in that singular association called Thugs, who are well known in Hindustan, and have of late years become very formidable in Malwa and adjoining provinces, with many of the petty chiefs of which this extraordinary society was, during its late troubles, intimately connected. A description of these robbers and their usual proceedings, while it shews their character, will suffice as an example of the bands by which the provinces of India, in the condition this country has lately been, are liable to be infested, or rather invaded. (II: 190)

Sleeman's *Ramaseeana*, a 'vocabulary' of the thugs, was widely reviewed in respected periodicals like the *Edinburgh Review* (1837) and the *Foreign Quarterly Review* (1838), clearly contributing to the picture of the thugs among the British readers. Indeed, 'Thuggee' became a household name in Britain due to Sleeman's meticulous engineering of the public discourse (wherein his writings played a prominent role) around the practice. Stewart Gordon in an 1969 essay wrote of Sleeman's role:

> It was the writing of William Sleeman and the Evangelical, crusading tone of the British Indian administration of the 1830's that played up these locally-organized, small-scale marauding groups (given the name 'Thugs' by the British) into a hideous, widespread religious conspiracy, somehow typical of India and Indian 'national character'.

> We cannot and will not know the nature of the 'Thugs' or any other marauding group of the eighteenth century until we return them to a historical and geographic setting, and view them in the context of the on-going structure and processes of power. (429)

Besides the accounts by Spry, Edrup, Holick and others, official campaigns of the British government were also documented in the form of detailed reports. These reports often included depositions by those who had turned approvers. These depositions had enabled the British to prosecute the captured thugs, since there was no other evidence for their crimes.

E. Thornton's *Illustrations of the History and Practices of the Thugs and Notices of Some of the Proceedings of the Government of India for the Suppression of the Crime of Thuggee* (1837), *Selections from the Records of the Government of India (Foreign Department)* (1858), Charles Hervey's *Report on the Crime of Thuggee by Means of Poisons in British Territory for the Years 1864, 1865, and 1866* (1868) and John William Kaye's massive *The Administration of the East India Company* (1853) compiled the reports of the campaigns. These texts enabled the British to demonstrate through public documents the civilisational mission of the Empire, for the campaign against thuggee was a campaign at erasing the scourge of the subcontinent and implement the rule of law for all its people. They served the additional purpose of showing the extent of thuggee in the form of detailed tables of incidents of thuggee in various provinces (Hervey's text organized the incidents by district to show how deep-seated and widespread the problem was). They also demonstrated the resounding success of the British campaigns against thugs and, by implication, the success and power of the British Empire in India. Letters and other communications between the officials, reprinted in many of these reports, were also useful in demonstrating the British will to exterminate Thuggee, and to communicate the resourcefulness, strength of character and moral rectitude of the officers.

While postcolonial studies readily treat thuggee as a colonial construction that justified British legal measures and the Empire itself, scholars such as Kim Wagner caution us that the thug was not entirely a colonial construction:

> there *was* a social reality in terms of Indian banditry, which the British in turn misrepresented. It would be naïve to assume that the sources offer a direct access to the past, but it is equally naïve to assume that they do not in any way reflect the past from which they emerged. (2009: 8, emphasis in original).

Thuggee thus provided the British statesman, politician, police officials a site for active intervention. As a social reality in the subcontinent, it fuelled colonial discourse that merged moral, social and legal components, indicting the thugs for their religious beliefs, their codes of conduct and their actions violative of the law. Perhaps matched only by the discourses and actions against sati, thuggee came to symbolise everything that was wrong with the social order in India – its absence of moral and ethical codes, its bloodlust, its superstition-ridden populace, among others. That later novelists such as John Masters (*The Deceivers*) continued to weave stories around thuggee also signals the endurance of the legends, myths and historical details around the practice.

References

Gordon, Stewart N. 'Scarf and Sword: Thugs, Marauders, and State-formation in 18th Century Malwa.' *The Indian Economic & Social History Review.* 6.4 (1969): 403–429.

Malcolm, John. *A Memoir of Central India Including Malwa and Adjoining Provinces.* London: Kingsbury, Parbury & Allen, 1823. 2 vols.

Wagner, Kim A. *Thuggee: Banditry and the British in Early Nineteenth-Century India*. Basingstoke: Palgrave-Macmillan, 2007.

______. 'Introduction'. In Wagner (ed.) *Stranglers and Bandits: A Historical Anthology*. Oxford: Oxford University Press, 2009. 1–48.

ACKNOWLEDGEMENTS

The Raj has been a perennial favourite when it comes to research and writing, and I cannot remember a year when I did *not* do some 'Raj work'.

Chandra Sekhar of Bloomsbury was very receptive to the project idea, and has been incisive and encouraging when it came to subjects like the volumes' organisation, content and final form—to him, this project owes much.

I express my thanks to journals and anthologies, and their editors and reviewers whose comments have enabled me to sharpen my thoughts on the Raj-topic-of-the-moment. Among journals, I acknowledge: *South Asia, South Asian Review, Anglo-Saxonica* and *Asiatic*. Among the anthologies, I acknowledge *Ireland's Imperial Connections*; *The Edinburgh History of Reading*; *The English Renaissance, Orientalism, and the Idea of Asia*; *Cultural Histories of India*. To Debra Johanyak and Walter S. Lim, Rita Banerjee, Daniel Roberts and Jonathan Wright, Mary Hammond and Jonathan Rose, editors of these fabulous anthologies, many thanks for your invitation to contribute and the work you put into the volumes of which I am now a part.

To Kate Teltscher, whose work *India Inscribed* showed me where to go way back in the mid-1990s, I owe an intellectual debt of enormous proportions.

I am also grateful to publishers and editors at Penguin, Bloomsbury, Palgrave-Macmillan, Edinburgh University Press, Orient BlackSwan, Wiley-Blackwell and Routledge for their comments, suggestions and, above all, interest in this area and my contributions to it.

To Soma Ghosh, Librarian (English) at the Salar Jung Museum, Hyderabad, and her constant efforts, all undertaken with cheer and grace, to obtain materials when I have worked there, immeasurable gratitude.

Many books germinate in conversations with Anna Kurian, who is always enthusiastic about any Raj-work I do, especially if they are multivolume projects. For the constant-traveller role that you assay with such commitment, solidarity and affection, it is my privilege, Anna, to acknowledge you.

Thank you, Molly ('Chechu'), for enquiring lovingly about her 'little one'.

Nandana Dutta has been unceasing in her interest in my work, and her always gentle and loving urging to think in certain ways, even as she tries to catch up with her reading of what I publish. To your attention, insights and perspicacity, Nandana—much, much gratitude.

Professor K. Narayana Chandran established, for some of us willing ones, the standards in academic scholarship and publishing—that he sustains these standards even now, after four decades, is nothing short of the marvellous. To KNC's indomitable spirit of inquiry and work ethic, and showing us the way to do things, I am very grateful.

Friends who drop in 'WhatsAppingly', regularly, to check on me—Neelu, Bhalla, Ajeet, Kulsoom, Om, Archana, Ashish, Krishna Ram, Sai Jawahar, Savita, Vaishali, Soma and Zahid—thank you.

To Nandini, Pranav, my parents and parents-in-law, I owe unquantifiable gratitude, for never complaining at the volume of work I take on, my frequently distracted state of being and, more importantly, for creating an extraordinarily supportive environment.

And thank you, Shubha, for obtaining, wizard-like, essays and journal articles in minutes, and for your enthusiasm for my work.

To the works of P.G. Wodehouse, Agatha Christie, Stephen King, the comics around Batman—my regular reading—many of which unwittingly capture the horror, the abyss and the comedy of academia, I can never express enough gratitude.

It is a pleasure to thank Atul Nair who compiled many of the materials meticulously.

I am grateful to the Institution of Eminence (IoE) project's Professional Development Fund.

J. Shakespeare

'Observations Regarding Badheks and T'hegs.'

Asiatic Researches 13 (1820): 282–292.

REGARDING BADHEKS AND T'HEGS,

Extracted from an offical report by Mr. John Shakespear, *Acting Superintendent of Police for the Western Provinces, dated the 30th April,* 1816.

THE moſt heinous robberies committed in theſe Provinces are perpetrated by gangs of *Badheks* and *Shighál Khors.* Theſe gangs are almoſt excluſively ſettled in the Diſtrict of *Aly Gher,* and in that part of the territory of the Nawab Vizier, bordering the Diſtrict of *Goracpúr.* After much inquiry I am diſpoſed to believe that the *Badheks* of *Aly Gher,* and the *Shighál Khors* of *Baraich,* are connected with each other; and are one and the ſame people; the name conſtituting the ſole diſtinction. Excluſive of the *Shighál Khors* eſtabliſhed in the country of the Nawab Vizier, the following tribes of Jackal eaters are notorious in the Weſtern Provinces:—*1ſt, Badheks,—2d, Kunjar,—3d, Gídia, 4th, Bauría,—5th, Harbúra.* All of theſe ſubſiſt by robbing, and are more or lefs attached to a vagrant life, eating the flefh of jackals, lizards, &c. When ftationary, they commonly refide with their families in temporary huts, conftructed of reeds and leaves, and erected in jungles and plains. The term *Budhek* is faid to be derived from the *Sanfcrit* word, " *Badh,*" " deftruction."—The following Diftich is taken from a *Hindee* Author.

" Hit anhit fab hot hyn, Tulfí dúr din pae,
" Badheo, Badhek mirg bán te rudhír ké dét butae."

Which may be rendered—

O Tulsí, friends become enemies in the days of misfortune; even as the blood of the ftricken deer ferves as a guide to the Huntfman (deftroyer).

The *Badheks* of *Aly Gher* and the *Shigal Khors* of *Goracpúr* are out-cafts of *Muffelman* as well as *Hindu* tribes; the majority however are *Rajpúts.* The records of this office fhew a fubdivifion of claffes amongft the *Badheks,* as the *Súdanki, Dúdhadhal, Jaran, Danpi, Ehipti, Badharah, Powar* and *Chowan,* the two laft of which are alfo the diftinguifhing names of *Rajput* tribes.

The *Badheks* are divided into feparate gangs, each confifting of from thirty to an hundred followers, headed by a jummadar; and thefe gangs occafionally unite for the purpofe of carrying on their depredations with greater certainty of fuccefs and difpatch. They are commonly protected by zemindars, who fupport their families during their abfence, and affift them when they are apprehended and get into trouble; becoming fecurity to the Police for their future good behaviour, and employing them oftenfibly as ryots; but, in fact, harboring and encouraging them in their predatory habits, for the fake of the proportion of plunder, which they invariably receive. They are alſo frequently ſupported by petty Mahajuns, who advance them money at an exorbitant intereſt.

Some of the *Badheks* ſhare ſuch booty as they obtain; others receive a monthly ſtipend of two or three rupees, from their jummadars, who alſo feed and maintain them at a conſiderable expenſe, ſupplying them with ſpirituous liquors, of which they drink inordinately. The jummadars have generally conſiderable ſums of money at their command, either for immediate expenditure, or for obtaining their releaſe by bribery, when apprehended.

Formerly numbers of *Badheks* infeſted different parts of the Diſtricts of *Alygher*, *Etawah*, *Furruckabad* and *Agra*. At preſent thoſe reſiding in the Company's Weſtern Provinces are ſettled on the eſtates of the Chieftains of *Moorſan*, *Hatras*, &c. in *Alygher*, and ſome few in the diſtrict of *Agra*. The reſt are eſtabliſhed in great numbers in pergunnahs *Atroula*, *Balrampur* and *Baraich*, in the North Eaſt quarter of the territory of the Nawab Vizier, and alſo in the vicinity of *Gohad*, *Gwalior*, *Bhertpur*, and the country to the weſtward of *Dehli*.—The gangs generally make excurſions once a year, in the proſecution of which they journey ſeveral hundred miles.—Thoſe in *Alygher* have been known to range to *Sahāranpur*, *Haridwar*, *Lucnow*, *Allahabad*, *Benares* and *Jaypur*; and thoſe in *Baraich* to *Chaprah* in the diſtrict of *Saran*, to *Hazārī Bāgh* in *Ramgher*, and to *Allahabad*. On ſome occaſions they travel ſeparately, and meet at a given ſpot, or they follow one another in detached parties, in which caſe, they faſten ſhreds of cloth to trees, or pile up mounds of earth or dung, as marks to guide thoſe of their brethren who follow their footſteps.—They travel, not unfrequently, diſguiſed as fakeers or Pilgrims, with the water of the *Ganges*, carrying in their *kawers*, or caſkets, heads of ſpears to arm themſelves! and food for their ſubſiſtence. At other times their *jamâdárs* journey through the country as merchants; accompanied by their gangs, and women as ſervants: with camels, carts, tents and doolies. Previouſly to their commencing theſe expeditions, they ſend out their ſpies, diſguiſed as religious mendicants, commonly as *byrágis*, to obtain intelligence in any town or city where they may determine to proceed. It is the buſineſs of theſe ſpies to gain correct information regarding the hoards of caſh or jewels in the houſes of merchants and others, or reſpecting diſpatches of treaſure. In the principal cities are to be found perſons ſtyling themſelves *jamâdárs*, who ſupply the bankers and merchants with hired peons, for the ſafe-guard of treaſure or merchandize. Some individuals of this deſcription have been obſerved to riſe to great opulence in a ſhort time. In ſeveral confeſſions of *Badheks* apprehended in *Furruckabad, Sáran* and other places, it is ſtated that the *Badhek* ſpies collude with thoſe jummadars; and inſtances are mentioned of the *Badheks* having themſelves been hired out by theſe *jamâdárs*; to ſerve as peons for the protection of the treaſure which they intended to plunder. The *ſarráfs* and *mahájans*, whether from falſe œconomy or from careleſſneſs, uſually ſend their money under very inſufficient eſcorts; and it is a common practice to attempt to remit and conceal a diſpatch by ſewing up the money in the clothes of the peons—When the ſpies have obtained information, they prepare bambus, as ſhafts for ſpears, which they bury under ground with torches for the uſe of the gang—They endeavor alſo to arrange for the reception of the gang, on their arrival, with ſome zemindar or local reſident, with whom they may have been formerly acquainted; or they ſelect ſome retired jungle or ravine where they may remain concealed till the time of action.—On the arrival of the gang the *jamâdár* arranges his plan with the ſpies.—They then quit their place of concealment, dig up the bamboos and torches, and fixing on their ſpear heads, proceed, as early in the dusk of the evening as possible, that they may have the night before them for retreat.—If a house is to be robbed, they station men to guard all the approaches, whilst they effect the robbery ; and they invariably murder or wound all who come in their way.—They are equally sanguinary with the guards escorting treasure ; and frequent instances have occurred of sepoys having been surprized and butchered at night.—In the doolies they carry off their wounded, as women, with the purdahs down ; and as in some of these robberies, *hajáms* or village barber surgeons have been apprehended with the gangs, it is probable that these persons accompany to dress their wounds—Immediately the robbery is effected, they travel the whole of the night, in the direction of their homes, with great rapidity ; and divide their booty on the following day, at the first favorable spot ; when they separate and return to their places of abode by different routes.

The class of *Shíghál Khors,* called *Kunjárs,* are said to have formerly been very notorious as dacoits.—There are however, very few of this class remaining in the western provinces, and those, for the most part, earn a livelihood by the manufacture of cord, baskets and by cutting wood, &c. &c. The *Bawría* and *Harbúra* classes of *Shíghál Khors* are particularly squalid, and scarcely human in their appearance. The greater part of them have for time to time, been expelled from the Company's territories, but there are still many remaining ; and numbers frequently make temporary incursions from the Mahratta States. These are the men who follow camps, and are particularly expert in cutting into, and stealing from tents. They are not so notorious as gang robbers, as famed for their skill as thieves and cut-purses ; robbing in crowds of people, and passing the stolen property from one to another, and practising other similar tricks to prevent detection.

THE *Gidias* are ſimilar in their habits to the two claſſes laſt mentioned, and are likewiſe famed for imitating the noiſe of animals, when they approach to rob, and for diſguiſing themſelves in ſkins to avoid detection.

OF theſe claſſes, the *Badheks* are by far the moſt numerous and deſtructive to the peace of the country; and the circumſtances under which they rob, combined with the precautions which they take, by giving two or three names to each individual, and uſing a cant peculiar to themſelves, render it extremely difficult to bring them to juſtice.

MUCH ſcepticiſm ſtill prevails regarding the exiſtence of any diſtinct claſs of people who are deſignated *T'hegs*. Perſons have been apprehended, tried and convicted, for highway robbery and murder, under circumſtances ſimilar to thoſe which diſtinguiſh the crimes of this deſcription aſcribed to the *T'hegs*; but no inſtance has come to my knowledge of any individual having been convicted of highway robbery and murder, againſt whom it has been eſtabliſhed that he was a profeſſed *T'heg*, who earned a ſubſiſtence by the commiſſion of this crime. The reſult of ſuch enquiries as I have made upon this ſubject, leaves, however, little room for doubt, that there are at preſent perſons reſiding in the Company's territories who practice this ſpecies of robbery as a profeſſion; various confeſſions in this office ſhew, that regular ſocieties of theſe men have had exiſtence, communicating together and making, at ſtated periods, a diviſion of their ſpoil.

THE term "*T'heg*" is uſually applied, in the weſtern provinces, to perſons who rob and murder travellers on the highways, either by poiſon, or the application of the cord or knife.—The literal meaning however, in its common acceptation, as given in the familiar proverb, is "villain," "raſcal," "knave," &c. which alſo is the ſignification applied to the term in GILCHRIST's Dictionary.—" *Bhágalpur ca Bhagalia, Cahálgeng ca T'heg, Patna ca Dewália, tinon nám zad:*" or, " the *Bhaugulpur* Cheats, the *Cahalgeng* Knaves, and the *Patna* Swindlers, are notorious." They are known also by different appellations in other parts of *India*, as would appear from the following extract from a work recently published.

FORBES'S ORIENTAL MEMOIRS.

" SARENGPUR is famous for a a manufactory of muslins for turbans and other cottons, which are cheaper than any we have met with. A *jat'hera* or religious fair, is occasionally kept here, at which our fellow traveller, SIAD MAHOMMED, a particular friend of SIR CHARLES MALLET's, was present on his last journey to *Delhi*; when several men were taken up for a most cruel method of robbery and murder, practised on travellers by a tribe called *P'hánsigárs* or stranglers, who join passengers frequenting the fair in bye-roads, or at other seasons, convenient for their purpose. Under the pretence of travelling the same way, they enter into conversation with the strangers, share their sweetmeats, and pay them other little attentions, until an opportunity offers of suddenly throwing a rope round their necks, with a slip knot, by which they dexterously contrive to strangle them on the spot."

IN the part of *India* to which the present report relates, there would appear to be five distinct classes of robbers of this description, who rob and murder on the highways.

1st Class.—THE high roads leading through *Etawah*, *Aly Gher*, and *Furrackabad* are, for the most part, the scenes of the atrocities committed by this class. To so great an extent did this crime prevail in former year, that during 1808 and 1809, not less than 67 bodies were taken out of wells in the ſingle diſtrict of *Etawah*. The gangs compoſing this claſs were eſtabliſhed and foſtered in the eſtates of the Chieftains Hi'ra Sinh, Bhagwant Sinh, and Thacu'r Dayara'm in *Aly Gher*, and of Himmet Sinh, the former Raja of *Eta* in the diſtrict of *Etawah*, and ſome detached parties alſo reſided in different parts of the three diſtricts above named. In 1811, a liſt of 68 perſons and ſeveral ſirdars called *jamâdárs*, compoſing theſe gangs, was given into this office by perſons who were induced to deliver themſelves up to Colonel Gardner, under the hope of pardon. They were all *Muſſelmans* and chiefly of the *Mewáti* tribe. By the confeſſions made by the members of theſe gangs, they appear to have carried on their malpractices in ſmall parties, aſſuming various diſguiſes, reſorting to the *Serais*, and accompanying travellers under ſpecious pretences, to have watched their opportunity, and to have deſtroyed their victims in retired places commonly by ſtrangulation, the knife being uſed alſo, to ſecure complete deſtruction, and the bodies being uſually thrown into wells or nullahs. Deleterious drugs are ſaid to be uſed only by novices in the buſineſs, the more experienced *Thegs* truſting rather to the certain effects of the knife or cord, than to the doubtful operation of poiſon. Theſe murders are moſt frequent in the hot winds, at which ſeaſon travellers are induced to ſtart on their journey before day light to avoid the heat.

2d Claſs.—This claſs conſiſts excluſively of *Hindus*, and chiefly of the *Lodeh* tribe.—They are ſtated to paſs themſelves on travellers as *brahmins* and *cayets*, and are reported to be much more numerous than the 1ſt claſs.—The ſcene of their depredations has been, for the moſt part, on the confines of *Etawah*, and the Weſtern thannahs of the *Cánpur* diſtrict, and they are ſtated to be oſtenſibly engaged in cultivating ſmall ſpots of land, though in fact ſupported by the more lu-

2 E

crative profeſſion of *T'heggy*. The murders committed by theſe people are effected by means ſimilar to thoſe practiſed by the 1ſt claſs.

3d Claſs.—This claſs was formerly ſettled in the pergunnahs of *Sindouſe* and *Perhara*, from whence they were expelled, and have ſince taken up their reſidence in *Mahratta* villages, on the confines of our territory, where the *aumils* of the native Governments are ſaid to derive a revenue from their depredations. From the examinations, it would appear, that theſe *T'hegs* are *Muſſelmans* and *Hindus* of various tribes. The murders committed by theſe gangs appear to be perpetrated more openly than thoſe committed by the firſt two claſſes; whole parties of travellers being deſtroyed together, and the bodies of theſe victims being frequently found unburied on the plains. The depradations of this claſs are ſaid to have formerly extended over different parts of the *Doab*, but latterly, to have been directed to the country near *Gwalior* and to the diſtrict of *Bundelcand*. It does not appear that the crime of murder by *T'hegs* was known in the diſtrict of *Bundelcand* prior to 1812, but, in conſequence of the diſperſion of the *Sindouſe T'hegs*, no leſs than 19 inſtances of the offence were aſcertained in 1813, in which 35 bodies were found with marks of the knife or cord. Very conſiderable gangs of theſe people are ſaid to be at preſent collected in the *Mahratta* ſtates. Mr. Wauchope, on the 21ſt inſtant, writes—"But a few weeks have elapſed ſince a party of 42 "travellers (men, women and children,) were every one ſtrangled by a "large body of *T'hegs*. The travellers were coming from *Jebbelpur* "towards *Purma*, and the murders took place about the frontier be-"tween the *Nagpur* and *Purma* country. Four of the miſcreants were "ſeized by an officer of the *Purma* Chief, &c. &c."

It would appear from examinations in this office, that the puniſhment for this offence in ſome of the *Mahratta* ſtates, is by encloſing the criminal alive in a pillar constructed of masonry. The joint magistrate of *Etawah* writes, that a gang of *T'hegs*, seized not long since by the Chieftain Mír Khan, were subjected to amputation of each hand, and to the loss of their noses.

4th Class.—Several instances of murder on the highways in the districts of *Allahabad, Ghazipur*, and *Juanpur*, will be observed in the detailed reports for the last year, said to have been perpetrated by persons assuming the garb of *bairagis*, who join travellers at *mat'hs* and accompany them on the road, take an opportunity of mixing the seeds of the *Datura* or other narcotic plant, with the hooka or food of the traveller, and plunder him when stupified or killed by the effects of the dose. These murders are not, I apprehend, committed by the persons termed *T'hegs*—as poisoning would appear to be the only means of destruction used by these robbers. At the same time, as they have prevailed for some years, particularly in the district of *Juanpur*, and the circumstances attending each case are nearly alike, there seems reason to believe, that some association, similar to that of the *T'hegs* of the *Doab*, is established in *Juanpur* and its vicinity. Pilgrims proceeding from the west and north west to *Gáya*, or to *Jagannath* in *Cuttack*, take *Benares* in their way, and pass through the district of *Juanpur*. In like manner pilgrims proceeding from the lower provinces, pass through *Juanpur*, in their way to *Haridwar*, or to *Mathura* and *Bindraban*. The circumstances of various roads meeting in this district, combined with the facilities afforded for escape by the proximity of the country of the Nawab Vizier, are probably the causes why this offence is more prevalent in *Juanpur* than elsewhere.

5th Class.—Travellers have been frequently found murdered in that part of the country placed under the joint magistrate stationed at *Ghazipur*. The bodies have commonly been discovered buried, and the same offence can be traced to the eastward, through the districts of *Saran* and *Tirhut*. In the detailed report on the state of the police, during the last year, in the jurisdiction of the joint magistrate of *Ghazipur*, a case will be found stated, in which it appeared from the magistrate's enquiries, that a fraternity of *gosains* had long been established in that quarter, who were said to entice travellers to sojourn at their *math*, particularly sepoys, and to murder them. It is not stated what means of destruction are used by these people; but in the examinations taken before Mr. CRACROFT, the zemindars would appear to be concerned with the *gosains* in these nefarious practices; and it is stated by a witness, that numbers of travellers have, for years, been made away with, in this quarter. The establishment of chokies, on the highways principally infested by these miscreants, and the employment of the village watch in aid of these chokies, are, in every respect, the most certain and efficient arrangements which can be devised for the suppression of this crime.

[Doctor] Sherwood

'Of the Murderers Called Phansigars' [1816].

Asiatic Researches 13 (1820): 250–282.

OF THE MURDERERS CALLED P'HANSIGARS.

BY DOCTOR SHERWOOD,

Communicated by Colonel McKenzie.

WHILE Europeans have journeyed through the extenſive territories ſubject to the Government of Fort St George, with a degree of ſecurity no where ſurpaſſed, the path of the native traveller has been beſet with perils little known or ſuſpected, into which, numbers annually falling, have myſteriouſly diſappeared; the victims of villains as ſubtile, rapacious, and cruel, as any who are to be met with in the records of human depravity.

THE *P'hánſigárs,* or ſtranglers, are thus deſignated from the Hinduſtani word *P'hánſi,* (a) a nooſe. In the more northern parts of *India,* theſe murderers are called *T'hegs,* (b) ſignifying deceivers: in the Tamul language, they are called *Ari Túlúcar,* (c) or muſſulman nooſers: in Canareſe, *Tanti Callerú,* (d) implying thieves who uſe a wire or catgut nooſe: and in Telagu, *Warlú Wahndlú* or *Warlú Vayſhay Wahndloo,* (e) meaning people who uſe the nooſe.

THERE is no reaſon to believe that Europeans were aware of the exiſtence of ſuch criminals as *P'hánſigárs,* until ſhortly after the conqueſt

---

(a) پھانسی

(b) ٹھگ

(c) [illegible]

(d) [illegible]

(e) [illegible]

[illegible]

of *Strangapatan*, in 1799; when, about a hundred were apprehended in the vicinity of *Bangalore*. They did not engage general attention; nor would it appear that they were suspected to belong to a distinct class of hereditary murderers and plunderers, settled in various parts of *India*, and alike remarkable for the singularity of their practice, and the extent of their depredations. In the year 1807, between *Chittoor* and *Arcot*, several *P'hánsigárs* were apprehended, belonging to a gang which had just returned, laden with booty from an expedition to *Travancore:* and information was then obtained, which ultimately led to the developement of the habits, artifices, and combinations of these atrocious delinquents.

The *P'hánsigárs* that infested the south of *India* a few years ago, were settled in *Mysore*, on the borders of that kingdom and the *Carnatic*, in the *Balaghat* districts, ceded to the Company by the Nizam in 1800; and they were particularly numerous in the *poliums* of *Chittoor*. The sequestered part of the country, which comprehended these *poliums*, maintaining little intercourse with the neighbouring districts, abounding in hills and fastnesses, and being immediately subject to several *polygars*, afforded the *P'hánsigárs* a convenient and secure retreat; and the protection of the *polygars* was extended to them, in common with other classes of robbers, in consideration of a settled contribution: or, which was more frequent, of sharing in the fruits of their rapacity.

It is impossible that such criminals as *P'hánsigárs*, living by systematic plans of depredation, could long remain in the same place in safety, unless their practices were encouraged or connived at by persons in authority. Hence, after the establishment of the Company's Government over the *Carnatic*, and the districts ceded by the Nizam, and the consequent extinction of the power and influence of the *po-*

lygars, some of whom had succeeded in rendering themselves virtually independent of the former government, these murderers very generally changed their abodes, and frequently assumed other names.

WHILE they lived under the protection of polygars and other petty local authorities, and among people whose habits were in some respects analogous to their own, it was unnecessary to dissemble that they subsisted by depredation. They and their families lived peaceably with their neighbours, whom they never attempted to molest, and between whom there subsisted a reciprocation of interest in the purchase and disposal of the plunder which the *P'hánsigárs* brought with them on returning from their expeditions. Afterwards, on the extension of the English Government, it was usual for the *P'hánsigárs*, while they continued their former practices, ostensibly to engage in the cultivation of land or some other occupation, to screen themselves from suspicion to which they must otherwise have been obnoxious.

P'HA'NSIGA'RS never commit robbery unaccompanied by murder, their practice being first to strangle and then to rifle their victims. It is also a principle with them to allow no one to escape of a party, however numerous, which they assail, that there may be no witnesses of their atrocities. The only admitted exception to this rule is in the instance of boys of very tender age, who are spared; adopted by the *P'hánsigárs*; and, on attaining the requisite age, initiated into their horrible mysteries.

A GANG of *P'hánsigárs* consists of from ten to fifty, or even a greater number of persons; a large majority of whom are Musselmans: but Hindu's, and particularly those of the Rajput tribe, are often associated with them. Bramins, too, though rarely, are found in the gangs. (f) Emerging from their haunts, they ſometimes perform long journeys, being abſent from home many months, and prowl along the eaſtern and weſtern coaſts to *Hyderabad* and *Cape Comorin.* In general, however, they do not roam to ſuch a diſtance; but make one or two excurſions every year. Their victims are almoſt excluſively travellers whom they fall in with on the road. Each gang has its *ſirdar* or leader, who directs its movements. Of a numerous gang, ſome uſually remain at home, while the reſt are engaged in the work of pillage and murder. Thoſe that are abroad are often divided into ſeparate parties of ten or fifteen perſons; who either follow each other at ſome diſtance, or, the parties taking different routes, they rendezvous at an appointed place in advance; meaſures being at the ſame time taken to ſecure a ſpeedy junction of the gang, ſhould this be requiſite for the purpoſe of attacking ſeveral travellers at once. Different gangs ſometimes act in concert, occaſionally appriſing one another of the approach of travellers whoſe deſtruction promiſes a rich booty.

P'HA'NSI'GARS have the appearance of ordinary inoffenſive travellers, and ſeldom aſſume any particular diſguiſe. They indeed not unfrequently pretend to be traders; and there is reaſon to believe, that they ſometimes come from the *dekhin* clothed in the garb of *bairagis.* Formerly, when *P'hánsigáry* was practiſed to a greater extent, and in a more daring manner than at preſent, the leader, eſpecially if enriched by former ſpoliations, often travelled on horſeback, with a tent, and paſſed for a perſon of conſequence or a wealthy merchant: otherwiſe, he appeared at firſt in a more humble character, and aſſumed in the courſe of his rapacious progreſs one of more importance, as he became poſſeſſed of horſes and bullocks; which, while they afforded him carriage for the plundered property ſubſerved the purpoſe of giving countenance and import to his feigned character.

(f) B[illegible]able, do not aſſiſt in the actual perpetration of murder, but are employed to procure intelligence, [illegible]g which their peculiar privileges afford them great facilities.

P'HANSIGÁRS are accuſtomed to wait at choultries on the high roads, or near to towns, where travellers are wont to reſt. They arrive at ſuch places and enter towns and villages in ſtraggling parties of three or four perſons, appearing to meet by accident and to have had no previous acquaintance. On ſuch occaſions, ſome of the gang are employed as emiſſaries to collect information, and eſpecially to learn if any perſons with property in their poſſeſſion are about to undertake a journey. They are often accompanied by children of ten years of age and upwards; who, while they perform menial offices, are initiated into the horrid practices of the *P'hánsigárs*, and contribute to prevent ſuſpicion of their real character. Skilled in the arts of deception, they enter into converſation and inſinuate themſelves, by obſequious attentions, into the confidence of travellers of all deſcriptions, to learn from them whence they come, whither and for what purpoſe they are journeying, and of what property they are poſſeſſed;—thus,

"—— under fair pretence of friendly ends,
And well placed words of glozing courteſy,
Baited with reaſons not unplauſible,
Wind them into the eaſy-hearted man;
And hug him into ſnares."

When the *P'hánsigárs* determine, after obtaining ſuch information as they deem requiſite, to attack a traveller, they uſually propoſe to him, under the ſpecious plea of mutual ſafety, or for the ſake of ſociety, to travel together; or elſe they follow him at a little diſtance, and, on arriving at a convenient place, and a fit opportunity preſenting for effectuating their purpoſe, one of the gang ſuddenly puts a rope or ſaſh round the neck of the unfortunate perſon, while others aſſiſt in depriving him of life.

Two *P'hánsigárs* are conſidered to be indiſpenſably neceſſary to effect the murder of one man, and commonly three are engaged. There is ſome variation in the manner in which the act is perpetrated, but the following is perhaps the moſt general. While travelling along, one of the *P'hánsigárs* suddenly puts the cloth round the neck of the person they mean to kill, and retains hold of one end, while the other end is seized by an accomplice; the instrument crossed behind the neck is drawn tight, the two *P'hánsigárs* pressing the head forwards; at the same time the third villain, in readiness behind the traveller, seizes his legs, and he is thrown forward upon the ground. In this situation he can make little resistance. The man holding the legs of the miserable sufferer, now kicks him in those parts of the body endowed with most sensibility, and he is quickly despatched.

Antecedently to the perpetration of the murder, some of the gang are sent in advance and some left in rear of the place, to keep watch and prevent intrusion by giving notice, on occasion, to those engaged in the act. Should any persons unexpectedly appear on the road, before the murdered body is buried, some artifice is practised to prevent discovery, such as covering the body with a cloth while lamentations are made professedly on account of the sickness or death of one of their comrades: or one of the watchers falls down, apparently writhing with pain, in order to excite the pity of the intruding travellers and to detain them from the scene of murder.

Such are the perseverance and caution of the *P'hánsigárs* that a convenient opportunity not offering, they will sometimes travel in company with, or pursue persons whom they have devoted to destruction, several days before they execute their intention. If circumstances favor them, they generally commit murder in a jungle or in an unfrequented part of the country, and near to a sandy place or a dry water course. A hole three or four feet in depth, in such a spot, is dug with facility; in which the body being placed, with the face downwards, it is shockingly mangled. Deep and continued gashes are often made in it in both sides, from the shoulders to the hands and to the feet, which lay open the abdomen, and divide the tendon at the heel. Wounds are also made between the ribs into the cheſt; and ſometimes, if the hole be ſhort, the knees are disjointed and the legs turned back upon the body. The hole is then filled with earth. The body is thus cut and disfigured to expedite its diſſolution, as well as to prevent its inflation; which, by raiſing or cauſing fiſſures in the ſuperincumbent ſand, might attract jackals, and lead to the expoſure of the corpſe. When the amount of the property is leſs than they expected to find, the villains ſometimes give vent to their diſappointment in wanton indignities on the dead body.

If, when a murder is perpetrated, a convenient place for interring the body be not near, or if the *P'hánsigárs* be apprehenſive of diſcovery, it is either tied in a ſack and carried to ſome ſpot, where it is not likely to be found, or it is put into a well; or, which is frequently practiced, a ſhallow hole is dug, in which the corpſe is buried, till a fit place for interring it can be diſcovered; when it is removed and cut in the manner already mentioned. If the traveller had a dog, it is alſo killed; leſt the faithful animal ſhould cauſe the diſcovery of the body of his murdered maſter. The office of mangling the dead body is uſually aſſigned to a particular perſon of the gang. The *P'hánsigárs* are always provided with knives and pickaxes, which they conceal from obſervation.

From the foregoing account it will be obvious, that the ſyſtem of the *P'hánsigárs* is but too well adapted for concealment. The precautions they take, the artifices they practice, the mode of deſtroying their victims, calculated, at once, to preclude almoſt the poſſibility of reſcue or eſcape—of witneſſes of the deed—of noiſe or cries for help—of effuſion of blood—and, in general, of all traces of murder:—theſe circumſtances conſpire to throw a veil of darkneſs over their atrocities.

I now proceed to notice various particulars, more fully illustrating the practices, habits, and character of these criminals.

It is not improbable that formerly a long string, with a running noose, might have been used by *P'hánsigárs* for seizing travellers, and that they robbed on horseback. But, be this as it may, a noose is now, I believe, never thrown by them from a distance, in this part of *India*. They sometimes use a short rope, with a loop at one end; but a turban or a *dot'hi*, (a long narrow cloth, or such worn about the waist,) are more commonly employed; these serve the purpose as effectually as a regularly prepared noose, with this advantage, that they do not tend to excite suspicion. When such a cloth is used, it is, previously to applying it, doubled to the length of two, or two and a half feet, and a knot is formed at the double extremity; and about eighteen inches from it, a slip knot is tied. In regulating the distance of the two knots, so that the intervening space when tightly twisted, may be adapted to embrace the neck, the *P'hánsigár* who prepares the instrument tries it upon his own knee. The two knots give the *P'hánsigárs* a firm hold of the cloth, and prevent its slipping through their hands in the act of applying it. After the person they attack has been brought to the ground, in the manner already described, the slip knot is loosed by the *P'hánsigár* who has hold of that part of the cloth, and he makes another fold of it round the neck; upon which, placing his foot, he draws the cloth tight, in a manner similar to that (to use the expression of my *P'hánsigár* informer,) "of packing a bundle of straw."

Sometimes the *P'hánsigárs* have not time to observe all the precautions I have mentioned in cutting and interring a body; apprehensions for their own safety inducing them to leave it slightly buried. Sometimes, also, when a murder is perpetrated in a part of the country which expoſes them to the riſk of obſervation, they put up a ſcreen, or the wall of a tent, and bury the body within the incloſure:—pretending, if enquiries are made, that their women are within the ſcreen. On ſuch occaſions theſe obdurate wretches do not heſitate to dreſs and eat their food on the very ſpot where their victim is inhumed.

If, which ſcarcely ever happens, a traveller eſcape from the perſons attempting to ſtrangle him, he incurs the hazard of being diſpatched by one of the parties on watch. Should he finally eſcape, or ſhould any other circumſtance occur to excite alarm, or apprehenſions of being ſeized, the gang immediately diſperſes; having previouſly agreed to re-aſſemble at an appointed time, at ſome diſtant place.

Travellers reſting in the ſame choultry with *P'hánsigárs* are ſometimes deſtroyed in the night, and their bodies conveyed to a diſtance and buried. On theſe occaſions a perſon is not always murdered when aſleep; as, while he is in a recumbent poſture, the *P'hánsigárs* find a difficulty in applying the cloth. The uſual practice is firſt to awaken him ſuddenly with an alarm of a ſnake or a ſcorpion, and then to ſtrangle him.

In attacking a traveller on horſeback, the *P'hánsigárs* range themſelves in the following manner. One of the gang goes in front of the horſe, and another has his ſtation in the rear; a third, walking by the ſide of the traveller, keeps him engaged in converſation till, finding that he is off his guard, he ſuddenly ſeizes the traveller by the arm and drags him to the ground; the horſe at the ſame time being ſeized by the foremoſt villain. The miſerable ſufferer is then ſtrangled in the uſual manner.

Against *P'hánsigárs* it muſt be obvious, that arms and the ordinary precautions taken againſt robbers, are unavailing. When a perſon is armed with a dagger, it is uſual for one of the villains to ſecure his hands. It ſometimes happens, that a party of travellers, conſiſting of ſeveral perſons, and poſſeſſed of valuable effects, are, while journeying in imaginary ſecurity, ſuddenly cut off; and the lifeleſs and deſpoiled bodies being removed and interred, not a veſtige of them appears. (*g*) Inſtances are ſaid to have occurred, of twelve and fourteen perſons being ſimultaneouſly deſtroyed. But ſuch occurrences muſt be rare; and, in general, the property taken is not conſiderable. Such, indeed, are the cruelty and cupidity of theſe deteſtable wretches, that, on the preſumption of every traveller poſſeſſing concealed treaſure, or ſome property, however trifling, even indigence affords not its wonted ſecurity.

Formerly, if good horſes, ſhawls, or other valuable articles, were among the booty, they were commonly reſerved for the *polygar*, in payment of protection. A portion of the plunder was uſually appropriated to defraying the expences of religious ceremonies; and, ſometimes, a part was alſo allotted for the benefit of the widows and families of deceaſed members of the gang. The reſidue of the booty, being divided into ſeveral parts, was uſually ſhared as follows:—to the leader, two ſhares; to the men actually concerned in perpetrating the murder, and to the perſon who cut the dead body, each one ſhare and a half; and to the remainder of the gang each one ſhare. The plunder was almoſt always carried home by the *P'hánsigárs* and ſold greatly below its value:—it was never diſpoſed of near to the place where the per-

(*g.*) Near *Sadras*, about ten years ago, three *golah* peons were killed, having on them money in different coins, to the amount of 16,000 rupees. In 1805, five perſons were killed in *Coimbatoor*, and caſh to the amount of about 2,500 pagodas, the property of the collector of the diſtrict, was taken. In the ſame year, two reſpectable natives, proceeding on horſeback from *Madras* to the *Malabar* coaſt, with five attendants, were all killed. In 1807, five perſons, beſides two others who had joined them on the road, were killed near *Bangalore*, and robbed of property to the amount of 1,000 pagodas, belonging to an officer of engineers. And, in 1815, three perſons were killed in the diſtrict of *Maſulipatam*, and 2,500 rupees taken.

ſon to whom it belonged was murdered, nor where it was likely to be recognized, of which the *P'hánsigárs* were enabled to judge by the information imparted to them by the credulous ſufferers.

THE frequent aſſociation of the moſt abject ſuperſtition, with the deepeſt guilt, has been often noticed. The juſtneſs of the obſervation is exemplified in the conduct of moſt—perhaps of all—claſſes of *Indian* delinquents, and remarkably ſo in that of the *P'hánsigárs.* Their ſyſtem, indeed, ſeems to be founded on the baſis of ſuperſtition. They pay the moſt ſervile regard to omens; and they never leave their abodes to go on an expedition, without a previous perſuaſion, derived from modes of devination in uſe among them, that it will be attended with ſucceſs. Though the *P'hánsigárs* are almoſt all *muſſulmans,* they have nevertheleſs univerſally adopted on certain occaſions, the idolatrous worſhip of *Hindu* deities. CALI' or MARRIATTA, (the goddeſs of ſmall-pox of the *Carnatic,*) is regarded as their tutelary deity, and is the object of their adoration. She is uſually invoked by them under the names of JAYÍ, or AYÍ, and of TULJAPURÍ. *(b)* Before an expedition is determined on an entertainment is given, when the ceremony of ſacrificing a ſheep to JYU is performed; and though perhaps not always yet it would ſeem generally, in the following manner. A ſilver or brazen image of the goddeſs, with certain paraphernalia pertaining to her;

(*b*) Colonel COLIN MACKINZIE, ſo well known for his ſucceſsful reſearches into *Indian* hiſtory and antiquities, obſerves, in a letter to me, "that it was the cuſtom of many of the ancient heads of families, that have raiſed themſelves by depredation to rank and power, to conciliate CA'LI'; hence the ſacrifices of human kind, of offerings of noſes, and ultimately of ſheep by the Rajahs of *Myſore*; and now the commutation of cocoanuts at the hill of *Myſore*, which derives its name from MAHE'SA-ASURA MARDANA', another name for CA'LI'.

"At *Chitteldroog* alſo the ancient *polygars* worſhipped and ſacrificed to CA'LI'; and even ſtill at *Tuljapúr*, on the weſtern ghauts, 300 miles weſt of *Hydrabad*, on the road to *Poonah*. I was there in March 1797. It is a celebrated temple of CA'LI', where the pooja is performed by a low tribe and not by bramins, who abhor theſe rites. It is even ſo much ſuſpected that infamous rites and human victims were offered there, that my head bramin (the late valued *Boriah*) horror-ſtruck by the accounts he received, urged my departure from *Tuljapúr* and was not eaſy till we got away."

and ſometimes, alſo, one of GANESʹA; and the images of a lizard and a ſnake, reptiles from which preſages are drawn; together with the implements of *P'hánsigárí* as a nooſe, knife, and pickaxe, being placed together, flowers are ſcattered over them, and offerings of fruit, cakes, ſpirit, &c. are made; odoriferous powders are burned, and prayers are offered for ſuccess. The head of the ſheep being cut off, it is placed, with a burning lamp upon it and the right fore foot in the mouth, before the image of JAYÍ, and the goddeſs is entreated to reveal to them, whether ſhe approves of the expedition they are meditating. Her conſent is ſuppoſed to be declared, ſhould certain tremulous or convulſive movements be obſerved, during the invocation, in the mouth and noſtrils, while ſome fluid is poured upon thoſe parts. But the abſence of thoſe agitations is conſidered as indicating the diſapprobation of the goddeſs, and the expedition is poſtponed.

ABOUT ten or twenty day's afterwards, the ceremony is repeated; and, if auſpicious inferences be drawn from it, the *P'hánsigárs* prepare to depart. But before they determine towards what quarter to proceed, ſome perſons of the gang are ſent on the high road, in the direction they wiſh to take, to obſerve the flight of crows and other birds, and to liſten to the chirping of lizards. Should ſucceſs be betokened, the ſame path is taken. If the ſigns be adverſe, the *ſirdar* ſends ſome of the gang to make obſervations on another road, or at a place where two roads meet; and theſe votaries of ſuperſtition proceed in that direction, which promiſes, as they infer, the beſt ſucceſs.

IN the courſe of their progreſs, they obſerve the ſame ſcrupulous regard to omens. Emboldened by favorable ones, they are greatly diſcouraged by thoſe of an oppoſite tendency. If they have not proceeded far from home, when unlucky ſigns are deſcried, they regard them as premonitions to return:—under other circumſtances they either perform certain ceremonies, or they halt for a few days, till the malignant influence, denoted by them, is ſuppoſed to be paſſed; or elſe they bend their courſe in a different direction. To the intervention of bad omens, a traveller, over whom deſtruction was impending, is ſometimes indebted for his ſafety. *(i)*

On returning alſo from a ſucceſsful expedition, ceremonies are performed to Jayí.

The *P'hánsigárs* keep the *Hindu* feſtivals of the *Dípávalí* and the *Deſſerah*, which they celebrate in a manner ſimilar to that obſerved among *Hindus*.

A tradition is current among *P'hánsigárs*, that about the period of the commencement of the *Cali Yug*, Mariatta co-operated with them ſo far, as to relieve them of the trouble of interring the dead bodies, by devouring them herſelf. On one occaſion, after deſtroying a traveller, the body was, as uſual, left unburied; and a novice, unguardedly looking behind him, ſaw the goddeſs in the act of feaſting upon it, half of it hanging out of her mouth. She, upon this, declared that ſhe would no longer devour thoſe whom the *P'hánsigárs* ſlaughtered; but ſhe con-

(i) It would be tedious to enumerate all the omens by which they allow themſelves to be influenced in their proceedings. I ſhall briefly mention a few of both kinds—proſperous and adverſe.

The following are favorable ſigns:—A lizard chirping, and a crow making a noiſe on a living tree on the left ſide. A tiger appearing is deemed rather a good ſign. The noiſe of a partridge on the right ſide, denotes that they will meet with good booty on the very ſpot, and they, therefore, are accuſtomed to make a halt.

Theſe betoken misfortune:—A hare or a ſnake croſſing the road before them. A crow ſitting and making a noiſe on a rock or a dead tree. An aſs braying while ſitting. An owl ſcreeching. The noiſe of a ſingle jackal. If a dog ſhould carry off the head of a ſheep which they have ſacrificed, they conſider it to betoken that they will get no booty for many years.

descended to present them with one of her teeth for a pickaxe, a rib for a knife, and the hem of her lower garment for a noose, and ordered them, for the future, to cut and bury the bodies of those whom they destroyed.

White and yellow being considered the favorite colors of their patroness, and those in which she is arrayed; the cloths for strangling are of one or other of these, to the exclusion, I believe, of all other colors.

Ridiculous as their superstitions must appear, they are not devoid of effect. They serve the important purposes of cementing the union of the gang; of kindling courage and confidence; and, by an appeal to religious texts deemed infallible, of imparting to their atrocities the semblance of divine sanction.

To the ascendancy of the same superstitious feeling is also to be ascribed the curious circumstance that *P'hánsigárs* are accustomed to refrain from murdering females, and persons of the *Camála* cast; which includes gold, iron, and brass, smiths, carpenters, and stone-cutters.) Washermen, potmakers, pariahs, chucklers, lepers, the blind and mutilated, a man driving a cow or a female goat, are also spared. These persons appear to be regarded either as the descendants or servants of Jayi; as her constant worshippers; or as having claims to the especial protection of the goddess, and are for these reasons exempted from slaughter.

When this rule is respected any one of these persons, travelling with others of different casts, proves a safeguard to the whole party; the same principle which prompts the *P'hánsigárs* to destroy every individual of a party, forbidding them to kill any unless the whole.

Many *P'hánsigárs*, who have become informers, have declared that they never knew any of the abovementioned perſons to have been deſtroyed, and conceived that no pecuniary temptation could be ſufficiently powerful to occaſion a violation of the rule. Others have ſtated that they had *heard* of a gang of *P'hánsigárs* who, having murdered a woman, never afterwards proſpered, and were at length deſtroyed. Notwithſtanding the reaſons for acquieſcing generally in the truth of the ſtatement, that women, and men of particular caſts, are ſpared, the following occurrences, in the latter of which not fewer, than nine perſons diſappeared, and who were almoſt beyond doubt murdered by *P'hánsigárs*, ſhew that their religious ſcruples on this point are, when the temptation is great, at leaſt ſometimes overcome.

In the latter end of 1800, Mohamed Rous, the ſubadar who commanded the eſcort of the Reſident of *Myſore*, being ordered to join the force then forming againſt the ſouthern *Polygars*, ſent ſome of his family, among whom were two, if not three, women, to *Madras*. They were never heard of until June 1801; when a man was ſeized at *Bangalore* having in his poſſeſſion a bullock which was recogniſed to have belonged to Mohamed Rous. This man was a *P'hánsigár*; and gave a clear account of the murder, by a gang to which he belonged, of the ſubadar's family.

The wife of Kistna Row, in company with his nephew, and attended by a bramin cook; two female ſervants, two private peons, and two *coolies*, ſet out from *Poonah* with four horſes to join Kistna Row, then at *Nagpúr*. They had nearly completed their journey, having arrived at a village about fifteen miles from the place of their deſtination, and ſent to apprize Kistna Row of their approach. Two perſons were ſent by him to conduct the party to *Nagpúr*; but ſubſequently to the departure of the travellers from the village abovementioned no intelligence could be obtained—no traces whatever could be difcovered of them; and though about four years have fince elapfed, all enquiries have been fruitlefs. (*k*)

The utility to fuch criminals as *Phánsigárs* of figns, and of words and phrafes not underftood by others, as channels of communication muft be obvious. It is accordingly found that feveral fuch are employed by them. Some of thofe in more frequent ufe I fhall mention; and the catalogue might have been eafily extended.

Drawing the back of the hand along the chin, from the throat outwards, implies that caution is requifite—that fome ftranger is approaching. Putting the open hand over the mouth and drawing it gently down implies that there is no longer caufe for alarm. If an advanced party of *Phánsigárs* overtake any traveller whom they defign to deftroy, but have need of more affiftance, they make certain marks on the road, by which thofe of the gang who follow underftand that they are required to haften forwards. A party in advance alfo leaves certain marks where a road branches off, as intimations to thofe who follow of the route their comrades have taken.

The following lift comprehends feveral flang terms and phrafes in ufe among them. This language they denominate *Pheraferi-ci-bót*; or, as the term may be rendered, the language of difpatch or emergency.

(*k*) I have ftated that nine perfons were cut off on this occafion, though there is fome reafon to believe that the party confifted of even a greater number.

Kistna Row had been formerly employed in the confidential fituation of Shirifhtedár under Colonel Read, when this gentleman held the Collectorfhip of the territories ceded by *Tippoo* on the conclufion of the war of 1793. He afterwards ferved under Colonel Close at the Refidency at *Poonah*; where he is ftill employed by the Britifh Government.

Yelú	one
Bítrí	two
Sancód	three
Wodlí	four
Panchúrú	five
Serlú and Cherú	ſix
Sat'húrú	ſeven
Deſrú	ten
Máhí	one hundred
Hácadé	one thouſand
Doácadé	two thouſand
Deſacádé	ten thouſand
Sitcalé	pagoda
Burcé	rupee
Chiltá	fanam
Sitac	gold
Cawúdga	ſilver
Cúrp	a horſe
Cúrpání	a mare
Newála	ſheep
Lamcání	a hare
Móz (*per*)	bullock
Agá-í	turban
Raclán (*per*)	jackal
Comuda (*h*)	cock

Comudí (*h*)	hen
Sendrí	coral
Pandúr-p'hálí	pearl
Shaic'h-jí or Mohamed Khan	muſſulman ſtranger
Bhítú	hindu ditto
Cantger (per)	watcher
C'halcári	intelligencer
Worawal	perſons appointed to ſeize horſemen
Mahí	pickaxe
Cát'hiní	knife for cutting the dead body
Rumál	a handkerchief worn as a turban (various articles used for strangling)
Cancha (*h*), D'hotí (*tel*)	ſaſhe (various articles used for strangling)
Newár (*h*)	tape (various articles used for strangling)
Nár Muctem	(various articles used for strangling)
Sir-ghant	chief knot
Der-ghant	$1\frac{1}{2}$ or ſlip knot
Mán	a convenient place for murdering
Cónt	name of an entertainment given by *P'hánsígárs* to their friends

---

	Literally	*P'hánsígár* acceptation
Nyamet	A delicacy	A rich man
Lacra	A ſtick	A man of no property
P'hankaná		Ditto

Dhol	**....A barber's drum**	....An old man
Man j'harcen do	**....Sweep the place**	....See that no perſon is near
Kante pante láo	**....Bring firewood**	....Take your allotted poſts
Pán ka rumal nicálo	**Take out the handkerchief with the beetle**	Get out the doti, &c.
Pán Khaó	**Eat beetle ....**	....Deſpatch him
Roná caro	....	Implies a ſlight burial, with the face downwards, the body whole, and covered only with ſufficient earth to conceal it.
Kedbí Gidbí, Dékho,	Look after the ſtraw.	Look after the corpſe; that is, the *P'hánsigárs* proceed to a village after the ſlight burial, and ſend out the appointed perſons to bury the body properly, keeping watch that no perſon is looking.
Kedba bahir pariya	The ſtraw is come out.	Jackals have taken out the corpſe: you muſt not go that way.
Bhavání Púter....	Deſcendents of Bhowani.	*P'hánsigárs?*
—— Pútúr	Town of Bhowani Púter.	*P'hánsigárs?*
		Uſed interrogatively to aſcertain, without the riſk of expoſing themſelves, whether perſons whom they meet on their journeys, and whom they ſuſpect to be of the ſame fraternity, are ſo or not. When caution is particularly requiſite, the queſtion is

put in the latter and leſs ſuſpicious ſhape. The firſt ſyllable *put* aſcertains the point of their connexion with *Bhaváni*, whilſt from the termination *úr*, which ſignifies a town or village, they would appear to a ſtranger to be enquiring only about ſome particular place.

P'HÁNSIGARS bring up all their male children to the profeſſion, unleſs bodily defects prevent them from following it. The method obſerved in initiating a boy, is very gradual. At the age of ten or twelve years, he is firſt permitted to accompany a party of *P'hánsigárs*. One of the gang, generally a near relation, becomes his *uſtád* or tutor; whom the child is taught to regard with great reſpect, and whom he uſually ſerves in a menial capacity, carrying a bundle, and dreſſing food for him. Frequently the father acts as the preceptor to his ſon. In the event of being queſtioned by travellers whom he may meet, the boy is enjoined to give no information further, than that they are proceeding from ſome one place to another. He is inſtructed to conſider his intereſt as oppoſed to that of ſociety in general; and to deprive a human being of life, is repreſented as an act merely analogous and equivalent to that of killing a fowl or a ſheep. At firſt, while a murder is committing, the boy is ſent to ſome diſtance from the ſcene, along with one of the watchers: then allowed to ſee only the dead body: afterwards more and more of the ſecret is imparted to him—and, at length, the whole is diſcloſed. In the mean time, a ſhare of the booty is uſually aſſigned to him. He is allowed afterwards to aſſiſt in matters of minor importance, while the murder is perpetrating: but, it is not until he has attained the age of 18, 20, or 22 years, according to the bodily ſtrength he may have acquired, and the prudence and reſolution he may have evinced, that he is deemed capable of applying the *dhouti*, nor is he allowed to do ſo, until he has been formally preſented with one by his *uſtád*. For this purpoſe a fortunate day being fixed upon, and the time of the *Deſſerah* is deemed particularly auſpicious, the preceptor takes his pupil apart and preſents him with a *dhóuti*, which he tells him to uſe in the name of JAYÍ; he obſerves to him that on it he is to rely for the means of ſubſiſtence, and he exhorts him to be diſcreet and courageous. On the concluſion of this ceremony his education is conſidered to be complete, he is deemed qualified to act as a *P'hánsígár*; and he applies the nooſe on the next occaſion that offers.

AFTER his initiation, a *P'hánsígár* continues to treat his preceptor with great reſpect. He occaſionally makes him preſents, and aſſiſts him in his old age; and, on meeting him after a long abſence, he touches his feet in token of reverence.

SUCH is the effect of the courſe of education I have deſcribed, ſtrengthened by habit, that *P'hánsígárs* become ſtrongly attached to their deteſtable occupation. They rarely, if ever, abandon it. *(l)* Some, narrowly eſcaping the merited vengeance of the law and releaſed from priſon under ſecurity, could not refrain from reſuming their old employment; and thoſe who, bending under the weight of years and infirmities, are no longer able to bear an active or principal part, continue to aid the cauſe by keeping watch, procuring intelligence, or dreſſing the food of their younger confederates.

THE bonds of ſocial union among *P'hánsígárs* are drawn ſtill cloſer by intermarriages. Though not of frequent occurrence, inſtances are

(l) Three are known to have engaged in the ſervice of the Company as ſepoys.

not wanting in which they have married into families deemed honeſt and reſpectable. The women are not ignorant of the proceedings of their huſbands. Perſons of mature age are very rarely admitted into the fraternity, and when this has been done, it was only after long and intimate intercourſe had enabled the *P'hánsigárs* fully to appreciate the character of their confederates.

To the influence of perſonal character are *P'hánsigárs* uſually indebted for becoming the heads of gangs. Like others, who follow lawleſs and abandoned courſes, the *P'hánsigárs* are profligate and improvident, and addicted to the uſe of *bang*; ſo that the wealth they may acquire, even though conſiderable, is ſoon waſted.

Whether any *P'hánsigár* were ever capitally puniſhed by the Nabobs of the *Carnatic*, I know not. One gang, ſettled in the polium of *Chargal*, near the *Paidnaigdrug Paſs*, between the upper and lower *Carnatic*, was apprehended about 17 years ago, and fined to the amount of 5,000 rupees by the *ſubahdar* of the province; a mode of puniſhment ſo far from being juſtifiable, that it could hardly have been impoſed except from ſordid motives: nor could it fail to give new impulſe to the activity of the *P'hánsigárs*, and to render them more than ever rapacious and ſecret in their barbarous practices.

Hyder Alli proceeded againſt theſe criminals in a very ſummary manner, and deſtroyed ſeveral of them. In the reign of Tippoo, ſome were ſentenced to hard labour, and others ſuffered mutilation of the limbs. While Purniah was *dewan* of *Myſore*, during the minority of the preſent Rajah, highway robbery being frequent, was made capital, and ſeveral *P'hansigárs* were executed.

It muſt be obvious that no eſtimate, except what is extremely vague and unſatisfactory, can be formed of the number of perſons that have annually fallen victims to *P'hánsigárs* in the south of *India*. The number has varied greatly at different periods. There is reason to believe, that from the time of the conquest of *Mysore* in 1799, to 1807 and 1808, the practice of *P'hánsigárí*, in this part of *India*, had reached its acme; and that hundreds of persons were annually destroyed. (*m*) The great political changes, which marked the commencement of that period, and the introduction of a new system of government in *Mysore*, the *Ceded Districts*, and the *Carnatic*, though infinitely preferable to the former, yet was it in many respects less jealous and vigilant, and afforded facilities of communication before unknown between distant countries, of which the *P'hánsigárs* and other criminals availed themselves to overspread the country: and it may be conjectured that many persons, deprived by the declension of the *Mohammedan* power of their wonted resources, were tempted to resort to criminal courses to obtain a subsistence.

The foregoing description of the *P'hánsigárs* is meant to be more particularly applicable to those gangs that were settled in the northern part of the *Carnatic* and in the *Ceded Districts*, antecedently to the year 1808. Since that time, they have become well known to the *English* courts of justice, and their habits have undergone some changes. Many have left the Company's territories and fled to those of the *Nizam*, and of the *Mahrattas*. But though the number of them is greatly diminished, *P'hánsigárs* still infest the dominions of the Company. The gangs,

(*m*) In one of his reports, the magistrate of *Chittúr* observes: —" I believe that some of the *P'hánsigárs* have been concerned in above two hundred murders; nor will this estimate appear extravagant, if it be remembered, that murder was their profession, frequently their only means of gaining a subsistence: every man of fifty years of age, has probably been actively engaged during twenty-five years of his life in murder, and on the most moderate computation, it may be reckoned, that he has made one excursion a year, and met each time with ten victims."

Yet, Francis Bartolemeo says, in a note page 69.—" During a residence of 13 or 14 years in *India*, I never heard of any traveller being robbed or murdered on the highway." —*Travels in India, translated by* Forster.

indeed, consist of fewer persons than formerly; their plans are less systematic, their range is less ample; they roam the country more secretly; more frequently changing their names and places of abode; and adopting other precautionary measures to screen themselves from justice. Unfortunately, few of the numerous *P'hánsigárs* that have at different times been apprehended, could be convicted in accordance with the evidence required by the *Mohammedan* criminal law; which admitting not the testimony of accomplices, and rarely the sufficiency of strong circumstantial evidence unless confirmed by the confession of the culprits, their adherence to protestations of innocence has alone, but too frequently, exempted them from punishment. Those that have been tried and released becoming greater adepts in deceit, have, together with their old propensities, carried with them a knowledge of the form of trial, and of the nature of the evidence requisite to their conviction.

The habits and proceedings of the *P'hánsigárs* it is reasonable to conclude have been modified and varied by different circumstances and events of a local or political nature in the several states infested by them, in some places approximating more than in others to the foregoing description. There is every reason to believe, that in the *Deccan*, and more particularly in the territories of the *Nizam*, *P'hánsigárs* are very numerous. They will be naturally encouraged to settle in greater numbers, and to carry on their practices with less caution and secrecy, in a country, a prey to anarchy or invasion, where the administration is feeble or corrupt, or where crimes are constantly committed with impunity. It is also not unreasonable to suppose, that they may occasionally act in concert with other classes of delinquents; and that their proceedings may sometimes be of a mixed nature, partaking of the peculiarities of those with whom they may be in league. In those countries too, where *P'hánsigári* has been long practised, it may be presumed, that the ordinary artifices will at length become known, and as the ſucceſs of thoſe murderers muſt chiefly depend on the ignorance of travellers of their devices, they will perhaps find it neceſſary to reſort to novel and unſuſpected ſtratagems.

I HAVE heard of no inſtance in which a European was murdered by *P'hánsigárs*. The manner in which they are accuſtomed to travel in *India* is perhaps generally ſufficient to exempt them from danger; added to which, apprehenſion of the conſequences of ſtrict enquiry and ſearch ſhould a European be miſſing, may be ſuppoſed to intimidate the *P'hánsigárs*, at leaſt in the dominions of the Company. Similar reaſons influence them in ſparing coolies and parties charged with the property of *Engliſh* gentlemen, combined with the conſideration that while ſuch articles would generally be uſeleſs to the *P'hánsigárs*, they would find difficulty in diſpoſing of them, and might incur imminent danger of detection in the attempt.

THAT the diſappearance of ſuch numbers of natives ſhould have excited ſo little intereſt and enquiry as not to have led to a general knowledge of thoſe combinations of criminals will naturally appear extraordinary. Such ignorance, certainly, could not have prevailed in *England*, where the abſence, if unaccounted for, of even a ſingle perſon, ſeldom fails to produce ſuſpicion, with conſecutive inveſtigation and diſcovery. In *India* the caſe is far otherwiſe; and ſuch an event, unleſs occurring to a perſon of ſome conſequence, would ſcarcely be known beyond the precincts of the place of reſidence or the village of the unfortunate ſufferer. Many that fall victims to the *P'hánsigárs* are the ſubjects of other and diſtant ſtates: many have no ſettled abodes. It muſt alſo be remembered that *P'hánsigárs* refrain from murdering the inhabitants of towns and villages near to which they are

2 A

halting; neither are they accuſtomed to murder near to their own habitations; circumſtances which not only prevent ſuſpicion attaching to them as the murderers, and to the local authority as protecting and ſharing the booty with them, but tend to throw it upon others, who reſide near to the ſpot whither a traveller may have been traced, and where he was laſt ſeen. Beſides, a perſon ſetting out on a journey is often unable to fix any period for his return; and though he ſhould not reviſit his home at the expected time, his delay will, for a while, excite little alarm in the minds of his friends. He is ſuppoſed to be unexpectedly detained—to be ill—to have met with ſome ordinary accident—to have deſerted his family—to have died. Should ſuſpicion ariſe that he has been murdered, the act is attributed to ordinary highway robbers, and it is but ſeldom that minute enquiries can be inſtituted by his bereaved relatives. But ſuppoſing that this is done, and the progreſs of the miſſing traveller traced to a particular place and not beyond it, ſtill ſuſpicion would be apt to attach to any, rather than to a few apparently inoffenſive travellers, journeying either for the purpoſe of traffic, as is imagined: or, as is often pretended, to ſee their relations—or, to be preſent at ſome marriage; and who, if ever noticed, have perhaps been long ſince forgotten. If, notwithſtanding all theſe improbabilities, ſuſpicion ſhould fall upon the actual perpetrators, where could they be found?

Thus with reſpect to ſepoys, who, having obtained leave of abſence, never rejoined their corps, the concluſion generally formed has been, that they had deſerted—when, in various inſtances, they had fallen ſacrifices to the wiles of the *P'hánsigárs*. The ſame obſervation is particularly applicable to *golah* peons, charged with the conveyance of money and valuables; many of whom having diſappeared, no doubt was entertained that they had abſconded, and appropriated the property to their own uſe. Even the apprehenſion, which an indiſtinct idea of danger tends to create in the minds of these and other travellers, would render them only more liable to fall into the snare. Less persuasion would be requisite to induce them to join a party of *P'hánsigárs;* prompted by the belief that they were thus providing, in the most effectual manner, for their own safety.

What constitutes the most odious feature in the character of these murderers, is, that prodigal as they are of human life, they can rarely claim the benefit of even the palliating circumstance of strong pecuniary temptation. They are equally strangers to compassion and remorse—they are never restrained from the commission of crimes by commiseration for the unfortunate traveller—and they are exempted from the compunctious visitings of conscience, which usually follow, sooner or later, the steps of guilt. "*P'hánsigárí,*" they observe, with cold indifference blended with a degree of surprize, when questioned on this subject, "is their *business;*" which, with reference to the tenets of fatalism, they conceive themselves to have been pre-ordained to follow. By an application of the same doctrine, they have compared themselves, not inaptly, to tigers; maintaining, that as these ferocious beasts are impelled by irresistible necessity, and fulfil the designs of nature in preying on other animals, so the appropriate victims of the *P'hánsigárs* are men; and that the destiny of those whom they kill, "was written on their foreheads."

This state of moral insensibility and debasement is yet calculated to give birth to pity, while it aggravates the horror with which we contemplate their atrocities. It ought not to be forgotten, that unlike many who adopt criminal courses, the *P'hánsigárs* had not previously to divest themselves of upright principles—to oppose their practice to their feelings; but that, on the contrary, having been trained up from their childhood to the profession, they acquired habits unfitting them for honeſt and induſtrious exertion; that a deteſtable ſuperſtition lent its ſanctions to their enormities; and that they did but obey the inſtructions, and imitate the examples, of their fathers.

The *T'hegs*, *(n)* in the more northern parts of *India*, may be divided into three claſſes. The firſt conſiſts chiefly of *Mohammedans* who originally reſided under the protection of zemindars of large eſtates, as Hura Sing, Dia Ram, &c. and in the diſtrict of *Etawah*; including alſo a few ſtragglers at other villages. The ſecond claſs is compoſed of *Hindus*, who are for the moſt part of the *Lodeh* caſt, and is much more numerous than the former. They reſided in great numbers in the eaſtern part of *Etawah*, and the adjoining diſtrict of *Cawnpore*, until alarmed by the active exertions of the magiſtrates, by whom many were apprehended. Theſe *T'hegs* had long eſcaped ſuſpicion by engaging in tillage, and by always carrying on their depredations at a diſtance from home. The third claſs is more conſiderable in reſpect to number, and extends over a larger tract of country than either of the foregoing claſſes. It conſiſts of a deſperate aſſociation of all caſts, which grew up in the *Pergunnahs* of *Sindouſe* and *Purhara*, and the neighbouring villages on the *Mahratta* territories. They travel in large bodies, and are more bold and adventurous than the *T'hegs* in the Company's provinces. Their predatory excurſions are chiefly confined to the country that lies to the eaſtward and ſouthward of *Gwalior*, and to the province of *Bundlecund*.

Thevenot, in the following paſſage, evidently alludes to the *P'hánsigárs* or *T'hegs*.

(n) The term *T'heg* is not unknown in the ſouth of *India*, but it is not applied to the *P'hánsigárs*, but to a claſs of delinquents to whom it ſeems more appropriate, viz. to cheats or ſwindlers, who, often appearing as pearl and coral ſellers, practice various fraudulent acts, particularly in ſubſtituting bad coins for good, which they receive under the pretence of giving or taking change.

" Though the road I have been ſpeaking of from *Delhi* to *Agra* be
" tolerable, yet hath it many inconveniences. One may meet with
" tygers, panthers, and lions upon it, and one had beſt alſo have a care
" of robbers, and above all things not to ſuffer any body to come
" near one upon the road. The cunningeſt robbers in the world are
" in that country. They uſe a certain ſlip with a running nooſe,
" which they can caſt with ſo much ſlight about a man's neck, when
" they are within reach of him, that they never fail, ſo that they
" ſtrangle him in a trice. They have another cunning trick alſo to
" catch travellers with. They ſend out a handſome woman upon the
" road, who with her hair diſhevelled ſeems to be all in tears, ſighing
" and complaining of ſome misfortune which ſhe pretends has befallen
" her. Now as ſhe takes the ſame way that the traveller goes, he eaſily
" falls into converſation with her, and finding her beautiful, offers her
" his aſſiſtance, which ſhe accepts; but he hath no ſooner taken her up
" behind him on horſeback, but ſhe throws the ſnare about his neck
" and ſtrangles him, or at leaſt ſtuns him, until the robbers (who lie hid)
" come running into her aſſiſtance and complete what ſhe hath begun.
" But beſides that, there are men in thoſe quarters ſo ſkilful in caſting
" the ſnare, that they ſucceed as well at a diſtance as near at hand; and
" if an ox or any other beaſt belonging to a *caravan* run away, as
" ſometimes it happens, they fail not to catch it by the neck." (o)

Travellers in the ſouth of *India* alſo are ſometimes decoyed through the allurements of women into ſituations, where they are murdered and plundered by perſons lying in wait for them; but, whether by that claſs of criminals who are properly called *P'hánsígárs*, I am uncertain. This method, as well as that of adminiſtering intoxicating and poiſonous mixtures to travellers, though inconſonant with the habits of the large

(o) Thevenot's Travels, part III. page 41.

gangs, who are not accompanied in their excurſions by women, may perhaps be reſorted to by ſmaller and more needy parties, who rob near to their own abodes, or who, having no fixed habitation, continually roam with their families from place to place.

WITH reſpect to the practice of throwing the nooſe from a diſtance, as mentioned by THEVENOT, and which is that of the *Binjaris* in *India*, to recover their ſtrayed bullocks, *(p)* I conclude it to be the ſame as was reſorted to in battle (according to FIRDAUSI) by the ancient *Perſians* and other *Aſiatic* nations, for ſeizing and binding their enemies, and dragging them off horſeback. The *cammand*, (literally a rope or nooſe,) ſaid to have been formed of ſilk, or of the dried ſkin or ſinews of animals, is mentioned in various parts of the SHAH NA'MAH. Thus, in narrating the exploits of the renowned champion RUSTUM, it is ſaid:—

امی رفت رستم چو پیل دژم   کمندی ببازو درون شصت خم

RUSTUM advanced like a furious elephant,
His *cammand* in his arm full ſixty coils.

(*p*) TAVERNIER, ſpeaking of the *Circaſſians*, obſerves:—" Ils ne ſe ſervent point de chiens ni d'oyſeaux pour la chaſſe, & quand ils y vont ils s'aſſemblent d'ordinaire ſept ou huit des principaux du village. Ils ont de si bons chevaux qu'a la courſe ils fatiguent la beſte & la forcent de ſe rendre. Chacun tient toute preste une corde qui a un nœud coulant & c'eſt atachee a l'arçon de la ſelle, & ils ſont si adroits a la jeter au col de la beſte qui ſe rend de laſſitude qu'il y en a peu qui leur echapent."—Tom I. Liv. Troisieme, Ch. XI.

The *laqui* of the *South American Indians*, enables them to ſtrike and entangle animals at the diſtance of 300 paces. It is a ſtrip of leather, five or ſix feet long, to each end of which is faſtened a ſtone about two pounds weight. The huntſman, who is on horſeback, holds one of theſe ſtones in his hand, and whirls the other round like a ſling as ſwiftly as poſſible, in order to hurl it with more force, when he throws it at the animal he has ſingled out, which he is almoſt certain of ſtriking.

The *laqui* of the *Spaniſh* peaſants of *South America*, in the uſe of which they are amazingly expert, differs from that uſed by the *Indians* in having a ſingle nooſe, in place of a ball at each end. It is their principal weapon, for they employ it on all occaſions, both in hunting and in their private quarrels. ULLOA ſays, that the *Spaniſh* peaſantry can ſtrike and halter the object of their attack, with almoſt unerring certainty, at the diſtance of 30 or 40 paces; but that a ſmall diſtance, ſuch as 10 or 15 paces, renders their dexterity in ſome meaſure ineffectual.—Vide Encyclo. Brewſt Art. Chili.

بیامد ز اولاد بگشاد بند به فتراک بست آن کیانی کمند

He loosed AULAD (*q*) from his bonds,
And tied his *Kyanian* (*r*) *cammand* to the bow of his saddle.

که از پشت زین شان بخم کمند ربودم سر و پای کردم به بند

For from their saddles, with the noose of my *cammand*,
I tore them, and bound fast their heads and feet.

بینداخت آن تاب داده کمند بیکی سواران بسی کرد بند

He threw the well-twisted *cammand*;
And caught many a horsemen on the same spot.

چو از دست رستم رها شد کمند سر تاجدار اندر آمد به بند

When the *cammand* issued from the hand of RUSTUM,
The crowned head (*s*) became imprisoned.

IN the same manner as the *cammand*, the *Pásan*, (*Tel.*) or *Pásan*, (*Tam.*) literally a rope, was also, it is probable, used by the ancient *Hindu* heroes in war. If the authority of the RÁMÁYANA were allowed to be sufficient to establish the point, it might be asserted that there were three sorts of *Pásas* known to the *Hindus*: two, viz. the noose of justice and the noose of death, pertaining to YAMA; and one, the noose of the water, to *Varuna*. They are mentioned in the following passage among the weapons presented by VISWAMITRA to RÁMA.

धर्म्मपाशंतथैवास्त्रंकालपाशञ्चदुर्ज्जयं ।
वारुणञ्चापितेपाशन्ददामिपरमार्च्चितं ।

(*q*) A prisoner to RUSTUM in the plains of *Mazenderán*—the *Persian* region of magic and romance.

(*r*) From the dynasty of ancient *Persian* Kings so named.

(*s*) Alluding to *Khacan* or the King of *China*, who, seated on his elephant, was taken prisoner by RUSTUM in a great battle, in which the former had come to the assistance of the *Turks* against the *Persians*.—See also D'Herbelot's Bib. Or. Art. Khathai, &c.

"I give thee the *Dherma-pása*, and also, the miſſile weapon *belonging to it;* the cruelly-conquering CA'LA-PÁSA, and the highly valued YARUN'A-PÁSA." (t)

SIVA is ſometimes, though very rarely, repreſented with the PÁSA; (v)—VISHN'U, as HARI, is invoked in the *B'hágavat*, and ſaid to hold it in one of his eight hands; and GAN'E'S'A, as the lord of wiles, ſtratagems, &c. is almoſt always repreſented with the PÁS'A.

How long the country ſouth of the KISTNA has been infeſted by *Phánsigárs* I know not, though it is certain that they have been ſettled in the *Poliums* of *Chittoor* for at leaſt a century. On this point the *P'hánsigárs* themſelves are quite ignorant, knowing in general little more than that their fathers and grand fathers followed the ſame horrid employment, and taught it to their children. There is however no reaſon to ſuppoſe that the practice in this part of *India*, is of great antiquity. It may alſo be a queſtion whether to the *Hindus* or to the *Muſſelmans* ought to be conſidered as attaching the reproach of inventing this deteſtable ſyſtem of pillage and murder. The reſpect paid by *Muſſalman P'hánsigárs* to the omens and modes of divination, and to the religious and idolatrous rites of the *Hindus*—a reſpect apparently not accidental, but which pervades, and ſeems interwoven with their whole ſyſtem—affords grounds for the belief, that to them, rather than to the *Muſſelmans*, is to be aſcribed the invention.

On the other hand it may be argued, that had theſe bands of murderers conſiſted primarily of *Hindus*, it would probably have appeared

(t) Book I. ſection 26.—The learned tranſlators of the RA'MA'YANA, ſtate the *pás'a* to have had the power of entangling or binding the foe, and ſuppoſe it to have been a kind of gin or net.

(v) A print, in which JAYU or SIVA, and QUENERADI or GAN'ES'A, are repreſented with the *pásham*, will be found in Picart's Cuſtoms and Religious Ceremonies, Vol. III. page 457.

that the practice was of considerable antiquity; in which case there could hardly have been that prevailing ignorance among the *Hindus* with regard to it, which is found to exist. It is a practice more in unison with the habits and customs of the *Musselmans* than with those of the *Hindus*. The gangs at least in the southern parts of *India*, consist chiefly of *Musselmans*, and similar practices, it has appeared, prevailed in *Hindustan* in the time of SHAH JEHAN and AURUNG-ZEB, and probably much anterior to the reigns of these monarchs, and have continued to the present day; and if, as I have been informed, *Arabia* and *Persia* be infested by *P'hánsigars*, little room is left to doubt that these murderers came along with the *Mohammedan* conquerors into *India*, and that they have followed the progress southward of the *Mohammedan* arms. In support of this opinion it may be observed, further, that in the more southern provinces which were never, or which fell latest, a prey to *Mohammedan* conquerors, *P'hánsigárs* do not appear even yet to have established themselves. I have not heard of any gangs being found to the south of *Salem* in *Baramahal*; and even these, there is reason to believe, but recently migrated thither from the *Poliums* of *Chittoor*, and the zillah of *Cuddapah*. With respect to the *Hindu* usages, adverting to the disposition observable among the lower orders of both nations to adopt the rites and customs of each other, they may have been introduced and eagerly received among ignorant and superstitious offenders, ever prone to embrace a scheme which serves the purpose of tranquillizing the mind without requiring the abandonment of criminal habits, either by *Hindu* converts to *Islamism*, or by such *Hindu* criminals as retaining their religion, attached themselves to bands of *P'hánsigárs*.

RICHARD C. SHERWOOD,

Surgeon on the Establishment of

Fort St. George.

December 1816.

W.H. Sleeman

Ramaseeana, or, *A Vocabulary of the Peculiar Language Used by the Thugs*. Calcutta: GH Huttmann, Military Orphan Press, 1836.

THE RAMASEEANA.

Aulae—A Thug, in contradistinction to Beetoo, any person not a Thug. When Thugs wish to ascertain whether the persons they meet are Thugs or not, they accost them with "*Aulae Khan Salam,*" if Musulmans; and "*Aulae Bhae Ram Ram,*" if Hindoo. This to any one but a Thug would seem the common salutation of "peace to thee, friend," but it would be instantly recognized by a Thug. Any man that should reply in the same manner would be quite safe.

Adhoreea—Any person who has separated himself from a party whom the Thugs have murdered or intend to murder, and thereby escaped them.

Ae ho to Ghyree Chulo—"If you are come, pray descend." The phrase most commonly used as the *J,hirnee* or signal for putting people to death, when every thing has been prepared for the purpose.

Agasee—A Turban. A Thug never moves out without his turban, except in Bengal perhaps. If a turban is set on fire, it threatens great evil, and the gang must, if near home, return, and wait seven days; if at a distance, an offering of goor is made, and the individual to whom the turban belonged, alone returns home. If the turban falls off it is an omen almost as bad, and requires the same sacrifices.

Agasee—Is also the term given for the cry of the kite. Heard in the day time, it is of little importance, and interpreted according to their rules for the *Thibaoo* and the *Pilhaoo*; but heard during the *Kootub*, or interval between the first watch and daybreak, it is called the *Kootub Agasee*, a dreadful omen. If in Camp, they get up and fly immediately, leaving untouched any person they may have inveigled, however wealthy. If they hear it after dark, but before the end of the first watch, they are not alarmed, as they consider the threatened evil to pass away in their sleep; literally the "omen gets suffocated under their sides as they turn in their sleep." It is the same with almost all bad omens that take place between evening and the end of the first watch.

Ardal—Among the Duckun Thugs, is the same as *Adhoreea* among those of Hindoostan.

Agureea—Descendants of the Thugs, who, after their expulsion from Delhie, resided for a time in the district of Agra, and thence spread over India; in contradistinction to those who went to different parts of India without resting at Agra. The *Buhleems* and *Tundels*, two of the seven original clans of Musulman Thugs, did not rest at Agra; and they are excluded. Their tradition is, that one of the Emperors of the house of Gouree expelled them all from Delhie, after the murder of a *Cheyla*, or slave of his, who had been long in league with them, but was murdered in consequence of a threat to betray them, made with a view to extort more money than they thought reasonable. The Emperor had them all marked on the *posteriors* with the stamp of the copper coin of the Empire.

Ansootore—Literally, "tear drops." Any shower of rain that falls before or after the four usual months of June, July, August and September. If it falls during the first day and night after entering on an expedition the gang must return, and open it anew. It is always a bad omen, and requires some sacrifices. See also Rukutbondee, or blood dropping. The Duckun Thugs call this shower *Now*.

Agasee Birar—Term among the Duckun Thugs for thunder. If it thunders while opening an expedition, and heavy rain falls, it is of no importance. If little or no rain falls the omen is bad, and they must suspend operations : after the expedition has been opened it is of no importance.

Ankura—One thousand of any thing.

Awk,hur—Any person maimed or deprived of the use of his limbs. In this sense it is peculiar to Duckun Thugs. Among Hindoostanees it signifies any bad omen. If they meet with such a maimed person on the road, the first day after they enter on an expedition, the gang must return, and open it anew. They never kill such maimed persons. There have been instances of it, but they are all supposed to have been followed by great calamities. See the case of Nawul Sing Jemadar, murdered at Biseynee—Appendix.

Anhur—Any metallic utensil for eating, drinking, or cooking.

Anjuna or *Anjruhna*—To sleep or pass the night.

Aentha—Silver money.

Angjhap—A term used by the Thugs of the Duckun for *Rehna*, or a temporary burial of bodies.

Ard,hul—Any bad omen ; the same as *Khurtul*. Both terms are confined to Duckun Thugs.

Balmeek—The author of one of the three *Ramaens* (or histories of the rape of *Seeta*, the wife of *Ram*, one of the incarnations of *Vishnoo*) which after its author is called the *Balmeek Ramaen*. The Thugs consider *Balmeek* to have been of their profession ; but, though they quote his name with reverence, they do not, I believe, invoke it in their offerings and sacrifices. A sketch of his life is given in each of the three *Ramaens*. His name was *Dojadh,un*, and he is said to have been a Brahmin by birth; to have been born at Kunoje in the latter end of the Sutjoog, or golden age; to have lost his parents when he was five years of age, and soon after to have joined some gangs of Bheel robbers, who, armed with bows and arrows, infested the roads about Chutterkote; to have married one of their daughters, and to have become the most noted robber and murderer of his day. From this course of life he is said to have been reclaimed by a miracle. Seven celebrated saints, at their holy place of abode, learned by inspiration that a Brahmin was thus disgracefully employed, and proceeded to the place to admonish him. He saw them approach, and as usual bent his bow, and demanded their money or their lives. "Why do you, a Brahmin by birth, follow this horrible "trade, and rob and murder innocent travellers?" "I have "a wife and children whom I love, on the top of yonder "hill; they want food, and I must provide it for them." "Go and ask those you love, and for whom you provide "food by the murder of innocent men, whether they are "willing to share with you in the crimes as well as in the "fruits." "And in the mean time you will make off. Many "a traveller has tried to escape me by similar tricks, but "I am not to be deceived." "We swear to remain till you "return." He went to his wife and children and asked the questions. They told him that they shared in what he brought to them, but he must be alone answerable for the means by which he acquired it. He returned to the saints, with a contrite heart, and implored their instructions. They told him to tarry where he stood till they should return, and continue to repeat the words, "*Mura, Mura, Mura,*" dead, dead, dead, which was familiar to him; knowing that he would in time convert it into *Ram, Ram, Ram,* God, God, God; and thinking that his soul was not yet fitted to repeat the holy name. He soon made the expected change, and continued to repeat *Ram, Ram, Ram,* for twelve thousand years, when the seven saints returned. Nothing but the bones remained, but they were erect, and repeating the holy name of *Ram.* White ants had built their hill over them, but on hearing their voice the skeleton assumed a form of Godlike beauty, and burst forth, as it is said, like the sun from behind a dark cloud. He became a man after God's own heart, and wrote his Ramaen by inspiration. *Balmee* signifies *ant hill,* and the *k* affixed signifies *born of,* and his name was changed from *Dojadhun* to *Balmeek.*

Bajeed—Safe, free from danger. When the Thugs have got their victims at the place where they intend to murder them, if the spies placed around, see all clear, they call out one of the following names, and the work of murder goes on. *Bajeed* or *Bajeed Khan, Deo* or *Deomun,* or *Deoseyn.* If the spies see a stranger approach and apprehend danger, they call out *Sheikh Jee,* or *Sheikh Mahummud,* or *Luchmun,* or *Luchmun Sing,* or *Luchee Ram,* or *Gunga Ram,* and the Thugs suspend operations. When one part of the gang advances with the travellers they intend to kill, and on the road meets other travellers, whom the party in the rear may conveniently murder, they tell them to bid their friends *Bajeed* or *Bajeed Khan,* and *Deo,* or *Deoman,* or *Deo Sing,* to make haste and overtake them. As soon as the gang behind hear this message they may fall upon and murder them, understanding by the signal that in advance the road is clear.

Baee or Dubaee—A frequented road.

Bae hojana—To become public; viz. the bodies of victims or other traces of their proceedings.

Byd,ha—**A man who has lost a limb or any member of his body. If they meet such a person during the first day of their expedition it is a bad omen, and requires sacrifices. Also any thing unbecoming the cast or condition of the person, and likely to lead to suspicion and danger. They seldom murder any person who has lost a limb, and attribute much of our success against them on the Nerbudda river, to the murder of Newal Sing, who had lost an arm, and his family at Biseynee, in 1820. See Biseynee case Saugor Sessions of 1831-32.**

Bagh—Bagdena—**Same as *Phooldena*, parole of rendezvous or meeting.**

Bagureea—**A class of Thugs who reside chiefly about Sooper, in the Gwalior territories. They are called also *K,hokhureeas*, and have followed the trade several generations, since their intermarriage with the emigrant Thugs from Delhie through Agra, or *Agureeas*.**

Boguma—**An old garment.**

Bugjana—**To become aware of the designs of the Thugs upon one.**

Bugna—**The same.**

Bâjunee—**A gun.**

Boj,ha—**The Thug who take the bodies of the murdered person to the grave.**

Bojhae—**The office of the Bojha.**

Bukote—**A strangler same as *Bhurtote*.**

Buk,h—**The word made use of by the Thugs when calling to each other to assemble after having been separated by accident or design. *Buk,h, Buk,h, Buk,h*, or come, come, come.**

Bahleem—**One of the seven original Thug clans. There are scarcely any of this clan to be found north of the Nerbudda.**

Beyl—**The place chosen for burying the victims.**

Beegha—Term among the Thugs of Behar and Bengal for a share of the spoil. From every booty they first set aside ten per cent. for the leaders, and five for the stranglers, however few or many; the remainder is divided into *Beeghas*, or shares. Their proportions are 1.2 for jemadar or leader—1.14 for a man who has attained the rank of strangler—1 for a person who has not attained that rank.

Beelha—A great enemy of Thugs: also a leper, or man deprived of his nose or ear; or any person much emaciated by sickness.

Beetula—A dog. Term peculiar to the *Jumaldehee*, *Lodaha* and *Moteea* Thugs of Behar and Bengal.

Bykureea—The spy or scout. Term used by the *Bongoos*, or river Thugs, the *Jumaldehees*, *Lodahas*, and *Moteeas* for *Tilha*.

Bykuree kurna—To act as a spy or scout—or *Bykuree* "*dek,hna*," to look out.

Beyl,ha.—The person who chooses the place for murdering.

Beylhae.—The office of choosing the place.

Beel Grain.—Term peculiar to Duckun Thugs.

Bhalee or Bhaloo.—The call of the jackal. There are three kind of calls from which the Thugs draw omens. The *Bhalee*, which they also call *Burhohee*, is the call of one jackal. The second is the general clamour of jackals, which people call their *lamentation*. This the Thugs call *Raureen*. The third, the *Ekareea*, or short call of a jackal, in which he seems to be cut short after an effort or two. Any one of these calls heard during the day threatens great evil, and the gang quits the country in which they hear it, leaving untouched any persons they have inveigled, however wealthy. The *Ekareea* is bad either by night or by day. The other two calls, when heard by night on opening the expedition, are interpreted according to the ordinary rules for the *Thibaoo* and *Pilhaoo*.

Bileea.—A brass cup ; technically a place for murdering or burying the victims.

Bileea-Manjuna.—Literally, to clean the brass cup. To choose the place for murder.

Bilgaree.—An extensive jungle or waste, very convenient for the purpose of murder.

Bhimjodha—The bird Chirrah Q. V. peculiar to some classes of Thugs.

Banee—Blood.

Baean Geedee Sona Leedee—A proverb of the Thugs. " A jackal crossing from right to left brings gold." If a jackal crosses the path of the Thug from the right to the left it promises good fortune. If from left to right bad.

Bungoo—The river Thug of Bengal. These men live chiefly in the district of Bhurdwan, on the banks of the Hoogly river. They move up and down the Ganges during the months of November, December, January, and February, always pretending to be going to or coming from holy places, such as Bunares, Allahabad, &c. &c. They inveigle people on board their boats, strangle them, and throw them into the river, having broken their spines to prevent the chance of their recovering. The leader of the gang has commonly his own boat, but he sometimes hires it for the season, and the owner of the boat gets the share of one man. The boats have a hole on each side through which they throw the bodies into the river; but they never stab or cut them, lest there should be signs of blood in the water to attract the attention of people in the boats by which they float on their way down the river. This class of Thugs is very numerous—from two to three hundred.

Bhans lena—To steal or defraud each other in the division of booty; peculiar to Duckun Thugs; same as *Kootkurna* among Hindoostan Thugs.

Bhontee—Calling of the kite while flying. It is a bad omen. If they see the dung of a kite falling in the air, it is considered to promise a valuable white booty, in silver or cloth.

Binderee—A sword.

Bindoo—A Hindoo.

Bunasna or Bunas Jana—To lose any thing, but particularly the road.

Bunij—Literally merchandize or goods; technically a traveller or any other person whom the Thugs consider worth murdering. He is their stock in trade.

Bunij Ladhna—Literally, to load the goods; technically, to murder the travellers.

Bunjaree—A cat. If a cat comes to them at their lodgings at night it promises good fortune.

Bungur—A Thug term peculiar to Duckun Thugs.

Buneana—To stain with blood a cloth or any other thing.

Bunar—Same as *Baee*. Bad news, untoward discovery of the Thugs proceedings: also a road become unsafe for Thugs.

Bhurtote—A strangler.

Bhurtotee—The office or duty of strangler. Thugs seldom attain this rank or office till they have been on many expeditions, and acquired the requisite courage or insensibility by slow degrees. At first they are almost always shocked and frightened; but after a time they say they lose all sympathy with the victims. A Thug leader, of most polished manners and great eloquence, being asked one day in my presence by a native gentleman, whether he never felt compunction in murdering innocent people, replied with a smile, "Does any man feel compunction in "following his trade; and are not all our trades assigned "us by providence." The native gentleman said, "How "many people have you in the course of your life killed "with your own hands at a rough guess?" "I have kill-"ed none! "Have you not been just describing to me a number of murders?" "Yes; but do you suppose I could "have committed them. Is any man killed from man's "killing? *Admee ke marne se koe murta.* Is it not "the hand of God that kills him? and are we not mere "instruments in the hand of God?" They are first employed as scouts; then as sextons; then as *shumseeas* or holders of hands; and lastly as *Bhurtotes*. When a man feels that he has sufficient courage and insensibility for the purpose, he solicits the oldest and most renowned Thug of the gang to make him his *cheyla*, or disciple. The Thug agrees to become his *gooroo*, or spiritual preceptor and when the gang falls in with a man of respectability but not much strength, fitted for the purpose, he tells the gooroo that he is prepared, with his permission, to try his hands upon him. While the traveller is asleep with the gang at their quarters, the gooroo takes his disciple into a neighbouring field followed by three or four old members of the gang. On reaching the spot chosen, they all face to the direction the gang intends to move, and the gooroo says, "*Oh Kalee, Kunkalee, Bhudkalee. Oh Kalee, Ma-"hakalee, Calcutta Walee.** If it seemeth to thee fit that

* The Thugs, and I understand all other Hindoos, believe Kalee to have first appeared upon the earth in Calcutta. They believe also that after she had, through the means of the Thugs created by her for the special purpose, destroyed the great Demon "*Rukut beej dana*" at Bindachul, on the eastern extremity of the Vindeya range, she carried the body to Calcutta and there buried it where her temple now stands. That place they consider to be her favorite seat where she *works more miracles* than

" the traveller now at our lodging should die by the hands " of this thy slave, vouchsafe us the *Thibaoo.*" If they get the auspice on the right within a certain time (half an

in all the rest of India. They have got a notion that in Calcutta even the Christians attend her worship, and make offerings to her temple ; and I believe the priests have always actually made offerings to her image on great occasions in the name of the Hon'ble Company out of the rents of the land with which Government has endowed the temple. European Gentlemen and Ladies frequently attend the nautches and feasts of her great days in the *Durga Pooja* ; and as these feasts are part of the religious ceremonies, this innocent curiosity is very liable to be misconstrued by people at a distance from the scene, and should not therefore be indulged. The Hindoos have a verse which they often repeat in their invocations. " *Kalee ! Calcutta walee ! tera buchun na jawe Khalee. Oh " Kalee, great goddess of Calcutta, may thy promise never be made in " vain.*" She is said to delight in the name of *Kunkalee*, or man-eater, and to be always drinking the blood of men and of Demons. The term means, I believe, the same thing as *Kunkalin*. They all believe Kalee to have been extremely black, and to have had features so terrifically hideous that no mortal man could dare to look upon them.

When Kalee or Parbuttee appears in company with her husband, Siwa or Mahadeo, she is represented as beautiful and fair, and is commonly called *Gouree*, or *the fair*. It was only when she came to destroy demons, or as the Goddess of war, that she is supposed to have put on these hideous shapes. In a beautiful piece of sculpture at Beragur on the Nerbudda river, she is represented as seated on a Bull behind her husband, whose dress and ornaments are, as usual, composed of snakes, very gracefully twisted and suspended around him. This piece of sculpture is called *Gouree Shunkur*, after her name *Gouree*, and that of Mahadeo, *Shunkur* ; and it is so much superior to any other they are accustomed to see, that the people, from the most learned to the most unlettered, implicitly believe that the God and Goddess came here, mounted as they now are, on a visit to the Nurbudda, from the mountain *Khylas*, and got their earthly parts turned into stone as a memorial of their visit, and will some day resume them.

The whole is cut out of one block of lava from a dyke in the marble rocks through which the Nurbudda flows beneath the temple which is consecrated to them. The wall of the court in which the temple stands is lined all round by the statues of some three score *Jognies*, or petty goddesses, who attend upon Parbuttee, about the size of life, cut out of

hour), it signifies her sanction; but if they have no sign, or the *dhilhaoo*, (or sign on the left) some other Thug must put the traveller to death, and the candidate for honor wait for another time.

Davey's sanction having been conveyed in the *Thibaoo*, they return to their quarters, and the *gooroo* takes a handkerchief, and, facing to the west, ties the knot in one end of it with a rupee or other piece of silver inserted. This knot they call the *Goor Ghat*, or *classic knot*, and no man who has not been thus ordained by the high priest, is permitted to tie it. *See Goor Ghat*. The disciple receives it respectfully from the high priest in his right hand, and stands over the victim, with a *shumseea*, or holder of hands, by his side. The travellers is roused on some pretence or other, and the disciple passes the handkerchief over his neck, at the signal given by the leader of the gang, and strangles him with the aid of his *shumseea*. Having finished his work, he bows down before his gooroo, and touches his feet with both hands, and does the same to all his relations and friends present, in gratitude for the honor he has attained. He opens the knot after he has heard or seen the *Thibaoo*, or auspice on the right, takes out the rupee and gives it, with all the other silver he has, to his gooroo, as a nuzur; and the gooroo adding what money he has at the time, purchases a rupee and a quarter's worth of goor for the *Tuponee*, and lays out the rest in sweetmeats. The *Tuponee* sacrifice is now performed under the neem, the mango, or

rocks of different kinds, with various faces and in various attitudes, and all mounted upon different *Bahuns*, or vehicles of birds and quadrupeds. They are all sadly mutilated, and the God and Goddess within are said to have been saved by a miracle from *Aurungebe* and his army, to whom these things are always attributed. At this temple an annual fair is held in the beginning of November.

the byr, if they are available, and if not, under any other tree except the babul, the sirsa *(mamosa series)* and the reonja. The new disciple now takes his seat among the *Bhurtotes* around the carpet, and receives his share of the consecrated sugar, and the sweetmeats are distributed to all the members of the gang of whatever grade. On his return home after the expedition he gives a feast to his gooroo and his family ; and if he has the means, to all his relations; and he presents his gooroo with an entire new suit of clothes for himself, and one for his wife, and others for his relations, if he can afford it. The gooroo after a certain interval, returns the compliment to him and his family, and the relation between them is ever after respected as the most sacred that can be formed. A Thug will often rather betray his father than the gooroo by whom he has been knighted.

The *Bhurtote* is not permitted to bathe on the day he has strangled any one: formerly no member of the gang was permitted to bathe on the day that a murder was committed, but now the stranglers alone are forbidden to do so.

Buhup, Buhupna, Buhapjana—To go, or escape; as a traveller from the snares of the Thugs, or Thugs from pursuit.

Bara Muttee—The call of the lizard. At whatever time and place they hear the call of the lizard, they consider it a very good omen. The fall of a lizard, upon a Thug is considered a very bad omen ; and if it falls upon any garment, that garment must be given away in charity. If it falls upon the ground it threatens nothing.

Baroonee—An old and venerable Thug woman, who is much respected by the fraternity.

I have heard of only one woman who has gone herself on Thug expeditions, and that is the wife of Bukhtawur Jemadar, of the Sooseea class of Thugs. She and her husband are still at large in the Jypore territory. She has often assisted her husband in strangling; and on one occasion strangled a man who had overpowered and stunned her husband. Mothers, I know, have often made their sons go on Thuggee when they would not otherwise have gone, and wives on some occasions their husbands; and I have heard of one woman in the Duckun who kept herself a small gang of Thugs; but Bukhtawur's wife is the only woman that has, as far as I can learn, gone on Thuggee herself.

Baroo—A Thug of respectability either from the celebrity of his Thug ancestors, or from his own character as a Thug.

Baruna, Barawnee kurna—To disperse on the approach of danger or separate into small parties to avoid suspicion.

Birar—The fighting of cats or their screams when fighting. Also the Duckun Thugs term for *Manj*.

Agaseebirar—Thunder: a term also peculiar to Duckun Thugs. *Agasee* signifies turban among both Duckun and Hindoostanee Thugs.

Bhurahur—A pitcher full of water. *Bhurehur* one empty.

If on leaving their homes on an expedition they meet a woman with a pitcher full of water on her head, it promises a safe return and prosperous journey; if empty, the reverse. The pitcher full promises still more if the female be with child.

Bhurka—Rupees. Peculiar to the Duckunees.

Bhurehur—An empty pitcher, and a bad omen when met on the road.

Bharakee—A gun.

Bhara—Dead bodies of the victims. Term peculiar to the Duckun Thugs. Hindoostanee Thugs call them *Ghurt,ha*.

Bora—A Thug; in contradistinction to *Beetoo*, any person not a Thug. This term is peculiar to the *Jumaldehee, Lodaha, Moteea* and *Bungoo* Thugs in Behar and Bengal.

Borkee—A knife.

Borkeeana, or *Borkee Marna*, or *Borkeeae dalna*—To stab with a knife.

Boreeahut or *Bore*—Loud talking, bellowing, uproar.

Borkee—The small deer. If a single small deer crosses their road from right to left, it threatens evil. If from left to right, it promises good; but its promises and threats are not considered important. A herd of small deer at all times and under all circumstances promise a meeting with other Thugs, and is considered good. The Duckun Thugs consider the crossing of the single deer either from left to right, or right to left a bad omen.

Boroha—New clothes: term peculiar to Duckun Thugs. Also a bundle or load of new cloths. Hindoostanee Thugs call it *seep*.

Burauk—The omen of the wolf or wolves crossing their road. If from left to right it threatens great evil. If from right to left it is a good omen. If its call be heard during the day, the gang must immediately quit the country in which they hear it. If between midnight and day light, it is bad; if between evening and midnight, indifferent; between midday and sunset, it is not so bad as between sunrise and midday. They call it the weeping *(Chimmama)* of the wolf, and consider the sound mournful. The single wolf portends more than a pair; and the *Burauk* is, whether for good or for bad, one of their most important omens.

Bursote.—One of the seven original clans of Thugs who were all Musulmans.

Burg—Any thing seen upon a man unbecoming his condition, and therefore likely to lead to suspicion.

Burgeela—An accomplice: one who knows the secrets of the Thugs and keeps them.

Burka—A leader or chief of Thugs, or one thoroughly instructed in the art; distinguished from *Kuboola*, a *Tyroo*. Also any man of rank.

The Thugs consider a *Burka* as capable of forming a gang of Thugs out of the rude materials around him in any part of India; and a Thug who has arrived at this degree of proficiency in the art ought not therefore to be left at large. A *Kuboola*, or *Tyroo*, they think, could do nothing if left to himself, and he might therefore be left at large without much danger to society, if he had no leader to join.

Buroee—An omen from the jackal's call—*See Bhalee*.

Buhra—Four travellers, or victims in the hands of Thugs.

Bees—A low call of the small owl repeated three or four times: called also *Chireya*. It always threatens evil.

Bhusmee—Fine earth or sand, particularly applicable to what is found in digging the graves for the victims: same as *Rewaroo*. Flour is also called by them *Bhusmee*.

Bhys—One of the seven original clans of Thugs.

Bisul purna—To be awkwardly handled in strangling: to have the *roomal* round the face or head instead of the neck. *Soosul purna*—to have it round the neck.

Bisnee—A Thug, pick-pocket, thief, or any one that lives by the plunder of others.

Bisendhee—Fetters. Also a *Thulee* or metal utensil of any kind.

Bisul—A person, intended to be killed, who has clothes round his neck and head, or other impediment to strangling. Also a man on whom the *roomal* falls untowardly, either on his head or face, or is otherwise untowardly handled in strangling. Also a Thug who has blood upon his clothes, or other signs of murder that may lead to suspicion. In all these and other senses *Sosul* is opposed to *Bisul.* Any Thug in whose hands victims have been often *Bisul,* is excluded from the office of strangler, on the ground of presumed unfitness for the duty.

Bous—A large gang of Thugs above twenty-five; same as *Kharoo.*

Beeta or Bheeta—A hundred.

Beetoo—Any person not a Thug, in contradistinction to *Aulae* a Thug.

Bhitree—A pair of travellers or victims.

Botoel—A body of travellers too large for the Thugs to manage: see *Tonkul.*

Bote hona—To become inveigled; fall into the snares of the Thugs; in contradistinction to *Chuk Jana* or *Iter-jana.*

Char—A *Bhurtote* or strangler. Term peculiar to the *Bungoos, Jumaldehees, Lodahas* and *Moteeas.*

Chareeae—*Bhurtotee,* the office or duty of strangler.

Cheeha—A coward, timid Thug, one who shews sympathy or fear.

Chibilna—To be released from confinement; distinguished from *Jhur jana,* to escape or brake prison.

Chandanee-kee-dhap—A dog seen dunging by moonlight; a very bad omen, which makes the gang suspend all operations for three days if possible, and make sacrifices.

Choukana—To examine or reconnoitre secretly.

Choukna or *Chouklena*—To see, inspect, examine.

Chookadena—Same as *Thibaedena.* To cause to sit down and look up; as travellers before strangling them. They direct their attention to the sky or some other object above them.

Chuk—Suspicion.

Chukbele—A place chosen for the murder too near to danger.

Chuk ho jana.—To become aware of the designs of Thugs and on one's guard; as travellers whom they are trying to inveigle.

Chukura—A small gold coin. This term is confined to Duckun Thugs.

Chulub—The interval between the time when the sun sets and about gunfire at night. Evening: *Chulub men Ladhna,* To kill in the evening.

Chuttoo-Dhuneea—Same as *Oorut Kawuree.*

Chamoo Jana—To be seized or arrested.

Chamlena—To seize or arrest.

Chimmama—The call of the wolf; considered a bad omen at all times, but particularly during the day. The gang must immediately halt, or go back, and quit that part of the country as soon as possible.

Chimmota—A boy.

Chimmotee—A girl.

Chummun—A Brahmin.

Chumoseea—A holder of hands. Term used by Duckun Thugs for *shumseea.*

Chummoseeae—The office or duty of *Chumoseea.*

Chumeeae.—The office or work of the *Chumeea,* viz. seizing the victim.

Chumeea—The person who seizes, or assists the *Chumosee* in seizing and keeping down the victim. There may be ten *Chumeeas,* but there can be only one *Chumosee.*

Chanda—Cloth.

Chandoo—An experienced and expert Thug.

Chingoreea—One of the sects or *Bharnts* of the Thug clans.

Chinha—A boy.

Chinguree—A clan of Moltanee Thugs; sometimes called Naicks, of the Musulman faith. They proceed on their expeditions in the characters of Brinjaras, with cows and bullocks laden with merchandize, which they expose for sale at their encampments, and thereby inveigle their victims. They use the rope of their bullocks instead of the *roomal* in strangling. They are an ancient tribe of Thugs, and take their wives and children on their expeditions. They destroy, it is said, their female children; and if they at any time preserve them, they never allow them to marry out of their tribe.

There are, it is said, more than a hundred families of these Moltanees in the neighbourhood of Hingolee. They do not associate with the other Thugs, but they use nearly the same technical language, and practise the same trade of murder. They have however a different ostensible employment in the hire of their bullocks, sale of wood and grain, &c. &c.

Chingana—A boy. Term peculiar to Duckun Thugs.

Choundh,na—To bind up in bundles booty or the dead bodies of victims.

Choundh Lena—To tie on the turban. *Agasee Choundh lena.*

Choundhee-Churana—To tie the arms behind.

Chowan—A woman. Term peculiar to Duckun Thugs.

Choundhee—Turband.

Cheeng—A sword. Term confined to Berar Thugs.

Chungar—A thief of any kind.

Cheek—A Gold Mohur.

Cheyhur—Jungle or forest.

Chirreya—A chirping of the small owlet, which Thugs consider a bad omen, whether made while the bird is sitting or flying; it is said to be a melancholy and low sound, seldom repeated. See *Puttoree.* Judae, Jemadar, who was considered to be one of the best augurers of his day, lived at *Murnae,* a celebrated Thug village, and it is said that, returning one morning from a walk in the fields, he told his friend that he had heard the *Chirreya* in a manner that indicated some great calamity at hand. That night or the night after Mr. Halhed is said to have attacked the village and Lieutenant Monsel was killed. It was I believe in November, 1812.

Chireeapotee—One of the sects of Thugs, said to be from the *Bhys* clan

Chira—The call of the *Roopareel,* or *Muhoka (Caculus Custaneous),* or the bird itself. Some Thugs call it also the *Bhinjhoda.*

Chirchera—The call of the Lizard. See *Bara Muttee.*

Chireyta—A Pundit, or any Marhata.

Chourukna—To inform or give information against any one.

Churagee—A Byragee—term peculiar to Duckun Thugs.

Churtee-Pholkee—The time between sunrise and midday: see *Pholkee.*

Cheesa—Any good or blessing from Heaven, but particularly a rich traveller.

Cheeota—Rupees.

Cheyt—Same as *Cheek.* A traveller who has discovered the designs of the Thugs. *Cheyt ho Jana—Cheek-ho-jana* —To become aware of their designs and on one's guard.

Chutaw—A share of the booty.

Chutae—The same.

Chutae Lena—To divide.

Deo—Used for the same purpose as *Bajeed khan.*

Deo Sing—The same.

Daee—The road—term peculiar to Duckun Thugs.

Duheea—The call or cry of the hare. They will perish in the jungles, they say, after hearing it, if they do not make sacrifices, and the hare or some other animal of the forest will drink water out of their skulls : if they kill any one whom they have with them at the time, they will find no booty on him, or what they find will tend to their ruin —See *Roopuneea*.

Duhee Phorkana—To gargle and squirt from the mouth sour milk. The means by which the evil threatened by the *Kalee kee Manj*, is averted in the morning.

Dada Dheera—A very ancient and canonized Thug of the Bhursote class whom they invoke in drinking spirits at certain religious ceremonies. They do not mention him with *Jora Naek* in the *Ghoor* offering, or *Tuponee* ; but they make votive offerings of ardent spirits to *Dada Dheera*. They promise an offering of spirits, and if they succeed in their prayers, they drink the spirits, if their caste permits; if not, they throw it on the ground with the expression of their thanks in prescribed phrases. *Dada Dheera's* tomb is visited as a holy shrine by Thugs at Kumona in Koel, where he was buried.

Dudh—A man who is not a Thug.—See *Beetoo*.

Dhagal—Papers.

Dhaga kurana or dena—To satisfy a suspecting chief or public functionary of the innocence of Thugs suspected.

Dhaga le ana—To search out and report what they require to learn from travellers.

Dhaga—An eliciting of the intentions of travellers ; or negociation with native chiefs, or any men in authority for protection, or for release when arrested.

Dhagsa—Hilly or jungly country. Term peculiar to Duckun Thugs.

W.H. Sleeman

Thugs, or, Phansigars of India. Philadelphia: Carey & Hart, 1839.

Phansigars have the appearance of ordinary inoffensive travellers, and seldom assume any particular disguise. They indeed not unfrequently pretend to be traders, and there is reason to believe that they sometimes come from the Dukhun clothed in the garb of Bairagis. Formerly, when Phansigary was practised to a greater extent, and in a more daring manner than at present, the leader, especially if enriched by former spoliations, often travelled on horseback, with a tent, and passed for a person of consequence or a wealthy merchant,

* In the districts between the Ganges and Jumna, there were some associations of Thugs that seldom went far from home, and who made short and frequent expeditions. So the Jumaldehee Thugs of Oude and the neighbouring districts, so some of the Thug families in Bundelcund. Generally, however, the Thugs north of the Nurbudda, have been in the habit of making long expeditions, and remaining absent from six to eight months on each. W. H. S.

sessed of valuable effects, are, while journeying in imaginary security, suddenly cut off; and the lifeless and despoiled bodies being removed and interred, not a vestige of them appears.* Instances are said to have occurred, of twelve and fourteen persons being simultaneously destroyed. But such occurrences must be rare; and, in general, the property taken is not considerable. Such, indeed, are the cruelty and cupidity of these detestable wretches, that, on the presumption of every traveller possessing concealed treasure, or some property, however trifling, even indigence affords not its wonted security.

Formerly, if good horses, shawls, or other valuable articles, were among the booty, they were commonly reserved for the Polygar, in payment of protection. A portion of the plunder was usually appropriated to defraying the expenses of religious ceremonies; and sometimes, a part was also allotted for the benefit of widows and families of deceased members of the gang. The residue of the booty, being divided into several parts, was usually shared as follows:—to the leader two shares; to the men actually concerned in perpetrating the murder, and to the person who cut the dead body, each one share and a half, and to the remainder of the gang

* Near Sadras, about ten years ago, three *golah* peons were killed, having on them money in different coins, to the amount of 16,000 rupees. In 1805, five persons were killed in Coimbatoor, and cash to the amount of 2,500 pagodas, the property of the Collector of the district, was taken. In the same year, two respectable natives, proceeding on horseback from Madras to the Malabar coast, with five attendants, were all killed. In 1807, five persons, besides two others who had joined them on the road, were killed near Bangalore, and robbed of property to the amount of 1,000 pagodas, belonging to an officer of engineers. And in 1815, three persons were killed in the district of Masulipatam, and 2,500 rupees taken.

such as not to render shelter necessary for nine months in the year; and none but single travellers or very small parties care for serais or houses. All who are rich enough to carry tents, or those who travel in tolerable numbers, usually prefer encamping under the shade of trees, at some distance from the dirty serais or villages; and when one party is so encamped under a shady grove, a single traveller, or even several together, will easily be induced to join them, and often ask permission to do so, for the sake of protection.

It is the existence of such customs which renders the operations of the Thugs so practicable.

Our readers will almost deem it impossible that such organised gangs of murderers, amounting to several thousands, could carry on their villainy almost undiscovered so long; for two or three centuries at least. The difficulty, however, nearly vanishes when we reflect on the mode of travelling in India, just described, and on the peculiar system of the Thugs. In the first place they seldom murder near their own homes; but even this would be a point of little importance when we consider, secondly, that travellers, and generally from a distant part of the country, are their victims: thirdly, that they invariably murder before they rob.

Lastly, they avoid exciting suspicion by being careful to leave behind them no marks even of a crime having been committed. The travellers who became their victims were men seeking for service; or returning home with the savings of years; merchants going on business to a distant town; or others journeying either for business or pleasure. They might be murdered in the morning twilight within half a mile of the serai or village in which they had passed the night; while the Thugs who watched and had marked them for their prey were encamped at a short distance. No one missed them: the people of the serai or village which they had left took it for granted that they had proceeded on their way; and those of the next halting-place in advance were ignorant of their approach. It is not till days, weeks, months, or even years had passed away that their relations, hearing nothing of their arrival at their intended destinations, make inquiries, and it is seldom that they can ascertain even the place about which the travellers were probably murdered. Unless the inquiry be made within a short time, and there may have been something in the appearance or equipage of the travellers to attract attention, the villagers and others who reside along the road would not recollect whether those inquired for had passed or not. But even supposing (as has occasionally occurred) that the relations succeed in tracing the travellers to a certain spot, beyond which all clue is lost; this gives a moral certainty that they have been murdered at no great distance, that is, within a few miles adjacent.—But how, within such a space, are they to pitch upon the spot where the bodies are interred?—and more,—where are the murderers? probably hundreds of miles away; and even should they by chance be again encamped on the very spot, what means are there of detection? In ordinary thefts, and by local thieves, the tracing and discovery of stolen property affords a very powerful means of bringing the matter home to the perpetrators; but this has but little effect against Thugs. They contrive to obtain full knowledge of the persons, residence, and destination of those they murder, and are careful not to dispose of any recognisable articles where they might by chance be perceived. Such as have any peculiar marks are destroyed.

Considering all these circumstances, it is not astonishing that so little has been done towards suppressing this association of miscreants. The fact is, that until these five or six years, no one had any correct notion of its extent: all that was known up to that period was, that travellers were occasionally enticed and murdered by people called Thugs, who assumed the garb of inoffensive wayfarers. By some extraordinary chance, such as one of the victims having made his escape, or some of the stolen property being unexpectedly recognised, or one of the gang having turned informer in consequence of a quarrel for the division of the spoil, a few of these miscreants were occasionally discovered and punished. Even had the various governments into which India is divided, been aware of the extent of the evil and anxious to destroy it, they would have been unable to do so: insulated efforts would have produced little or no benefit; the jealousies which existed would have prevented their combining for the purpose; and for a century and a half or more, there has not existed any paramount power which could devise a general plan of operations, and compel the rest to submit to it.

Other causes are not wanting which tended to prevent any attempts being made, even in detail, to arrest the proceedings of the different gangs of Thugs. Some of the native chiefs knowingly harboured and protected them as a source of revenue from which they derived considerable sums annually out of the profits of their plunder. The

Thugs lived in villages like other people, and generally cultivated small portions of ground to maintain appearances: so that the native chiefs, if questioned, pretended of course to know nothing of their real character; asserting that these people lived, cultivated, and paid their rent like others, and accounting for the absence of most of the male population during several months, by saying that they went for service and returned periodically with the amount of their earnings. In other cases, native chiefs who would have readily punished a gang of thieves when apprehended, were deterred from doing so by superstitious dread. The Thugs always endeavoured to impress the belief that they were acting according to the injunctions of their deity Bhowanee, and that all who opposed them would feel the vengeance of their goddess. The few instances in which Thugs were put to death by native chiefs were generally cases of personal vengeance, because these villains had murdered some relation or dependent of the chief, and were by good fortune apprehended immediately, "in the red-hand." It has unfortunately in several instances occurred that after punishing Thugs, the chief himself, his son, or some relation has died within a short time: whether some of the Thug fraternity took secret means to insure such an occurrence, cannot be ascertained; but they seized all such opportunities to substantiate the belief which they endeavoured to inculcate. In general, a native chief would merely extort a sum of money from the Thugs, or keep them in confinement for a short time, after which they were released; and not unfrequently they were discharged at once. Their own superstition however, as has just been explained, is now beginning to operate against them.

The following will show what extraordinary proceedings occur sometimes in India. A dispatch of dollars to the value of four thousand pounds sterling, made on account of a rich merchant of Indoor, Dhun Raj, was carried off by Thugs, who murdered the attendant guards, near a place called Burwaha Ghaut, on the Nerbudda. He contrived to ascertain who the Thugs were, and, being a man of considerable influence, to occasion their arrest and detention in gaol by the native chiefs in whose jurisdiction they lived: after some time an agreement was made with the Thugs to release them, if they would refund the money or its amount.

Some paid out of the fruits of former expeditions, others borrowed in anticipation of future success; and those who had neither money nor credit, pledged themselves to pay part of their future earnings.

The Thugs durst not break their engagements for fear of Dhun Raj, and after some time he realized the full sum of which he had been plundered. Finding, however, that he could turn his power and influence to so good an account, he began to assume the character of a patron of Thugs: he had always some of the principal leaders about his person, and yearly exacted large sums of money from the principal gangs in return for his protection, threatened those who refused with arrest and punishment: and such was his influence, that he could procure the release of a gang from almost any gaol in central India.

Though the British Indian government was free from the superstitions or the corruptions which prevented the native chiefs from punishing Thugs, it was not the less hampered by prejudices of its own, and by real difficulties which lay in the way of the object desired. Regarding the prejudices alluded to, it is necessary to explain a little of the secret springs that actuated the government. The members at the head of the administration have always had a tolerably correct idea of the oppressive nature of the British rule in India, and of the light in which it is held by the natives; but it has always been a primary object to prevent this knowledge from reaching the English public. To effect this, the reports forwarded to the Court of Directors, have always descanted on the admirable system of internal government which has been established in their territories; the blessings which the native subjects enjoy; and their consequent gratitude. The feeling descends through the various ranks of government servants, who generally take their cue accordingly. It may be observed too, that the majority of the officers of government, civil or military, are extremely ignorant of the natives of India, and of their real sentiments; and are therefore easily misled by a few designing favourites, who alone possess their ear, and have their own ends to serve.

To acknowledge, even had they been fully aware of it, the existence of such an evil as Thuggee over the whole of the British provinces, was by no means agreeable to the government, it would have contradicted their repeated assertions and representations. If an evil could be suppressed quietly and without incurring any additional expense, it would have been a source of deep satisfaction; but the proceedings of government have almost warranted a belief that they would prefer the existence of an evil, provided it were not generally known, even to the discovery of a remedy, if this should tend to produce a considerable sensation and excite inquiry. We could at least instance several public officers who have brought considerable annoyance upon themselves by too broadly bringing to notice the existence of evils, or the enormous extent to which crimes of the deepest dye, such as murders, gang robbery, and others, are perpetrated. Appearances are, however, kept up. The zeal and ability of the officer are praised, and his praiseworthy motives duly appreciated;—but then come certain remarks indicating an "apprehension of his being misinformed;" doubts that "the evil is not so bad as he has represented;" with a concluding observation that copies of the correspondence will be sent to the superintendent of police, judge of circuit, or some superior officer, who will be desired to report on the subject. This individual, if he have any tact, or any thing to hope or fear from the favour of government, frames his report according to what he sees is wished or expected from him; states the district to be not in worse order than others (which perhaps is true enough, owing to the vigorous measures of the magistrate in question, by which crime has been abated); and, by a careful adjustment of words and phrases, contrives to do away entirely with the impression which, in accordance with truth, ought to have been received. Occasionally, where the magistrate has persisted in his representations, the affair has actually ended by his removal, while his successor has reaped the full benefit of his exertions, and gained the entire credit of them.

A strong instance of the way in which the ends of justice may be defeated by a mistaken anxiety in public officers to gain a good name with the government by making it appear that crime does not exist, occurred in the district of Chupra in 1827. Two men were murdered by a gang of Thugs, who, almost immediately after, got drunk and quarrelled. Four of them in consequence gave information against the others, who were arrested with the property of the murdered men in their possession; these were committed for trial, and the four first allowed to turn King's evidence. The state of the case is as follows:—There was, first, the evidence of the approvers; second, the deposition of the wives of the men, who swore to the property found; and thirdly, the men accused of being Thugs could give no satisfactory account of themselves. The defence was merely a denial, and an assertion that the property claimed by the widows was their (the prisoners') own. The judgment given will scarce be credited by our readers. The prisoners were released; the approvers and the police were severely punished for perjury and for oppression; government was led to believe that no such crime as Thuggee existed in that part of the country; and the magistrate, Mr. Pringle, who had been active in apprehending many Thugs, and had reported the same, received a severe reprimand.

One fact yet remains to be mentioned, which will show the difficulties of the case. The judge, Mr. Elliot, ordered the property which was claimed by the widows to be retained in court, while all the rest of the property found on the prisoners was returned to them. Now, for whom was the above to be retained? It could not belong to any third person, but either to the prisoners or to the murdered men. If the judge disbelieved the whole story for the prosecution, and deemed the prisoners innocent, he should have restored to them this property along with the rest that was found upon them, and which they claimed as their own. If he believed the statement of the widows, that those things belonged to their husbands, then must the prisoners have been punished as the murderers, and the property would have been given to the widows. This little fact is one of those which either show a strange perversion of judgment, or denote a vacillation of mind indicating that the judge himself felt that all was not right in the orders he gave.* The truth of all that was stated on the part of the prosecution has since been fully proved by depositions of other Thug approvers; and not only so, but that Thuggee existed to a great extent in those districts, at the very time that Mr. Elliot was assuring government that no such crime occurred.

Many of the English magistrates were actuated by the same feelings. Some would not allow that Thuggee could exist in their districts, and even were excessively indignant at such statements being made by the officers employed in the suppression of this crime: they were perfectly astounded, when men dispatched by those officers proceeded to dig up the bodies of persons recently murdered in various places, sometimes within a short distance of the police functionary's residence. Others admitted that such a thing might occur occasionally; while a few boldly and openly stated what they had discovered, and gave much valuable information. Our limits do not permit us to add here, extracts from the official papers: we must,

* No mention of this order to retain that portion of the property is to be found in Capt. Sleeman's book. We derive it from a statement publicly made by Mr. Pringle.

therefore, refer our readers to various letters from Mr. Wright, a Madras magistrate.

But even if all the English magistrates in India had been aware of and cordially co-operated with each other, they would have effected little towards the suppression of Thuggee. The ordinary tribunals and modes of proceeding, which answered in some degree for the detection and punishment of ordinary offenders, were of little avail against Thugs. Except in the rare instance of a gang being apprehended with stolen property in possession, which the relations of the murdered persons were there to identify, the only witnesses who could ever be brought against them were some of their own fraternity; and the evidence of men whose preliminary step must be to confess themselves the most ruthless villains in existence, is naturally received with distrust, of which the case commemorated by Mr. Pringle is a memorable example, and doubtless may plead for the judge.

Such being the English mode of proceeding, it is no wonder that approvers and informers were slow to come forward; for no sooner did they lose the protection of the functionaries, than they were murdered by their accomplices. The dilatoriness and inefficiency of the courts; the great power which the subordinate police and court officers possess to disguise the real merits of a case; the influence which the Thugs contrived to obtain over these by means of bribes; the few instances in which stolen property or bodies were discovered; all conspired to increase the difficulty under which the ordinary magistrates laboured in detecting the perpetrators of this crime. But even where the bodies were found in wells, which was a common way of disposing of them when in a hurry or likely to be disturbed, in the Doab, Oude, and other parts, the owner of the ground and his neighbuors generally buried them as quickly as possible that the police officers might know nothing of the matter; and if these did become acquainted with the circumstance, a bribe would usually prevent their reporting it to the magistrate. The farmers and others had just grounds for what they did, owing to the strange mode in which the English government conducts its police affairs. In such cases as those now mentioned the common practice is to summon to court the owners of the neighbouring lands, and many of the neighbours;—at a distance, perhaps, from ten to eighty miles, and to fine them severely as a matter of course, if they could not produce the perpetrators of the murders.

But even when an insulated gang was actually brought to justice, it was but a drop in the ocean towards the suppression of Thuggee:—nor would, nor will any thing effect this, but a general system, which shall be in operation all over India.

W.H. Sleeman

Report on the Depredations Committed by the Thug Gangs of Upper and Central India.

Calcutta: GH Huttmann, Military Orphan Press, 1840.

EXPEDITIONS

OF THE

MALWA AND KHANDEISH GANGS,

IN 1828-29.

Report of an Expedition into Malwa and Khandeish by some Gangs from Bundelcund and Gwalior, amounting to one hundred and twenty persons, under Bhujjoo, Khoshal, Khoorkoo and Dulsah, in the year 1828-29.

1. Bhujjoo Jemadar with eight Thugs, and Khoshal with eighteen, left their homes, and proceeding through Bhilsa crossed the Nerbudda at Chimpanee and reached Berhanpore; here Khorkoo Jemadar with forty, and Dulsa with thirty, joined them—they proceeded through Aurungabad, Lahoree and Bamboree, to within four stages of Poonah, without killing any one. They returned to Ankee Jhankee, two stages beyond Dholeea, where they met two Rajpoots—leaving that place before day light next morning, they put them to death at a place a coss and a half from their encampment on the road to Dholeea.

2. After this they came to Walagon, where they met a Rajpoot, and bringing him to the village of Rae, spent the night there—proceeding about one coss next morning, before day light they killed him.

3. The gang came on to Dholeea, where, in February 1829, they fell in with seven Treasure Bearers. They

followed them and reached Amulnair, and thence to Choupara, on the Taptee, to Dhoree, without getting the Treasure Bearers into their power. On the fourth day the Rokureeas reached Dharee, about ten in the morning, and cooked their dinner on the bank of the river. The Thugs did the same at a distance. After they had dined, the Treasure Bearers went on about mid-day, and two coss from the place, about 2 P. M., the Thugs overtook them in a jungle and killed them; but they only found six, one having gone on—they left the bodies exposed and made off with the Treasure—fifteen of them were seized by the Police of the country under Captain Hodges, the Magistrate of Kandeish, and the remainder reached their homes in safety.

A total of nine men murdered in this expedition.

Report of an Expedition made in Berar and Khandeish by some Gangs from Bundelcund and Gwalior, amounting to two hundred and twenty, under Feeringeea, Phoolsa, Tijjun, Buhorena, Gungadeen, Hurreea and others.

1. Feringeea with twenty-three, Phoolsa thirteen, Tijjun twenty-four, left their homes at Gorha in Jhansee, and at Bhilsa met Buhorena with five, making a gang of sixty-five Thugs. They crossed the Nerbudda at Kherepore, and reached Roojana in Deogur, on the road to Nagpore. There they met a traveller, inveigled him to their camp from the village, and murdered him. Phoolsa was arrested by the people of the village.

2. The gang went on to Omrowtee, and on the road they met Rambuksh, Rae Sing, and Heera approver, on their way back from the Dhoree affair, who recommended

them to fly, as the Police was in pursuit. They went on to Omrowtee from this place. Tijjun twenty, and Buhorena five, left the gang and returned. Feringeea went on to Nadgow to Sonee; where he met five men on their way back to Lucknow, with Images and Busts for sale—with them were Gungadeen with seven, Hureea approver five, Lall Khan, Jemadar, eight, and Adhar, Jemadar, five. All united and came with the travellers to Bham, leaving that place the next morning, they killed them at a place half a coss distant.

3. After this affair they went to Mungrook; leaving that place the next day, on the road to Hydrabad they met Tilokee Sing Havildar and four Sipahees on their way to Singheerampoor, in Jhansee. Returned with them the next day and killed them at a place two coss distant.

4. After the last affair they went to Phaleegow, on the road to Hydrabad, where they met two Hindoos and five Mussulmen—coming on with them to a place two coss north of Phaleegow, they put them to death.

5. Proceeded to Phandegow, where they met Hosein Khan, Jemadar, with ten, and Sheik Kurreem, approver, with twenty—coming on with four travellers. These four men were killed at the encampment.

6. Went through Nandair to Gungakhere, where they met three travellers—took them on to Sehloo, and leaving that place next morning murdered them.

7. Went to Jhalna, and on preparing to set out the next morning, four men came up and accompanied them to a village between Jhalna and Boregow, and leaving that place the following morning killed them.

8. After this affair they came to Barora, a village on the road to Omrowtee, where they fell in with four men, whom they killed next morning, one and a half coss on the road to Lakunwara.

9. They then proceeded on the Omrowtee road to Basum where they met three men—leaving the place with them the next day they killed them one coss distant.

10. Coming on they met six men, whom they accompanied to a village six or seven coss from Basum, and leaving this next morning they killed them at one and a half coss on the road to Purureea.

11. The gang proceeded to Soonee, where they met four Kowrutties. They were Sepähees who had taken that disguise for security—coming on next day they killed them half a coss from Soonee.

12. After the last affair they went to Omrowtee, where they met two travellers,—came on to a village seven coss from Omrowtee on the Nagpore road, and put them to death in camp.

13. Returned to Omrowtee and there met Zoolfakar (hung at Saugor) with seven men, all joined and went to Burwulagow, on the road to Hydrabad, where they met a Punditanee and two attendants. Took them on to Boregow, and leaving that next morning put them to death about one coss distant.

14. They reached Korinja and there met four Seiks—leaving this place next day they killed them at a place one coss this side.

15. The gang returned to Omrowtee where they fell in with Mojahid Khan (hung at Jubulpore 1835,) with twenty, Kalee Khan (still at large) with eight: all united, and brought nine travellers to Mojhuree, where they killed them.

16. After the last affair the men of the Deccan returned towards Hydrabad, and Feringeea and followers came to Meinpanee, in Baitool, where they fell in with two Hindoos and a Mussulman, and coming on a coss with them next morning they killed them.

17. After this the gangs dispersed and returned home, except Feringeea and two followers, who came to Saugor and there met Ghasee Khan Duffadar, with three companions. They left Saugor with these three men, and in three days reached Kheree in Churkaree territory, on the road to Calpee. There they met Zoolfakar Approver with nineteen, on his way from his home at Purwaha in Jhansee —Zoolfakar had murdered a Tailor, his wife, son and daughter at Kuneara, in the Myhere territory,—they were on their way from Allahabad to Nagpore.

18. All the gang, except those who returned home, went to Jeitpore, where they fell in with one Mussulman, whom they took on half a coss and then murdered.

19. They went to Khopnewaree, where they met a man on his way from Mhow—taking him to a nullah one coss distant, next morning they killed him.

20. After this they came to the village of Jumaneea, close by the Sudder Bazar at Saugor, where they met two Mussulmen Merchants, with horses for sale, from Bhopaul. They killed them at their encampment and buried their bodies under a hill at some distance.

21. After this affair Hyaut and Noorkhan returned home and Zoolfakar and his men went on to Rahtgurh, where they met a Kahar, and taking him on, a coss and a half, next day, towards Saugor, killed him. Afraid of the search for Thugs on that road they came back to Khyra, in Churkaree, where they met Feringeea, who pointed out his companions (Ghasee Khan Duffadar and his companions) as a good prize. They went on with them to Chutterpore, where they met Omeda and Sewdeen Sing Jemadars, they all joined and proceeded with the travellers to Jytpore, and thence taking them on half a coss put them to death, after which they dispersed and returned to their homes.

A total of seventy-seven men and three women murdered in this expedition.

Report of an Expedition made into Bundelcund and the Saugor Territories by some Gangs from Bundelcund and Gwalior, to the amount of two hundred, under Inaeut, Zalim, Ashroff, Bukut, Bheeka and others, in the year 1829.

1. Inaeut with twenty Thugs, Zalim ten, and Ashroff ten, left Guteara, in Jhansee, and going to Mundula, in Punna, killed two Shop-keepers going to Punna with cloth.

2. Came on to Biseynee, Bukut Jemadar (hung at Saugor), Bukut 2d (transported), Bikha (still at large), and Bhugee Lodhee (transported), with a gang of twenty-four Thugs. They had with them four Sepahees. The whole united and went on with them half a coss on the road to Khopnewaree and put them to death.

3. They returned to Biseynee, where they fell in with three Treasure Bearers, and leaving Biseynee with them put them to death—after this affair they returned to their homes.

4. Inaeut had been at home only four days when Bhola Buneea Approver came to him with a party of four Thugs, and they opened a second expedition. Inaeut had twenty, Lall Mahomed six, and Bhola four. They came to Biseynee, where they fell in with Bhowanee, the son of Mukka, with forty Thugs. Soon after they had joined a Moonshee, by name Bhowanee Sing, came, upon his way, from Soonee, they went to Jhoojhar Ghat, where he was put to death with his four companions.

5. Went thence to Chutterpore, where they fell in with two Hindoos and a Mussulman, Sepahees, on their way to

the Dooab—they went on with them to Sitaree, a little west of Jytpore, and going on with them next morning put them to death.

6. Thence went to Loghasee, where they fell in with three other Sepahees on their way home, they took them on to Jytpore, where they met Khuluk Jemadar, Bhowanee, son of Runna, Dhokul Jemadar, Noorkhan and others, with a gang of sixty Thugs. All made a gang of one hundred and fifty, and going on with the Sepahees, half a coss from Jytpore, put them to death.

7. After this some went to their homes, but Inaeut, Peer Mahomed and Lall Mahomed came to Goolgunge with a party of forty, and there met two Pundits taking cloths to Jhansee—going on with them to Khurgapore, in Tehree, and half a coss from that place on the Jhansee road, they put them to death.

8. They came to Khopnewarree, in Punna, and there met two travellers going to the Dooab. Deeba Buneea joined them with four men—and going on one coss from Khopnewarree, put them to death.

9. Going on one coss on the road to Punnah, they met two men, a Buneea and his companion—going on with them to the boundary of Muhoba village, they killed them.

10. After this affair Inaeut went home. Bhola Buneea soon after came again to Inaeut, and they proceeded together. Inaeut with twenty men and Bhola with five, they reached Biseynee. Here they met a man from Nehreepunguree, in Banda, who had been to see his son at Jubulpore, and had arrived near his home. They took him on half a coss on the road to Khopa and put him to death.

11. They returned and came through Biseynee to Shuhgurh, where they fell in with Gholab, alias Koman, and nine, Bhika, son of Sunum, with five, Bodha two, and

Khyratee with three. All united, and soon after a man came up with a camel and a Sepahee—they took them to Pareyna, in Punna, and put them to death.

12. Went back to Khopa where Bhikah, Lall Mahomed and Bhoda left them, and returned to their homes—on their way they fell in at Hadjeegur, with two treasure bearers, and there murdered them.

13. Inaeut was joined at Khopa by Rambuksh, son of Punna, with five Thugs, Meherban five, Persaud five and Dhokul five. All united and came to Biseynee—here two Blacksmiths, two Shop-keepers and a Trooper came up. They took them on some distance on the Khopa road and murdered them.

14. They proceeded through Punna to Sohawul, where they met three travellers on their way to the Dooab. Inaeut sent on twenty Thugs with Esuree, who took them on two coss, east of Kothee Sohawul, and killed them. Inaeut and the rest came to Sunkur Killa, in Oocheyra, where they met a traveller and put him to death at night in camp. After this they went to Myhere and there met Bhukun Khan with eight followers.

15. Proceeded to Sewagunge, on the road from Jubulpore to Mirzapore, here the twenty men rejoined them, Inaeut was soon after seized by some approvers from Jubulpore, going with the 73rd to Bandah. Rambuksh, Dibba, Miherban, Persaud and Esuree fled towards Mirzapore, and at Oomerpatun killed six Goosaens from Elichpore to Benares.

16. After the arrest of Inaeut, Chand Khan and Dulelee, his brother, with Bhekun Khan (approver) fled to Belehree with all his gang, and there fell in with two Kawrutties, two Tailors and a woman. Took them on to Biseynee, where two other travellers joined them, and they took the whole seven on to the nullah, where they had

murdered five men on the road to Khopa, and there put them to death—after this affair they returned home.

A total of fifty-two men and one woman murdered in this expedition.

Report of an Expedition made by a Gang of seventy Thugs from Bundelcund and Gwalior under Buduloo, Purmsook, Muneeram, Heera, Rambuksh and Chotee, in the year 1829.

1. Buduloo, Purmsook, Muneeram, Heera and Rambuksh with fifty Thugs from Bundelcund, crossed the Nurbudda, at Chiepanee, and proceeded to Boorhanpore and thence to Chowka Phoolmaree, where they fell in with a traveller. Taking him on one coss and a half they killed him. This is the man whose sitrengees were brought to Saugor.

2. They went to Aurungabad, where they fell in with two Rajpoots going from that place to Naggur, they took them on two coss and put them to death and went on to Naggur.

3. At Naggur they fell in with three travellers. They took them on two coss, put them to death and went on to Poonah. From a village four coss this side of Poonah, they retraced their steps and struck off on the road to Nasick.

4. At Nasick they met Chotee, who had escaped from Beharee Lall Seith and reached that place with a gang of twenty Thugs. He had gone to Barodah and there killed a Rajpoot.

5. At Nasick the gangs joined and fell in with two travellers. Taking them on one and a half coss, they killed them and thence Chotee returned to Nasick, while the rest went to Barodah and thence to Tuppa.

6. At Tuppa they fell in with Soorut Sing Tomandar and four attendants. One and a half coss from Tuppa, on the road to Echawur, they put them to death. After this they dispersed and returned to their respective homes.

7. Chotee fell in with two women at Nasick in search of service—he accompanied them to a village, one stage on the other side of Nasick, and killed them both.

8. They returned through Nasick to Barodah, where they fell in with two Rajpoots, one Lodhee and one Aheer. They went on with them to Chanee, where they killed all four in camp.

9. After this affair they went on to the banks of the Mehee river in Guzerat, whence they returned to the Khyra cantonments—here they fell in with two men on their way to Bhurtpore—going on with them to a village two coss distant, they killed them.

10. They went back to Barodah where they fell in with five Sepahees—came on with them to Makhunee where they murdered them in their camp. After this affair they heard of the execution of Makhun, Gungadeen and their gang at Jowra, and in alarm returned to their respective homes.

A total of twenty-seven men killed in this expedition.

Report of an Expedition into Berar by a gang of forty Thugs, under Bhodae, Bukut, Moreea, Soorjun Aheer, Jowahir, Nunhooa Weaver, and Mandhata, in the year 1829.

1. Bodhee (hung at Saugor), Bukut, Moreea, Soorjun Aheer, Jowahir, Nunhooa and Mandhata with forty Thugs from Jhansee and Gwalior, set out and reached Rughoogur in Bhopaul, where they met two travellers, took them on one coss on the road to Jowra, and there put them to death.

2. After this they crossed the Nerbudda river at the Pugulana Ghat and reached Omrowtee, where they found four men in search of service—they took them to Bham, pretending to be able to get service for them—and thence going on half a coss put them to death.

They came back to Bham and were dividing the booty when the people of Dunraj Seith came and arrested twenty-two of the gang, the rest escaped. They remained in confinement four months when they heard that orders had been sent from Jubulpore for them, and dreading the consequences of coming here, they broke their prison and got off. They were not in irons and remained merely to negociate for the cost of their release.

Dirgpal Subahdar had returned from his expedition into Guzerat, and having had a dispute with his associates he went to Narain Raw, Subah of Gwalior, and got a guard to seize Durroo and Motee—having heard this, these two men fled and came in the same character to Jubulpore whence Durroo got a guard and arrested Dirgpal and Ramchund. Durroo and these two men were sent from Jubulpore to Jowra, where Durroo was hung and Dirgpal sent to Gwalior and released. He was again seized in 1831, and executed at Saugor in 1832.

A total of six men murdered in this expedition.

Report of an Expedition into Rajpootana by some gangs under Bhimmee, Saadut Khan and other Jemadars, with a gang of Thugs, in the year 1828-29.

1. Eight years ago, Bhimmee Jemadar with twenty-two Thugs, after observing the usual omens, left their homes in the Jhansee district on a Thuggee expedition. They

reached Secundra, four coss from Jypore, in ten days, where they met Saadut Khan, (approver) Aman, Setar Khan, (hung) Bheka and Chundee Jemadars, (still at large). Shortly after this they fell in with four travellers, two Hindoo Blacksmiths and two women from Jypore en route to Allahabad—Bejee Sing Jemadar acted as Sothai or inveigler, and won their confidence, and they proceeded in their company next morning. After proceeding a short distance, east of the village of Mangouh, they were all strangled, and their bodies buried in the sand, but were exhumed by the wild beasts a few days afterwards and discovered by the civil authorities.

2. After this affair they proceeded to Leik in Jypore, and while encamped outside the city, Bigae Sing introduced a traveller to them—a party of the gang set out with him in the morning and effected their designs on him after proceeding about a coss on the Agra road, and rejoined the main gang.

3. They then arrived at Jypore in five days, where Setar Khan won the confidence of two travellers en route to Bhurtpore. They left this place with them next morning, and murdered them on arriving at a mangoe grove, one coss distant.

4. They struck off to the Delhie road and while resting near a nullah, were overtaken by three travellers, Mussulmen, proceeding from Neemuch to Delhie, accompanied them to a mangoe tope, three coss from Achreole, and, after the congregation they found assembled there had been dispersed, they strangled them and interred their bodies in an adjacent field.

5. On the following morning they reached Achreole, and while encamped in the Serai, were joined by Peearjee Jemadar, with twenty-two Thugs, of the Soseea caste. Shortly after four Rajpoots from Gwalior came up én-

route to Lahore, who had with them two horses about 400 rupees value. Gholab Khan afterwards inveigled three more travellers, one a Sewar belonging to a Corps of Local Horse, returning from leave, and the other two from Jyepore, en-route to Kurnal. The same day Sutar Khan won the confidence of six more travellers, two Bheesties (or water carriers), one Mussulman and three Hindoos from the Dekhan, en-route to Delhi. Gholab Khan set out with the three travellers in the Delhi direction, and after descending a Pass, two coss from Achrole, killed them in a heavy jungle, threw their bodies into a nullah and covered them over with stones.

6. Sutar Khan and forty Thugs set out with the six travellers shortly after Gholab Khan and his party; and on arriving at the spot where the above murder was perpetrated, the travellers became alarmed at seeing the Sewar's horse without its owner and ran off, but the gang followed, soon after overtook and strangled them; when brought their bodies to the place where the three men had been interred. These bodies were discovered by the local authorities. Bhimee Jemadar then set out with his own gang and the remaining four travellers; but were obliged to forego their intentions on account of the lateness in leaving their ground, and they consequently proceeded to Munear Thana, where the parties who had preceded them were encamped. Having previously taken the precaution to leave two Thugs, Kudar Buksha and Mungra Sooseea, near the place where the nine men were murdered, to give them intelligence in case the bodies should be discovered. In the evening they detached seven men to bury them more securely; but before these men reached the place, they saw a concourse of people collected round the dead bodies, and lost no time in giving the gang intelligence, and they immediately made off, leaving their four victims behind unhurt,

they halted at the Ghasee Thana, and divided the spoils acquired on the expedition; after which the Sooseea Thugs left the gang, and the remainder proceeded via Ulroul and Rujghur to Dhoosa, whence Laek and Doorjun (approvers) went to their homes, and the remainder toward Jypore. They halted at Lallsoute, where they met Bhowaneea (nose cut) and Omna Dacoits, who informed the Police of their being Thugs, and caused their apprehension: but they obtained their release after delivering up their property.

A total of seventeen men and two women murdered in this expedition.

Report of an Expedition into Rajpootana by a gang of Thugs under Chutter, Ameer Allee, Imamee, and Kalee Khan, in January 1829.

1. At half a coss distant from the village of Sasmere, they met two shopkeepers on their way from Indore—halted with them during the night, and, going on with them next morning, murdered them at a water course a short distance from the village.

2. They then went towards the Mukundeea Pass, there met two travellers from Indore, halted with them during the night, and the next morning went on with them to Burnoon, in the Khotah territory—set out again at day break next morning, and murdered them under a tree. They next proceeded to Lukheree and Niea Sheher, in the Jypore territory, and there met a party of six Koeleea Thugs,—

3. Whom they joined, and formed a gang of thirteen. They then went to Milana, thence towards Indore—on the road met four Brahmins, went on with them to Khosalghur,

where they passed the night; started the next morning, and murdered them, about a coss and half distant, in the plain.

4. After this affair the Koeleea Thugs returned to their homes, to spend the Hooley festival. Two months after this expedition, in the month of March 1829, Imamee opened another expedition with a party of twenty-six Thugs, and proceeded to Garwasa, in the Jypore territory, there met two Bunjarus, set out with them next morning, and murdered them near a water course, a coss from the village—proceeded to the village and sent back four men to bury their bodies securely.

5. Proceeded on the road to Dhoosa; the following morning halted at a village one and a half coss distant, there fell in with a traveller, murdered him about midnight and afterwards proceeded to Dhoosa.

6. There met an Affghan; proceeded with him towards Lalsont; halted at a village—left it about midnight, strangled him at the banks of a water course, and went on to Lalsont.

7. At Lalsont they met a Sepahee, proceeded with him to the next stage and encamped there—left it about midnight, and murdered him on the march.

8. Then took the road to Agra, and while halted at a Chokie, fell in with a Duffadar and three Nujeebs—halted with them at a village; proceeded towards Dholpore Baree the next morning, and strangled them in a nullah; got from them four Bullocks, which they disposed of.

9. Went towards Nugora and met a traveller a short distance this side of the village, on his way home from Neemuch, and murdered him.

10. From Nagura went to Madhoorajpore and were then joined by five Soosea Thugs, and soon after fell in with nine travellers on their way home—set out from Madhoorajpore in company with the travellers towards Jypore, and murdered them about one coss from the town.

11. Halted that day at a village where they were joined by five travellers on their way to their homes,—came on with them to Gararwas, and, leaving that place before day light, murdered them in the open plain, and buried their bodies in a water course which they, in the dark, took for the Bele selected by their people for the murder. It proved however to be a place much frequented by the villagers—on discovering their mistake they sent back some of their party to see whether the bodies might be discovered; and they found that they had been dug up by jackalls, and that a concourse of people had collected round them. They returned forthwith to the gang, who immediately dispersed but rendezvoused some days afterwards at Karowlie, where a division of the plunder took place, the Soosea Thugs did not rejoin them.

12. On the road to Karowlie, they fell in with a Chuprassee of the Insurance office, on his return to Calcutta from Mhow, where he had delivered some books to Captain Burns on the 20th July 1829—he encamped with them at Rujooghur, and going on with them next morning, he was murdered.

13. They then came to Peepala and then to Tuppa; there met a Havildar, two Sepahees and two of their relations going to their homes in Oude; they induced them to join their party and encamped with them at Konoee in the Bhopaul territory; started with them the following morning and murdered them half a coss from the village. This was their last affair. Of the men present in this expedition fifteen were soon after apprehended, of whom five were executed; three made approvers, and the remainder sentenced to imprisonment for life.

A total of thirty-eight men murdered in this expedition.

A total of two hundred and twenty-six men and six women murdered during the different expeditions this season.

Names of the Principal Leaders of the Gangs engaged in the foregoing Expeditions for 1829.

No.	Names of the Leaders.	Caste.	Resident.	Remarks.	No. of Thugs.
1	Sooper Sing,	Mussulman,	Gwalior,	Hung at Saugor in 1832,	20
2	Khoosala,	Ditto,	Ditto,	Transported from Saugor 1832,	10
3	Dulsa Jemadar,	Ditto,	Ditto,	Died at his home in 1830,	10
4	Khoorkooa ditto,	Ditto,	Ditto,	Transported from Saugor in 1832,	40
5	Rae Sing ditto,	Ditto,	Jhansee,	Hung at Saugor in 1832,	30
6	Purumna ditto,	Ditto,	Cawnpore,	Ditto ditto,	8
7	Kullooa ditto,	Lohar,	Candeish,	At large,	6
8	Nungoo ditto,	Barber,	Bundelcund,	Ditto,	6
9	Feringeea ditto,	Brahmin,	Gwalior,	Approver,	23
10	Tejun ditto,	Ditto,	Ditto,	Hung at Saugor in 1832,	24
11	Phoolsa ditto,	Ditto,	Ditto,	Approver,	13
12	Buhorena ditto,	Lodhee,	Huttah,	Died in Hydrabad Jail in 1832,	5
13	Heera ditto,	Aheer,	Gwalior,	Approver, died 1832,	
14	Gungadeen,	Lodhee,	Sumthur,	Hung at Jowra in December 1829,	7
15	Hureea,	Rajpoot,	Hingolee,	Approver,	5
16	Lal Khan,	Mussulman,	Calpee,	Hung at Saugor in 1832,	8
17	Adhur,	Rajpoot,	Baitool,	Ditto ditto,	5
18	Hoosain Khan Jemadar,	Mussulman,	Hydrabad,	Hung at Jubulpore in July 1835,	10
19	Sheik Meerun ditto,	Ditto,	Ditto,	Approver, died in 1837,	20
20	Zoolfakar ditto,	Ditto,	Saugor,	Hung at Saugor in 1832,	7
21	Mojahet Khan ditto,	Ditto,	Hydrabad,	Hung at Jubulpore in 1835,	20
22	Fureed Khan ditto,	Ditto,	Ditto,	Ditto ditto,	20
23	Kalee Khan ditto,	Ditto,	Ditto,	Died in Jubulpore Jail in 1835,	8
24	Zoolfukar ditto,	Ditto,	Punna,	Approver,	19
25	Noorkhan,	Ditto,	Jhansee,	Hung at Jubulpore in 1835,	

No.	Names of Leaders.	Caste.	Resident.	Remarks.	No. of Thugs.
26	Omed Jemadar,	Lodhee,	Cawnpore,	Hung at Saugor in 1832,	9
27	Sewdeen ditto,	Ditto,	Ditto,	Approver,	9
28	Inaeut ditto,	Mussulman,	Jhansee,	Ditto,	20
29	Zalim ditto,	Ditto,	Tehree,	Died at his home in 1835,	10
30	Ashraff,	Ditto,	Gwalior,	At large,	10
31	Bukut Jemadar,	Lodhee,	Sumthur,	Hung at Saugor in 1832,	6
32	Bukut ditto,	Brahmin,	Gwalior.	Transported from Saugor in 1832,	6
33	Bheka ditto,	Mussulman	Jhansee,	At large,	6
34	Bhugee ditto,	Lodhee,	Cawnpore,	Died in Saugor Jail in 1833,	6
35	Khuluk ditto,	Ditto,	Ditto,	Hung at Saugor in 1833,	20
36	Bhowanee,	Ditto,	Jhalone,	Approver,	10
37	Dhokul,	Ditto,	Cawnpore,	Hung at Saugor in 1833,	20
38	Bhola Buneea,	Buneea,	Jhalone,	Approver,	5
39	Kohman,	Mussulman,	Jhansee,	Ditto,	9
40	Boodha,	Ditto,	Ditto,	Transported from Saugor in 1832,	2
41	Khyratee,	Ditto,	Saugor,	Died in Saugor Jail ditto,	3
42	Rambux,	Lodhee,	Feruckabad,	Approver,	5
43	Persaud,	Ditto,	Ditto,	Ditto,	5
44	Deeba,	Buneea,	Ditto,	Ditto,	5
45	Mihrban,	Lodhee,	Cawnpore,	Ditto,	5
46	Esuree,	Ditto,	Ditto,	Ditto,	5
47	Dhunooa,	Ditto,	Ditto,	Hung at Jubulpore in 1836,	10
48	Hurlal,	Ditto,	Ditto,	Hung at Saugor in 1833,	10
49	Bhikhun Khan,	Mussulman,	Calpee,	Approver,	8
50	Chand Khan,	Ditto,	Jhansee,	Hung at Saugor in 1832,	
51	Dulele Khan,	Ditto,	Ditto,	Ditto ditto,	
52	Budloo Jemadar,	Lodhee,	Ditto,	Ditto ditto,	10

53	**Purumsookh,**	Brahmin,	Gwalior,	Hung at Saugor in 1832,	10
54	**Muneeram,**	Lodhee,	Jhansee,	Ditto ditto,	10
55	**Heera.**	Aheer,	Ditto,	Approver, died ditto,	10
56	**Rambux Jemadar,**	Brahmin,	Gwalior,	At large,	10
57	**Chotee ditto,**	Ditto,	Jhansee,	Approver,	20
58	**Bhudai ditto,**	Ditto,	Ditto,	Hung at Saugor in 1832,	5
59	**Bukut Moreea,**	Ditto,	Gwalior,	At large,	5
60	Soorjun,	Aheer,	Ditto,	Ditto,	5
61	Jowahir,	Rajpoot,	Indore,	Approver,	10
62	Nunhooa,	Kolee,	Gwalior,	Ditto,	5
63	Mandhata,	Lodhee,	Etawah,	Ditto,	10
64	Dirgpaul Sobahdar,	Brahmin,	Gwalior,	Hung at Saugor in 1832,	
65	Motee Jemadar,	Lodhee,	Ditto,	Ditto ditto,	
66	Durroo ditto,	Mussulman,	Sindouse,	Hung at Jowra in 1830,	
67	Sutar Khan,	Ditto,	Dholepore,	Hung at Saugor in 1832,	
68	Bhimee Jemadar,	Lodhee,	Gwalior,	Approver,	22
69	Sahadut ditto,	Mussulman,	Ditto,	Ditto,	
70	Peearjee ditto,	Naik,	Jeypore,	Ditto,	22
71	Ainan ditto,	Mussulman,	Gwalior,	Hung at Saugor in 1832,	
72	Chutter ditto,	Aheer,	Ditto,	Ditto ditto,	
73	Kunhye ditto,	Ditto,	Ditto,	Died in Joudpore 1833,	
74	Kulooa,	Rajpoot,	Ditto,	Killed by a Zemindar in attempting to arrest him at Gwalior in 1835,	20
75	Bhika Jemadar,	Mewatee,	Ditto,	At large,	
76	Kalee Khan,	Mussulman,	Koel,	Hung 1837,	
77	Emamee,	Ditto,	Gwalior,	Approver,	
78	Ameer Allee,	Ditto,	Ditto,	Ditto,	
79	Punoo,	Ditto,	Ditto,	Ditto,	
80	Kalee Khan,	Ditto,	Nursingpore,	Died in Saugor Jail in 1832,	
81	Chutter,	Aheer,	Gwalior,	Hung at Saugor ditto,	
82	Chudamee,	Mussulman,	Nursingpore,	Ditto ditto,	

REPORT

OF A

THUG EXPEDITION

In the Year 1831.

Report of a Thug Expedition in the year 1831,
Rambuksh, Deveedeen, with Twenty-five

No. of List.	Names and jurisdiction of the place where the Murder was perpetrated.	No. and Sex of the Murdered.		Date of the Murder.	Intended destination of the Murdered.		Supposed value of the property robbed.
		Men.	Women.		From	To	
315	Poorwa, in Cawnpore,	1	0	January, 1831,	Benares,	Mynpooree,	50 rupees.
316	Sooltangunge, in Mynpooree,	1	0	Ditto,	Kurnal,	Cawnpore,	100 rupees.
317	Mallawa,	2	0	Ditto,	Loodhiana,	Ditto,	150 rupees.
318	Somp, in the Coel district,	2	0	Ditto,	Ditto,	Eastward,	200 rupees.
319	Khoorjah, in Anoopshuhur,	2	0	Ditto,	Ditto,	Mirzapore,	100 rupees.
320	Boorhana,	2	0	Ditto,	Kurnal,	Cawnpore,	200 rupees, a sword and musket.

under the following leaders: Mehrban, . Thugs, and other Leaders.

REMARKS.

In January 1831, Mehrban, Rambuksh, Daveedeen and other leaders with twenty-five Thugs, assembled at Rajee Mhow in Furruckhabad, and set out on an expedition. In the course of three or four days they arrived at Bithoor, and when next morning they were about to set out towards the east, a bird chirped, without repeating its cry—alarmed at this monitary omen, the Thugs agreed among themselves, that it would be dangerous to pursue the proposed route, and they accordingly took the road to the west. They went and rested at Poorwa in Cawnpore, where they fell in with a Hindoo from Benares on his way to Mynpooree, mounted on a pony, whom they decoyed, and next morning having taken him a mile out of the village, put him to death. His body was thrown into a well.

After the murder, they proceeded on towards Secundra, which place they reached in two days—on the road onwards next day they were joined by another gang of fifteen Lodhee Thugs under Budlee, Hurlall and Lallah Lochun jemadars.

This gang had, a short time previously, set out from Chouda-ka-Poorwa in Cawnpore, and proceeded in the first instance to Sooltangunge in Mynpooree. There they had decoyed a Brahmin from Kurnal on his way to Cawnpore, whom they strangled next morning, and threw his body into a well a mile or so distant from the village.

They then went to Mallawa and inveigled two travellers, by caste shepherds who had come from Loodhiana, intending to go to Cawnpore. The travellers were taken out next morning and strangled at a well two miles off, and their bodies thrown into it.

Having proceeded onwards they reached Somp, in the Coel district, where Lalla Lochun decoyed two troopers, by caste Mahomedans, from Loodhiana, travelling eastward. They were strangled next morning on the road two miles from the village, and their bodies buried.

Their next stage was to Koorjah in Anoopshuhur; and there they fell in with and decoyed two travellers, shop-keepers by trade, who came from Loodhiana, on their way to Mirzapore. They were put to death next morning as usual, and their bodies buried.

After this the gang reached Boorhana. There they found two Hindoos from Kurnal on their way to Cawnpore, whom they induced to take up their quarters with them. Next morning the travellers were taken to a river which runs near the town, and having been put to death, their bodies were thrown into the stream.

***Report of a Thug Expedition in the year of* 1831,**
Rambuksh, Deveedeen, with Twenty-fire

No. of List.	Names and jurisdiction of the place where the Murder was perpetrated.	No. and Sex of the Murdered.		Date of the Murder.	Intended destination of the Murdered.		Supposed value of the property robbed.
		Men.	Women.		From	To	
321	Jhinjana,	1	0	That Season of 1831,	Loodhiana,	Oude,	100 rupees.
322	Bidolee, near Kurnal,	1	0	Ditto,	Lahore,	Allahabad,	50 rupees.
323	Kerooa,	2	0	Ditto,	Ditto,	Lucknow,	300 rupees.
324	Haupper,	1	0	Ditto,	Kurnal,	Cawnpore,	150 rupees.
325	Near Secundra,	3	0	Ditto,	Meerut,	Ditto,	5 copper coins, and some old clothes.
326	Ditto,	2	0	Ditto,	Hurdwar,	Allahabad,	300 rupees.
327	Near Buldeojee,	2	0	Ditto,	Baroda,	Byswara,	50 rupees.

under the following leaders: Mehrban, Thugs, and other Leaders.

REMARKS.

The gang next proceeded to Jhinjana, and met a traveller, by caste a Hindoo, who came from Loodhiana on his way to the Oude State, whom they decoyed; and taking him out next morning a mile from the town, they strangled him, and threw his body into a well.

The Thugs proceeded in the same direction as far as Bidolee near Kurnal, whence having turned back they came to a village ten miles distant. They found a traveller, by caste herdsman, who was going from Lahore to Allahabad. He was decoyed and next morning put to death on the way-side, where his body was also buried.

Passing through Sirdhana, the capital of the Begum Sumroo, they went to Kerooa, where they fell in with two travellers from Lahore, who were proceeding to Lucknow. They were Hindoos by caste, and were persuaded to join the gang, who put them to death next morning as usual, and buried their bodies about two miles from the village.

Having visited Meerut, the Thugs went to Happur and decoyed a traveller, by caste Hindoo, who was going from Kurnal to Cawnpore, who was conducted out next morning and strangled two miles off. The body was buried.

After this they arrived by easy stages at Coel, from whence they again took the road to Secundra. Before reaching the latter place they overtook three Hindoos, by caste Kuhars, who were travelling from Meerut to Cawnpore. These men were decoyed and the gang had not proceeded many paces when they fell in with Deveedeen jemadar, Mehrban and others, who had murdered the Hindoo as already described. This party of Thugs had two Ganges water-carriers with them, whom they had also just decoyed, and who were on their way from Hurdwar to Allahabad. It was agreed that Deveedeen and ten Thugs should join Lalla Lochun's party, and that the rest of his gang should rendezvous at Shamlee. The five travellers passed the night at Secundra, whither they were accompanied by the murdering party. Next morning early the Ganges water-carriers were taken out first, and put to death two miles from the town. The bodies were buried. Next the Kuhars were led out to their fate, and having been conducted to a tank four miles off, they were strangled and their bodies buried on the brink.

After completing the murders they went to Buldeojee, and fell in with two travellers, a Rajpoot and a Cow-keeper, on their way from Barodah to Byswara, who were decoyed, and next morning having been taken to a well two miles from the village, they were strangled, and their bodies thrown into the water.

Report of a Thug Expedition in the year 1831;
Rambuksh, Deveedeen, with Twenty-five

No. of List.	Names and jurisdiction of the place where the Murder was perpetrated.	No. and Sex of the Murdered.		Date of the Murder.	Intended destination of the Murdered.		Supposed value of the property robbed.
		Men.	Women.		From	To	
328	Bohgaon, in the Mynpooree district,	2	0	That Season of 1831,	Baroda,	Byswara,	50 rupees.
329	Near Kurreer,	3	0	Ditto,	Kurnal,	Cawnpore,	50 rupees.
330	Mukhun-ka-seraee, in Mynpooree,	1	0	Ditto,	Muttra,	Ditto,	25 rupees.
331	Ajeetgunge, in the Mynpooree zillah,	2	0	Ditto,	....	Benares,	6 Gold mohurs, and other property, all worth 150 rupees.

under the following leaders: Mehrban, Thugs, and other Leaders.

REMARKS.

Lalla Lochun jemadar's gang of fifteen Thugs separated at this place from Deveedeen's party, and took the road homewards; while the latter proceeded to keep their appointment with their companies at Shamlee.

Lalla Lochun's party travelled on towards Bohgaon in the Mynpooree district, which place they reached in the course of some days. They fell in with two Brahmins from Benares on their way to Byswara, whom they decoyed, and having passed the night with them at Bohgaon, they put them to death next morning, and threw their bodies into a well two miles off. After the murder this gang reached home without any other adventure.

Part of Deveedeen's gang under Mehrban Sing left Secundra, and proceeded at once to Shamlee, where they remained in expectation of Deveedeen's arrival. After the murder at Bohgaon, Deveedeen and his companions went directly to Shamlee, and were welcomed with great delight by the rest of the gang, who had begun to entertain apprehensions for their safety.

Next day, they all set out again, and proceeded as far as Bidolee, without meeting with any success in their search after victims. They therefore turned back and came to Kurreer, where they fell in with three shoe-makers travelling from Kurnal to Cawnpore, whom they decoyed, and next morning escorted a couple of miles on their way, and then put to death. The bodies were thrown into a well.

Marching onwards by regular stages, the Thugs, in the course of some days, arrived at Mukhun-ka-seraee, in Mynpooree, and inveigled a Hindoo traveller on his way from Muttra to Cawnpore. He passed the night in their company, and next morning was strangled a mile out of the town, and his body thrown into a well.

They went on to Shukoorabad, slept there, and next day proceeded onwards. About eight o'clock in the morning, they reached a tank near Arown in the Mynpooree zillah, and fell in with two travellers, by caste Lodhees, on their way to Benares. They were decoyed, conducted to Ajeetgunge, where they passed the night, and next morning were put to death outside the town, and their bodies thrown into a well.

After the murder, they went to Mudpore, and there Deveedeen and Mehrban were recognized by a Brahmin, who knew them to be Thugs. The Brahmin gave information in the town, and a number of people came out, seized Rambuksh, Deveedeen, Bhowanee and Mohun, and made them over to the thanadar of the Police, who forwarded them to the magistrate at Mynpooree. These four men were detained on suspicion for six months, after

***Report of a Thug Expedition in the year* 1831,**
Rambuksh, Deveedeen, with Twenty-five

No. of List.	Names and jurisdiction of the place where the Murder was perpetrated.	No. and Sex of the Murdered.		Date of the Murder.	Intended destination of the Murdered.		Supposed value of the property robbed.
		Men.	Women.		From	To	
332	Barha, in Cawnpore,	1	0	That Season of 1831,	Bundelkhund,	Benares,	20 rupees, a pony.
333	Baba Wallagaon,	2	0	Ditto,	Oude,	Mhow,	100 rupees.
334	Near Burwara,	2	0	Ditto,	Lucknow,	Saugor,	80 rupees.
335	Near Muhoba,	2	0	Ditto,	Mhow,	....	150 rupees.
336	Near Oomree,	2	0	Ditto,	Dekhan,	Northward,	40 Rs. cash, 36 rupees worth a silver armlet.

under the following leaders: Mehrban, Thugs, and other Leaders.

REMARKS.

which intelligence having intermediately been conveyed to Saugor of their imprisonment, they were made over to a party sent from that place to receive them. Of the number three were admitted approvers at Saugor, and the fourth, Mohun, was tried and sentenced.

The remainder of the gang, on perceiving that their leaders were captured, dispersed and returned home.

At the same time that the above proceedings were being carried on, (in January, 1831,) another gang of thirty Thugs, under Bhowanee, Dhowkul, and Shunkur jemadars assembled at Motee-ka-Poorwa in Furruckabad, and set out on an expedition; they went as far as Barha in Cawnpore, and there fell in with their first victim, a Hindoo, on his way from Bundelkhund to Benares, who was decoyed; and having passed the night with the Thugs, was put to death next morning in a field, and his body securely buried.

The gang crossed the Jumna at Calpee, and were joined while in the boat by a sepahee and another man, both Hindoos, on their way from Oude to Mhow in Malwa. They agreed to travel with the Thugs, and went and slept at Baba Wallagaon. Next morning they were strangled, and their bodies buried in a water-course.

After this affair they went on to Keitah in Bundelkhund. There they managed to decoy two travellers, a Brahmin and a Kuhar, who were going from Lucknow to Saugor, and conducted them to Killowa. Having slept there, the travellers were taken near to Burwara next morning, and then put to death. The bodies were buried.

The gang went on to Chutterpore, and rested near the well called Meetah Kooa. They fell in with two shepherds, who were going from Mhow to their homes in the Dooab, and took them to a hamlet near Muhoaba, where they passed the night. Next morning the travellers were put death, two miles from the village.

They next arrived at Rahut, and rested in a garden. There they were joined by Bhikka, son of Sunnum jemadar, with nine Thugs from Sindouse, and soon afterwards, two Hindoos from the Dekhan, on their way northward, came to the same place and were decoyed. They were taken to Oomreea, and the next morning setting out again the Thugs put them to death at a nullah two miles off, and buried their bodies. The remains have been disinterred, and the case tried by the Agent to the Governor General S. and N. T.

Report of a Thug Expedition in the year 1831, Rambuksh, Deveedeen, with Twenty-five

No. of List.	Names and jurisdiction of the place where the Murder was perpetrated	No. and Sex of the Murdered.		Date of the Murder.	Intended destination of the Murdered.		Supposed value of the property robbed.
		Men.	Women.		From	To	
337	Kunnooa Khairah and Baba Wallagaon,	4	0	That Season of 1831,	Keitah,	Cawnpore,	180 rupees.
338	Oude State,	2	0	Ditto,	Saugor,	Beyrajh,	100 rupees.
339	Near Futtehgunge,	2	0	Ditto,	....	Sultanpore,	60 rupees.
340	Bulla,	2	0	Ditto,	Gwalior,	Bulla,	125 rupees, and a pony
341	Moraya,	1	0	Ditto,	....	Sultanpore,	50 rupees.

under the following leaders: Mehrban, Thugs, and other Leaders.

REMARKS.

The Sindouse Thugs now took their leave of the Loodhees of the Dooab, who proceeded to Jullalpore, and at the river near it they met and decoyed two Hindoos travelling from Keitah to Cawnpore. The party had scarcely got clear of the bed of the river, when two Bhisties (water-carriers) from Keitah, also proceeding to Cawnpore, came up, and being addressed were persuaded to join the gang. The Thugs divided themselves into two parties. One took the two water-carriers to Kunnooa Khairah, and the other the two Hindoos to Baba Wallagaon. Next morning all four were put to death in the usual manner. The bodies were buried in both instances.

Having visited Calpee the gang returned home, without any further adventures.

In the month of March, 1831, Khuluk, Dhowkul, and Bhowanee jemadars, with six Thugs collected together, and went to Maita-ka-Poorwa, in the Furruckhabad district. They arrived at Sirsaya Ghat on the Ganges, where their numbers were increased by the junction of Shewdeen, Runna, and others, seven Thugs, all crossed the river Ganges and entered the Oude State. They soon afterwards decoyed two travellers, Hindoos by caste, from Saugor, on their way to Bhurach who passed the night in their company, and next morning were put to death as usual. The bodies were thrown into a well.

They then went on to Futtehgunge, there they fell in with two Hindoos, who were going to Sultanpore, who were decoyed, and next morning put to death two miles from the village. The bodies were thrown into a well.

After the murder they proceeded slowly onwards and were joined by Gunga Buneea, a Thug, who had come out in search of them, and continued their journey unsuccessfully as regarded victims till they reached Runjeet-ka-Poorwa. There they decoyed two cowherds from Gwalior, on their way to Bulla, and took them to Bassa Peepeerea and rested. Soon afterwards a gang of twenty Jumaldee Thugs of Oude, under Mehrban, Ruhman, and others came to the same place. All the Thugs set out next day with the travellers—they proceeded onwards till nightfall, when they arrived within a mile of Bulla. The travellers already imagined themselves safe at home and had even invited their murderers to partake of their evening meal at their own houses, when the fatal signal was given and they were put to death in the usual manner. The bodies were buried in a dry water-course.

The gangs went and slept at Moraya: there they met a barber on his way to Sultanpore, whom they decoyed, and next morning strangled a mile or two from the village, burying his body in the sand.

Report of a Thug Expedition in the year 1831, Rambuksh, Deveedeen, with Twenty-five

No. of List.	Names and jurisdiction of the place where the Murder was perpetrated.	No. and Sex of the Murdered.		Date of the Murder.	Intended destination of the Murdered.		Supposed value of the property robbed.
		Men.	Women.		From	To	
342	Hydergurh,	4	0	That Season of 1831,	....	Jounpore,	300 rupees.
343	Supowlee, in the Gwalior State,	2	0	Ditto,	Gwalior,	Jhalone,	50 rupees.
	Meeting of Sindouse Thugs.						
344	Near Nowr,	2	0	1831,	Gwalior,	Oude territory,	100 rupees.
345	Sobhana, in the Coel district,	2	0	Ditto,	Mynpooree,	Subathoo,	100 rupees.

under the following leaders: Mehrban, Thugs, and other Leaders.

REMARKS.

Hydurgurh was their next day's journey; and while there four travellers, by caste Hindoos, fell into their hands. These men were proceeding to Jounpore. Next morning the travellers were conducted out of the village, and strangled at a well two miles off, into which their bodies were thrown.

After this murder, the two gangs of Jumaldhees and Lodhees separated, and went to their respective homes without perpetrating any other murder.

In the month of March 1831, a gang of twenty-two Thugs was collected by Shunker and Hurlal jemadars at Kurrooa in Furruckhabad. They determined to proceed into Bundelkhund, and crossed the Jumna at Shergurh. Here they were joined by Bhola Buneea, and two other Thugs, and all went to Supowlee in the Gwalior State. A Brahmin and a Kuhar, on their way from Gwalior to the neighbourhood of Jhalone, were decoyed at that place, and next morning were taken out and strangled in a field in which their bodies were buried.

The gang then proceeded to Rampooree. There they decoyed two travellers, a Brahmin and a Buneea, who were going from Gwalior to the Oude territory, and took them with them next day to Nowr, where they passed the night in the bazar. A gang of twenty-seven Thugs from Sindouse under Bukbut Mooreah, Thukoree, Zalim and other leaders happened to be at the same place, and were invited to assist at the murder of the travellers, who were taken out a short distance next morning and put to death. The bodies were thrown into a well.

N. B. These remains of bodies have been pointed out by Bhola Buneea approver, and exhumed—the case was tried by the Agent to the Governor General at Jubulpore. The murder has been ascertained to have been committed on the 24th March 1831. Having completed this murder, the gang returned home.

In the month of May, 1831, Uchul, Bukshel and twenty-five Thugs met Bahareepore, and agreed to try their fortune together on an expedition. It was determined that ten Thugs of the number should set out at once, and the remaining fifteen should join them at Sirhind twenty days afterwards. The ten Thugs first went to Sobhna, in the Coel district, where they fell in with two Hindoo travellers of the Kaet caste, on their way from Mynpooree to Subathoo, who were decoyed and induced to join the party. The same day twenty Thugs under Lalla Lochun jemadar came to Sobhna, and rested for the day outside of the village. The two gangs interchanged enquiries, but those inside of the village did not reveal to their friends outside, that they had any travellers in their train. Next morning early, the travellers

Report of a Thug Expedition in the year 1831, Rambuksh, Deveedeen, with Twenty-five

No. of List.	Names and jurisdiction of the place where the Murder was perpetrated.	No. and Sex of the Murdered.		Date of the Murder.	Intended destination of the Murdered.		Supposed value of the property robbed.
		Men.	Women.		From	To	
346	Near Goorsaheegunge,	2	0	That Season of 1831,	Muttra,	Byswara,	200 rupees, and a pony.
347	Koorjah,	2	0	Ditto,	Delhi,	Ditto,	200 rupees.
348	Jhinjanah,	3	0	Ditto,	Loodhiana,	Cawnpore,	150 rupees.
349	Semgurh,	3	0	Ditto,	Loodhiana,	Cawnpore,	300 rupees.
350	Bunjara-ka-seraee,	2	0	Ditto,	Lahore,	Gya,	500 Rs. cash, 2 horses, &c.

under the following leaders: Mehrban, Thugs, and other Leaders.

REMARKS.

---

were inveigled out and put to death, a couple of miles from the village. The bodies were buried. Having completed the murder, the gang returned and joined the other party under Lalla Lochun jemadar.

It appears that Lalla Lochun jemadar with his twenty Thugs, having set out from Jiddee-ka-Poorwa in the Furruckhabad district, went to Goorsahee Gunge, where they decoyed two Brahmin sepahees on their way from Muttra to Byswara, and put them to death next morning a mile from the village, and threw their bodies into a well.

After this they went at once to Sobhna and joined Uchul jemadar's party, as has been above related.

The two parties having united went to Koorja. There they met with two travellers, by caste Brahmins, on their way from Delhi to Byswara, whom they inveigled into their company, and having conducted them out next morning to a well two miles off, they strangled them and threw their bodies into the water.

Proceeding onwards, the gangs passed through Boolundshuhur, Meerut and Sirdhana to Bidolee. They had not even undressed themselves after three days' journey at the last places, when three sepahees, Hindoos by caste, arrived there from Loodhiana, on their way to Cawnpore. They were decoyed by Uchul jemadar, and the gang proceeded onwards with them to Jhinjana, where they all halted to sleep. Early next morning the travellers were taken two miles from the village, and having been strangled, their bodies were thrown into a well.

After the murder the gang went on to Kurnal, and thence to Semgurh, where they decoyed three travellers, by caste Hulwahees, or confectioners, on their way from Loodhiana to Cawnpore, and induced them to pass the night in their company. The travellers were strangled next morning some distance from the village, and their bodies buried.

The gang went on by the usual stages to Dooraha seraee near Loodhiana, without meeting with any further success, and therefore turned back; and having travelled eight miles sat down at a well by the way side to rest themselves. Two horsemen, Sheikhs, from Lahore, on their road to the sacred shrine at Gya, came up to the same place, and were easily persuaded by the Thugs to prosecute the journey in their company. They were conducted on the same day to Bunjara-ka-seraee, where they all slept, and next morning setting out again, the travellers were put to death a couple miles off, and their bodies buried.

***Report of a Thug Expedition in the year* 1831,**
Rambuksh, Deveedeen, with Twenty-five

No. of List.	Names and jurisdiction of the place where the Murder was perpetrated.	No. and Sex of the Murdered.		Date of the Murder.	Intended destination of the Murdered.		Supposed value of the property robbed.
		Men.	Women.		From	To	
351	Kurreer,	6	0	That Season of 1831,	Loodhiana,	Byswara,	450 rupees.
352	Buxar,	2	0	Ditto,	Delhi,	Lucknow,	150 rupees.
353	Tiggur,	5	0	Ditto,	Meerut,	Ditto,	500 rupees.
354	Kumorah Dumora,	4	0	Ditto,	Ditto,	Lucknow,	250 rupees.
355	Banska Ruttra,	3	0	Ditto,	Bareilly,	Shajahanpore,	4000 rupees.

under the following leaders: Mehrban, Thugs, and other Leaders.

REMARKS.

They had proceeded but a short distance onwards after completing this murder, when the fifteen Thugs alluded to above, of Uchul jemadar's gang, arrived and joined the gang. All agreed to turn back and try their luck to the eastward, and having passed through Kurnal, they arrived at Shamlee, where they fell in with six travellers, by caste Bhurbhoojas, on their way from Loodhiana to Byswara, who fell an easy prey to the Thugs. They were taken to the village of Kurreer, where they passed the night, and next morning were strangled a short distance from the village. The bodies were buried.

The gang then went on to Hauper, from whence twenty Thugs of their number took leave and went home, with a promise to rejoin in the course of fifteen or twenty days at a shrine in the Oude State. The next day the remainder of the gang set out in the direction of Boolundshuhur, and in the way fell in with two Kuhars proceeding from Delhi to Lucknow, who were decoyed and conducted to Buxar. Next morning early the travellers were strangled some distance from the village, and their bodies thrown into a well.

They all went on to Goormuktessir, on the Ganges, and embarked on the ferry-boat to cross the Ganges. Five travellers, Kuhars by caste, on their way from Meerut to Lucknow, had taken advantage of the same opportunity of crossing the river, and being addressed by some of the Thugs were easily persuaded to join their party. They all went to Tiggera, where they slept, and next morning the travellers were put to death on the bank of the river. Four of the bodies were buried in a ravine on the bank, but as it began to rain the fifth was thrown into the stream.

They proceeded next through Moradabad to Kumora Dhumora on the road to Bareilly, overtook and succeeded in decoying four travellers, by caste Hindoos, on their way from Meerut to Lucknow. The next morning the travellers were put to death outside of the village, and their bodies buried.

Having completed this murder the gang went to Bareilly, and taking the road to Shujahanpore, arrived at Futtehgunge. Next day they proceeded six miles further on and sat down at a well near a tank to refresh themselves, when three treasure carriers from Bareilly, on their way to Shujehanpore, came up to the well and commenced to bathe themselves. They consisted of a Musulman and two Hindoos, and their names have since been ascertained to have been Bhooree Khan, Myaram and Saligram. The circumstance of their being the conveyers of specie could not for a moment be concealed from the Thugs, whose cupidity led them instantly to discover the fact. They were addressed and decoyed, and beguiling the road with their insinuating discourse, the Thugs conducted the treasure-carriers to Bans-ka-Kuttra, where they all slept. Next morning the travellers were strangled about a mile from that place, and

Report of a Thug Expedition in the year 1831, Rambuksh, Deveedeen, with Twenty-five

No. of List.	Names and jurisdiction of the place where the Murder was perpetrated.	No. and Sex of the Murdered.		Date of the Murder.	Intended destination of the Murdered.		Supposed value of the property robbed.
		Men.	Women.		From	To	
356	Koorowlee, in the Mynpooree district,	1	0	That Season of 1831,	Meerut,	Cawnpore,	15 rupees.
357	Moghul-ka-saraee,	3	0	Ditto,	Muttra,	Lahore,	100 rupees.
358	Near Sirhind,	6	0	Ditto,	....	....	300 rupees.

under the following leaders: Mehrban, Thugs, and other Leaders.

REMARKS.

---

the dead bodies were thrown two into one well, and the third into another. They then pursued their way. The traveller whose body was thrown singly into the well, by name Myaram, was not quite dead, and the cold water acting upon his frame, recovered him from the state of suffocation in which he had been left by the Thugs. He managed to scramble out of the well after the departure of the Thugs, and running into the village gave instant information to the Police authorities. The thanadar mounted his horse and attended by his Police runners followed in pursuit of the gang. The majority of the Thugs had got safe to Shahabad, but twelve of the number, as follows, having lagged behind, fell into the thanadar's hands:

Lalla Lochun jemadar—Buldee—Bukshee jemadar—Himunchula—Seetla—Heerooa—Hurrea—Sukkoo—Mooradea—Dhya Lodhee—Purshadooa—Uchul jemadar.

These were overtaken, and eleven of them were secured. The twelfth, Uchul jemadar, eluded the Police, and fled to Shahabad, where he gave information to the main gang, who immediately set off homewards. These eleven men had a bag of 600 rupees in their possession, which they threw away as soon as they were seized, and on being searched nothing was found in their possession. The thanadar put them all into confinement. It so happened that a man soon after went to the spot, where the money had been thrown away, to cut grass, and found the bag of rupees, which the Thugs now say he appropriated, without their daring to point out the fact to their captors. These eleven men were detained in confinement for six months and then released.

In the month of September or October, 1831, Runnooa moonshee, Uchul and Hurlal jemadars, with a gang of thirty Thugs, assembled at Behareepore, in the Furruckhabad district, and set out on an expedition. They went first to Koorowlee in Mynpooree, where they decoyed a traveller, Hindoo by caste, on his way from Meerut to Cawnpore, whom they kept near them all day, and next morning put to death at a well a mile from the village, throwing his body into the water.

The gang went onwards and reached Moghul-ka-seraee by regular stages. There they fell in with three travellers, by caste Sheiks, on their way from Muttra to Lahore, whom they inveigled and induced to join the gang. They were put to death next morning about two miles from the village, and their bodies buried.

After this the Thugs went to Loodhiana, and met six travellers, about to leave that place for the Oude territory, Runnooa moonshee decoyed them and agreed to travel in their company. The whole gang accordingly turned back

Report of a Thug Expedition in the year 1831,
Rambuksh, Deveedeen, with Twenty-five

No. of List.	Names and jurisdiction of the place where the Murder was perpetrated.	No. and Sex of the Murdered.		Date of the Murder.	Intended destination of the Murdered.		Supposed value of the property robbed.
		Men.	Women.		From	To	
359	Near Kurnal,	3	0	That Season of 1831,	Lahore,	Hurdwar,	400 rupees.
360	Near Goolchutter,	4	0	Ditto,	West,	Banda,	500 rupees, a horse worth 50 rupees, 2 dogs.
361	Near Boorhana,	2	0	Ditto,	Lahore,	Benares,	100 rupees.
362	Tukkeah,	2	0	Ditto,	Meerut,	Sultanpore,	100 rupees.
363	Near Hussungunge,	6	0	Ditto,	Ditto,	Jugdespore,	500 rupees.

under the following leaders: Mehrban, Thugs, and other Leaders.

REMARKS.

and accompanied the travellers to a village, a little to the west of Sirhind, where they slept. Early next morning the travellers were strangled a mile or two off, and their bodies buried in a tank.

They again turned back and proceeded for two or three stages to the vicinity of Umballa, where they were sitting on the bank of a stream—when three travellers on their way from Lahore to Hurdwar, came up and were decoyed and taken to Umballa. They slept there, and next morning went towards Kurnal, passing the next night in a village, name unknown. Next morning the travellers were as usual strangled, and their bodies buried on the bank of a stream some distance off.

The gang next proceeded to Goolchutter, where they managed to inveigle four Hindoos travelling on their way from the west to Banda. They had two dogs with them which they were taking to the Chief of Banda. They took them to a village ten miles off, where they slept, and next morning the travellers were put to death in the usual manner two miles from the village, and their bodies buried.

Having crossed the Jumna, the Thugs arrived at Boorhana in the Begum Sumroo's territory, where they decoyed two Brahmins travelling from Lahore to Benares, and took them to a village four miles off to sleep. Next morning they were escorted two miles on their way and then strangled. The bodies were buried in the bed of a stream.

After this affair the gang returned home without any further adventure.

About the same time that the before-mentioned gang was out Keseeree subadar and Shewdeen jemadar with a gang of thirteen Lodhee Thugs left Byns-ka-Poorwa in Oude, and set out on an expedition. They first went to Tukkeah, where they fell in with two travellers, by caste Hindoos, on their way from Meerut to Sooltanpore, whom they decoyed. Soon after a gang of sixteen Jumaldhee Thugs from Oude under Sirdar jemadar arrived at the same place, and joined the Lodhees. Next morning early the travellers were conducted to a garden a mile off and strangled. The bodies were thrown into a well.

Having gone on to Hussungunge, the gang was joined by another party of six Thugs under Dhambul jemadar and Ouseeree, (approver.) Soon after six Mahomedans from Meerut on their way to Jugdespore in Oude, came to the same place, and being addressed by Keseeree subadar, were easily drawn into his snare. Next morning the travellers were strangled only a mile from the village, and their bodies thrown into a well.

Report of a Thug Expedition in the year 1831, Rambuksh, Deveedeen, with Twenty-five

No. of List.	Names and jurisdiction of the place where the Murder was perpetrated.	No. and Sex of the Murdered.		Date of the Murder.	Intended destination of the Murdered.		Supposed value of the property robbed.
		Men.	Women.		From	To	
364	Etawah,	2	0	That Season of 1831,	Saugor,	Koonda,	100 rupees.
365	Near Bhunter,	1	0	Ditto,	Dekhan,	Sultanpore,	30 rupees.
366	Bhaukaira,	2	0	Ditto,	Ditto,	....	100 rupees.
367	Ruhmutgunge,	1	0	Ditto,	Cawnpore,	Jugdespore,	40 rupees.
368	Futtehgunge,	2	0	Ditto,	Meerut,	Sultanpore,	50 rupees.
369	Nuwabgunge,	1	0	Ditto,	Nusseerabad,	Goruckpore,	30 rupees, 2 bullocks.
370	Subdhulgunge	1	0	Ditto,	Lucknow,	Ajoodhea,	12 rupees.
371	Gossaingunge,	2	0	Ditto,	West,	Sultanpore,	60 rupees.
372	Bhicknapore,	4	0	Ditto,	Muttra,	Byswara,	300 rupees.

under the following leaders: Mehrban, Thugs, and other Leaders.

REMARKS.

The gang now crossed the Ganges, and proceeded to Etawah, where they found two Hindoos travelling from Saugor to Koonda, who were decoyed and next morning put to death as usual some distance off. The bodies were thrown into a well.

They then went to Bhunter, and decoyed a Hindoo travelling from the Dekhan to Sooltanpore Having passed the night there, the traveller was strangled next morning two miles from the village, and his body thrown into a well.

They next went to Bhaukhaira, were they fell in with two travellers from the Dekhan, whom they decoyed and took out next morning a distance of two miles, and then strangled them. The bodies were thrown into a well.

After this affair the gang went to Ruhmutgunge, where they decoyed a traveller, by caste Mussulman, on his way from Cawnpore to Jugdespore. During the day twenty-five more Jumaldhee Thugs from Oude under Futhee, Hyder and Dhossoo jemadars came and joined the gang. The Thugs next morning conducted their victim to a tank two miles off, and then put him to death. His body was buried.

They then went on to Futtehgunge, where they fell in with two travellers, by caste Chumars, who were employed as grooms, and were on their way from Meerut to Sooltanpore. They were decoyed and next morning put to death a mile from the village. The bodies were buried.

Having proceeded to Nuwabgunge, they fell in with a Hindoo on his way from Nusseerabad to Goruckpore, whom they decoyed, and next morning strangled, as usual, outside of the village. The body was thrown into a well.

The Thugs then proceeded to Subdhulgunge and decoyed a traveller, by caste a gardener, on his way from Lucknow to Ajoodhea. He was decoyed and next morning despatched a mile outside of the village, in the usual manner. His body was thrown into a well.

They next went to Gosaeengunge, where they met two travellers from the west on their way to Sooltanpore, whom they decoyed, and next morning took out a mile from the village, where they were strangled at a well, into which the bodies were thrown.

After this, Futteh jemadar and his gang took another direction, and the rest of the Thugs went to Bhicknapore, where they decoyed four Hindoos

Report of a Thug Expedition in the year 1831,
Rambuksh, Deveedeen, with Twenty-five

No. of List.	Names and jurisdiction of the place where the Murder was perpetrated.	No. and Sex of the Murdered.		Date of the Murder.	Intended destination of the Murdered.		Supposed value of the property robbed.
		Men.	Women.		From	To	
373	Chupra,	2	0	That Season of 1831,	Delhie,	Oude Provinces,	50 rupees, and a pony.
374	Juhangeerabad,	4	0	Ditto,	Loodhiana,	Futtehpore,	250 rupees.
375	Malagurh,	3	0	Ditto,	....	Kurnal,	100 rupees.
376	Rajhpore, in the Putteeala State,	3	0	Ditto,	Loodhiana,	Eastward,	300 rupees.
377	Kunheyah,	3	0	Ditto,	Amritsir,	Furruckhabad,	100 rupees.
378	Doorhaha,	3	0	Ditto,	Lahore,	Ditto,	150 rupees.

under the following leaders: Mehrban, Thugs, and other Leaders.

REMARKS.

---

travelling from Muttra to Byswara. Next morning they were conducted a mile out of the village and strangled. The bodies were thrown into a well.

Having completed this murder the Thugs returned to their respective homes.

In the month of October, 1831, Runnooa moonshee, Bukshee jemadar and others, assembled a gang of thirty-five Thugs at Behareepore in the Furruckhabad district, and determined on trying their fortune again on the roads. They went first to Chupra, where the moonshee decoyed two Hindoos from Delhi on their way to the Oude Provinces, whom the Thugs took out next morning to a tank a mile from the village and strangled. The bodies were thrown into a well.

They then proceeded to Juhangeerabad, where they fell in with four Hindoos travelling from Loodhiana to Futtehpore, who were decoyed and accommodated with a resting place near one of the Thug jemadars. Next morning before daylight, they went on their way again and the travellers were put to death at the distance of a couple of miles. The bodies were thrown into a well.

The gang went on to Boolundshuhur, and there they decoyed three Hindoo travellers on their way to Kurnal, whom they took with them to Malagurh. They slept there and next morning the travellers were put to death at a stream about two miles off, and the bodies thrown into a well.

Proceeding onwards the Thugs passed through Kurnal, and arrived at Rajhpore in the Putteeala State. They there fell in with three travellers, by caste Brahmins, from Loodhiana, going eastwards, who were decoyed and next morning being conducted a mile on their way were put to death, and their bodies buried on the bank of a stream.

After this the Thugs went to the seraee at Kunheya, where they found three travellers resting, who had come from Amritsir on their way to Furruckhabad. They were decoyed, and taken out next morning a mile or two on the road, and then put to death. The bodies were buried.

The gang went on to Doorada and put up in the seraee. Three travellers, one a Pundit and two Kuhars, were resting there. They had come from Lahore intending to go to Furruckhabad, and were persuaded to join the Thugs. Next morning they were strangled about a mile from the village, and their bodies buried in a field.

Report of a Thug Expedition in the year 1831, Rambuksh, Deveedeen, with Twenty-five

No. of List.	Names and jurisdiction of the place where the Murder was perpetrated.	No. and Sex of the Murdered.		Date of the Murder.	Intended destination of the Murdered.		Supposed value of the property robbed.
		Men.	Women.		From	To	
379	Near Sirhind,	6	0	That Season of 1831,	Lahore,	Dhoondea,	900 rupees.
380	Bunjara-ka-seraee,	2	0	Ditto,	Loodhiana,	Cawnpore,	50 rupees cash, and clothes, &c
381	Umballa,	2	0	Ditto,	Ditto,	Furruckhabad,	100 rupees.
382	Dahoo Manjarah,	4	0	Ditto,	....	....	500 rupees.
383	Kurreeakhaira,	3	0	Ditto,	Lahore,	Byswara,	250 rupees.
384	Near Goolchutter,	2	0	Ditto,	Loodhiana,	Furruckhabad,	100 rupees.

under the following leaders : Mehrban, Thugs, and other Leaders.

REMARKS.

Having arrived at Loodhiana, the gang rested at the house of Bhageeah Bhuteeara for two days. On the third day they turned back to the eastward, and had scarcely got out of the town, when they were joined by six travellers, by caste Hindoos, from Lahore, on their way to Dhoondea. Runnooa moonshee entered into conversation with and decoyed them. They went on together for two days, and on the third day took them to a village, a short distance from Sirhind, where they slept, and next morning the murder was completed about three miles from that place. The bodies were buried.

After that the gang went to Bunjara-ka-seraee and fell in with two Kuhars from Loodhiana on their way to Cawnpore, who were decoyed and next morning put to death as usual a short distance from the village. The bodies were buried.

They next went to Umballa, and met two water-carriers on their way from Loodhiana to Furruckhabad, who were persuaded to continue their journey in company with the Thugs Early next morning the travellers were taken out two miles from the town and strangled. The bodies were buried, and have since been disinterred on the showing of Heera approver.

The gang then went to Muchunda where they found four travellers, one a Mewatee named Makhun, and three Koormees (Hindoos,) whom Uchul jemadar managed to inveigle out of the village, and next day they were conducted to Dahoo Manjira, where they all passed the night, and early on the ensuing morning the travellers were put to death about two miles off, and their bodies buried. These four bodies have since been pointed out and exhumed.

After the murder the gang went on to Shahabad, where three Hindoos, on their way from Lahore to Byswara, fell into the snares of the Thugs and next day accompanied them to Kurreeakhaira The succeeding morning the travellers were strangled about two miles from the village, and their bodies buried.

After this murder seven Thugs left the gang, went home with money for their families, agreeing to rejoin at the ford of the Jumna at Kurnal. The remainder went to Goolchutter. They then decoyed two Hindoos from Loodhiana, on their way to Furruckhabad, whom they took next morning to a village ten miles off, and rested there. Early next morning the travellers were escorted a mile out of the village and strangled. Their bodies were buried.

Report of a Thug Expedition in the year 1831, Rambuksh, Deveedeen, with Twenty-five

No. of List.	Names and jurisdiction of the place where the Murder was perpetrated.	No. and Sex of the Murdered.		Date of the Murder.	Intended destination of the Murdered.		Supposed value of the property robbed.
		Men.	Women.		From	To	
385	Near Bugroor,	4	0	That Season of 1831,	Amritsir,	....	500 rs cash, 2 horses worth 120 rupees, a matchlock.
386	Bidolee,	2	0	Ditto,	Loodhiana,	Furruckhabad,	50 rupees cash, 10 rupees property.
387	Gurheya,	3	0	Ditto,	Kurnal,	Byswara,	150 rupees.
388	Mallawah, in Mynpooree,	2	0	Ditto,	Mynpooree,	Coel,	40 rupees.
389	Near Khoorjah, in the Boolundshuhur zillah,	2	0	Ditto,	Loodhiana,	Byswara,	100 rupees.

under the following leaders: Mehrban, Thugs, and other Leaders.

REMARKS.

The gang arrived at Kurnal and halted there. Then they went to the ford at Sneikhpoora on the Jumna, where they fell in with four travellers, Hindoos, from Amritsir, whom they decoyed, and having taken a coss on the river, they were met by the Thugs, who had been to their homes and returned. All went to Bugroor and rested there, and before daylight next morning, the travellers were strangled about a mile from the village, and their bodies thrown into a well. They have since been discovered in the place indicated by Heera approver.

They next went to Bidolee, where they found two shoe-makers on their way from Loodhiana to Furruckhabad, whom they decoyed and next morning early put to death two miles from the village. The bodies were buried in a tank.

Proceeding onwards the Thugs passed through Jhinjana to Shamlee, at which place three cowherds from Kurnal, intending to go to Byswara, were resting and bathing themselves. The Thugs seeing they were travellers also engaged in their ablutions at the same spot, and then accompanied the cowherds to Gurheya, where they passed the night. Before daylight next morning the travellers were escorted out a distance of a couple of miles from the village in the Begum Sumroo's territory and strangled. The bodies were thrown into a well.

N. B The remains of these bodies have been pointed out by Eseree approver, and the case committed to trial in the Court of the Agent Governor General.

After this affair the gang returned home without any further adventure.

While the proceedings beforementioned were going on, another gang of thirty Thugs under Shunker, Hurlal, and Shewdeen jemadars, set out during the month of October, 1831, from Sooltangunge, and proceeded to Mullawah, in the Mynpooree district. At the last named place they found two Bunneahs, who were going from the town of Mynpooree to Coel, whom they persuaded to travel with them and next morning put to death a mile from the village, throwing their bodies into a well.

After quitting the scene of murder, the gang met another party of nineteen Thugs under Budlee and Mandhata, who agreed to pursue their journey in company with them. This gang had set out a short time before from Jodee-ka-Poorwa, and having passed through Coel, had gone to Koorja, in the Boolundshuhur district. They found resting in the caravansera two travellers,

***Report of a Thug Expedition in the year* 1831,**
Rambuksh, Deveedeen, with Twenty-five

No. of List.	Names and jurisdiction of the place where the Murder was perpetrated.	No. and Sex of the Murdered.		Date of the Murder.	Intended destination of the Murdered.		Supposed value of the property robbed.
		Men.	Women.		From	To	
390	Goolowtee,	1	0	That Season of 1831,	Lahore,	Oude,	100 rupees.
391	Boorhana,	3	0	Ditto,	Kurnal	Cawnpore,	150 rupees.
392	Near Coel,	2	0	Ditto,	Ditto,	Benares,	100 rupees cash, 50 rupees property.
393	Soorujpore, in Boolundshuhur,	2	0	Ditto,	Hansi,	Cawnpore,	80 rupees.
394	Goolowtee,	2	0	Ditto,	Kurnal,	Ditto,	40 rupees.
395	Near Goolchutter,	4	0	Ditto,	Loodhiana,	Ditto,	22 rupees.

under the following leaders: Mehrban, Thugs, and other Leaders.

REMARKS.

a Brahmin and a Rajpoot, who had come from Loodhiana on their way to Byswara. They agreed to travel with the Thugs, who took them out next morning, and strangled them two miles from the seraee. The bodies were buried. They then went to Goolowtee and put up in the seraee—where a traveller, by caste a Rajpoot, on his way from Lahore to Oude, came and joined them. He was decoyed, and next morning strangled two miles from the village. The body was buried.

After this murder they went on to Boorhana, and took up their quarters in the seraee. Three travellers, Kuhars, on their way from Kurnal to Cawnpore, were resting there, whom the Thugs inveigled, and taking with them next morning strangled a mile out of the village. The bodies were buried.

They turned back again after this affair, and re-visited Coel, where they fell in with two travellers, on their way from Kurnal to Benares. They came and joined the Thugs of their own accord, and were invited to travel with them. They were taken the same day to a small village near a Police thana, six miles from Coel, where they passed the night, and next morning were put to death two miles on their way. The bodies were buried.

While the gang was going eastward after completing this murder, they fell in with the party under Shunker and other jemadars as above described.

After mutual enquiries had passed between the two gangs, it was agreed that their entire numbers should be divided into two parties, who should conduct their proceedings independently of each other, though for the common benefit of both.

Budlee jemadar's party went to Soorujpore in Boolundshuhur, and having rested in the seraee found there two travellers, on their way from Hansi to Cawnpore, whom they decoyed, and next morning strangled outside of the village at the distance of two miles. The bodies were buried.

They then went to Shamlee, where they again fell in with Shunker jemadar's gang, who on parting had gone to Goolowtee, where they decoyed two Hindoo travellers, on their way from Kurnal to Cawnpore. Next morning early the travellers were put to death, as usual, a mile from the village. The bodies were thrown into a well.

The united gangs proceeded to Kurnal, and thence came to a village near Goolchutter, where they sat down in a garden. One of the Thugs had fallen in with two travellers, by caste barbers, whom he decoyed and brought to join the Thugs—and Hurlal jemadar inveigled two cow-herds, who, all four, were

***Report of a Thug Expedition in the year* 1831,**
Rambuksh, Deveedeen, with Twenty-five

No. of List.	Names and jurisdiction of the place where the Murder was perpetrated.	No. and Sex of the Murdered.		Date of the Murder.	Intended destination of the Murdered.		Supposed value of the property robbed.
		Men.	Women.		From	To	
396	Near Secundra,	2	0	That Season of 1831,	Kurnal,	Cawnpore,	150 rupees.
397	Jhinjana,	2	0	Ditto,	Loodhiana,	Byswara,	250 rupees.
398	Khoorjah, zillah Boolundshuhur,	2	0	Ditto,	Kurnal,	Ditto,	300 rupees.
399	Horagaon,	2	0	Ditto,	Lucknow,	Kurnal,	200 rupees,

under the following leaders: Mehrban, Thugs, and other Leaders.

REMARKS.

on their way from Loodhiana to Cawnpore It was determined to pass the night in the garden, where all made themselves comfortable under the trees. During the night the four travellers were strangled on their beds, and their bodies were buried in the garden.

Next day the gang went to the seraee at Kunhya, where they discovered two treasure carriers; and having placed spies to watch their movements, they followed them till on the second day they arrived at Umballa. There, one of the Thugs named Shewdeen, managed to introduce himself to one of the treasure carriers, and made him a present of a new pair of shoes. While the present was making, another Thug incautiously lifted up the bundle, belonging to the treasure carriers to discover its weight, on which the owner, (proverbially careful from the nature of this employment,) took the alarm, and told his Thug friends that he intended to proceed no further than Umballa—leaving the gang in despair at the loss both of their new pair of shoes and the anticipated booty.

The gang went on to Kurnal, where they again separated into two parties. Dibba jemadar with half the Thugs went towards Muttra, and the remainder, under Budlee jemadar, took the road to Cawnpore.

The party under Budlee having arrived within four miles of Secundra, fell in with two travellers, by caste Kayuts or scribes, on their way from Kurnal to Cawnpore, whom they engaged in conversation, and took with them to Secundra, where all passed the night. Early next morning the travellers were roused and conducted out of the village, and at the distance of two miles from it they were put to death, and their bodies buried in a marsh After this affair Budlee's gang proceeded home without perpetrating any other murder.

The party of Thugs under Gopal and Baichoo jemadars, which parted from the main gang at Kurnal, first proceeded to Jhinjana, where they fell in with two travellers, on their way from Loodhiana to Byswara, who were induced to join the Thugs, who took them out about two miles, and then strangled them. The bodies were thrown into a well.

They next went to Khoorjah, zillah Boolundshuhur, and soon after their arrival two travellers, Hindoos, from Kurnal, intending to go to Byswara, came and took up their quarters in the seraee. They were decoyed and next morning put to death some distance from the town. The bodies were buried. This gang then returned home without further adventure.

In the mean time Mehrban, Hurlal, Bhola Bunneah and other Thugs, who had separated from the main gang at Kurnal, proceeded by way of Panniput to a village called Horagaon, where they rested in a Faqueer's garden. They

Report of a Thug Expedition in the year **1831,**
Rambuksh, Deveedeen, with Twenty-five

No. of List.	Names and jurisdiction of the place where the Murder was perpetrated.	No. and Sex of the Murdered.		Date of the Murder.	Intended destination of the Murdered.		Supposed value of the property robbed.
		Men.	Women.		From	To	
400	Cheretta,	2	0	That Season of 1831,	Gwalior.	Cawnpore,	50 rupees
401	Rajee Mhow,	2	0	Ditto,	Benares,	Westward,	50 rupees.
402	Kureagaon,	8	0	Ditto,	....	Eastward,	100 rupees in cash, 50 rupees property, and a fighting ram.

Jubulpore, Superintendent's Office,
The 31st March, 1840.

under the following leaders: Mehrban, Thugs, and other Leaders.

REMARKS.

found there two Hindoo Brinjaras from Lucknow, on their way to Kurnal, whom they decoyed, and next morning escorted about two miles on their way, and then strangled them. The bodies were thrown in a well.

After this affair, all the Thugs, with the exception of six, returned to their homes. Bhola Bunneeah led this small band, which took the road to Gwalior, where they arrived in fifteen days. They thence proceeded to the village of Cheratta, where they were soon afterwards joined by two travellers, both from Gwalior, on their way to the vicinity of Cawnpore. One of these men was a Mahomedan mendicant, and the other a Brahmin named Gunesh. They were decoyed and next morning early, having been taken to a field two miles off, on the road side—they were put to death, and their bodies buried.

The six Thugs then returned home again.

N. B. The above affair was established by the proceedings of Mr. J. C. Wilson, of the Civil Service, while engaged in the arrest of these gangs in the Dooab.

In the month of December, 1831, Mehrban jemadar accompanied by four followers, set out in search of adventures. They went, in the first instance, to Kora Jehanabad, but as they were going thence in an easterly direction, a wolf crossed their path; which being looked upon by Thugs as an exceedingly unfavorable omen, they turned back, and proceeded to Poorra in the Cawnpore district There they were joined by Pershad jemadar (approver) with ten Thugs, who had just left Rajee Mhow, intending to go on an expedition. Soon afterwards Khulluck and Bhowanee jemadars of Thugs, with nine followers, came to the same place from Metee-ka-Poorwa, so that the party was increased to twenty-six Thugs. During the day two Hindoo travellers from Benares, intending to go to westward, arrived at the village and were inveigled; and early next morning were put to death at a well a mile off, and their bodies thrown into it.

The gang went on to Kureagaon and Soowrujpore, where they fell in with three travellers, by caste Hindoos, who were going to the eastward. They were decoyed, and next morning early were conducted some distance to the banks of the Ganges, where theywere strangled and their bodies committed to the stream.

The Thugs then turned back and went home again.

After this expedition, it has been ascertained that Bhowanee jemadar, who was the greatest leader of Thugs in his time, died at home.

P. A. REYNOLDS,
Superintendent for the Suppression of Thuggee.

List of Thugs who were concerned in the above Murders.

No.	Name of Thugs.	Parentage.	Caste.	Remarks.
1	Uchall Jemadar,	Son of Gunsham,	Lodhee,	Hanged at Jubulpore, in 1835.
	Cheyne Jemadar,	Bukha,	Ditto,	Died while out on Thuggee.
	Runjeet alias Daveedeen,	Kurhoree,	Ditto,	Died in Jail at Saugor.
	Dhunna, the whiskered Jemadar,	Chidda,	Ditto,	Hanged at Jubulpore, 1836.
5	Nowul Jemadar,	Punchum,	Ditto,	Ditto Saugor, 1833.
	Dhunna,	Madaree,	Ditto,	Approver.
	Bukshee Jemadar,	Rutta,	Ditto,	Ditto.
	Esseeree,	Ditto.	Ditto,	Ditto.
	Heera,	Sumadhan,	Ditto,	Ditto.
10	Shewdeen,	Assa,	Ditto,	Ditto.
	Dhunna,	Kashee,	Ditto,	Transported from Saugor.
	Chidda,	Ramkissen,	Ditto,	Ditto Jubulpore.
	Heera,	Tijja,	Ditto,	Hanged at Cawnpore.
	Lalsa,		Ditto,	At large.
15	Soomair,	Muthoulee,	Ditto,	Approver (dead.)
	Keseeree Subadar,	Buddo,	Ditto,	Hanged at Jubulpore, 1835.
	Tijja,	Ditto,	Ditto,	Approver.
	Khooshallee,		Ditto,	Ditto.
	Rumma,	Munna,	Ditto,	Ditto.
20	Bulla,	Ditto,	Ditto,	Ditto.
	Bukhtawer,	Koonj,	Ditto,	Died at home.
	Khulluck Jemadar,	Rutta,	Ditto,	Hanged at Saugor, 1833.
	Dhowkul Jemadar,	Chutta,	Ditto,	Ditto.
	Lalla Lochun,	Koonj,	Ditto,	Hanged at Jubulpore, 1835.

25	Gunna,	Huns,	Lodhee,	Transported.
	Bukka,	Heera,	Ditto,	Ditto.
	Anward.	Mudaree,	Ditto,	Ditto.
	Budlee,	Dya,...	Ditto,	Died while on an expedition.
	Shunker Jemadar,	Dyaram,	Buneah,	Hanged at Jubulpore, 1835.
30	Dibba,	Ditto,	Ditto,	Approver.
	Dummee,		Ditto,	Transported,
	Oomeid Kobra.		Lodhee,	At large.
	Ram Buksh Jemadar,	Runna,	Ditto,	Approver.
	Daveedeen Jemadar,	Ditto,	Ditto,	Approver (died.)
35	Girdharee,	Ramlal,	Brahmin,	Approver.
	Summa,	Bhugwant,	Lodhee,	Ditto.
	Sumbha,	Ghassee,	Ditto,	Ditto.
	Dijja,	Mansa,	Ditto,	Hanged at Jubulpore, 1836.
	Nowla,	Oomeid,	Ditto,	Transported.
40	Himmunchula	Runnooa Moonshee,	Ditto,	Approver.
	Dhunna,		Ditto,	Ditto.
	Purusram Jemadar,	Oodey,	Ditto,	Died at Jubulpore.
	Surawan,	Ditto,	Ditto,	At large.
	Hurlal Jemadar,	Sookha,	Ditto,	Hanged at Saugor, 1833.
45	Dhumma,		Ditto,	Approver.
	Binda,		Ditto.	Transported from Jubulpore.
	Atmaram,	Son of Dhya,	Ditto,	Ditto.
	Oodey,	Mukka,	Ditto,	Approver.
	Gopal,	Dhya,	Ditto,	Ditto.
50	Moollooa,	Sookhtee,	Ditto,	Ditto.
	Bhowanee Jemadar,	Mukka,	Ditto,	Died at home.
	Pershaud Jemadar,	Runna,	Ditto,	Approver.
	Ummer Jemadar,	Madaree,	Ditto,	Transported,
	Mukkooa,		Ditto,	Ditto.
55	Gunesh,	Mukhan,	Ditto,	Died at Saugor.
	Bichoo Jemadar,	Ruttee,	Ditto,	Approver.
	Suroop,	Gunesh,	Ditto,	Transported from Jubulpore.

No	Name of Thugs.	Parentage.	Caste.	Remarks.
	Dureawo,	Gunesh,	Lodhee,	Transported from Jubulpore.
	Shewa,		Ditto,	Approver.
60	Mohun,		Ditto,	Ditto.
	Mandhata,	Dulput,	Ditto,	Ditto.
	Mandhata, 2d,		Ditto,	Ditto.
	Runnooa Moonshee Jemadar,	Jeysook,	Ditto,	Hanged at Jubulpore, 1835.
	Gumbhooa,		Bunneah,	At large.
65	Dhunna,	Hurree,	Lodhee,	Approver.
	Seetla,	Chidda,	Ditto,	Died while out on Thuggee.
	Neehalooa,		Ditto,	Transported from Jubulpore.
	Boodhooa,		Ditto,	Ditto ditto.
	Budla,		Ditto,	Ditto ditto.
70	Bhola,	Son of Mukka,	Ditto,	Approver.
	Khoosheal,	Mutta,	Ditto,	Transported from Jubulpore.
	Desraj,		Kachee,	Ditto from Saugor
	Jowihur,		Rajpoot,	Ditto ditto.
	Bukshee,		Abkar,	Hanged at Saugor, 1833.
75	Himma,		Brahmin,	Ditto ditto.
	Budlee Jemadar,	Suntoke,	Lodhee,	Approver.
	Deorae Jemadar,		Ditto,	Died at home.
	Teeka,	Nundee,	Ditto,	Approver.
	Heera,	Ramdeen Jemadar,	Ditto,	Ditto.
80	Magooa,	Chidda,	Ditto,	Ditto.
	Cheyne,		Ditto,	At large.
	Anoop,	Cheyne,	Ditto,	Transported.
	Bhola,	Mudaree,	Ditto,	Ditto.
	Bikka,	Ditto,	Ditto,	Approver (dead.)
85	Peareelal,	Mudden,	Kayet,	At large.

No.	Name	Father	Caste	Fate
	Pershaud,	Dya,	Bukhal,	Transported.
	Pershaud, 2d,		Lodhee,	Ditto.
	Bujja.	Oomeid Jemadar,	Ditto,	Ditto.
	Layuk,	Kishen,	Ditto,	Hanged at Saugor, 1833.
90	Hurrea	Adopted of Lalla Lochun,	Ditto,	Died at home.
	Dhowkula.		Ditto,	At large.
	Ram Buksh,	Ramkissen,	Ditto,	Ditto.
	Letchmuna,	Ditto,	Ditto,	Ditto.
	Ramkissen,		Ditto,	Ditto.
95	Jowihur,	Ram Singh.	Ditto,	Ditto.
	Chittooa,	Oomeid,	Ditto,	Hanged at Cawnpore.
	Bukshea.	Ditto,	Ditto,	Transported.
	Ramdeen Jemadar,	Runna.	Ditto,	Hanged at Cawnpore.
	Goolabee,	Bukhtawer,	Ditto,	Ditto Barielly.
100	Shewdeen Jemadar,	Ditto.	Ditto,	Transported.
	Ghazee.	Bhugwant.	Ditto,	Ditto.
	Maheen Lal,	Dhya,	Ditto,	Ditto.
	Shewdeen,	Munsa,	Ditto,	Ditto.
	Rambuksh,	Pirthee,	Ditto,	Hanged at Saugor.
105	Mudaree,	Suntoke.	Ditto,	Ditto.
	Hoolassee,	Munsookh.	Ditto,	Ditto.
	Bhimma,	Ditto,	Ditto,	Ditto.
	Dhunna,	Hissa,	Ditto,	Ditto.
	Mungle,	Suntoke,	Ditto,	Transported.
110	Makhun Jemadar,	Kishen,	Ditto,	Approver.
	Khooshallea,	Uchul Jemadar.	Ditto,	Transported from Jubulpore.
	Asa.	Benee,	Ditto,	Ditto ditto.
	Mohun,	Dhya,	Ditto,	Ditto ditto.
	Budlee,	Ditto.	Ditto,	Ditto ditto.
115	Mudaree,	Mutta,	Ditto,	Died at Jubulpore.
	Doorgooa.	Ducha,	Ditto,	Transported.
	Jowihur,	Dhowkul,	Ditto,	At large.
	Chittooa,	Oomeid,	Ditto,	Hanged at Cawnpore.

No.	Name of Thugs.	Parentage.	Caste.	Remarks.
	Rumma,	Hunsa,	Lodhee,	Approver (dead.)
120	Gurrooa.	Dhya,	Ditto,	At large.
	Munnooa,	Oomeid,	Ditto,	Ditto.
	Pemmooa,	....	Kuhar,	Ditto.
	Dooburrea,	Koosal,	Lodhee,	Ditto.
	Gumbhooa,	....	Ditto,	Ditto.
125	Mehrban,	Bijjaeen,	Ditto,	Approver.
	Heera,	Oomeid,	Ditto,	Ditto.

P. A. REYNOLDS,
Superintendent for the
Suppression of Thuggee.

JUBULPORE, SUPERINTENDENT'S OFFICE,
The 31st March, 1840.

J.A.R. Stevenson

'Some Account of the Phansigars, or Gang-Robbers and of the Shudgarshids, or Tribes of Jugglers.' *Journal of the Royal Asiatic Society* 1 (1834): 280–283.

ART. XXII.—*Some Account of the P'hansigárs, or Gang-robbers, and of the Shúdgarshids, or Tribe of Jugglers, by* JAMES ARTHUR ROBERT STEVENSON, Esq., *of the Madras Civil Service.—(Communicated by the Bombay Branch Royal Asiatic Society.)*

Read 1*st of February*, 1834.

THE *P'hansigárs** are a tribe of, perhaps, the most deliberate and decided villains that stain the face of the earth. I hardly know whether they should be called a tribe, for they have no distinct religion or prejudices: they admit into their fraternity persons of all castes and persuasions; and the gangs which are found in different parts of the country appear to have no general knowledge of, or connexion with, each other, further than the diabolical compact existing among a few of the members who may at any period have acted in concert in their trade of villany. The following few particulars I gathered from the examination of part of a large gang which inhabited a village on the western frontier of the NIZÁMS country, not very far from Bíjápúr.

The number of males in this troop amounted to about sixty, almost all of whom had families and houses in Dúdgí, which they considered as their head-quarters. They were subject to two *náiks*, or chiefs, who planned their expeditions, and regulated the division of booty, being themselves entitled to a double share: they were also responsible to the *pattél*, or head of the village, for the payment of a regular tribute, the price of his protection and silence. The greatest proportion of this gang were Muhammedans; but there were among them Rájapúts, and other castes. Their ostensible employment was agriculture and daily labour; but their only actual means of subsistence was the plunder obtained by the murder of their fellow-creatures. When their means of debauchery and indulgence became limited by the expenditure and waste of their ill-gotten wealth, fresh expeditions were ordered, and parties sent to make circuits in different directions, all the plunder being brought to their head-quarters to be shared. They were sworn to a fair division, to secrecy, and to inviolable fidelity to each other. Their standing rules were never to rob without first depriving their victim of life, never to attack by open force, and never to leave the smallest traces of their crimes; the bodies of the murdered being entirely defaced or deeply buried, and the property sent to a distant market. As all their murders are perpetrated by means of strangulation, no marks of blood are left on the spot; and

* From the Hindústání word *P'hánsí*, a noose.

so well have they generally kept their resolves and contrived their crimes, and so faithful have they generally proved to each other, that there are but few instances of *P'hansigárs* being convicted in a court of justice, although they have been repeatedly apprehended. A departure from their rules (the commission of a daring robbery which was quite out of their line) led to the seizure of the gang to which I have alluded.

Their methods of proceeding in their own horrid trade are various; but the chief object in view is to lull their victim into a sense of security before they proceed to deprive him of life, which is, as before remarked, always effected by strangulation. When a favourable opportunity presents itself, one of the party throws a noose, which is made with a tightly twisted handkerchief,* round the destined sufferer's neck; an accomplice immediately strikes the person on the inside of his knees, so as to knock him off his legs, and thus throw the whole weight of his body on the noose; and a very few seconds puts an end to the unfortunate man's struggles. The plan generally adopted by the *P'hansigárs* is to pretend to travellers, or to Company's sipahis proceeding to their homes on leave of absence, to have met them by chance, and to agree to pursue their journey together. They likewise fall into conversation with travellers whom they may meet on the road, or in the choultries and halting-places, and frequently share their provisions with them, proposing, at last, that, as they are all travelling the same road, they should, for the sake of companionship and mutual security, travel together. The first favourable opportunity that offers itself on the road is seized to murder the deluded traveller; but so cautious and wary is the *P'hansigár*, that he will often accompany his victim several days' march before he can find a place and an opportunity sufficiently safe for his purpose.

Another mode of luring the traveller to his destruction is by the assistance of a woman. They select a pretty-looking girl of their tribe, and place her near some retired road, where she watches until she observes an object of prey fit for her purpose. She has a pitiful story ready to explain the cause of her having been left thus alone in the jungles, and seldom fails to interest the unfortunate listener, who almost always falls into the snare that is laid for him. The girl sometimes excites his passions, and having seduced him into a favourable spot, herself fastens the fatal noose, her companions being always near enough to afford timely aid. The traveller, if mounted, will perhaps

* This cloth, or handkerchief, is stated to be always of a white or a yellow colour, those being the favourite colours of their tutelary deity, MARIATTA, the goddess of small-pox in Malabar.

offer to take the girl up on his horse, to assist her in overtaking the party she says she has lost; but before he has advanced many paces, the murderess casts the snare round his neck, and, throwing herself from the horse, drags her protector to the ground, where he is speedily despatched by the ever-ready accomplices.*

One of the *P'hansigárs* to whom I have alluded in the commencement of this paper turned king's evidence, and was very particular in his details. He said, that during their last tour of a fortnight they had murdered sixteen individuals; and he also mentioned a circumstance which will tend to shew the barbarity with which they carry on their terrible system. The party of *P'hansigárs* had retired to rest in a pagoda, in which a *Laskar*† had also taken up his quarters for the night, during the course of which he was murdered. The assassins dug a hole in the *sanctum* of the pagoda, in which to bury the corpse, but they found that it was too small to admit the body; they consequently dismembered it, and then succeeded in thrusting the mangled pieces into the hole.

The booty for which these horrid murders are committed is often so trifling—sometimes not exceeding one rupee, or the clothes on the person's body—that it appears as if the *P'hansigárs* found a delight and a pastime in such deeds of blood. This seems more probable, as I found from their cant phrases (of which I collected a few examples, since lost), that they had ludicrous names for the convulsive struggles of their expiring victims, as well as for murder, the noose, and the different acts attending their diabolical trade. An old woman, one of the tribe, repeated them to me with a great deal of glee. She, as well as most of the other females, made no secret of their vocation, and appeared to think that there was nothing wrong in it. When asked of what caste they were? they answered *P'hansigárs*. How do you get your livelihood? By *p'hansigáring*. Are you not ashamed of your way of life? have you never followed any other trade? No, this is the same trade that our fathers followed; if we don't *p'hansigár*, how are we to live?

I fear that many gangs of these miscreants still exist; they have been for the most part hunted out of the British territory, but they are said to carry on an uninterrupted career in the *Nizám's country*, and in other independent provinces. The forms of law have allowed many to escape, or have obliged the magistrates to let loose on their

* Females, and persons of some particular castes and occupations, are considered by the *P'hansigárs* as exempted from their attacks, being, as they imagine, in some way connected with their goddess.

† A camp servant, whose general business is to attend to the pitching of tents, &c.

fellow-creatures beings who are a disgrace to the lowest order of the human race—in fact, they are a race of vampires undeserving of the name of man.*

The *Shúdgárshid* is a tribe of jugglers and fortune-tellers, who wander about the Dekkan, and, probably, other parts of the country, where, however, they are not known by this name, but generally, I believe, by that of *Gáródi* (juggler), which is the denomination of the caste in the *Vijnáneswára Sástra*. The *Karnataka* term of *Shúdgárshid* is derived from *Shúdgár* (a burning or burial-ground) and *shid* (proficient, ready) it being their habit to prowl about these places to collect certain pieces of human bone, with which they are supposed to work charms and incantations. The tribe is looked upon with much awe and detestation, and the fear of exciting the wrath of any of its members, generally secures a ready compliance with their demands for charity. On this, however, they do not place their only reliance, they are notorious for kidnapping children, and also for an abominable traffic, consisting in the sale of sinews extracted from the breasts, the wrists, and the ankles of females; these are supposed to be preservative charms from all evil: but, in order that they may possess this virtue to the full extent, they must be taken from the person of a woman who has been very lately delivered. An instance of this practice occurred at *Shólapúr* a few years ago;—a rich merchant named DÉVELÁT had a married daughter (LAKSHMI) who resided in his house, and who had been confined of her first child about ten days, when she was suddenly missed. The infant was found in its cradle, but no search was successful in discovering the unfortunate mother. It was at last remembered by some member of the family, that on the morning of the day on which the girl was missed a female *Shúdgárshid* had been at the house, and had told the fortunes of several of the inmates. Knowing the habits of these people, apprehensions and anxiety regarding the fate of the lost LAKSHMI were excited to their height, as it was deemed beyond doubt that she had been enticed away, and had fallen a victim to the *Shúdgárshid*, who was immediately seized; but nothing could be learnt from her, for she denied ever having seen the girl. In the course, however, of the inquiries and cross-questioning of the friends—probably not conducted in the mildest manner—some words dropped from the juggler

* In the *Asiatic Researches*, vol. xiii. p. 250, will be found an ample and detailed account of the *P'hansigárs*, *T'hegs*, *Bádheks*, &c. all different classes of gang robbers in India, furnished by Dr. Sherwood, Mr. J. Shakespear, &c. The former gentleman gives several specimens of the cant phrases of the *P'hansigárs;* a sort of language termed by them *Pheraseri-ki-bát*, "the language of despatch."

regarding a neighbouring tank. This induced the parties to proceed there and to examine its waters, in which the body of the unfortunate girl was quickly found; the sinews from the breast, ankles, and wrists, had been extracted, but no further marks of violence were visible. The event was now made known to the civil authorities, but the *Shúdgárshid* continued firm in her denial of all knowledge of the affair, nor was any other information regarding the fate of the unhappy LAKSHMI ever obtained. The caste of *Shúdgárshid* is said to have sprung from the union of a woman of the *Pátráwat* (stone-cutter) tribe, and of a *Kúlu* or *Kabír* (boat-man). *Kabír Rishi*, the author or compiler of one of the *Védas*, taught the art of magic to some of the first of this race, who have now lost the greater part of their original skill. The deity which they conceive chiefly entitled to their worship is the goddess CHOWDI, whose principal shrine is in Malabar, where, I understand, the caste is most numerous. North of the *Krishna* they worship KÁMAKSHIKA, a goddess whose chief pagoda is in Kandahár.

The descendants of a *Mahá purushá* named MALSIDÁYA, a *Jungam* of *Parvati Malkárgin* on the *Krishna*, are still looked upon by the *Shúdgárshids* as their *gúrús*. It is related that two *Shids*, LING SHID and MUSEM SHID used to sit in the burial-grounds at Delhi up to their necks in the earth; and that at night, by the power of their incantations, they caused the dead to rise and to wander as evil spirits through the city. The *Mahá purushá*, MALSIDÁYA, famed for the strict observance of all his religious and moral duties, and for the severity of his penances, visited Delhi, and by the divine aid accorded to him in reward of his piety, counteracted the deeds of the *Shúdgárshids*, and finally cast out the evil spirits. The *Shids* fell at his feet, acknowledged his superior power, and bound themselves and their posterity to consider and to obey him and his descendants as their *gúrús*. Up to this day, the *Shúdgárshids* are said, once a-year, to visit the descendants of MALSIDÁYA at their *Matts* in *Parvati Malkárgin*, to make their offerings to the *Jangams*, and to receive from them the small bags in which they carry their charms. There is also in *Miritch*, in the southern Mahratta country, a shrine much visited by the *Shúdgárshids*. It is the tomb of a Muhammedan saint called SHEINNA MIR VAIGAMBAR, who, tradition says, was endowed with supernatural powers to enable him to overcome a washerman named GANGA DHÓBI, who was deeply skilled in the art of magic, and exerted it to oppress and torment the *Shúdgárshids* and all the minor professors of the art.

ERRATA TO VOLUME I.

Page 9, line 17, *for* raking stern, *read* raking stem.
.. 10, .. 14, *for* prow stern, *read* prow stem.
.. —, .. 29, *for* stern head, *read* stem head.
.. 11, .. 34, *for* ditto, *read* ditto.
.. 12, .. 23, *for* ditto, *read* ditto.
.. —, .. 31, *for* ditto, *read* ditto.
.. 13, .. 5, *for* ditto, *read* ditto.
.. 22, *for Sindhú, read Sindhu.*
.. —, *for Sindhúdés, read Sindhudés.*
.. 23, .. 3 from below, *for Púrána, read Purána*, and in other parts of the Number.
.. —, last line, *for Tohfat al Girám, read Tuhfat al Giráni;* and in other parts of the Number.
.. 24, .. 22 from the top, *for Sirowar, read Sarowar*, (recurring in the note.)
.. 25, .. 5 from below, *for* Susi, *read Sasi.*
.. 26, .. 3 .... *for Oriti, read Oritæ.*
.. 29, last line, *for Láryía, read Larica.*
.. 30, .. 5 from the top, *for Akbári, read Akbari.*
.. 32, *for Ságára, read Ságara.*
.. 46, .. 17 from the top, *for* pharasaical, *read* pharisaical.
.. 48, .. 1 .... *for Pánchayat, read Pancháyat.*
.. —, .. 2 from below, *for Dharamádhikari, read* Dharmádhikárí.
.. 88, .. 7 from the top, *for* SÍVA, read SIVA.
.. —, .. 12 .... *for* DÚRGA, *read* DURGÁ.
.. 91, .. 7 .... *for Nava Ráttiri, read Nava Rátra.*
.. 117, .. 22 .... *for* AKBÁR, *read* AKBAR (repeatedly).
.. —, .. — .... *for* ARANGZÍB, *read* AURANGZÍB (repeatedly).
.. 118, .. 17 from below, *for Habib-as-sír, read Habíb-as-siyar.*
.. 122, .. 7 .... *for midiním, read mediním.*
.. 126, .. 2 .... *for Serumenrai, read* (properly) *Surra-man-rad.*
.. 132, .. 10 .... *for Himaláya, read Himálaya.*
.. 135, .. 7 from above, *for Aromea, read* (usually) *Urmiah, Oormeah.*
.. 138, last line, *for Patalipura, read Pátaliputra.*
.. 171, .. 11 from the bottom, *for* COSMOS, *read* COSMAS.
.. 173, .. 22 ...... *for* NEBUCHADREZZAR, *read* NEBUCHADNEZZAR.
.. 200, .. 6 ...... *for Púrán, read Purán,* } all through.
.. —, .. — ...... *for Púrána, read Purána,* } all through.
.. 233, .. 18 & 33 from the top, *for* ALLÁ-UD-DÍN, *read* ALA-UD-DÍN.
.. 234, .. 6 .... *for* RIZÁK, *read* RIZZÁK.
.. —, .. 5 .... *for Ságára, read Ságara.*
.. —, .. 12 . .. *for* AKBÁR, *read* AKBAR (all through).
.. 236, .. 21 .... *for Mánsura, read Mansúra.*
.. 267, .. 7 from the bottom, *for sabhásúdd'ha, read sabhásudd'ha.*
.. 278, .. 8 ...... *for srid'han, read stríd'han* (several times).
.. 284, .. 18 from the top, *for purushá, read purusha.*
.. 294, .. 13 ...... *for Bháratá-Várshán, read Bhárata-varshan.*
.. 307, .. 9 ...... *for* REMUSÁT, *read* RÉMUSAT.
.. 327, .. 15 ...... *for Zodaic, read Zodiac.*
.. 330, .. 2 from the bottom, *for Badukhíhán, read Badakhshán.*
.. lxxi .. 15 ...... *for Tim, read T.*
.. — .. 10 ...... *for Sástrá, read Sástri.*

END OF VOL. I.

H.H. Spry

'Some Accounts of the Gang Murderers of Central India, Commonly Called Thugs; Accompanying the Skulls of Seven of Them.'

The Phrenological Journal and Miscellany 8 (March 1834): 511–524.

ARTICLE III.

SOME ACCOUNT OF THE GANG-MURDERERS OF CENTRAL INDIA, COMMONLY CALLED THUGS; ACCOMPANYING THE SKULLS OF SEVEN OF THEM. By HENRY HARPUR SPRY, Esq. Bengal Medical Service, Saugor.

THE skulls I have the pleasure of forwarding for the Phrenological Society, through the kind favour of Mr Swinton, were taken from among a party of one hundred criminals executed at Saugor, in Central India, by order of the Supreme Government, in the months of June and July 1832, for thuggee or strangling.

Unacquainted as most in Europe must be with the practices of the thugs, I purpose entering into a short history of the class generally, and into a more detailed account of those individuals whose skulls accompany this paper. The thugs or stranglers are composed of Hindoos and Mahomedans, who make murdering their fellow creatures the business of their lives. These wretches are considered to have appeared in India with the first Mahomedan conquerors, and they are distinctly ascertained to have existed in great numbers in the reign of Akbur the Great; no less than five hundred prisoners being executed in one province by order of that Emperor. They are for the most part brought up from infancy to regard thuggee as their calling, and they set about it with the callous indifference incidental to such an impression. Caste, that barrier to intellectual innovation, has for them the same charms it has for the rest of their brethren. Indeed, the stupid adherence of all classes to the habits and customs of their forefathers must be seen to be believed; and I really am disposed to think many boys go on the roads as thugs, because their fathers did, and not from any inherent ferocity of disposition. As, however, the men whose skulls I send herewith were notorious characters during their lifetime, it is more than probable they had a natural inclination for the work of death. I think that, on examination, the development will be found to justify such a conclusion.

The thugs put an implicit confidence in omens. Among them the partridge *, the shama, the deer, the jackall, the jackass, &c. are either good or bad omens; and again, the same animal or bird appearing or calling on the right hand or the left constitutes it a good or bad omen. They leave their homes in bands at the end of the rainy season, and direct their steps to their high priest or gooroo, generally an old thug (no matter whether Hindoo or Mussulman), who has retired from the trade, and lives upon the contributions of his descendants or disciples, who look up to him with great reverence for advice and instruction, and to whose decision they bend in all cases of doubt or dispute. On this old man they confer presents. They have a *kodalee* or pickaxe, consecrated by solemn religious rites, which they carry with them. The bearer of this sacred *kodalee* is considered to fill a post of high honour: one of the many virtues ascribed to it is, that it can prevent the spirits of the murdered rising from the graves which are dug with it. All oaths of the members of the gang are administered upon this instrument.

Having performed the ceremonies of consecration, they proceed to rendezvous at some place previously fixed on, where the gangs make their final arrangements for the season, such as fixing on

* So attached are they to the partridge that they keep them in cages, and when a thug is brought in a prisoner he prays to be allowed to keep his partridge

their private signals, and so on. Before breaking into parties or gangs, they muster between three and four hundred strong. Without some explanation, it might appear strange that so large a body of men, when collected, should not arouse suspicion. The fact is, that, during the Pindaree power in Central India, marauders of every description were abroad; travellers were consequently obliged to go in large parties, and the thugs could, under the same pretence, assemble in equally large bands. Since the conclusion of the Mahratta war, the attention of the Supreme Government has not, until lately, been particularly directed to the suppression of these monsters; and the fear of the thugs has still induced travellers to go in company,—thus unintentionally prolonging the thug system, and, as Shakspeare beautifully has it,

—— "What they undid, did."

Their homes are situated in the Bhopaul, Oude, Gwalior, and Bundelkund states, as well as in the Company's possessions in the Doab; and the directions they take are the three great thoroughfares of the Deccan, Scindias, and Holkar's country, down to the sea and the Delhi country. They remain out, infesting the roads, for eight months every year, or till they obtain some valuable booty, when each man generally betakes himself to his own home, and passes the remainder of the year ostensibly in cultivating the ground. Nearly all are married, and their wives conduct their household affairs during their absence, and take charge of the jewels and other property brought or sent home by them. On the road the person of a Brahmin is no longer held sacred, and to kill him is considered no greater sin than the murder of another. Indeed, a large number of thugs are Brahmins.

Wholesale dealers in human blood as these vagabonds are, it is not to be wondered at, that, while abroad, they indulge in every carnal propensity; and it has happened more than once that a gang has split from the leaders, quarrelling about a favourite. A knowledge of these practices coming to their wives' ears, they sometimes leave their husbands and go off with other men. When they are once fairly on the roads, they never shave or eat *pawn* till they have killed their first traveller. It is an invariable rule with them never to rob travellers till they have first strangled them; and it is really wonderful to observe how trifling the object of temptation sometimes is which induces them to commit the crime. Two Brahmins were murdered by a gang of forty thugs, and the only booty shared by them was two brass pots and a dish. Careful distinctions are drawn between those fit to throw the angocha (or handkerchief used in strangling) and those who are only aspirants; the latter, for the first few expeditions are not considered sufficiently hardened to witness the strangling of the victims, and are employed therefore as grave-diggers and scouts, and in the performance of other subordinate and menial duties. The former are called "Bhurtotes," and the latter "Shumseeahs." In each gang there are two or three smooth-spoken men, who are usually deputed to join the ill-fated travellers. Dirgpaul was one. They generally contrive in the space of a short time to lull the suspicions of the most cautious, and by degrees to introduce the rest of the gang: at this time, if some fortuitous circumstance favour their purpose, a grand repast is proposed, and the expense readily borne by the thugs; after dinner, some two or three will play the guitar, the rest of the party sitting round smoking and talking. Having by this means lulled all suspicion, the private signal is given, the fatal cloth is thrown round the neck, and in the moment of hilarity and apparent security, the helpless travellers are strangled, unpitied and unheard. One man throws the handkerchief, while two hold the hands; and it is not unusual, if a victim is more restive than ordinary, to give him a kick below, which immediately knocks him prostrate, and the work of death is completed. The bodies are now cast into the graves prepared to receive them; and the gang, having collected the booty, generally decamp. The beds of rivulets are often selected as sites for the graves, but not always. Sometimes they bury the bodies in mango groves, or under large tamarind or burr trees; and the accuracy with which these men will, after a lapse of several years, point out the spot where the murdered bodies are laid, is truly astonishing.

As if to mock and ridicule the solemn institutions of man, these wretches affect to have a presiding deity over them. On their return from their murderous expeditions, they conceive it necessary to propitiate the goddess Bhowanee *, whom they regard as the arbitress of their destinies, and whose mercenary and crafty priesthood, ever ready to minister to the weaknesses and superstitions of her followers, do not scruple to lend themselves to the vices of these wretches, and wink at their horrible deeds. It is well known that these priests give information to the thugs of the movements of travellers, and the despatch of treasure. They suggest expeditions, and promise the murderers, in the name of their goddess, immunity and wealth, provided a due share of the guilty spoil be offered up at her shrine. If they die by the sword, in the exercise, with her sanction, of their murderous vocation, she promises them paradise, with all its most exquisite delights. Bhowanee's temple at Bindachurun, a few

* This goddess is also worshipped under the name of Devee Doorga, and Kalee. She is considered to preside over smallpox, cholera, and all other pestilential diseases.

miles west of Mirzapore, on the Ganges, is constantly filled with murderers from every quarter of India, who go thither to offer up in person a share of their ill-gotten wealth.

It seems strange that the Mahomedan thugs should put faith in the attributes of Bhowanee; but all who enter on thuggee appear to embrace the Hindoo creed so far; and indeed every Mussulman, when cholera or smallpox is raging, thinks proper to stop and pay his devotions on passing Bhowanee's temple.

What has here been said of the ministers of Bhowanee, applies, I am sorry to say, equally to the whole Hindoo priesthood of India; and, before closing these general remarks, I cannot refrain from quoting the words of the Abbé Dubois, a man most competent to give an opinion. What he said of them fifty years ago is equally applicable at the present day. He says, "That, when they find themselves involved in trouble, there is no falsehood or perjury which they will not employ for the purpose of extricating themselves. Nor is this to be wondered at, since they are not ashamed to declare openly, that untruth and false swearing are virtuous and meritorious deeds, when they tend to their own advantage. When such horrible morality is taught by the theologians of India, is it to be wondered at that falsehood should be so predominant among the people?" How little astonishing is it, then, that we find a class of fellow creatures, like the thugs, so sunk in the depths of infamy, when the people are led by such unprincipled teachers!

To conclude. The thug character appears made up of inconsistencies. I have seen them alive to the most tender feelings of human nature,—agitated at the mention of a wife or brother's danger; yet, on the roads, their hearts may be said to be as hard as adamant. No appeal, however moving—no recollection, however grateful—arrests their merciless grasp; and the cries of the infant at the breast, and of the fond and doating parent, are equally disregarded.

SOME ACCOUNT OF THE INDIVIDUAL THUGS WHOSE SKULLS HAVE BEEN PRESENTED TO THE PHRENOLOGICAL SOCIETY.

1. *Dirgpaul, Brahmin, son of Newul, Brahmin.*—This man, from his great daring and success, was distinguished among the thugs by the title of *Subahdar*. His ancestors have been thugs for many generations, and his brother Luchman is a thug leader. It is necessary to premise, that the murders herein mentioned are not a tithe of the scenes these men have been engaged in; but only those of which the evidence is officially recorded in the Government office, as taken before Captain Sleeman, the po-

litical officer at Saugor, to whose indefatigable zeal in suppressing the thugs the Government owes so much.

The first affair at which Dirgpaul figures is in the year 1817, at the murder of a pundit at Selodha, a village north-west of Saugor one march. The body of the pundit, with those of some others in the same grave, was disinterred by Captain Sleeman. He was next concerned in the murder of fourteen shopkeepers at Seronge, and got 2000 rupees, about equivalent to L. 180 Sterling. The day after, seventeen Rohillas, marching through this part of the country, fell in with the gang, and were likewise strangled by Dirgpaul and his party.

In 1821, he was concerned in the murder of four police guards, at a place called Bhanpore; the bodies were buried in a rivulet. The following day, a native officer of Holkar's army, with four troopers, came up, and they also were strangled, and the bodies buried under mango trees. Four days subsequent to these murders, they fell in with a Nawaub, whose name was Amber Khan, and his wife and ten soldiers, all of whom were murdered by this gang. Just as they had completed their work, eleven *cowhattees* *, or carriers of Ganges water, came up, who, suspecting what they had been about, let out a hint of the kind. The consequence was, that the gang of thugs fell on them also, and the whole party were strangled. Their bodies were buried in some empty houses close by; and the bones of these twenty-three unfortunate victims have lately been dug up by Captain Sleeman's people, and an inquest held on them by the native local authorities.

In 1823 he was a principal in the murder of eleven men, one woman, and one girl, in all thirteen, on their way from Poona towards Indore. The gang of thugs amounted to 150. Dirgpaul was the man who cajoled the party, and persuaded them to march in company with them. The booty on this occasion was 1000 rupees.

After halting a day at this place of murder, they were joined by more treasure-bearers, travelling with four ponies. In a sequestered spot, at mid-day, the whole were murdered, and the bodies thrown into the jungle. The treasure found on them amounted to 25,000 rupees (L. 2400.)

The last act recorded of Dirgpaul was the murder of a native officer of rank, in the service of the Queen of Oodipore, called Loll Singh, of his wife, a female servant, and six men followers. The thugs mustered 250 strong, 50 of whom were under the command of Dirgpaul, who was the principal man in concerting the murders with another notorious leader. The subahdar Loll

* So sacred is the muddy Ganges water held throughout India, that hundreds of people are annually employed in carrying it over the country. All Hindoos are sworn on the water of the "sacred Ganges" in our courts of justice.

Singh rode a mare, and his wife was nursing an infant boy. The thugs kept in company with the travellers for some days, and, by one of the leaders riding a horse whose tail was docked, they persuaded the subahdar that they were sepoys, and that the rider got the horse from his European officer. Having intoxicated him with opium and stramonium, the thugs fell on him and his companions a little after dusk, and the whole were killed, with the exception of the infant, whom Dirgpaul kept and adopted. This child was brought in with the prisoner, and a fine little fellow he is. He is now being educated at the Saugor Government School, at the expense of government.

This man had a singular leer on his countenance: when he was under trial for his life, and, subsequently, when sentence of death was being passed on him, it did not forsake him; and, with his little wooden spindle twisting cotton, he affected a carelessness, at once unnatural and indecent. He was executed with twenty-nine others, on the morning of the 30th June 1832; and though his *courage* was great, his *caution* prevented him from being too precipitate. Six carts conveyed them to the place of execution, which was outside the town of Saugor, about a mile and a half from the jail. The gibbets were erected temporarily, and formed three sides of a square. The posts supporting the cross-poles were fixed into stone walls, about five feet high, and, from the edge of one stone wall to the other, a beam was placed for the wretched men to stand on after ascending the ladders. The nooses were all ready, hanging from the cross-beams, and each man as he landed on the platform selected his rope. Considering it an everlasting disgrace to their names to die by the hands of the common hangman, the condemned thugs no sooner take hold of the halter, than they push their heads into the noose, and, with loud shouts and cheers, adjust the knot behind the ear, jump off, and launch themselves into eternity! The beam against which the ladders are resting, is the platform on which they stand, and which is withdrawn; but the men are all off swinging before this can be done. Dirgpaul waited to see nearly all his companions off, and I well remember the last look he took of them before he swung himself from the fatal beam.

2. *Gunga Bishun, jemadar, son of Doorga Pershad, Brahmin.*—This man was a Brahmin. On being brought in, he denied being a thug, but acknowledged he had served Beharee Loll, the banker, in recovering a part of his lost treasure; something in the manner, I suppose, in which the members of the notorious *bone shops* in London act between the robbers and the robbed.

Feringia, one of the approvers, states that Gunga Bishun was considered a very skilful thug, and was a man whom the thugs employed to inveigle travellers, and induce them to join their party. It was this man who first inveigled the subahdar Loll Singh, whose murder is related in Dirgpaul's case, (No. 1.) "He had great influence over Sepoys," one of the informers said, "and could always bring them to their destruction."

He was at the murder of thirteen treasure carriers, at a place called Choupara. The following is the deposition of Chotee Brahmin, a notorious thug leader, admitted as King's evidence, as taken before Captain Sleeman, September 23. 1831.

"About seven or eight years ago, I left my home on an expedition to the south-west, with six leaders and their followers. We proceeded to Aseerghur, where we fell in with Dirgpaul (No. 1.), now in Saugor jail, with his gang of twenty-five thugs. We joined, and proceeded together to Borhampore, and thence to Hydalabad, where we met Makun Jemadar (who has since been hung at Indore) with 150 followers. We joined them, and proceeded on to Aurungabad, in the Deccan, where we halted two days, and then proceeded on the Poona road to the river Gunga Gadowlee. We proceeded on to a village called Chalagou, and, on leaving it for Dollea, we fell in with six men, escorting treasure to Ojeyn on two ponies, and two ponies unladen. We came on with them to Dorea, but they suspected us, and would not move till they found an escort proceeding with a family towards Ojeyn. We found at Dhoreea eleven Marwarrees, or men from Marwar, on their way to Jyepore, and they were soon persuaded to join us by Dirgpaul (No. 1.), and the treasure-bearers were left behind. We left Dhoreea and proceeded on, twenty-five miles, to Amneyra, where we halted on the bank of a river. About nine o'clock at night they were all strangled, and buried on the bank; and we found on them 1000 rupees. We halted at this place a day, and fell in with fourteen more Marwarrees, on their way from Poonah to Ojeyn, with four ponies, two loaded with gold, and the other two with brass boxes. Some of us moved before and some behind them. About fifteen miles from the former place of murder, near the Tapty River, we strangled all the fourteen at mid-day, and threw the bodies into the jungle. The treasure amounted to 25,000 rupees (L. 2400). The brass-boxes we buried in the bank. At night twelve of the party returned and buried the bodies."

Gunga Bishun was concerned in the murder of a Calcutta carrier, who had brought a parcel of books to Mhow; also in the murder of a havildar (sergeant) and four sepoys, at Koondee, in June 1829, on their way to their homes. He was a principal concerned in the following murders. "Deposition of Imamee, approver, taken August 2. 1831. One year and half ago, two shopkeepers, on their way to Saugor, halted at a well near the village of Deshuttee, and about a gun-shot from a grove, in which a gang of thugs, of whom I was one, were encamped. Ram Buksh and Munneeraw went to the well, and prevailed upon them to join us. We started at midnight; and, at a stream about four miles from Deshuttee, to the east, they were strangled, and their bodies buried in the bed of the stream. We got from them bundles of tinsels, and each shared nine bundles and seven rupees. Also a pony, which Durreean got and afterwards sold."

The following is the evidence of the father of one of the victims:—

"Deposition of Dameedut Brahmin, from Guzerat, taken August 18. 1831.—I have been for the last ten or twelve years settled at the village of Omuyta, one stage north of Baroda. Many years after my settlement, Mehesur, the husband of my daughter, came on a visit, and remained with me three years. He, during this time, went to Surat, and there purchased various kinds of lace and silver, to the amount of 450 rupees, to sell at Saugor. About fifteen months ago he left me with Jyphal Brahmin of Omuyta for Saugor. Hearing nothing from them for three months, I wrote to my son Kirpa Suntur at Saugor, who informed me that nothing had been heard of them. I soon after came off in search of them, but found traces no further than Dunno, one stage on this side of Baroda. I came on four stages farther, towards Oodipore, but discovering no traces, returned to Omuyta. Some months after, I came off to visit my family at Saugor; and, hearing a proclamation about two men killed by thugs, with gold and silver lace, I came to inquire, and found that the two men killed at Deshuttee were my son-in-law and Jyphal. My son had a bay pony." The tears flowed down the old man's cheeks while he listened to the detail given of the murder of his son-in-law by Imamee.

Another deposition, of Chotee Jemadar, regarding this man, is as follows:—

"In the month of October last year (1830), I left home with two or three thugs, on an expedition towards Kotah. At Sakheree we met Fouj Khan Jemadar with fifteen thugs, and we proceeded together towards Jypore. At Chorsoo we found Bechoo Jemadar with sixty thugs, all from the Company's territories in the Dooab. They were encamped on the bank of a tank with seven travellers (sepoys) on their way from Ajmere to their homes, whom Bechoo and his gang had persuaded to join. From this ground Kutman, one of Bechoo's party, was sent on to select a place to murder the sepoys, and he fixed on the bed of a rivulet, about three miles distant from Charsoo. We all left our ground about midnight, and when we reached the bed of the river, the signal was given, and the seven sepoys were strangled. 300 rupees shared."

Proceeding on, they killed three people at Bera, and shared 200 rupees.

At Salsont, four travellers were strangled at a fakeer's hut. The fakeer was sent into the village to purchase food, and during his absence the murders were committed. 400 rupees in money, and 100 rupees' worth of property, shared.

At Kaleeghatee, five Rajpoots were strangled under a burr-tree. 125 rupees and two swords shared.

At Secundra four travellers were strangled, and the bodies buried in the bed of a rivulet. ' 125 rupees found upon them. " We sent back, three days afterwards," continues the deponent, " to ascertain how the graves were looking, and we found the wild beasts had torn the bodies up, and the villagers had seen them."

Gunga Bishun was one of a gang at the murder of some sepoys at Dhar. There were ten of them on their way to their homes on furlough. Duneeaw, an approver, states: " We encamped in the grove, outside the town. We made acquaintance with them during the day, and five of the ten were persuaded to come and sleep with us. We started on the road towards Mhow, about midnight, and, at a rivulet about two miles from Dhar, near some tamarind trees, strangled the five. I was employed to bury the bodies. We got 500 rupees booty. We went on towards the Mhow cantonments, and a little distance from the place we separated into two parties; one went into the cantonment-bazar, and the other passed outside. The five sepoys, whom we could not persuade to join us, came up, and recognised us, and reporting the circumstance to the officer commanding, the party was seized, and sent to the Resident at Indore (Mr Wellesley); but he, not deeming the proof against them sufficient, liberated them."

The last act of this murderer I have to record is the strangling a pundit and a sepoy at another village, called Deshuttee, in 1828.

3. *Soopher Sing*, alias *Khan Mahomed*, alias *Bujoo*.—On being brought in, he denied being a thug. Is a resident of Gwalior. Punna, an approver, says he is the son of Odeyt Thug, and is a thug by trade. Kalleean Singh, another approver, says the prisoner is a jemadar, or leader of thugs; that he was once a Rajpoot, but is now a Mussulman.

The first mention I find made of this man is at the murder of a pundit, in the year 1817, with Dirgpaul (No. 1.), near Saugor, and, a short time after, of sixteen treasure carriers, a few miles from the town of Reylee, in the Saugor territories. He was one who helped to strangle them. The gang amounted to 108 men, and each man shared 100 rupees in money, besides corals and other things.

Soopher Singh was the leader of fifty thugs in the murder of the subahdar Loll Singh, before alluded to; of the eight thugs who threw the strangling cord this man was one.

This man was with Gunga Bishun (No. 2.) at the murder of the Calcutta Chaprassee in 1829, near the cantonments of Mhow. They got from the unfortunate man eighteen rupees, a pony, and the brass plate he wore. The latter was found upon Soopher Singh. He was present likewise at the murder of the havildar and four companions, which took place six days afterwards, at Koondee, in the Kotah territory. In this last murder the thugs shared 1500 rupees among them. He was engaged in the murder of a pundit and a Brahmin at Deshuttee, in 1828-29. He was also one of the gang who strangled Amber Khan, (a connexion of the Nawaub Jaffier Khan) with his family, at Joura, and afterwards twelve Ganges water-carriers, the bodies of whom were buried in some empty houses, and subsequently dug up, as mentioned in the case of Dirgpaul (No. 1.)

In 1828, he was leader of a gang of thugs in Candeish, and fell in with nine persons going towards Jypore with pearls and gold. Thirty thugs followed these people for three days, without having an opportunity of murdering them. On reaching the village of Dhoree, they strangled eight out of the nine; one escaped, and gave the alarm to the neighbouring police-guard, and seventeen thugs were caught. Out of these, five were hung, four released, and eight transported. The pearls, according to the merchants to whom they belonged, were of the value of 72,322 rupees (L. 7000); and, besides the pearls, the people had treasure in gold mohurs and Venetian ducats.

Sooper Singh was a principal concerned in the murder of a risaldar, a woman, and fourteen companions, at Chapara, on their way from Hydrabad. Each thug shared seventeen rupees. Four poor travellers came up before the murders were completed, and, to prevent them communicating what they saw, they were also strangled; thus making twenty in all. Two of the poor men were going one way, and two another. . They did not reach the spot together. "The two that came up first," the informer goes on to say, "we made to sit down; when we had murdered the risaldar and his companions, and when the second two came to the top of the pass, at the foot of which we were, our people persuaded them we had had a dispute, and induced them to descend, which at first they were unwilling to do. When the leaders came up from the murders they were then engaged in, they insisted on strangling these four poor men, who submitted in silence to their doom."

4. *Hosein Alee Khan*, alias *Hosein Yar Khan*.—Hosein Alee was a Mussulman, and all the informers agree in saying, his forefathers have been thugs for many generations.

This man was a principal in the murder of the Nawaub Amber Khan, in which Dirgpaul (No. 1.) and Soopher Singh (No. 3.) were concerned, and of the twelve Ganges water-carriers. He was also concerned in the murder of the Calcutta Chaprassee, and a few days after of the havildar and four companions at Kondee, as described in Soopher Singh's case (No. 3.)

He was a principal concerned in the Chourahete affair. About ten years ago a brazier of Gurrawara, in the Nerbudda territory, was on his way to Hoshingabad, with a daughter about seven years of age, his wife, his wife's brother, and his own brother. The gang inveigled the party to join them, and they proceeded towards Hoshingabad; but in the jungle, about one coss from the village, and between that and Chourahete, at twelve o'clock in the day, they were all strangled, and the bodies buried near the place. They got about forty brass utensils of different sorts, and two bullocks. The bullocks they let go, but they were subsequently found in the jungle, and brought to Major Macpherson, then in civil charge of the Jubbalpore district. The bodies were dug up by the wild beasts.

This man Hosein Alee was a leader in the Beseynee gang, by whom eleven persons were murdered on their return home from Nagpore. Of the eleven there were two girls, to whom the thugs became attached, and they marched in company together from Nagpore as far as Jubbalpore. Here suspicion falling on them, the whole were searched, and the gold and silver ornaments observed on the girls, which the thugs had not before seen, induced them to determine on killing them. The party left Jubbalpore the following day, and proceeded on some forty miles. On the banks of a rivulet the thugs fell on them and murdered the whole. The bodies were concealed under stones, the ground being too hard to dig deep. They got 1000 rupees worth of gold and silver ornaments, and some other property.

5. *Keramut Khan*, alias *Kurreem Khan.*—Keramut Khan was the son of Asalut Khan, and was a Mussulman. He was well known to the approvers as a thug by trade, and the family have been thugs for many generations. He was with his father in the murder of some treasure-carriers belonging to a rich banker called Dhunraj Leth, the particulars of which are given in depositions so similar to those already quoted, that it is unnecessary to do more than allude to them.

This man was moreover concerned in the murders of Amber Khan, a relation of the Nawaub of Jowra, with his followers, and afterwards twelve Ganges water-carriers, as detailed in Dirgpaul's (No. 1.) case. He was also a party concerned in the murder of the brazier about seven years ago, near Chourahete, with his wife and daughter, his wife's brother, and his own brother, as detailed in Hosein Alee's case (No. 4.) A short time before these murders, the leaders quarrelled about three catamites, when they divided and took separate roads.

6. *Buksha, Mussulman, Jemadar of Thugs.*—Buksha was not executed. He died during confinement in the Saugor jail, and was never sentenced.

When he was first brought in, he acknowledged being a thug formerly, but stated he had left off the trade for ten years.

An approver named Punna, states he joined this man's gang of thugs about fifteen years ago, and proceeded to a town between Saugor and Jubbalpore, where, falling in with another gang, he left Buksha, who went on an independent expedition. Motee, a notorious thug (since hung), states this man was concerned in the murders of six men with treasure in 1830, in the Punna States of Bundlekund, and 8000 rupees were found on them. Gunga, an approver, says Buksha is a thug, and has no other trade.

This man was engaged in the murders of five men from Bombay (a serjeant and four sepoys), at the village of Golgunge, about sixty miles from Saugor. He had thirty followers with him, and the umbrella of the havildar was brought into court. A few hours after the murders had been committed, Lieutenant Wintle, adjutant 71st Regiment, N. I., came up and saw the murdered bodies lying in the jungle.

Doulut, the approver, who was sent to seize him with a guard, states, "We seized Buksha as he was leaving his house to run for the hills. I used to go on thuggee with him, and, among a thousand thugs, he is the most celebrated. I have been with him for eight years." Buksha was notorious among the thugs for his bravery, and it is said he would attack a horseman single-handed and strangle him. Many other murders are mentioned, but the particulars are not recorded.

7. *Golab Khan*, alias *Bussola, son of Meeah Khan.*—This man is a Mussulman, and is the adopted son of Dhurum Khan, a scoundrel who was a native officer at the Mynpooree jail, and, under pretence of going to catch thugs, headed a large gang himself, and travelled over the country with impunity, by virtue of the writ he possessed from the Mynporee magistrate. He was concerned in the murder of fourteen goseins (religious mendicants) nineteen years ago. He is notorious among all the thugs, and the approvers say he strangles a man by himself, and has done it often.

He was one of the Burwahaghat gang who murdered the camel-men in Dhunraj the banker's affair detailed in Keramut Khan's (No. 5.) history. He was also with the Akala gang in

1827, when the Subahdar Loll Singh and his family were murdered, as detailed in Dirgpaul's (No. 1.) history.

He was with the gang who murdered Amber Khan with his companions, and subsequently twelve Ganges water-carriers, as detailed in Dirgpaul's (No. 1.) history, and was again with Dirgpaul at the murder of a havildar and four companions, in the year 1826.

Several other expeditions are mentioned by the approvers, in which this man was concerned, but the particulars are not recorded.

For a great deal of the matter contained in the foregoing paper, I am indebted to the excellent report of F. C. Smith, Esq. the Governor-General's agent on the Nerbudda, and to the valuable evidence of the habits and customs of these people, recorded by Captain Sleeman, political officer at Saugor, who has been specially deputed by Lord Bentinck, to devote his time in effecting their extermination.

The zealous exertions of these two gentlemen, in this cause of humanity, are beyond all praise. H. H. SPRY.

REMARKS ON THE SKULLS AND CHARACTER OF THE THUGS. BY MR ROBERT COX.

The Scotch phrenologists are certainly much indebted to Dr Spry for his luminous and interesting account of this extraordinary race of men, and for the pains which he has taken in preparing the skulls of seven of the executed criminals.* It may be useful to offer a few remarks on these skulls, and to compare their configuration, with the particulars mentioned in Dr Spry's paper.

Heads are divided by phrenologists into three classes: the *first* includes those in which the organs of the propensities and lower sentiments predominate much over the organs of the faculties peculiar to man; that is to say, where Amativeness, Combativeness, Destructiveness, Secretiveness, Acquisitiveness, Self-Esteem, Love of Approbation, and Cautiousness, or most of them, are larger than Benevolence, Conscientiousness, Vene-

* George Swinton, Esq., Chief Secretary to the Supreme Government in India, to whom all the reports of the thug trials were made, was induced, by the interest which he takes in Phrenology, to request Mr Smith, the agent to the Governor-General by whom the criminals were tried and sentenced, to procure from Dr Spry the skulls of some of them for the phrenologists of Scotland. Dr Spry, accordingly, was so kind as to prepare seven of the skulls, and to draw up, also at Mr Swinton's suggestion, the account now printed. The skulls and manuscript were brought to this country by Mr Swinton, who is now resident in Edinburgh. It is much to be desired that gentlemen whose official situations put it in their power to add to our knowledge of human nature, would imitate the liberality and zeal of Mr Swinton and Dr Spry.

ration, Ideality, and the organs of Reflection :—heads in the *second* class are of exactly the opposite description, and indicate a preponderance of the moral feelings and reflection ;—while the *third* is composed of heads in which neither order of organs greatly predominates. A man whose head belongs to the first of these classes, is naturally endowed with base, selfish, and grovelling dispositions, and falls into criminal and vicious practices, in spite of the best education. He in whom the organs of the moral sentiments and reflective intellect predominate, is " a law unto himself," resists temptation to evil doing, and remains uncorrupted even among associates of the most depraved dispositions. When there is little disproportion between the organs of the propensities and those of the peculiarly human faculties, the individual is much the creature of circumstances, and is good or bad according to the society in which he is trained, the ideas instilled into his mind, and the example and motives set before him. To the first class belong most of these skulls of thugs. The mass of the posterior and basilar regions is large ; the coronal region is too small to enable the moral faculties to exercise sufficient restraint over the propensities ; and hence the natural tendencies of the individuals were to selfish and immoral courses of action. Two of them, however, Hosein and Gunga, are superior to the other five, and belong to the third class, or that in which the character is determined by external circumstances. One peculiarity however is, that Destructiveness is not a predominant organ in any of them ; and yet they were murderers. This fact, although it might appear to a superficial observer in opposition to their character, is in reality perfectly consistent with it. When Destructiveness is the predominant organ in the head of an individual, he delights in taking away life from " ruffian thirst for blood ;" but the thugs murdered obviously for the sake of robbing, and under the influence of other motives, to be immediately explained ; and also because they had been trained to this mode of life from their infancy. The skulls shew that combination of large organs of the animal propensities with comparatively moderate organs of the moral sentiments, which predisposes individuals to any mode of self-gratification and indulgence, without restraining them by regard to the rights and welfare of others. The thugs belong to the class of characters in which I would place the captains and crews of slave-ships, and also the more desperate among soldiers ; that is to say, men who individually are not quite so prone to cruelty, that they would of themselves have embarked in a murderous enterprize unsolicited ; but who, when temptation is presented to them, feel little or no compunction in yielding to it.

These skulls are of smaller size than the European average. The following is a Table of the developments and dimensions.

DEVELOPMENTS.							
ORGANS.	1. Dirgpaul.	2. Gunga Bishun.	3. Soopher Sing.	4. Hoseïn Alee.	5. Keramut Khan.	6. Buksha.	7. Bussola or Golub.
1. Amativeness	15	17	14	15	17	17	16
2. Philoprogenitiveness	19	17	17	14	16	16	19
3. Concentrativeness	15	14	13	13	16	16	14
4. Adhesiveness	16	15	15	16	15	15	13
5. Combativeness	17	15	17	15	18	17	17
6. Destructiveness	16	15	15	17	16	16	16
7. Secretiveness	16	15	16	17	16	16	15
8. Acquisitiveness	16	15	16	16	16	16	15
9. Constructiveness	16	15	15	15	15	17	16
10. Self-Esteem	18	18	15	18	17	15	17
11. Love of Approbation	16	17	16	18	15	14	15
12. Cautiousness	19	18	15	18	16	17	17
13. Benevolence	12	13	14	15	13	13	14
14. Veneration	16	15	16	16	14	15	16
15. Firmness	16	18	13	16	18	14	17
16. Conscientiousness	10	13	13	16	13	12	11
17. Hope	12	13	13	16	13	13	12
18. Wonder	12	14	15	14	14	12	12
19. Ideality	12	13	15	15	15	14	12
20. Wit	12	12	14	13	12	13	14
21. Imitation	12	14	14	15	13	13	13
22. Individuality	16	17	14	16	16	16	16
23. Form	15	15	13	15	14	16	14
24. Size	14	14	14	14	16	13	14
25. Weight	14	13	13	13	13	13	14
26. Colouring	13	13	13	12	13	10	12
27. Locality	16	16	14	16	16	16	14
28. Number	14	13	14	13	12	10	10
29. Order	12	14	13	13	12	10	10
30. Eventuality	15	16	14	15	12	16	12
31. Time	13	14	14	13	13	12	11
32. Tune	15	14	15	12	13	12	12
34. Comparison	13	14	14	15	12	14	14
35. Causality	13	14	15	15	12	14	14
DIMENSIONS.							
From—							
Individuality to Philoprogenitiveness,	$7\frac{3}{8}$	$7\frac{1}{8}$	7	$6\frac{7}{8}$	$7\frac{1}{8}$	7	$7\frac{1}{4}$
Ear to Individuality, ...	$4\frac{1}{4}$	$4\frac{1}{4}$	$4\frac{1}{4}$	$4\frac{1}{2}$	$4\frac{3}{8}$	$4\frac{1}{4}$	$4\frac{1}{4}$
...... Benevolence, ...	$4\frac{3}{4}$	$4\frac{7}{8}$	$4\frac{7}{8}$	5	$4\frac{3}{4}$	$4\frac{7}{8}$	$4\frac{7}{8}$
...... Firmness, ...	5	5	$4\frac{7}{8}$	$5\frac{1}{8}$	$4\frac{7}{8}$	$4\frac{7}{8}$	5
...... Philoprogenitiveness, ...	$4\frac{1}{4}$	4	$3\frac{7}{8}$	$3\frac{3}{4}$	$4\frac{1}{8}$	$3\frac{3}{4}$	4
Destructiveness to Destructiveness,	5	$4\frac{7}{8}$	$4\frac{7}{8}$	$4\frac{7}{8}$	$4\frac{7}{8}$	5	$4\frac{7}{8}$
Secretiveness to Secretiveness, . .	$5\frac{1}{8}$	5	5	$5\frac{1}{4}$	5	$5\frac{1}{8}$	$4\frac{7}{8}$
Cautiousness to Cautiousness, . .	$5\frac{1}{4}$	$5\frac{1}{8}$	$4\frac{5}{8}$	5	$4\frac{1}{2}$	$4\frac{7}{8}$	$4\frac{7}{8}$
Constructiveness to Constructiveness,	$4\frac{1}{4}$	4	$4\frac{1}{4}$	$4\frac{1}{4}$	$4\frac{1}{4}$	$4\frac{1}{4}$	4
Ideality to Ideality, ...	$3\frac{7}{8}$	$3\frac{7}{8}$	$3\frac{3}{4}$	$3\frac{7}{8}$	$3\frac{5}{8}$	$3\frac{3}{4}$	$3\frac{1}{2}$
Mastoid process to Mastoid process,	$4\frac{1}{2}$	$4\frac{1}{4}$	$4\frac{1}{8}$	$4\frac{1}{4}$	$4\frac{1}{2}$	$4\frac{1}{4}$	$4\frac{1}{4}$

NOTE.—The numbers refer to the following scale:—2. Idiocy; 4. Very small; 6. Small; 8. Rather small; 10. Moderate; 12. Rather full; 14. Full; 16. Rather large; 18. Large; 20. Very large. The *dimensions* are stated in inches.

Circumstances more suitable for the cultivation of the lower feelings and unfavourable for the strengthening of Benevolence and Conscientiousness, than those of the thugs, it is impossible to conceive; even Veneration and Love of Approbation, which, when rightly directed, serve to regulate the selfish feelings, are here rendered the prompters of Destructiveness and Acquisitiveness. It is not merely the size of the organs of these last two propensities that we are to regard; for in many cases the practices of the thugs are little if at all dictated by them. Dr Spry states it as his opinion—and the opinion exactly accords with my own conclusion, drawn from the examination of the skulls —that " many boys go on the roads as thugs because their fathers did, and not from any inherent ferocity of disposition." The influence of the priests is very great in leading to the enormities detailed by Dr Spry. When the *instructors* of the people are men " not ashamed to declare openly that untruth and false-swearing are virtuous and meritorious deeds when they tend to their own advantage," it is far from wonderful that the naturally weak morality of the *instructed* should become still more weak. Nor is it at all surprising, that the authority of men looked up to with awe, and their promises of eternal felicity, should be very influential in giving life and vigour to the animal propensities. In a letter published in the *Calcutta Literary Gazette*, and reprinted in the *Calcutta Magazine* for September 1832, (p. 508), Captain Sleeman thus alludes to some of the practices of the thugs, and the motives by which they are actuated. The correspondence between his remarks and what has already been said as to the non-predominance of Destructiveness in the heads, is very striking:—" It is an organized system of civil and religious polity" among the thugs, " to receive converts from all religions and sects, and to urge them to the murder of their fellow-creatures, under the assurance of high rewards in this world and the next; and sad experience teaches us how prone mankind have been in all ages and nations, to prey upon the lives and properties of each other, under such assurances, or under any sanction of law, human or divine, which they deem sufficient. Under a sentence of law, the executioner for a few shillings takes the lives of the fairest and most amiable of their species. Under a declaration of war, nations and families that have been living together in the strictest terms of amity, are instantly prepared to destroy each other, without the slightest feeling of compunction. When the Pope authorized the murder of the unhappy Americans by the Spaniards, they were sacrificed to Christ and the Apostles with sanguinary avidity; and when Henry the Lion of Germany, the brother-in-law of Richard Cœur de Lion of England, was put to the ban of the empire, his friends and neighbours rushed in upon his dominions with the awakened avidity of savages, and put to the sword almost every being that they could not sell at the hammer, not excepting the nuns of the convents. The page of history abounds with instances illustrative of the evil propensities of our nature under circumstances that relieve us from the necessity of respecting the lives, feelings, and possessions of our fellow-creatures, even among the most polished nations of the earth."

That Love of Approbation is a powerful stimulant to the commission of the atrocities of the thugs, is pretty obvious from what Captain Sleeman tells in the following passage, extracted from the letter just quoted. "After a man has passed through the different grades, and shewn that he has sufficient of dexterity, and of what we may call nerve or resolution, and they call 'hard-breastedness,' to strangle a victim himself, the priest, before all the gang assembled on a certain day, before they set out on their annual expeditions, presents him with the *romal* (the handkerchief with which the strangling is performed),—tells him how many of his family have signalized themselves by the use of it,—how much his friends expect from his courage and conduct;—and implores the goddess to vouchsafe her support to his laudable ambition and endeavours to distinguish himself in her service. The investiture with the *romal* is *knighthood* to these monsters; it is the highest object of their ambition; not only because the man who strangles has so much a head over and above the share which falls to him in the division of the spoil, but because it implies the recognition by his comrades of the qualities of courage, strength, and dexterity, which all are anxious to be famed for. The ceremony costs the candidate about forty rupees, and is performed by the *goroo* or high priest of the gang, who is commonly an old thug, no matter whether Mussulman or Hindoo, who has retired from service, and lives upon the contributions of his descendants or disciples." The high regard which the thugs pay to caste, proceeds chiefly from Love of Approbation, combined with Self-Esteem. Mr Smith tells us, that, "in the moment of death, even, the thug will be found scrupulously attentive to the preservation of his caste, and will plead as earnestly, or more so, to be spared the indignity of being touched by the low caste hangmen, as for the preservation of his life."

Cautiousness, which is strong, seems a powerful ally of Destructiveness in leading to the perpetration of the murders. "The maxim," says Captain Sleeman, "that '*dead men tell no tales*,' is repeated, and invariably acted upon, by these people, and they never rob a man till they have murdered him." Cautiousness, in fact, marks the whole of their proceedings. We are told by Captain Sleeman, that "the person invested with the *romal* has long used it in play before the practised eye of his *goroo*, and has been long accustomed to see others use it in earnest; but it is still thought necessary to select for him easy victims at first, and they do not employ him indiscriminately like the others, till he has shewn his powers in the death of two or three travellers of feeble form or timid bearing." Mr Smith mentions in his report, that " they decline murdering the *chuprassies* (native runners) of government, except under peculiar circumstances, as they dread the inquiry which might result. They also seldom meddle with Europeans, for the same reason. It was only after many years of success, that they ventured, about three years ago, to murder, near Banda, an invalid sergeant. In 1823, they deliberated whether they should destroy two officers passing by dawk, but the question was negatived; 1*st*, because the *saheb log* (gentlemen) seldom carry valuables with them in dawk trips; 2*d*, because they always carry pistols; 3*d*, because their destruction would draw too much publicity on their proceedings." There is much cautiousness in the mode in which unsuspecting travellers are lured into their clutches. The care with which the bodies are interred is equally characteristic. The beds of rivulets are generally selected as the burying places least likely to be discovered. It will be observed from the table of developments, that Dirgpaul had the largest Cautiousness of all the seven. Dr Spry mentions that Dirgpaul was the man who cajoled a party of thirteen people, and persuaded them to march in company with the thugs. At his execution, we are farther told, " his caution prevented him from being too precipitate." His Love of Approbation is rather large. Dirgpaul's leer was probably the effect of his large Self-Esteem.

The sexual feeling, as the table shews, must have been strong in most of the seven thugs. On this subject, Mr Spry says: " It is not to be wondered at that these vagabonds, while abroad, indulge in every carnal propensity; and it has happened more than once, that a gang has split from the leaders, quarrelling about a favourite. A knowledge of these practices coming to their wives' ears, they sometimes leave their husbands and go with other men." " Nearly all are married." Dr Paterson mentions, in the Transactions of the Phrenological Society, p. 441, that " the Hindoo cerebellum is uniformly well developed," and that the people are exceedingly jealous. " Polygamy and unnatural desires," he says, " abound."

Philoprogenitiveness is a large organ, especially in the cases of Dirgpaul and Bussola. Adhesiveness also is fully developed: Mr Smith's report contains the following passage: " The thug will lament, with unfeigned sorrow, the death of a relation or friend, and will do any thing, even to the surrender of himself to justice, to extricate his wife and children from imprisonment." " Feringeeâ, the Jemadar of thugs, avows, with what truth I know not, that he would have surrendered himself after the Bhilsah affair, if he had met the party of Nujeebs who had charge of his family; and he has more than once burst into a flood of tears, on Captain Sleeman's alluding to his relations, who were condemned in the Bhilsah trial, and hanged at Jubbulpoor." Dirgpaul, who has the largest Philoprogenitivness of the whole, spared and adopted an infant belonging to a company of whom every other individual was murdered. This is a fine illustration of the independent existence of Benevolence and Philoprogenitiveness. Dr Paterson mentions that the latter organ "is uniformly very fully developed in the Hindoo. According to my observations, males and females possess it in the same proportion. It is manifested by the Hindoos in their predilection for domestic quiet; in the happiness they seem to feel when surrounded by their children; in their terms of endearment; in the spirit of their lullabies; and in their frequent and ardent embraces." (Phren. Trans. p. 441.)

The development of Individuality and Locality corresponds with the memory and power of observation which the thugs manifest. Mr Smith observes: "The extraordinary ability displayed by the thugs, in ascertaining the characters, trade, name, residence, and intentions of their victims; the adroitness with which they worm themselves into their confidence; and the strong recollection of facts which have occurred many years ago, all display, in a wonderful manner, the tact and ability of their leaders, and the scientific and lasting principles on which the association is founded." It is remarked by Dr Spry, that "the accuracy with which these men will, after a lapse of several years, point out the spot where the murdered bodies are laid, is truly surprising."

Conscientiousness is in most instances developed only in a moderate degree. In the heads of Dirgpaul and Bussola it is remarkably deficient. The only tolerable Conscientiousness is that of Hosein. The whole of Dr Spry's paper is a commentary on this; and I shall merely add, in the words of Mr Smith, that to the thugs "gratitude is unknown; and the bosom-friend and benefactor,—nay, their preservers from prison and death, as has been too often exemplified in the late trials,—are remorselessly sacrificed at the shrine of wealth." The disregard of truth among the Hindoos is notorious. Sir William Jones has been heard to say, that, in the bazaars of Calcutta, he could purchase affidavits cheaper than asparagus.

In conclusion, it may be confidently affirmed, that so far as our information extends, the heads and characters of these seven thugs exactly correspond.

Lt. Reynolds

'On the Thugs.' *The New Monthly Magazine* 38 (1833): 277–287.

ON THE THUGS*.

RECEIVED FROM AN OFFICER IN THE SERVICE OF HIS HIGHNESS THE NIZAM.

The Thugs form a perfectly distinct class of persons, who subsist almost entirely upon the produce of the murders they are in the habit of committing. They appear to have derived their denomination from the practice usually adopted by them of decoying the persons they fix upon to destroy, to join their party; and then, taking advantage of the confidence they endeavour to inspire, to strangle their unsuspecting victims. They are also known by the name of Phanseegurs; and in the north-eastern part of the Nizam's dominions, are usually called "Kockbunds." There are several peculiarities in the habits of the Thugs, in their mode of causing death, and in the precautions they adopt for the prevention of discovery, that distinguish them from every other class of delinquents; and it may be considered a general rule whereby to judge of them, that they affect to disclaim the practice of petty theft, housebreaking, and indeed every species of stealing that has not been preceded by the perpetration of murder.

The Thugs adopt no other method of killing but strangulation; and the implement made use of for this purpose is a handkerchief, or any other convenient strip of cloth. The manner in which the deed is done will be described hereafter. They never attempt to rob a traveller until they have, in the first instance, deprived him of life: after the commission of a murder, they invariably bury the body immediately, if time and opportunity serve, or otherwise conceal it; and never leave a corpse uninterred in the highway, unless they happen to be disturbed†.

---

* Pronounced Túg, but with a slight aspirate.

† The Thugs were known in the time of the Emperor Akbar of Delhi, by whom many were executed. They were first known to the British Government in 1812,

To trace the origin of this practice would now be a matter of some difficulty, for if the assertions of the Thugs themselves are entitled to any credit, it has been in vogue from time immemorial; and they pretend that its institution is coeval with the creation of the world. Like most other inhuman practices, the traditions regarding it are mixed up with tales of Hindoo superstition; and the Thugs would wish to make it appear that, in immolating the numberless victims that yearly fall by their hands, they are only obeying the injunctions of the deity of their worship, to whom they say they are offering an acceptable sacrifice. The object of their worship is the Goddess Kalee, or Bhowanee, and there is a temple at Binda Chul, near Mirzapoor, to which the Thugs usually send considerable offerings, and the establishment of priests at their shrine are entirely of their community. Bhowanee, it seems, once formed the determination of extirpating the human race, and sacrified all but her own disciples. But she discovered, to her astonishment, that, through the intervention of the Creating Power, whenever human blood was shed, a fresh subject immediately started into existence to supply the vacancy. She therefore formed an image, into which she instilled the principles of life, and calling together her disciples, instructed them in the art of depriving that being of life by strangling it with a handkerchief. This method was found upon trial to be effectual, and the goddess directed her worshippers to adopt it, and to murder, without distinction, all who should fall into their hands, promising herself to dispose of the bodies of their victims, whose property she bestowed on her followers; and to be present at, and to preside over and to protect them on those occasions, so that none should be able to prevail against them.

Thus, say the Thugs, was our own order established, and we originally took no care of the bodies of those who fell by our hands, but abandoned them wherever they were strangled, until one man, more curious than the rest, ventured to watch the body he had murdered, in the expectation of seeing the manner in which it was disposed of. The goddess of his worship descended, as usual, to carry away the corpse, but, observing that this man was on the watch, she relinquished her purpose; and calling him, angrily rebuked him for his temerity; telling him she could no longer perform her promise regarding the bodies of the murdered, which his associates must hereafter dispose of in the best way they could. Hence, say they, arose the practice invariably followed by the Thugs of burying the dead; and to this circumstance principally is to be attributed the extraordinary manner in which their atrocities have

---

and then many were hung in Bundelkund. Again, in 1817, they attracted notice by their horrible acts, and twelve villages in Bundelkund, which were peopled almost entirely by them, were taken by a force sent against them. They were then dispersed, but assembled in various parts in Sindhia's and the Nagpoor country, also in Holkar's dominions. From 1817 till 1831 they were not molested; and, in consequence, increased greatly in the latter year. Measures were taken to suppress them, which have been attended with great success in this year. One hundred and eleven have been executed at Jubbulpoor, and upwards of 400 transported for life to the eastern settlement of Pinang, and upwards of 600 are now in jail at Saugor to take their trial at the next sessions at Jubbulpoor. Their apprehension, and their consequent disclosures, gave the means of those in this part of the country being pointed out. Mr. Reynolds, the officer who has the work here, has apprehended more than 100 in less than six months, and is catching others almost daily.

remained unknown, for with such circumspection and secresy do they proceed to work, and such order and regularity is there in all their operations, that it is next to impossible a murder should ever be discovered.

Absurd as the foregoing relation may appear, it has had this effect on the mind of the Thugs, that they do not seem to be visited with any of those feelings of remorse or compunction at the inhuman deeds in which they have participated that are commonly supposed to be, at some period of their lives, the portion of all who have trafficked in human blood. On the contrary, they dwell with satisfaction on the recollection of their various and successful exploits; and refer with no small degree of pride and exultation to the instances in which they have been personally engaged, especially if the number of their victims has been great, or the plunder they have acquired has been extensive.

Notwithstanding the adherence to Hindoo rites of worship observable among the Thugs, a very considerable number of them are Mussulmans. No judgment of the birth or caste of a Thug can, however, be formed from his name; for it not unfrequently happens that a Hindoo Thug has a Mussulman name with a Hindoo *alias* attached to it, and *vice versâ* with respect to the Thugs who are by birth Mahommedans. In almost every instance the Thugs have more than one appellation by which they are known. Of the number of Mussulman Thugs, some are to be found of every sect, Sheiks, Sezed, Mogul, and Pathan; and among the Hindoo, the castes chiefly to be met with are Brahmins, Rajhpoots, Lodhees, Ocheers, and Kolees. In a gang of Thugs some of every one of these castes may be found all connected together by the peculiar plan of murder practised by them, all subject to the same regulations, and all, both Mussulmans and Hindoos, joining in the worship of Bhowanee.

They usually move in large parties, often amounting to 100 or 200 persons, and resort to all sort of subterfuges for the purpose of concealing their real profession. If they are travelling southward, they represent themselves to be either proceeding in quest of service, or on their way to rejoin the regiments they belong to in this part of the country. When, on the contrary, their route lies towards the north, they represent themselves to be Sepoys from corps of the Bombay or Nizam's army, who are going on leave to Hindustan. The gangs do not always consist of persons who are Thugs by birth. It is customary for them to entice, by the promise of monthly pay or the hopes of amassing money that are held out, many persons, who are ignorant of the deeds of death that are to be perpetrated for the attainment of these objects, until made aware of the reality by seeing the victims of their cupidity fall under the hands of the stranglers; and the Thugs declare that novices have occasionally been so horrified at the sight, as to have effected their immediate escape. Others, more callous to the commission of crime, are not deterred from the pursuit of wealth by the frightful means adopted to obtain it, and remaining with the gang, too soon begin personally to assist in the perpetration of murder.

Many of the most notorious Thugs are the adopted children of others of the same class. They make it a rule, when a murder is committed, never to spare the life of any one, either male or female, who is old enough to remember and relate the particulars of the deed. But in the event of their meeting with children of such a tender age as to make it impossible they should be enabled to relate the fact, they generally spare their lives, and, adopting them, bring them up to the trade of Thugs. These men of course eventually become acquainted with the fact of the murder of their fathers and mothers, by the very persons with whom they have dwelt since their childhood, but are still not deterred from following the same dreadful trade. It might be supposed, that a class of persons whose hearts must be effectually hardened against all the better feelings of humanity, would encounter few scruples of conscience in the commission of the horrid deeds whereby they subsist; but, in point of fact, they are as much the slaves of superstition, and as much directed by the observance of omens in the commission of murder, as the most inoffensive of the natives of India are in the ordinary affairs of their lives.

The chief symbol of worship among the Thugs is a khadule, or pick-axe of iron. It is known among them by the name of *hishun*, *kussee*, and *mahee*. With every gang there is carried a *hishun*, which is, in fact, their standard, and the bearer of it is entitled to particular privileges. Previous to commencing an expedition, the jemadars of the party celebrate a poojah to the hishun, which is typical of the deity of their worship. The ceremonies differ little from the usual rites of Hindoos on similar occasions. A Hindoo Thug of good caste is employed in making a quantity of the cakes called poories, which, being consecrated, are distributed among the assembly. The hishun is bathed and perfumed in the smoke of burning benjamin, and is afterwards made over to the *hishun wulluh*, who receives it in a piece of cloth kept for that purpose. It is then taken out into the open fields, in the expectation of an omen being observed. The hishun is deposited in a convenient spot in the direction the party intends to proceed, and certain persons are deputed to keep watch over it. There are particular birds and beasts that are looked upon by the Thugs as the revealers of omens, to whose calls and movements their attention is, on this occasion, particularly directed. Among the number are the owl, the jay, the jackall, the ass, &c. &c. If one of these calls out, or moves to the right hand side, the omen is looked upon as favourable; but if to the left, it is considered unfavourable, and the project is abandoned. It is not unusual for the Thugs to look for a favourable omen previous to the commission of a murder, and they are frequently deterred from carrying their intentions immediately into effect by the observance of an unfavourable sign, such as a snake crossing their path when in pursuit of a victim, or the circumstance of any of the animals before mentioned calling out on their left hand sides. This, no doubt, accounts for the Thugs so often keeping company with travellers for many days previous to murdering them, although they had determined upon their sacrifice from the moment of their first joining the party. The omen is denominated *sugoor* by the Thugs, a corruption, no doubt, of the Persian *shugoôr*.

In the event of an expedition proving more than ordinarily successful, a poojah is usually made to Bhowanee, and a portion of the spoil taken by the gang is set aside for the purpose of being sent to the pagoda before alluded to, as an offering to the goddess. Propitiatory offerings are also made, and various ceremonies performed, before the *khodulee*, or *hishun*, should the Thugs have failed in obtaining any plunder for a length of time.

In every gang of Thugs there are to be found one or more jemadars, who appear to hold that rank not by the choice of their followers, but in consequence of their wealth and influence in their respective villages, and having assembled their immediate followers in the vicinity of their homes. The profits of a jemadar are of course greater than those of his followers; he receives six and a half or seven per cent. on all silver coin, and other property not hereafter specified, and then shares in the remainder in common with the other Thugs of the party. When gold is obtained in coin or in mass, the tenth part is taken by the jemadar previous to dividing it; and he has a tithe of all pearls, shawls, gold embroidered cloths, brass and copper pots, horses, &c. The jemadar acts as master of the ceremonies when the poojah is performed, and he assigns to every Thug the particular duty he is to undertake in the commission of every murder that is determined on. These duties are performed in succession by all the Thugs of the party, and to the regularity and system that exists among them is to be attributed the unparalleled success that has attended their proceedings. Next to the jemadar, the most important person is the *bhuttoat*, or strangler, who carries the handkerchief with which the Thugs usually murder their victims. This implement is merely a piece of fine, strong cotton cloth, about a yard long; at one end a knot is tied, and the cloth is slightly twisted, and kept ready for use in front of the waistcoat of the person carrying it. There is no doubt but that all Thugs are expert in the use of the handkerchief, which is called boomal, or paloo; but if they are to be believed, only particular persons are called upon, or permitted to perform this office. When a large gang is collected, the most able-bodied and alert of their number are fixed upon as bhuttoats, and they are made the bearers of the handkerchief only after the performance of various and often expensive ceremonies, and only on the observance of a favourable omen. The old and experienced Thugs are usually denominated gooroo bhow, and the junior Thugs make a merit of attending upon them, filling their hookahs, shampooing their bodies, and performing the most menial offices. They gradually become initiated into all the mysteries of the art, and if they prove to be powerful men, these disciples of the *gooroo* are made bhuttoats. The Thugs say, that if one of their class was alone, and had never strangled a person, he would not presume to make use of the handkerchief until he observed a favourable omen. The ceremonies observed in making a bhuttoat are the same as those described in carrying out the hishun, in room of which the handkerchief is on this occasion substituted, and an offering of pence (copper coin), cocoa-nut, turmeric, red ochre, &c., &c., is made. When a murder is to be committed, the bhuttoat usually follows the particular person whom he has been nominated by the jemadar to strangle; and, on the preconcerted signal being given, the handkerchief is seized with the knot in the *left hand*, the right hand being about nine inches farther up, in which manner it is thrown over the head of the person to be strangled from behind; the two hands are crossed as the victim falls, and such is the certainty with which the deed is done, as the Thugs frequently declare, that before the body falls to the ground the eyes start out of the head, and life becomes extinct. Should the person to be strangled prove a powerful man, or the bhuttoat inexpert, another Thug lays hold of the end of the handkerchief, and the work is completed. The perfection of the act is said to be, when several persons are simultaneously murdered without any of them having time to utter a cry, or to be aware of the fate of their comrades.

Favourable opportunities are given for bhuttoats to make their first essay in the art of strangling. When a single traveller is met with, a novice is instructed to make a trial of his skill; the party sets off during the night, and stops while it is still dark to drink water or to smoke. While seated for the purpose, the jemadar inquires what time of the night it may be, and the Thugs look up at the stars to ascertain. This being the preconcerted signal, the bhuttoat is immediately on the alert, and the unsuspecting traveller, on looking up at the heavens, in common with the rest of the party, offers his neck to the ready handkerchief, and becomes an easy prey to his murderer. The bhuttoat receives eight annas (half a rupee) extra for every murder that is committed, and if the plunder is great, some article of value is assigned to him over and above his share. The persons intended to be murdered are called by different names, according to their sect, profession, wealth, &c. &c.; a victim having much property is entitled "*niamud*," and they are also often called bunj. To aid the bhuttoat in the preparation of a murder, another Thug is especially appointed under the denomination of samsecah. His business is to seize the person to be strangled by the wrists if he be on foot, and by one of his legs if he be on horseback, and so to pull him down. A samsecah is told off to each traveller, and he places himself in a convenient situation near him to be ready when required. In the event of the traveller being mounted on horseback, another Thug assists under the denomination of "bhugdurra;" his business is to lay hold of the horse's bridle, and to check it as soon as the signal for murder is given.

One of the most necessary persons to a gang of Thugs is he who goes by the name of tillăee. The Thugs do not always depend upon chance for obtaining plunder, or roam about in the expectation of meeting travellers, but frequently take up their quarters in or near a large town, or some great thoroughfare, from whence they make expeditions, according to the information obtained by the tillăees. These men are chosen from among the most smooth-spoken and intelligent of their number, and their chief duty is to gain information. For this purpose they are decked out in the garb of respectable persons, whose appearance and manners they must have the art of assuming. They frequent the bazaars of the town near which their associates are encamped, and endeavour to pick up intelligence of the intended dispatch or expected arrival of goods or treasure, of which information is forthwith given to the gang, who send out a party to intercept them. Inquiry is also made for any party of travellers who may have arrived, and who put up in the suraee, or elsewhere. Every art is brought into practice to scrape an acquaintance with these people. They are given to understand that the tillăee is travelling the same road. An opportunity is taken to throw out hints regarding the unsafeness of the roads, and the frequency of murders and robberies; an acquaintance with some of the friends or relatives of the travellers is feigned, and an invitation from them to partake of the repast that has been prepared where the tillăee has put up,—the conveniences of which and the superiority of the water are abundantly praised. The result is, that the travellers are inveigled into joining the gang of Thugs, and they are feasted and treated with every politeness and consideration by the very wretches who are at the time plotting their murder, and calculating the share they shall acquire in the division of their property. What the feelings must be of men who are actuated by motives so entirely opposed to their apparent kindness of behaviour, it is difficult to imagine; and I know not whether most to admire the address with which they conceal their murderous intentions, or to detest the infernal apathy with which they can eat out of the same dish, and drink of the very cup, that is partaken of by their future victims!

It is on the perfection which they have attained in the art of acting as tillăees that the Thugs pride themselves, and they frequently boast that it is only once necessary to have an opportunity of conversing with a traveller, to be able to mark him as an easy victim, whenever they choose to murder him. Instances sometimes occur where a party of Thugs find their victims too numerous for them while they remain in a body, and they are seldom at a loss for expedients to create dissensions, and a consequent division among them. If all their arts of intrigue and cajolery fail in producing the desired effect, an occasion is taken advantage of to ply the travellers with intoxicating liquors; a quarrel is got up, and from words they proceed to blows, which end in the dissension of the company, who, proceeding by different roads, fall an easier prey to their remorseless destroyers. Having enticed the travellers into the snare they have laid for them, the next object is to choose a convenient spot for their murder. This, in their technical language, is called a *bhil*, and is usually fixed upon some distance from a village on the banks of a small stream, where the trees and underwood afford a shelter from the view of occasional passengers. The Thug who is sent on this duty is called a *bhilla*, and having fixed on the place, he either returns to the encampment of his party, or meets them on the way to report the result of his inquiry. If the bhilla returns to the camp with his report, the *suggaees*, or grave-diggers, are sent out with him to prepare a grave for the interment of the persons it is intended to murder. Arrangements are previously made so that the party in company with the travellers shall not arrive at the bhil too soon. At the particular spot agreed on, the bhilla meets the party. The jemadar calls out to him "Bhilla naujeh?" (Have you cleared out the hole?) The bhilla replies "Naujeh," on which the concerted signal is given that serves as the death-warrant of the unsuspecting travellers, who are forthwith strangled. While some are employed in rifling the bodies, others assist in carrying them away to the ready-prepared graves. The suggaees perform the office of burying the dead, and the remainder of the gang proceeds on its journey, having with them a certain number of the tillăees or watchmen on the look-out to prevent their being disturbed. Should a casual passenger appear, the tillăee gently throws a stone among the suggaees, who immediately desist, and crouch on the ground until the danger is averted. After the interment is completed, the suggaees rejoin their party, but it is not unusual to have one or more of the tillăees to keep watch to prevent the bodies being disinterred by beasts of prey; and if a discovery should be made by the village people, to give instant information to their companions, in order that they might have an opportunity of getting out of the way.

It often happens that the arrangements and precautions above-mentioned cannot be entered into; that travellers are casually met with on the road, and hastily murdered, and as carelessly interred. In these cases, if the opportunity is afforded them, the Thugs always have some one to keep watch at the place; and, rather than run the risk of detection, by the bodies being dug up by wild animals, they return, and re-inter them. If the ground is strong, they never touch the corpse; but if the soil is of that loose texture as to render it probable that the bodies, in swelling, will burst the graves, they generally transfix them with knives or spears, which effectually prevents that result.

When the Thugs may choose to strangle their victims in some more exposed situation,—as in a garden near a village where they may have put up for the night,—they resort to further precautions to prevent discovery. The grave is on this occasion prepared on the spot, after the murder has been committed; and the corpse having been deposited therein, the superfluous soil is carried away in baskets, and strewn in the neighbouring fields; the place is watered and beaten down, and it is ultimately plastered over with wet cow-dung, and *choolahs*, or fire-places for cooking, are made on the spot. If the party find it necessary to decamp, they light fires in the choolahs, that they may have the appearance of having been used to cook in. Should they determine on staying, they use the choolahs to cook their food in on the succeeding day, having few qualms of conscience to prevent their enjoying the victuals prepared on a spot, the associations attendant on which might be considered too revolting for even a Thug to dwell on.

The parties of Thugs being often very large, they have many beasts of burthen in their train—as bullocks, ponies, and sometimes even camels. If they remain at a place where they have committed a murder, and do not construct fire-places, they take the precaution of tying their cattle on the spot. The Thugs say they can always recognize the fire-places of their own class, there being peculiar marks about them, which are made to serve as directions to the next party that comes that way. The Thugs always prefer burying their victims at some distance from the public road; and therefore, as soon as the bodies of the murdered persons have been stripped of the property found on them, they are carried on the shoulders of the suggaes to the spot selected for interring them. They say they are more careless about the concealment of corpses in the Nizam's country than elsewhere; for they are always so secure from molestation, that they have frequently left bodies exposed without running any risk, as no one takes the trouble of inquiring about them.

The division of spoil does not usually take place immediately after a murder, but every one secures a portion of the property on the spot; and when a convenient opportunity occurs, each produces the articles he has been the bearer of, and a division is made by the jemadar, whose share is, in the first instance, deducted; then the bhuttoat's; next the sumseahs and bhugdurras claim the extra reward for each murder they have assisted at; the tilläee receives the perquisite which is his due for inveigling a traveller into their snares; the suggaee takes his recompense for the trouble he had in digging the grave; and the residue is divided, share and share alike, among the whole gang. It may be supposed that the cupidity of individual Thugs may occasionally lead them to attempt to defraud their comrades, by secreting an article of value at the time the murdered bodies are plundered; but they say that the whole class are bound by an inviolable oath to produce, for general appropriation to the common stock, everything that may fall into their hands while engaged with a particular party.

The division of plunder, as may be supposed, often leads to the most violent disputes, which it is astonishing do not end in bloodshed. But it might almost be supposed the Thugs have a prejudice against spilling blood; for, when pursued, they refrain from making use of the weapons they usually bear, even in defence of their own persons. The most wanton prodigality occurs when plunder is divided; and occasionally the most valuable shawls and brocades are torn into small strips and distributed amongst the gang, should any difference of opinion arise as to their appropriation. The Thugs say this is also done that every person may run the same risk, for such an article could not be shared among them until converted into money, and some danger is attendant upon the transaction. They appear invariably to destroy all hoondies* that fall into their hands, as well as many other articles that are likely to lead to detection. Ready money is what they chiefly look for, and when they have a choice of victims, the possessors of gold and silver would certainly be fixed upon in preference to others. In consequence, it seems to have been a general practice among the Bundelcund Thugs to waylay the parties of sepoys of the Bombay and Nizam's armies, while going on leave to Hindoostan, for the sake of the specie they are usually the bearers of; and they remark, that of the many sepoys who are supposed by their officers to have abandoned the service, while their friends and relatives consider them to be still with their regiments, they alone can tell the fate, the whole number being strangled by their hands. The immense wealth that has, at various times, fallen into the hands of these miscreants, has been expended in the grossest extravagance and debauchery, and, as may be supposed, their ill-gotten gains remain but a short time in their possession.

The Thugs have in use among them, not exactly a language of their own, but they have sets of slang terms and phrases which give them the means of holding a conversation with persons of their own class, without any chance of being understood by the uninitiated. Their term of salutation, whereby also they recognise each other, if they casually meet without being personally acquainted, is, *ali khan bhaee salaam.* What appears most extraordinary is, the manner in which the Thugs recollect the names of their comrades, as well as their persons; and they declare, that though the name of any one of a gang may have escaped their recollection, they never forget the person of a Thug who has assisted with them in the perpetration of a murder. The Thugs, indeed, seem to know each other almost intuitively; and the quickness with which the recognition is made is almost enough to warrant the supposition, that a sort of Freemasonry has been established among them.

To facilitate their plan of operations, the Thugs have established a regular system of intelligence and communication throughout the countries they have been in the practice of frequenting, and they become acquainted, with astonishing celerity, with proceedings of their comrades in all directions. They omit no opportunity of making inquiries regarding the progress of other gangs, and are equally particular in supplying the requisite information of their own movements. For this purpose they have connected themselves with several persons residing in the Nizam's dominions, as patails† and cultivators of villages, many of the

* Bills of exchange. † Headmen of villages.

latter of whom follow the profession of Thugs in conjunction with their agricultural pursuits.

The Marwarries* and other bankers are also frequently the channels of communication between Thugs, and there is no doubt of their being the purchasers of the property of the murdered. The religious medicants throughout the country occasionally assist in this measure, by becoming the receivers of messages from bands of Thugs, to be delivered to the next party that comes that way; with this view also they have adopted the practice of forming *choolahs*, or fireplaces of a particular construction, to serve as marks of their progress through the country. When a party of Thugs come to a road that branches off in two directions, they adopt the precaution of making a mark, for the guidance of their associates who may come after them, in the following manner:—the soil in a convenient spot is carefully smoothed, and the print of a foot is distinctly stamped upon it. A Thug on seeing this mark, which he naturally searches for, knows by the direction in which it points which track has been followed by those that have preceded him.

The peculiar designation by which they are known is a point in which the Thugs are particularly tenacious, and they attach an importance and even respectability to their profession, that they say no other class of delinquents is entitled to. The denomination of *thief* is one that is particularly obnoxious to them, and they never refrain from soliciting the erasure of the term, and the substitution of that of Thug, whenever it may occur in a paper regarding them, declaring that, so far from following so disgraceful a practice as theft, they scorn the name, and can prove themselves to be as honest and trustworthy as any one else, when occasion requires it.

It seems their ambition to be considered respectable persons; and with this view they expend much of their gains on their personal decoration. Even those who have been seized and admitted as approvers, or informers against their comrades, in fact, king's evidence, are more solicitous about their dress and decent appearance than anything else. They mostly seem to be men of mild and unobtrusive manners, possessing a cheerfulness of disposition entirely opposed to the violent passions and ferocious demeanour that are usually associated with the idea of a professed murderer.

Such is the extent to which this dreadful system has been carried that no idea can be formed of the expenditure of human life to which it has given occasion, or the immensity of the wealth that has been acquired by its adoption. When it is taken into consideration that many of the Thugs already seized confess to their having, for the last twenty-five and thirty years, annually made a tour with parties of more than a hundred men, and with no other object than that of murder and rapine; that they boast of having successively put their tens and twenties to death daily; and that they say an enumeration of all the lives they have personally assisted to destroy would swell the catalogue to hundreds, and, as some declare, to thousands †—some conception of the horrid reality may be formed; of the amount of the property that they have yearly made away

* Inhabitants of Marwar, generally bankers and traders.

† Ameer Ali, an approver and noted Thug, now at this place, declares and glories in having been present at the murder of 719 persons, whose property is estimated at two lacs and a half of rupees!

with, it must be impossible to form any calculation; for, independent of the thousands in ready money, jewels and bullion, the loads of valuable cloths, and every description of merchandise, that continually fall into their hands, the hoondies that they invariably destroy must amount to a considerable sum.

The impunity with which the Thugs have heretofore carried on their merciless proceedings, the facility they have possessed of recruiting their numbers—which are restricted to no particular caste or sect—the security they have had of escaping detection, and the ease with which they have usually purchased their release, when seized by the officers of the weak native governments, in whose dominions they have usually committed their greatest depredations, have altogether so tended to confirm the system, and to disseminate it to the fearful extent to which it has now attained, that the life of no single traveller on any of the roads in the country has been safe, and but a slight chance has been afforded to large parties of escaping the fangs of the blood-thirsty demons who have frequented them.

E. Thornton

Illustrations of the history and practices of the Thugs and Notices of Some of the Proceedings of the Government of India for the Suppression of the Crime of Thuggee.

London: W.H. Allen, 1837.

ILLUSTRATIONS

OF THE

HISTORY AND PRACTICES

OF THE

THUGS.

CHAP. I.

THE existence of large bodies of men having no other means of subsistence than those afforded by plunder, is, in all countries, too common to excite surprise; and, unhappily, organized bands of assassins are not peculiar to India! The associations of murderers known by the name of Thugs present, however, so many remarkable points of character and manners, that curiosity may reasonably be excited to inquire into the history, and ascertain the feelings, opinions, and motives of persons differing, in many respects, so widely even from all other followers of their own horrible occupation.

In different parts of India, these ruffians assume, and have been designated by, various names, derived either from the mode by which they dispatch their victims—from the purpose for which they destroy life, or from the arts by which they inveigle their prey to destruction. In the more northern parts of India, these murderers are called Thugs, the name by which they are most generally known among Europeans. This term signifies "deceiver." In some provinces to the southward, according to Dr. Sherwood, they have obtained the name of Phansigars, or "stranglers," from the Hindostanee word *phansi*, a "noose." By the same authority it is stated, that in the Tamul language they are called Ari Tulucar, or Mussulman "noosers"; in Canarese, Tanti Calleru, implying "thieves who use a wire or cat-gut noose"; and in Telagu, Warlu Wahndlu, or Warlu Vayshay Wahndloo, meaning "people who use the noose."

It is remarkable, that, after an intercourse with India of nearly two centuries, and the exercise of sovereignty over a large part of the country for no inconsiderable period, the English should have been ignorant of the existence and habits of a body so dangerous to the public peace. This, however, seems to have been the case: and it may be regarded as affording a strong proof, how little progress was made by the Europeans, during a long series of years, in knowledge of the people among whom they resided, and over whom they exercised the functions of rulers.

There is reason to conclude, that the British Government knew nothing of the Thugs until shortly after the conquest of Seringapatam, in 1799, when about a hundred were apprehended in the vicinity of Bangalore. They did not engage general attention; nor would it appear that they were suspected to belong to a distinct class of hereditary murderers and plunderers, settled in various parts of India, and alike remarkable for the singularity of their practice and the extent of their depredations. In the year 1807, between Chittoor and Arcot, several Thugs were apprehended, belonging to a gang which had just returned laden with booty from an expedition to Travancore; and information was then obtained, which ultimately led to the developement of the habits, artifices, and combinations of these atrocious delinquents.

The Thugs that invested the south of India some years ago were settled in Mysore, on the borders of that province and the Carnatic, in the Balaghat districts ceded to the Company by the Nizam in 1800; and they were particularly numerous in the Poliums of Chittoor. The sequestered part of the country which comprehended these Poliums maintained little intercourse with the neighbouring districts, abounding in hills and fastnesses; and, being immediately subject to several Polygars, afforded the Thugs a convenient and sure retreat. The protection of the Polygars was extended to them, in common with other classes of robbers, in consideration of a settled contribution, or, which was more frequent, of sharing in the fruits of their rapacity.

It is impossible that such criminals as the Thugs, living by systematic plans of depredation, could long remain in the same place in safety, unless their practices were encouraged or connived at by persons in authority. Hence, after the establishment of the Company's Government over the Carnatic and the districts ceded by the Nizam, and the consequent extinction of the power and influence of the Polygars, some of whom had succeeded in rendering themselves virtually independent of the former government, many of these murderers changed their abodes, and assumed other names: others, who remained, endeavoured to shelter themselves by subterfuge and dissimulation.

While they lived under the protection of Polygars and other petty local authorities, and among people whose habits were in some respects analogous to their own, it was unnecessary to conceal that they subsisted by depredation. They and their families lived peaceably with their neighbours, whom they never attempted to molest. Between them there subsisted a reciprocation of interest, in the purchase and disposal of the plunder which the Thugs brought with them, on returning from their expeditions. Conscience in the East is neither very delicate nor very enlightened; and if any scruples arose, the countervailing profit would more than balance them. The Thugs at all times engaged in the tillage of land, even under the native chiefs, when they had settled habitations. They either sowed the lands, or prepared them for seed, during the season that they remained at home; and left the care of them to their women and children, in their absence. This peaceful pursuit afforded them a screen, on the extension of the English Government, and, while pursuing their criminal practices, enabled them to appear dependent on honest and laudable industry.

According to Dr. Sherwood, who wrote in 1816, and whose acquaintance with Thuggee appears to have been founded principally upon observations made in the territories subject to the Presidency of Fort St. George, a gang consisted of from ten to fifty, or sometimes a greater number. Captain Sleeman states, that the gangs have often contained two or three hundred; but, in such instances, they commonly follow each other in small parties of ten or twenty, upon roads parallel to each other, being prepared to concentrate, on any point, when necessary. Different parties frequently act in concert, apprising one another of the approach of travellers whose destruction promises a valuable booty. They assume the appearance of ordinary inoffensive travellers: sometimes they pretend to be traders; and, if enriched by former spoliations, travel on horseback, with tents, and pass for wealthy merchants, or other persons of consequence. Sometimes they commence their route in more humble characters; but acquiring, in their rapacious progress, horses and bullocks, these at once furnish them with the means of transporting the remainder of their plunder, and of making pretensions to higher degrees of wealth and station.

Thugs are accustomed to wait at choultries, on the high roads, or near towns where travellers rest. They arrive at such places, and enter towns and villages, in straggling parties of three or four persons, appearing to meet by accident, and to have no previous acquaintance. On such occasions, some of the gang are employed as emissaries, to collect information, and especially to learn if any persons with property in their possession are about to undertake a journey. They are often accompanied by children of ten years of age and upwards; who, while they perform menial offices, are gradually initiated into the horrid practices of Thuggee, and contribute to prevent suspicion of their real character. Skilled in the arts of deception, they enter into conversation, and insinuate themselves by obsequious attentions into the confidence of travellers of all descriptions, to learn from them whence they came, whither and for what purpose they are journeying, and of what property they are possessed. When, after obtaining such information as they deem requisite, the Thugs determine to attack a traveller, they usually propose to him, under the specious plea of mutual safety, or for the sake of society, to travel together; or else they follow him at a little distance, and, when a fit opportunity appears for effecting their purpose, one of the gang suddenly throws a rope or sash round the neck of the unfortunate victim, while the rest contribute, in various ways, to aid the murderous work.

Intrepidity does not appear to be a characteristic of the Thugs; and, in truth, it is a quality not to be looked for in assassins by profession. A superiority in physical force is generally regarded as an indispensable preliminary to success. Two Thugs, at the least, are thought necessary for the murder of one man; and more commonly three are engaged. Some Thugs pride themselves upon being able to strangle a man single handed; and this is esteemed a most honourable distinction. To ascribe to a Thug this power, is the highest compliment that can be paid him. A single Thug who had succeeded in pulling a man from his horse, and strangling him, conferred a distinction upon his family which ennobled it in the eyes of their fellows for many generations. Such a man was Buckshee, and a few others; but the majority of the Thugs are, and ever have been, firm adherents of the maxim, that "discretion is the better part of valour."

Some variations have existed in the manner of perpetrating the murders; but the following seems to be the most general. While travelling along, one of the gang suddenly throws the rope or cloth round the neck of the devoted individual, and retains hold of one end; the other end being seized by an accomplice. The instrument of death, crossed behind the neck, is then drawn very tight, the two Thugs who hold it pressing the head of the victim forwards: a third villain, who is in readiness behind the traveller, seizes him by the legs, and he is thus thrown on the ground. In this situation there is little opportunity of resistance. The operation of the noose is aided by kicks inflicted in the manner most likely to produce vital injury, and the sufferer is thus quickly dispatched.

The best precautions are taken to guard against discovery or surprise. Before the perpetration of the murder, some of the gang are sent in advance, and some left in rear of the place, to keep watch, to prevent intrusion, and to give warning, if occasion requires, to those engaged in the act. Should any persons unexpectedly appear on the ground before the murdered body is buried, some artifice is practised to prevent discovery; such as, covering the body with a cloth, while loud lamentations are made, professedly on account of the sickness or death of one of their comrades; or one of the watchers will fall down, apparently writhing with pain, in order to excite the pity of the intruding travellers, and to detain them from the scene of murder.

Such are the perseverance and caution of the Thugs, that, in the absence of a convenient opportunity, they have been known to travel in company with persons whom they have devoted to destruction, for several days before they executed their intention. If circumstances favour them, they generally commit the murder in a jungle, or in an unfrequented part of the country, and near a sandy place or dry water-course. Particular tracts are chosen, in every part of India, where they may exercise their horrid profession with the greatest convenience and security. Much-frequented roads, passing through extensive jungles, where the ground is soft for the grave, or the jungle thick to cover them, and where the local authorities took no notice of the bodies, were favourite spots. The Thugs speak of such places with the same affection and enthusiasm as other men would of the most delightful scenes of their early life.

In these chosen spots, a hole, three or four feet in depth, usually forms the grave of the unhappy traveller, who is placed in it with his face downwards. The barbarous character of the Thugs is displayed in their treatment of the wretched remains of the murdered persons. Though death brings a termination of suffering, it does not put an end to the outrages of the murderers. Long and deep gashes are made in various parts of the bodies: sometimes the limbs are disjointed, and the figure distorted into unusual positions. These outrages arise from various motives. Their intention generally is, to expedite the decomposition of the body, and to prevent its inflation, which, by causing fissures in the superincumbent sand, might attract jackals, and thus lead to the discovery of the corpse. Sometimes, however, these deeds have been the result of disappointment, and the emanations of a petty and unmanly revenge. When the amount of plunder is less than had been expected, the villains have frequently vented their displeasure in wanton indignities on the unconscious remains of the dead.

If, when a murder is perpetrated, a convenient place for interring the body be not near, or if the Thugs be apprehensive of discovery, it is either tied in a sack, and carried to some spot where it is not likely to be found, or is put into a well. In Oude, where the fields are almost all irrigated from wells, the bodies were generally thrown into them; and when the cultivators discovered these relics of crime, they hardly ever thought it worth while to ask how they came there, so accustomed were they to find them. In Bengal and Behar, where the most frequented roads pass along or frequently across rivers, the bodies are cast into those rivers.

If none of these expedients be advisable, a shallow hole is dug, in which the corpse is buried, till a fit place for interring it can be discovered; when it is removed, and cut in the manner already mentioned. If compelled to perform the interment under circumstances which subject them to the risk of observation, the Thugs put up a screen on the wall for a tent, and bury the body within the enclosure; pretending, if inquiries are made, that their women are within the screen. If the traveller had a dog, it is killed, lest the affection of the animal should cause the discovery of the body of his murdered master. The office of mangling the dead body is usually assigned to a particular person of the gang. The Thugs are always provided with knives and pickaxes, which they conceal from observation.

It will thus be seen, that the system of the Thugs is well devised to secure that concealment so necessary to the continued success of their horrid practices. The mode of destroying their victims, and of disposing of their remains, almost preclude the possibility of rescue or escape, of witnesses to the deed, of noise or cries for help, of effusion of blood, and, indeed, of any trace of the crime. An impenetrable veil of darkness is thrown over their atrocities.

It has been supposed, that formerly a long string with a running noose was used by the Thugs for seizing travellers, and that they robbed on horseback. These practices do not at present, however, appear to be common. They sometimes use a short rope, with a loop at one end: but a turban, or sash, are more usually employed, as these answer the atrocious purpose in view as well as a regularly-prepared noose, and have the additional recommendation of exciting no suspicion. When a waist-cloth or sash is used, it is previously doubled to the length of two feet, or two feet and a half: a knot is formed at the double extremity, and a slip-knot tied about eighteen inches from it. In regulating the distance of the two knots, so that the intervening space, when tightly twisted, may be adapted to embrace the neck, the Thug who prepares the instrument ties it upon his own knee. The two knots give a firm hold of the cloth, and prevent its slipping through the hands in the act of applying it. After the person attacked has been brought to the ground, the slip-knot is loosed by the Thug who has hold of that part of the cloth: and he makes another fold of it round the neck; upon which placing his foot, he draws the cloth tight, in a manner similar to that—to use the expression of a Thug informer—"of packing a bundle of straw."

If, which scarcely ever happens, a traveller escape from the persons attempting to strangle him, he incurs the hazard of being dispatched by one of the parties on watch. These men have swords, and will endeavour to cut down any man who escapes from the stranglers. Should he finally escape, or should any other circumstance occur to excite alarm or apprehensions of being seized, the gang immediately disperses, having previously agreed to re-assemble, at an appointed time, at some distant place.

Travellers resting in the same choultry with Thugs are sometimes destroyed in the night. On these occasions, a person is not always murdered when asleep; as, while he is in a recumbent posture, the stranglers find a difficulty in applying the cloth. The usual practice is, first, to awaken him suddenly, with an alarm of a snake or a scorpion, and then to strangle him.

In attacking a traveller on horseback, the Thugs range themselves in the following manner: one of the gang goes in front of the horse, and another has his station in the rear; a third, walking by the side of the traveller, keeps him engaged in conversation, till, finding that he is off his guard, he suddenly seizes the victim by the arm, and drags him to the ground, the horse at the same time being seized by the foremost villain: the miserable sufferer is then strangled in the usual manner.

Against Thugs, it must be obvious, that arms, and the ordinary precautions taken against robbers, are unavailing. ' When a person is armed with a dagger, it is usual for one of the villains to secure his hands. It sometimes happens, that entire parties of travellers, consisting of several persons possessed of valuable effects, are, while journeying in imaginary security, suddenly cut off; and the lifeless and despoiled bodies being removed and interred, not a vestige of them appears. Instances have occurred, of twelve and fourteen persons being simultaneously destroyed; but such occurrences must be rare.

Occasionally, the booty obtained is considerable. Near Sadras, about eleven years ago, three *golah* peons were killed, having on them money, in different coins, to the amount of 16,000 rupees. In 1805, five persons were killed in Coimbatoor, and cash to the amount of 2500 pagodas, the property of the Collector of the district, was taken. In the same year, two respectable natives proceeding on horseback from Madras to the Malabar coast, with five attendants, were all killed. In 1807, five persons, besides two others who had joined them on the road, were killed near Bangalore, and robbed of property to the amount of 1000 pagodas, belonging to an officer of Engineers. And in 1815, three persons were killed in the district of Masulipatam, and 2500 rupees taken. Very frequently, however, the property taken is but small; and such are the cruelty and cupidity of these wretches, that, on the presumption of every traveller possessing concealed treasure, or some property, however trifling, the greatest apparent indigence does not always afford security.

The plunder was sometimes carried home; sometimes disposed of on the road. If the murdered person resided near the place of his assassination, the property was carried to a distance: if, as was more commonly the case, he was a stranger, the ruffians did not scruple to offer the fruits of their rapine in the immediate vicinity of their crime: the only precaution taken was, that the place of sale should be in advance of that where the murder was committed, and not a village where the traveller had previously been seen.

The mode of dividing the plunder is probably various. Dr. Sherwood says, that formerly, if good horses, shawls, or other valuable articles, were among the booty, they were commonly reserved for the Polygar, in payment of protection. A portion of the plunder was usually appropriated to defraying the expenses of religious ceremonies; and, sometimes, a part was also allotted for the benefit of widows and families of deceased members of the gang. The residue of the booty, being divided into several parts, was generally shared as follows;—to the leader, two shares; to the men actually concerned in perpetrating the murder, and to the person who cut the dead body, each one share and a half; and to the remainder of the gang, each one share.

According to Captain Sleeman, when there are ten

or more articles of the same kind, the tenth is assigned to the leader, before the general division takes place: if the nature of the property does not admit of decimation, one anna in the rupee is assessed upon its value, for the benefit of the leader. After this deduction, and the payment of a small extra allowance to the stranglers, grave-choosers, diggers, and other officers, the remainder is divided by lot, called, in the Thug dialect, *Kouree, Phenkua, Marna,* or *Dalna.* It is usual to make three allotments of the spoil, and to divide the gang into three equal parties. A cowry is then given to each party, by whom it is marked. The cowries are then placed in the hands of a man who is kept ignorant of the parties to whom they respectively belong; and the final decision is made by his placing one of the cowries upon each parcel of the plunder. The parties then take possession of the shares thus consigned to them, and divide the produce among the individuals.

The operations of the Thugs are facilitated, and their designs cloked, by a peculiar dialect: they have recourse, also, to a variety of signs, both for concealment, and for the purpose of communicating with comrades beyond the influence of speech. Drawing the back of the hand along the chin, from the throat outwards, implies that caution is requisite—that some stranger is approaching. Putting the open hand over the mouth, and drawing it gently down, implies that there is no longer cause for alarm. If an advanced party of Thugs overtake any traveller whom they design to destroy, but have need of more assistance, they make certain marks on the roads, by which those of the gang who follow understand that they are required to hasten forwards. A party in advance also leaves certain marks, where a road branches off, as intimations to those who are behind. They draw their feet along the dust, in the direction they have taken; and if their friends are to follow quickly, they leave the dust piled up at the end of the line where the foot drops, or make a hole in the dust with the heel. If the road afford no dust, they leave two stones, placed one upon the other, in the line they have taken; and strew a few leaves of trees along the road. If their co-adjutors are to make haste, they make a very long line of leaves. They have many other signs, for similar purposes.

Of the number of persons who fall victims to these lawless associations, it is obvious that no estimate can be proved, deserving of the slightest confidence. The number has, without doubt, varied greatly at different periods. There is reason to believe, that from the time of the conquest of Mysore in 1799, to 1807 and 1808, the practice, in that part of India, reached its height, and that hundreds of persons were annually destroyed. In one of his reports, the Magistrate of Chittoor observes: "I believe that some of the Phansigars have been concerned in above two hundred murders: nor will this estimate appear extravagant, if it be remembered, that murder was their profession, frequently their only means of gaining a subsistence: every man of fifty years of age has probably been actively engaged during twenty-five years of his life in murder; and, on the most moderate computation, it may be reckoned that he has made one excursion a year, and met each time with ten victims."

Francis Bartolomeo says: "During a residence of thirteen or fourteen years in India, I never heard of any traveller being robbed or murdered on the highway;"—but other travellers, whose experience was less agreeable, attest that the practice of Thuggee is not of recent introduction. Thevenot, in the following passage, evidently alludes to it:—"Though the road I have been speaking of, from Delhi to Agra, be tolerable, yet hath it many inconveniences. One may meet with tigers, panthers, and lions upon it; and one had best, also, have a care of robbers, and, above all things, not to suffer any body to come near one upon the road. The cunningest robbers in the world are in that country. They use a certain slip with a running noose, which they can cast with so much sleight about a man's neck, when they are within reach of him, that they never fail, so that they strangle him in a trice. They have another cunning trick, also, to catch travellers with. They send out a handsome woman upon the road, who, with her hair dishevelled, seems to be all in tears, sighing and complaining of some misfortunes which she pretends has befallen her. Now, as she takes the same way that the traveller goes, he easily falls into conversation with her, and, finding her beautiful, offers her his assistance, which she accepts: but he hath no sooner taken her up behind him on horseback, but she throws the snare about his neck and strangles him; or at least stuns him, until the robbers, who lie hid, come running to her assistance, and complete what she hath begun. But, besides that, there are men in those quarters so skilful in casting the snare, that they succeed as well at a distance as near at hand; and if an ox, or any other beast belonging to a caravan, run away, as sometimes it happens, they fail not to catch it by the neck."

The modern Thugs have recourse to numerous artifices to entrap their victims; but there is reason to think that the allurements of female fascination are now not often resorted to. Their customs with regard to their women, however, vary much. The Thugs, who reside in fixed habitations, rarely allow their women to accompany them. The wandering bands, who seem to retain more of the usages of their ancestors, are attended and aided by their females.

To a European reader it must appear extraordinary, that the constant disappearance of such numbers of natives should have excited so little interest and inquiry, as not to have led to a general knowledge of these combinations of criminals. Such ignorance, perhaps, could not have prevailed in England, where it might be supposed that the absence, if unaccounted for, of even a single person, must produce suspicion, with consequent investigation and discovery. But even in England it has recently been made evident, that numbers of persons may disappear from the scene of their ordinary avocations without producing much surprise or any alarm. In India, the probability of such disappearance is far greater; and such an event, unless occurring to a person of some consequence, would scarcely be known beyond the precincts of the place of residence, or the village of the unfortunate sufferer, nor much observed there. Many that fall victims to the Thugs are the subjects of other and distant states: many have no settled abodes. It must also be remembered, that the Thugs usually refrain from murdering the inhabitants of towns and villages near which they are halting; neither are they accustomed to murder near their own habitations; circumstances which not only prevent suspicion attaching to them as the murderers, and to the local authority as protecting and sharing the booty with them, but tend to throw it upon others, who reside near the spot to which a traveller may have been traced, and where he was last seen. Besides, a person setting out on a journey is often unable to fix any period for his return; and though he should not revisit his home at the expected time, his delay will, for a while, excite little alarm in the minds of his friends. He is supposed to be unexpectedly detained—to be ill—to have met with some ordinary accident—to have deserted his family—to have died. Should suspicion arise that he has been murdered, the act is attributed to ordinary highway robbers; and it is but seldom that minute inquiries can be instituted by his bereaved relatives. But supposing that this is done, and the progress of the missing traveller traced to a particular place, and not beyond it, still suspicion would be apt to attach to any, rather than to a few apparently inoffensive travellers—journeying either for the purpose of traffic, as is imagined, or, as is often pretended, to see their relations, or to be present at some marriage; and who, if ever noticed, have perhaps been long since forgotten. If, notwithstanding all these improbabilities, suspicion should fall upon the actual perpetrators, where could they be found?

Thus with respect to Sepoys, who, having obtained leave of absence, never rejoined their corps, the conclusion generally formed has been, that they had deserted; when, in various instances, they had fallen sacrifices to the wiles of the Thugs.

The same observation is particularly applicable to golah peons, charged with the conveyance of money and valuables; many of whom having disappeared, no doubt was entertained that they had absconded, and appropriated the property to their own use. Even the apprehension which an indistinct idea of danger tends to create in the minds of these and other travellers would render them only more liable to fall into the snare: less persuasion would be requisite to induce them to join a party of Thugs, prompted by the belief that they were thus providing, in the most effectual manner, for their own safety.

The profession of a Thug, like almost every thing in India, is hereditary—the fraternity, however, receiving occasional reinforcements from strangers: but these are admitted with great caution, and seldom after they have attained mature age. Rank is acquired by methods not dissimilar to those which procure the same advantage elsewhere. On Captain Sleeman's inquiring, of an approver, what gave a man the rank of Jemadar, the latter answered, that a man who has always at command the means of advancing a month or two's subsistence to a gang, will be called so;—a strong and resolute man, whose ancestors have been for many generations Thugs, will soon get the title;—or a very wise man, whose advice in difficult cases has weight with the gang;—or one who has influence over local authorities, or the native officers of courts of justice ;—or a man of handsome appearance and high bearing, who can feign the man of rank well. By such means a man is enabled to get around him a few who will consent to give him the fees and title of Jemadar; but it requires very high and numerous qualifications to gain a man the title of Subahdar. Wealth, influence, talents, and high descent, it thus appears, have the same power among Thugs which they have elsewhere; and, in the absence of all these, impudent pretension will answer the purpose of the adventurer who has confidence enough to assume it. In this respect, at least, the polity of the Thugs presents but a counterpart of what is passing elsewhere.

In contemplating the organization of these hordes of murderers, it is difficult to conceive how they continue to subsist. It might be hoped, that when the villains who have grown grey in the practice of assassination descend with their weight of crime to the grave, some difficulty would be found in perpetuating the succession—that the profession would decay, from the reluctance of the young and uncontaminated to enter it. The initiation, however, is progressive; and the force of habit gradually overcomes the natural repugnance which, in every human breast, would at first withdraw the hand from the destruction of human life. The children of Thugs, during their more tender years, are, it appears, kept in ignorance of the occupation of their fathers. After a time, they are permitted to accompany them; but a veil is thrown over the darker scenes of the drama. To the novice, indeed, the expedition presents nothing but an aspect of pleasure. He is mounted on a pony; and being, by the laws of the Thugs, entitled to his share of the booty, he receives a portion of it, in presents suited to his years—the delight attending the acquisition being unalloyed by any consciousness of the means by which it has been obtained. The truth reveals itself by degrees. In a short time, the tyro becomes aware that his presents are the fruits of robbery. After a while, he has reason to suspect that robbery is aggravated by a fouler crime: at length, suspicion passes into certainty: and finally, the pupil is permitted to witness the exercise of the frightful handicraft which he is destined to pursue. The moral contamination is now complete; but it is long before the disciple is entrusted with the performance of the last atrocity. He passes through a long course of preparatory study; being first employed as a scout, next as a sexton, then as a holder of the limbs, before he is in any case thought worthy of being elevated to the dignity of a strangler.

A too precipitate disclosure of the frightful truth has sometimes produced fatal consequences. The following affecting story, related by a Thug who had become approver against his comrades, will illustrate this; and there is reason to believe that the case is not altogether without parallel. It is admitted, indeed, that others have occurred resembling it in kind, though falling short of it in degree:—"About twelve years ago," said the narrator, "my cousin, Aman Subahdar, took out with us my cousin Kurhora, brother of Omrow approver, a lad of fourteen, for the first time. He was mounted upon a pretty pony; and Hursooka, an adopted son of Aman's, was appointed to take charge of the boy. We fell in with five Sieks; and when we set out before daylight in the morning, Hursooka, who had been already on three expeditions, was ordered to take the bridle, and keep the boy in the rear, out of sight and hearing. The boy became alarmed and impatient, got away from Hursooka, and galloped up at the instant the '*Ihirnee*,' or signal for murder, was given. He heard the screams of the men, and saw them all strangled. He was seized with a trembling, and fell from his pony: he became immediately delirious, was dreadfully alarmed at the turbans of the murdered men, and, when any one touched or spoke to him, talked wildly about the murders, screamed as if in sleep, and trembled violently. We could not get him forward; and, after burying the bodies, Aman, myself, and a few others, sat by him while the gang went on: we were very fond of him, and tried all we could to tranquillize him, but he never recovered his senses, and before evening he died.—I have seen many instances of feelings greatly shocked at the sight of the first murder, but never one so strong as this. Kurhora was a very fine boy; and Hursooka took his death much to heart, and turned Byragee. He is now at some temple on the banks of the Nerbudda river."

One of the most remarkable features in this narrative is the expression of affection for the unhappy boy, by a man steeped in blood and guilt. The difficulty of supposing the better affections of the heart to subsist in conjunction with the exercise of the trade of murder led Captain Sleeman to ask the individual who related the story, if the children of Thugs continued to reverence their fathers after they became acquainted with their occupation. The answer was brief and decisive, and apparently given without any feeling that the fact averred required explanation, or was calculated to excite surprize. The party interrogated calmly replied, "The same: we love them, and they love us." Such is the inconsistency of human nature!

The indiscriminate slaughter in which these miscreants might be tempted to indulge, is in some degree restrained by superstition. It is deemed unlucky to kill certain castes and classes; and their members are therefore usually respected. The most important and extended exception to the general rule of murder is that of the female sex. Thugs, who have any real regard to the principles which they profess to respect, never take the lives of women. It cannot, however, be supposed that such a rule should be invariably observed by such persons as form the society of Thugs; and, in fact, it is constantly violated. "Among us," said one of the approvers interrogated by Captain Sleeman, "it is a rule never to kill a woman; but if a rich old woman is found, the gang sometimes get a man to strangle her, by giving him an extra share of the booty, and inducing him to take the responsibility upon himself. We have sometimes killed other prohibited people, particularly those of low caste, whom we ought not even to have touched."

The Thugs of Hindostan, it is said, are less scrupulous about the murder of women than those of the Deccan; and even with the former, the practice is alleged to be rather of recent origin. It has been seen, that age has had some share in determining the fate of females; and it appears, from the confessions of some of the criminals, that the possession of beauty has been allowed to operate as a protection. Feringcea, a Hindostan Thug, says: "I and my cousin Aman Sabahdar were with a gang of 150 Thugs, on an expedition through Rajpootana, about thirteen years ago, when we met a handmaid of the Peshwa Bajee Row's, on her way from Poona to Cawnpore. We intended to kill her and her followers; but we found her very beautiful; and after having her, and her party, three days within our grasp, and knowing that they had a lac and a half of rupees' worth of property, in jewels and other things, with them, we let her and all her party go: we had talked to her, and felt love towards her, for she was very beautiful."—Beauty, however, does not always disarm these murderers. Another beautiful female, respecting whom the same witness was questioned, was sacrificed without remorse. Feringcea endeavoured to throw the guilt of this transaction upon the Mussulmans of the gang, and to exonerate those of his own creed from participation. "We none of us," said he, "ventured near the palanquin: the Mussulmans were the only men who approached her before the murder."—The comparative forbearance of the Hindoos, in all similar transactions, is a point that was strongly urged by many of the witnesses. Being questioned as to the murder of a female named Kalee Bebee, which had excited some interest, the account given was such as to clear the Hindoo portion of the gang from the guilt of engaging in the act, and even to represent them as actively opposing it; but it does not appear that their conscientiousness extended to the length of finally declining all participation in the spoil, and a few superstitious ceremonies soon reconciled all differences. If the evidence of the approver is to be credited, disputes arose between the Mussulmans and the Hindoos, both before and after the murder. The Mussulmans insisted upon killing the lady, as she had four thousand rupees' worth of property with her: the Hindoos would not agree. She was killed, however, with all her followers, twelve in number: but it is added, that, in the first instance, the Hindoos refused to take any part of the booty—that the two parties even came to blows;—at last, the Hindoos gave in, and consented to share in all, but the clothes and ornaments which the women wore. This compromise between cupidity and superstition put an end to the dispute for a time; but when Pursaram Benhman, one of the Hindoo conspirators, returned home, Rae Sing, his brother, refused to eat, drink, or smoke with him, till he had purged himself from this great sin; and he, with two others, gave a feast that cost them a thousand rupees each. This feast, at which four or five thousand Brahmans were assembled, made all right.

Some associations pride themselves upon their purity in this respect. One of the Behar Thugs being asked if that body ever murdered women, answered, with much warmth, "Never! we should not murder a woman, if she had a lac of rupees upon her." A member of the Doab fraternity, who was present, immediately added, "Nor would the Doab Thugs, if she had two lacs upon her."

Among the privileged classes, are, washermen and poets, professors of dancing, blacksmiths and carpenters, musicians, oil-venders, and sweepers, Ganges water-carriers if they have the water actually with them, but if their pots be empty they are subject to the general law of destruction, Madaree Fakeers, and, in some districts, Sieks. The maimed and the leprous are also spared; but perhaps the origin of the latter exemption is ascribable to the fear of contamination, rather than to humanity. The sacred cow, in the eyes of all Hindoos who have any pretensions to consistency, is a protection to its possessor: art is however sometimes resorted to, for the purpose of removing this impediment to business. A party of Thugs projected the murder of fourteen persons, including several women; but the design could not be carried into effect, because the victims had a cow with them. With some difficulty, they were persuaded to sell the cow to the Thugs; who, to induce the travellers to consent to the sale, pretended that they had vowed to make an offering of a cow at Shaphore, and were much in want of one. The cow was actually presented to a Brahman at Shaphore; and the obstacle being removed, the whole of the unsuspecting travellers, including the females, were, two or three hours afterwards, strangled. Such are the fruits of the horrible creed which overspreads and darkens so large a portion of the East!

CHAP. III.

The dark and cheerless night of superstition, which has long clouded the moral vision of India, has given rise to institutions and practices so horrible and fantastic, that, without the most convincing evidence, their existence could not be credited by minds trained under happier circumstances than those which prevail in the East. That giant power, which has held the human race in chains wherever the pure and unadulterated doctrines of Revelation have not penetrated, has in India revelled in the wantonness of prosperity; the foundations of delusion have been laid wide and deep; the poison of a false and brutalizing creed has been insinuated into every action of daily life; the most obvious distinctions of right and wrong have been obliterated; and men have been encouraged to believe, that, while stifling the best and strongest feelings of nature, and violating the plainest rules of social duty, they were but fulfilling their destined part in the scheme of the world, and even paying homage to those invisible forms which they were bound, both by conscience and interest, to reverence.

The fact of the existence of the cold-blooded miscreants who in India make a trade of assassination, is sufficiently horrible: but when it is added, that their occupation is sanctified by the national religion—that the Thugs regard themselves as engaged in the especial service of one of the dark divinities of the Hindoo creed—that the instruments of murder are in their eyes holy—and that their faith in the protection of their goddess, and the perpetuity of their craft, is not to be shaken—we must be struck by the reflection, that we have opened a page in the history of man, fearful and humiliating beyond the ordinary records of iniquity.

The genius of Paganism, which has deified every vice, and thus provided a justification of the indulgence of every evil propensity, has furnished the Thugs with a patron goddess, worthy of those whom she is believed to protect. Of Kalee, the deity of destruction, they are the most devout and assiduous worshippers: in her name they practise their execrable art; and their victims are held to be immolated in her honour.

This horrible divinity they believe to have formerly co-operated more directly with her votaries the Thugs, by disposing of the bodies of those whom they destroyed. Kalee, however, chose to be secret in her operations; and the Thugs were prohibited from looking back, to see what she was about. All was well, so long as they observed this rule; but the services of the goddess as a sextoness were lost through the carelessness or indiscreet curiosity of one of the association. Of the circumstances attendant on this mischance, there are different versions; and at least two are in pretty general circulation. According to one, prevalent in the Deccan, a party of Thugs, having destroyed a traveller, left the body, as usual, unburied, in perfect confidence of receiving the wonted aid from the goddess. A novice, however, unguardedly looking behind him, saw the patroness of the Thugs in the act of feasting on the corpse, one half of it hanging out of her mouth. According to another report, the person looking back was a slave; and the goddess was engaged, not in satisfying the demands of hunger, or gratifying a taste for luxury, by swallowing the murdered traveller, but in tossing the body into the air;—for what purpose does not appear. The offence to the goddess is said, also, to have been aggravated by the fact, that she was not attired with sufficient strictness to satisfy her sense of decorum. Both tales agree, in representing the goddess as highly displeased, and as visiting her displeasure upon her servants, the Thugs, by condemning them to bury their victims themselves. According to the Southern version indeed, like a wise and beneficent potentate, she tempered justice with mercy; for though she refused any longer to relieve the earth of the loathsome burdens with which her worshippers encumbered it, she was so considerate as to present her friends with one of her teeth for a pickaxe, a rib for a knife, and the hem of her lower garment for a noose. Whether or not this origin of the pickaxe be generally received, it is certain that this instrument is held by the Thugs throughout India in the highest veneration. Its fabrication is superintended with the greatest care; and it is consecrated to the holy duty to which it is destined, with many ceremonies. In the first place, a lucky day must be fixed upon: the leader of the gang then instructs a smith to make the required tool, and the process is conducted with the most profound secrecy. The door is peremptorily closed against all intrusion; the leader never quits the forge while the manufacture is going on; and the smith must engage in no other work, till his sacred task is completed. The pickaxe being made, must next be consecrated. Certain days of the week are deemed more auspicious for this purpose than the rest: Monday, Tuesday, Wednesday, and Friday, enjoy the distinction. Care is taken that the shadow of no living thing may fall on the axe, as this would contaminate the devoted implement, and frustrate all the pains that had been taken in its formation. A Doctor most deeply versed in the learning of the Thugs undertakes the solemn office of consecration. He sits down with his face to the West, and receives the pickaxe in a brass dish. The instrument which is to supply the want occasioned by the cessation of the goddess's personal labours is first washed in water, which is received into a pit dug for the purpose. The pickaxe then receives three further ablutions; the material employed in each being more expensive and valuable than that used in the first. The second washing is made with a mixture of sugar and water; the third with sour milk; and the fourth with ardent spirits. The pickaxe is then marked, from the head to the point, with seven spots. In performing this operation, the material used is neither very valuable nor very dignified, it being nothing but common red-lead. The brass dish, on which the pickaxe was handed to the officiating Thug, now comes into play again: the pickaxe is placed upon it, with a cocoa-nut, some cloves, white sandal-wood, sugar, and a few other articles. A fire is next kindled, and the fuel must consist of dried cow-dung, and the wood of the Mango or Byr tree. All the articles deposited in the brass pan are, with the exception of the cocoa-nut, thrown into the fire; and when the flame rises, the Thug priest, holding the pickaxe with both hands, passes it seven times through the fire. The cocoa-nut is now stripped of its outer coat, and placed on the ground. The comptroller of the pickaxe, holding it by the point, then says, "Shall I strike?" The bystanders signifying their assent, he strikes the cocoa-nut with the butt end of the pickaxe, and breaks it, exclaiming, "All hail, mighty Davy (the goddess), great Mother of us all!" The surrounding spectators respond, "All hail, Davy! and prosper the Thugs!" This is a most interesting and exciting moment to the Thugs; for upon the hardness of the nut, the skill of the operator, and the accidental circumstances which may affect the force or direction of the blow, depend the realization of the hopes of the community. If the cocoa-nut be not severed at one blow, all the labour is thrown away; the goddess is understood to be unpropitious; another day must be selected for the repetition of the ceremonies, and all the trouble be incurred again. If, however, the nut is cleft at once, the proof of the approval of the goddess is indisputable. The whole of the shell, and some of the kernel of the nut, is thrown into the fire; the pickaxe is carefully tied up in a clean white cloth, and, being placed on the ground to the West, the assembled spectators, turning in that direction, prostrate themselves in adoration before "that which their own fingers have made"; that which the labour of the smith might have fashioned with equal facility into an object of reverence or of contempt; and which, while it receives divine honours, is destined to assist in a series of acts, at once horrible by their guilt, and disgusting by their loathsomeness.

The ceremony of prostration concluded, all present receive a portion of the cocoa-nut: the fragments are then collected, and thrown into the pit which had been previously prepared, lest, if they remained on the ground, the sacred relics might be outraged by the defiling touch of some human foot.

These ceremonies, elaborate as they are, suffice only for a single expedition. At the commencement of every fresh series of adventures, they must be repeated.

When the sacred pickaxe is thus prepared, the next point is, to place it in safe custody: it is not every Thug who can be trusted with it. The person who bears it is selected, principally, for his shrewdness, caution, and sobriety. It is, however, only when on a journey that it is entrusted to human care at all. When in camp, it is deposited in the earth, under the especial protection of the goddess. When buried, it is always placed with the point towards the direction in which the party intend to proceed; and they have the fullest confidence, that if another course is to be preferred, the point will be found to have veered round so as to indicate the better way. Certain classes of the Thugs, when halting, throw their instrument into a well; and the received belief is, that, when wanted, it will come up of itself, if summoned in due form.

Of course, the instructed know better ; but all *profess* implicit belief in the miraculous egress of the pickaxe from the well into which it is thrown. One of the Thugs, interrogated by Captain Sleeman, said: "We have all of us seen the sacred pickaxe spring in the morning from the well into which it had been thrown overnight, and come to the hands of the man who carried it, at his call: nay, we have seen the pickaxes of different gangs all come up of themselves, from the same well, at the same time, and go to their several bearers." On being reminded of the extraordinary feats performed by jugglers, the Thug replied, with great energy: "What! shall not a hundred generations of Thugs be able to distinguish the tricks of man from the miracles of God? Is there not the difference of heaven and earth between them? Is not one a mere trick; and the other a miracle, witnessed by hundreds assembled at the same time?" —Captain Sleeman then said to another Thug: "Sahib Khan, you are more sober than Nasir; have you ever seen it?" The answer was: "On one expedition only. I was obliged to fly from Telingana when Major Parker and Captain Sheriff made their inroad upon us (Gurdee), and I went and joined the Arcot gangs. During a whole expedition that I made with them, Imam Khan and his brother carried the pickaxes; and I heard them, repeatedly, in the morning call them from the well into which they had thrown them overnight, and saw the pickaxes come of themselves from the well, and fall into their aprons, which they held open *thus*"— here he exhibited the mode.

No one acquainted with the almost superhuman dexterity of Indian jugglers will feel much surprise at these feats. Their prevalence only shews the extent to which delusion may be carried, in a country where human intellect has been long prostrated by a brutalizing superstition.

When the pickaxe is buried, no foot must touch the earth which covers it; nor must it, at any time, be approached by an unclean animal, or any object which bears contamination. After each time that it has been used for the preparation of a grave, it must be submitted to the purification of the bath.

If the pickaxe fall from the hand of the man who bears it, dismay spreads through the gang. The omen is regarded as of the most fearful description: its horrors are aggravated by the uncertainty, as to the nature of the approaching evil, and even as to the party upon whom it is to descend. The omen may indicate the death of the individual who had the care of the sacred weapon, and who, through heedlessness, or misfortune, or unavoidable fatality, suffered it to drop from his embrace: or it may forebode some dreadful reverse to the fortunes of the gang. Measures are immediately taken to frustrate the evil token; and the first step is, to deprive the unhappy pickaxe-bearer of his office.

The enterprise in hand, whatever it might be, is immediately abandoned; and the pickaxe must undergo a fresh consecration. Even these precautions are insufficient to restore things to their original state: the misfortune operates, upon the gang to whom it happens, as a sentence of excommunication from the society of all faithful Thugs. No other party will ever associate with one whose pickaxe has fallen, lest they should be involved in the evil which is apprehended to the "doomed ones."

The pickaxe affords the most solemn sanction of an oath among these murderers; and if any sanction can bind their consciences, it is, perhaps, the only one capable of effecting that purpose. Compared with it, neither the water of the Ganges weighs with the Hindoo, nor the Koran with the Mussulman. When the sacred pickaxe is not at hand, recourse is had to various expedients to remedy the want, and to give validity to the administration of an oath. A piece of cloth is made up into the form of the pickaxe, and duly consecrated: the person sworn then places his hand upon it, or holds it in both hands; and, after the administration of the oath, drinks water in which the representative of the revealed instrument has been washed. In other instances, he goes before the image of the goddess, with the emblem of the pickaxe in his hand, and there takes the oath. If a cloth is not conveniently to be had, even mud, moulded into the proper form, and duly submitted to the ceremonies of consecration, will answer the purposes. "If any man swears to a falsehood upon a pickaxe properly consecrated," said the Thugs, "we will consent to be hanged if he survive the time appointed. Appoint one, two, or three days, when he swears, and we pledge ourselves that he does not live a moment beyond the time: he will die a horrid death; his head will turn round, his face towards the back; and he will writhe in torture till he dies." The infliction of this miserable fate, some, even of the most intelligent of the Thug fraternity, declared that they had often seen. The pickaxe is, in short, the standard, round which all the gloomy family of Thug superstitions rally: it is regarded as the great source of security and prosperity: — the instrument of strangulation is held in esteem; but that of burial, in infinitely more—the Thugs think of it with enthusiasm. "Do we not," said one, interrogated by Captain Sleeman, "do we not worship it every seventh day? Is it not our standard? Is its sound ever heard, when digging the grave, by any but a Thug? And can any man even swear to a falsehood upon it?"—"How could we dig graves," asked another, "with any other instrument? This is the one appointed by Davy (the goddess), and consecrated; and we should never have survived the attempt to use any other."—" No man," it was added, " but a Thug, who has been a strangler, and is remarkable for his cleanliness and decorum, is permitted to carry it."

But though the pickaxe is the great symbol of their profession, and the devout object of their care, the respect in which it is held is but one of the degrading and frightful superstitions by which these murderers steel their hearts to encounter the horrors of their wretched profession.

CHAP. IV.

THE authority for the mode of murder practised by the Thugs is traced, like all their other usages, to the tremendous goddess whom they serve. It seems, that, in remote ages, a demon infested the earth, and devoured mankind as soon as created. The proportions of this devouring monster were so gigantic, that the water did not reach his waist in the most unfathomable parts of the ocean; and he strode over the world unrestrained, rioting in the destruction of the human race. The world was thus kept unpeopled, until the goddess of the Thugs came to the rescue. She attacked the demon, and cut him down; but from every drop of his blood another demon arose: and though the goddess continued to cut down these rising demons with wonderful alacrity and scientific skill, fresh broods of demons sprung from their blood, as from that of their progenitors; and the diabolical race consequently multiplied with fearful rapidity. The never-ending labour of cutting down demons, whose number was only increased by this operation of pruning, at length fatigued and disheartened the goddess; she found it indispensably necessary to make a change in her tactics;—and here the tale, which is thus far universally received, becomes subject to variations. It is admitted by all Hindoos, that the demons multiplied in the manner described, until the goddess found some means of putting a stop to this "surplus population": but there is a difference of belief as to the mode. The orthodox opinion is, that when the goddess found the drops of blood thus rapidly passing into demons—a fact which, with all her divine attributes, it seems she only learned by experience—she hit upon a very happy expedient to prevent the blood reaching the earth, where the demoniacal conversion took place. Being furnished with a tongue of extraordinary dimensions, she, after every blow, promptly and carefully licked the blood away. A "preventive check" being thus placed upon the further propagation of demons, the goddess was enabled to destroy those previously existing, at her leisure:—such is the commonly-received account of the goddess's dexterity and address. That of the Thugs is varied, for the purpose of affording a superhuman sanction to their mode of assassination. According to Thug mythology, the goddess, when she became embarrassed by the constant reinforcements of the demon army which accrued from her labours, relinquished all personal efforts for their suppression, and formed two men from the perspiration brushed from her arms. To each of these men she gave a handkerchief; how fabricated, at a time when reels and looms were not, is a question open to the discussion of the learned. With these handkerchiefs, the goddess's two lieutenants were commanded to put all the demons to death, without shedding a drop of blood. It does not appear why the goddess might not thus have plied the handkerchief herself: it may be presumed that she was too much exhausted by her previous exertions. Her commands, however, were faithfully executed; and the demons were all strangled without delay.

There is some difficulty in understanding how demons so powerful succumbed thus readily to two agents, who, though sprung from an exudation of the goddess's arms, were, as appears by the sequel of the tale, merely children of mortality: but the difficulty never seems to have occurred to the Thugs, whose faith, like that of the mass of their countrymen, is of a very unscrupulous character. The story is wound up with such poetical justice as might be expected in a Hindoo legend. The champions, having vanquished all the demons, offered, like honest men, to return the handkerchiefs; but their patroness, in the spirit of a grateful goddess, desired that they would retain them, not merely as memorials of their heroism, but as the implements of a lucrative trade in which their descendants were to labour and thrive. They were not only permitted, but commanded, to strangle men, as they had strangled demons. They forebore, indeed, to exercise this privilege for a long period: so say the Thugs. Several generations passed before Thuggee became practised as a profession. Whether this forbearance was founded on the principle according to which a sportsman suffers game to accumulate, is not stated. The privilege slept; but though dormant, it was not lost; and in due time it was abundantly exercised. The lapse between the grant of the patent and the use of it might tend to raise a presumption against its having been granted; but Hindoo casuists are not accustomed to scrutinize evidence with the severity which prevails in Westminster Hall.

Thus, according to the creed of the Thugs, did their order arise; and thus originated their mode of operation. The assistance once afforded by the goddess in removing the bodies, and the means by which this favour was forfeited, have already been noticed.

It has been mentioned, that the high office of a strangler is not attained until after a noviciate of considerable length. When the disciple has been sufficiently prepared, or at least when he believes that the conquest of natural feeling is so far complete as to enable him to perform without shrinking that which he has learned to contemplate without horror, he applies to one of the most experienced and respected of the gang to become his *gooroo.* This word appears to be derived from the *goor*, or "coarse sugar," which forms an important ingredient in the ceremonies of initiation; and the office of the person honoured with this title is, to introduce the aspirant to the actual exercise of his profession; to instruct him in the science of hangmanship; and to preside over the rites by which the pupil is to be consecrated to his diabolical work. Precautions are taken that the young beginner may not be embarrassed by difficulties. A victim is selected for his first essay in guilt, whose strength is below the average; and the chosen period of operation is at the moment when the senses of the traveller are bewildered by being suddenly roused from sleep. While the latter is reposing himself, the preparation takes place. The gooroo takes the pupil into a field, accompanied by three or four of the older members of the gang. The ceremonies commence by the whole party facing in the direction in which they intend to move. The gooroo then proceeds to take the auspices. Having invoked a favourable sign from the goddess, half an hour is allowed for the fulfilment of their wishes. If, in the course of that time, the required sign is obtained, all is well, and the goddess is believed to regard the attempt of the young Thug with benignity; but if no sign is obtained, or if it is of an unfavourable nature, the ambition of the novice is for that time disappointed, and the destined victim must fall by hands already practised in the murderous work.

If the sanction of the goddess be indicated, the group retire, in high spirits, to the place where the sleeping traveller awaits his death. The gooroo then, turning to the west, takes a handkerchief, and ties at one end a knot, in which he encloses a rupee. This knot is of a peculiar description, and the privilege of tying it confined to those who have been regularly introduced to their occupation. The clumsy intruder, who has not participated in the advantages derived from a regular apprenticeship to the art, leaves the end of the *roomal* exposed: the more accomplished practitioner manifests his science and elegance by concealing the end within the knot. This is the mark of his regular induction, and the ribbon of the order to which he has the honour to belong.

The knot being duly tied by the gooroo, the roomal is delivered to the incipient strangler, who receives it with all the reverence due to so precious a gift, bestowed by such venerated hands. The interest of the scene now increases. The executioner, attended by a *ghumgeea,* or holder of hands, stands before his victim, whose tranquil state is but an emblem of that deeper sleep which is about to seal his eyes for ever. His last earthly slumber is gradually interrupted—the victim is roused for slaughter—the fatal noose is cast over his neck by the hand of the youthful assassin, and, with the aid of the attendant ruffian, the work is soon completed. One human being has passed into eternity ;—another has taken the last step in guilt and infamy !

The horrible work is over ; and, so far from being actuated by any sensations of pity or remorse, the wretch, who has attested the strength of his nerves and the weakness of his moral perceptions, knows no feeling but that of delight flowing from gratified ambition. To his instructor, guide, and priest, his gratitude is boundless : he bows before his gooroo, and touches his feet with both hands, in token of the deepest and most affectionate respect. But his gratitude, if confined to the person of his preceptor, would be felt to be inadequate and niggardly : the relations and friends of the reverend man are entitled to share the warm feelings of the now-accomplished assassin ; and to them he tenders the same homage which he has previously paid to his father in crime.

The *thibaoo*, or happy auspice, is once more anxiously looked for ; and as soon as it is afforded, the newly-admitted strangler opens the knot tied in the handkerchief by the hands of his tutor, and takes out the rupee which had been placed within it. This coin, with all the other silver which he has, the pupil presents to the preceptor : the latter adds his own stock of money to the offering, and, after setting apart one rupee and a quarter to the purchase of *goor* (coarse sugar) for the Tapoonee, the remainder is expended in sweatmeats.

The Tapoonee is a solemn sacrifice, performed after every murder. The goor (sugar) is placed upon a blanket or sheet, spread upon a clean spot. On the cloth near the goor is deposited the consecrated pickaxe, and a piece of silver for an offering. The Thug whose reputation for professional learning stands the highest, and who is supposed to enjoy the largest share of the favour of the goddess, also takes his place on the cloth, with his face to the west: the most accomplished and scientific stranglers are associated with him in this place of honour. The number of this select body must be an even one; but its extent is limited only by the size of the cloth. Those of the higher grade, who are unable to find accommodation among their brethren, and the vulgar herd who have no claim to distinction, arrange themselves around the covering which bears the sacrifice, and those who preside over it. The leader then makes a hole in the ground, and, having poured into it a little of the goor, clasps his hands in the attitude of fervent devotion, and, raising them in harmony with his up-turned eyes to heaven, gives utterance to the following prayer :—" Great goddess ! as you vouchsafed one lac and sixty thousand rupees to Joora Naig and Koduck Bunwanee in their need, so we pray thee fulfil our desires !" The enumeration of the precise number of thousands bestowed by the goddess upon her favourites is not very poetical; but the petition is so entirely accordant with Thug feeling, that no doubt can be entertained as to the sincerity with which it is offered. All the assembled followers repeat the prayer after the leader; and the latter, after sprinkling water on the pit and pickaxe, puts a little of the goor upon the head of each Thug who has been so fortunate as to obtain a seat upon the carpet. The signal for strangling is now given, as if a murder were actually about to be committed; and the Thugs who have received the portions of goor, eat them in solemn silence. The most perfect stillness prevails, till these privileged persons have swallowed the precious morsels distributed to them, and diluted the repast by drinking some water. The goor is now given to all whose rank entitles them to partake of it; the greatest care being taken that no part shall fall to the ground. If, in spite of watchfulness, such a mischance should occur, the fallen fragments are punctiliously collected, and put into the pit. The misfortune is alleviated, as far as human prudence can go, by at least preserving the hapless relics of the sugar consecrated to murder, from contamination by the foot of man.

The sacred goor is not imparted to all Thugs indiscriminately: two conditions are necessary, to qualify them for a share of it. The participant must be in a state of freedom—servitude barring his admission to the privilege: the only remaining disqualification is found in innocence of murder, either actual or comparative. None but the practical assassin can be allowed to partake of the sacred goor: no one but he whose hands have performed the office of strangling is thought worthy of the food which derives its sanctity from the prayers of stranglers, aided, it is to be supposed, by the deglutition of the privileged, to which a portion of it has been submitted. For those who cannot boast the name of freemen, or whom youth or fear or ill-fortune has withheld from performing on any of their fellow men the honourable act of strangulation, some sugar is set apart, before it acquires its holy character. This the excluded eat, at the time when their more-favoured associates are gratified by the taste of the sanctified article.

On the performance of this ceremony, after the maiden effort of a newly-admitted strangler, the proselyte of course takes his place among the select, and receives his share of consecrated sugar. The sweetmeats which have been provided are distributed among the gang generally.

The expedition being closed, and the members of the community having retired to their quarters, the happy individual, who has passed from a state of pupilage into the maturity of a practised assassin, entertains his gooroo at a feast as magnificent as his circumstances will afford. If he have the means of defraying the expense, not only the immediate members of the gooroo's family, but all his relations, are invited, and the grateful murderer equips his tutor, from head to foot, with a complete array of new vestments: the same compliment is paid to the gooroo's lady, and sometimes to all his relatives. The hospitality of the gooroo is exercised, in return, by inviting his pupil to a future meeting. The connexion between them is henceforward indissoluble; and the most intimate and sacred relations of nature are considered as nothing, in comparison with it. A Thug will rather betray his father, than the gooroo by whom he has been introduced to the honours of his profession.

The dignity and sanctity with which murder is invested by the creed of the Thugs—and a mode of murder, too, marked by cowardice and meanness no less than the blackest atrocity—afford lamentable proof of the inseparable connexion subsisting between the corruption of religion and the corruption of morals. To obliterate all religious feeling from the heart of man is a difficult, if not an impossible task: to substitute superstitious belief for reasonable faith, is, unhappily, a very easy one; and sound morals invariably disappear with sound religion. Indeed, between false religion and false morals there is a mutual action and re-action.

The wayward desires of man lead him to indulge in that which true religion forbids: he therefore seeks shelter in a false one. Again, superstition sanctions, and even commands, practices, against which pure morality revolts: hence the moral judgment is depraved, the restraints of conscience abolished, and that feeling, which should conduct men to all that is good and pure and excellent, becomes the pilot to every vice, and the prompter of the most horrible crimes.

The effect of the consecrated sugar or goor is believed to be irresistible. Captain Sleeman, having reproached some of the fraternity on account of a murder marked by many ferocious and unmanly features, one of the party replied: "We all feel pity sometimes; but the goor of the Tuponee changes our nature: it would change the nature of a horse. Let any man once taste of that goor, and he will be a Thug, though he know all the trades and have all the wealth in the world. I never wanted food: my mother's family was opulent—her relations high in office. I have been high in office myself; and became so great a favourite wherever I went, that I was sure of promotion; yet I was always miserable when absent from my gang, and obliged to return to Thuggee. My father made me taste of that fatal goor when I was yet a mere boy: and if I were to live a thousand years, I should never be able to follow any other trade."

The Tuponee is not the only sacrifice offered by the Thugs to their patroness. Throughout India, another feast is observed; but to which, in Hindostan, no peculiar name appears to be allotted; it being called *Kurhae kurna,* or *Kurhahee dena*—terms indiscriminately applied, by all classes of persons, to a feast of any kind. In the Deccan it is honoured by the especial name of *Kote*. The requisites for the due celebration of this festival are goats—for the feast must be graced by an animal sacrifice—rice, ghee (butter), spices, and spirits. These being collected, the parties assemble in a room, the doors and windows of which must be so closed as to exclude all observation from without. The floor must be carefully cleaned, and then covered with an incrustation of cow-dung. In the centre, a square is drawn, with a mixture of turmeric and lime. Upon this square is spread a white sheet; and upon the sheet, the rice, after being boiled, is deposited. Upon the rice is placed the half of a cocoa-nut, filled with ghee; in which is inserted two wicks, lying across each other, each lighted at both ends, so as to afford four lights. If a cocoa-nut cannot be found, a vessel of dough of the same form will answer. This kind of lamp is occasionally made by all classes of people, and is called *chou mukh:* it is only in the Deccan, however, that the form of the lamp is an object of attention. In Hindostan they are less particular:

and there also the drawing of the square is omitted.

Upon the white sheet is now placed the consecrated pickaxe and the knife of the gang, with all the spirits brought for the feast. The selection of the goats is the next point; more than will be required are provided, in order that the goddess may have the advantage of a pick. Two are selected, black, and perfect in all their parts. They are bathed, washed, and made to face the west: and if they shake themselves lustily, to throw off the moisture from their bodies, this makes the Thugs happy, and seals the fate of the goats—they are immediately sacrificed, as having been accepted by Davy. If one only shakes himself, the omen is sufficient, and both are sacrificed—if neither of them, it is a sign that Davy has rejected both; and the party eat the rice and drink the spirits, but postpone the sacrifice to another day, regarding the feast in the light of a simple meal. This they do if any other bad omen is observed on that day, considering the goddess to be displeased with something.

The mode of sacrificing the goats varies; and the variations are not, like those affecting the square, and the form of the lamp, governed by locality: the custom is determined by the peculiar creed which the party of Thugs happen to profess. Mahometans cut the throats of the animals, during the repetition of a certain form of devotion: Hindoos strike off their heads. It has been mentioned, that the fate of these animals depends upon the receipt of a propitious sign from the goddess; and the duration of life in the rejected animals is involved in the same chance. If the desired sign be obtained by the honoured beasts shaking themselves with good will, not only are they sacrificed, but all the other goats purchased for the occasion, albeit unworthy of being devoted to the goddess, share the fate of their more illustrious fellows. They do not die with equal honour: the chosen pair ministers to the glory of the goddess of Destruction: the remainder die, but it is only to gratify the appetites of the Thug fraternity, by whom they are forthwith eaten. The withholding of the required sign, however, operates as a reprieve for the lives of all; and the meaner, as well as the nobler and more perfect animals, are permitted to live till a future day.

If the feast take place, a pit is dug, into which is thrown the skins, bones, and offal; for nothing brought in for this sacred feast must be seen by any living thing but a Thug eligible to partake of it. So important is care upon this point, and so fearful are the results which follow unfavourable omens at this sacrifice, that every part of the proceeding is watched with the most intense anxiety. If any man not a Thug see the lamps, or any part of the preparations; or if fire falls on the white sheet, and burns any part of it; or any animal touches the bones or offal; the leader of the gang must die within the year, and all the members be involved in some great calamity.

Secrecy is indispensable: when they are on an expedition, the Thugs must conceal themselves and their ceremonies by means of curtains, if they have not walls. After feasting, they must all wash their hands and faces over the pit, and then fill it up securely.

The expenses of this feast are defrayed commonly by subscription, when it is called the *Punchaetee Kote.* It is not confined to any particular season, but is most common during the Hooly or Dusera festivals, at which time it may take place on any day of the week; at other times, it is confined to Tuesdays and Fridays. Sometimes the feast is given by the leader or any individual member of a gang. No Thug is eligible to partake of it, in any part of India, till he has attained the rank of a Strangler; unless his family have been Thugs for at least two generations. The existence of contamination in the camp prevents its celebration at all.

The superstitions of the Thugs are all of Hindoo origin: yet Mahometans adopt them with a belief equally implicit, and a devotion equally ardent. The greater number of the Thugs in the South of

India are said to be Mahometans: not only do they profess to embrace the creed of Mecca, but, to a considerable extent, they follow it consistently. They marry, inherit, eat, and drink, according to the Koran: their devotions are statedly performed as the rule of Mahometan orthodoxy prescribes; and the Paradise to which their hopes are directed, is that pourtrayed by the cold, unspiritual, and sensual imagination of the false prophet to whom they profess allegiance: yet they pay divine honours to the impersonation of Destruction, which, in the eyes of all sound Mahometans, must be idolatry— a crime severely denounced in the Koran, and held by all good Mussulmans in abhorrence. These inconsistencies they find it hard to reconcile: sometimes they deny the worship of the goddess—the fact, however, is indisputable. At other times they seek to identify the patroness of the Thugs with a heroine of their own creed, to the great scandal of their brethren not initiated in the mysteries of Thuggee. Their mode of escaping the difficulties, in which they are involved by the inconsistency of their creed with their practice, is illustrated by a conversation held by Captain Sleeman with some Mahometan Thugs.

Q. (by Capt. S.) "Has Bhowanee (the goddess) been anywhere named in the Koran?"

Sahib. "No where."

Here (says Captain S.) a Mussulman Thug from Hindostan interposed; and said, he thought Bhowanee, and Fatima, the daughter of Mahommed, and wife of Alee, were one and the same person; and that it was Fatima who invented the use of the roomal, to strangle the great demon Rukut-beej-dana: which led to a discussion between him and some of my Mussulman native officers, who did not like to find the amiable Fatima made a goddess of Thuggee—an "Iphigenia in Tauris." The Thug was a sturdy wrangler; and, in the estimation of his associate Thugs, had, I think, the best of the argument.

Q. "Then has Bhowanee any thing to do with your Paradise?"

Sahib. "Nothing."

Q. "She has no influence upon your future state?"

Sahib. "None."

Q. "Does Mahommed, your prophet, anywhere sanction crimes like yours;—the murder in cold blood of your fellow-creatures, for the sake of their money?"

Sahib. "No."

Q. "Does he not say that such crimes will be punished by God in the next world?"

Sahib. "Yes."

Q. "Then do you never feel any dread of punishment hereafter."

Sahib. " Never: we never murder unless the omens are favourable: and we consider favourable omens as the mandates of the deity."

Q. " What deity?"

Sahib. " Bhowanee."

Q. " But Bhowanee, you say, has no influence upon the welfare, or otherwise, of your soul hereafter?"

Sahib. " None, we believe; but she influences our fates in this world; and what she orders in this world, we believe that God will not punish in the next."

The conjoint adoration of the deities of different and discordant creeds is neither new nor uncommon in the East. In the Old Testament, various instances are recorded, in which nations, as well as individuals, paid a divided homage to the True God and to a multiplicity of idols: and in various parts of India, the Mahometans, from having long been surrounded by a Hindoo population, have been led to adopt many of their opinions and practices. The principle, indeed, upon which this approximation is formed, is not peculiar to the East. Everywhere, time not only abates the fervour both of religious and sectarian zeal, but causes many of the distinctive marks of original difference to disappear, and tinges the entire mass with the colour of the party which, either from numbers or activity, acquires an ascendant. The natural tendency of man to superstition gives to that gloomy power, in any form, an extraordinary facility of access to his heart. The weak and the wicked alike flee to it for a refuge: the former, from a morbid apprehension of undefined evil; the latter, from the upbraidings of conscious guilt. To the one class, superstition presents the alluring prospect of perfect assurance, in place of the humble faith and hope which are the characteristics of genuine piety: to the other, she holds out the offer of peace of mind upon easier terms than true Religion proposes. It is not a subject for surprise, then, that, at all periods, the votaries of Superstition, in its multiform ramifications, should have far outnumbered the faithful adherents of Religious Truth: the errors of the understanding, and the depravity of the will, are continually furnishing their recruits to swell the myriad ranks of the army of Superstition.

The principle which assigns the distribution of good and evil, in this world, to an inferior divinity is not very dissimilar from one which, in Christian countries, has been maintained by grave writers;—which excludes the Superior Being from the ordinary course of human affairs, leaving them to chance and accident, and human passion; and confines His providence to an occasional interference in what are considered great emergencies in this life, and to the final retribution of good and evil in the life to come.

CHAP. VI.

THE outline which has been given of the general character and habits of the Thugs will now be best illustrated by reference to some of the details elicited by the inquiries of the European Authorities.

In 1833, several Thugs were put on trial, and convicted, before the Zillah Court in Benares.

The following are extracts from the report of the Session Judge to the Court of Nizamut Adawlut :—

" The prisoners are Thugs, and were concerned in three expeditions, during the month of Jeit 1240 Fuslee; corresponding to part of June and July, 1833, in which six persons were murdered.

" The Thanadar of Juggut Gunge, with the Foujdaree Nazis, and the spies Goplah and Bhuggoo, went to Rajah-ka-Tullao, described as a halting-place of the prisoners and others, who were proved to have purchased various articles of food from the grocers' shops, and to have slept there. Towards morning they took their departure, accompanied by a Mussulman traveller, and, leaving the high road at Sarai Mohun to the right, followed a pathway for about a mile, where, having found a convenient place, they strangled the traveller, and threw his body into a well. The Thanadar and his party proceeded to the well which was pointed out; and on examining the Goraits of the neighbouring village, it appeared that there had been a body taken out in the month of Jeit, which had been concealed by the Zemindar's orders all day in some sugar-canes, and at night thrown into the Sambhar Nullah: some bones were found in the nullah, which were declared to be human, and supposed to be those of the murdered traveller.

"The second Thuggee expedition occurred in the jurisdiction of the Kilia-Khonah Thannah. The shopkeepers there sold spices, &c. to some of the Thugs who passed the night at the Dhurm Salah of Bukt-Pooree at Kupuldhara. There were about five-and-twenty Thugs, and two Mussulmen travellers with them, with three bullocks. They all left before day-break; and having proceeded about a mile towards the Ganges, the two travellers were strangled, and their bodies thrown into the river.

"The third Thuggee excursion took place in Hurooah Thannah's jurisdiction. Three persons were strangled, and the bodies thrown into Hurdoo Dhobey's well; in searching which, three sculls, several human bones, and a pair of shoes, the latter evidently a sepoy's, were discovered.

" As the atrocious crime of Phansigare, or Thuggee, is fortunately very uncommon in this district, and no instance has occurred during the periods I have been resident at Benares, I shall submit, for the Court's consideration, the evidence of two of the witnesses, and likewise the confession of the prisoner Shumsherah ; which last was given before the magistrate, and affords, perhaps, a clearer insight into their proceedings.

" The first witness to the fact, in each of these cases, is Bhuggoo : his evidence, however, is so contradictory, and agrees so baldly with the deposition given before the magistrate, that I prefer sending the examination of the second witness, Kadir Khan, a Patan, son of Jumum Khan, inhabitant of Moujah Punnah, purgunah Moneah, Zillah Patna, aged forty-three years, formerly a cultivator, but for the last twenty-one years a Thug by profession.

" 'In the month of Aghun, 1240, he says, Fuslee, Shumsherah, Oozerah, Moradun, Bukus, Asmut, Mehar Ali, and myself, went on a Thuggee expedition to the westward, and reached the Oude territory. At Chand Pertaubpoor we met Chuta Thug, in company with a traveller who was afterwards strangled, and eleven rupees with two or four cloths found on him. We journeyed onto Allahabad, and thence eastward. Near Burount we met Goplah Beekah, and nine other Thugs, and they accompanied us to Mirza Morad's Serai. There we found Mohur Singh, a Jemadar of Thugs, with ten others, whose names I do not remember. We all went on together, and rested at night near the temple at Rajah-ka-Tullao. On the road we met a traveller, whom Mohur Singh entered into conversation with, and persuaded to join our party. At the last quarter of the night we renewed our march, and, quitting the high road near Serai, Mohur followed a pathway for about half a cose, and strangled the traveller. Seven rupees, with two or four cloths, were taken, and Goury and Mehar Ali threw the corpse into a well.

" 'After walking some distance in the direction of Benares, we overtook two Mussulmen travellers with three bullocks. They went in with us to our halting-place, the Dhurm Salah, at Kupuldharah. Towards daybreak we departed; and about a mile off, near the banks of the Ganges, Mohur Singh and Goury strangled the travellers. We found on them five rupees, a sword, and two or three pieces of cloths. Mohur Singh took all, and drove the bullocks on before us. Our people threw the bodies into the river. After taking some refreshment, we proceeded to Sydpoor: there Salaroo, a Burkundaz, recognised Mohur Singh, who, in consequence, gave him five rupees. The three bullocks were sent by Mohur Singh to his home. From Sydpoor we went to Kytee; and the next day to Rajghât. Very early the following morning we proceeded towards the west: it was then the month of Jeit, and the period of the Ghazymeean festival. When we reached a tank, we found two Sepoys and a Bearer sitting there. We drank toddy with them; and all went on together. Mohur Singh asked them where they came from, and whither they were going. They replied, "From the east towards the west." Mohur Singh said, "I am also going towards the west." In the evening, we halted at the Hurooah Bazar. When one quarter of the night only remained, we continued our journey, and went two miles on the Punch Cossy road, where there is a pucka well, with two mangoe-trees near it: there Moma and Imam Bux strangled the travellers; I standing by. Thirty rupees, ten pieces of cloths, and two brass pots, were found on them: there was also a horse and a mare. We were then twenty-five persons. Some of us threw the bodies into the well. My share was a doputta, and a rupee eight annas: the other Thugs had their proportion. I took the mare, and Mohur Singh the horse. From thence my companions and myself separated from the gang, and went home: the other Thugs likewise travelled in the direction of their homes. After being at home for some days, the Tomandar and Foujdaree Nazir of the city of Patna apprehended me. I was never taken up before, during the twenty-one years I have practised Thuggee. I have been in many excursions, in Oude and to the eastward; but excepting the three expeditions above alluded to, I have never done any thing in the Benares division. I have spent all my share of the plunder. The mare was taken from my house to the Patna Adawlut. There are only eight men connected with me in this business. Their names are, Moradhun, Bukus of Siveree, Shumsherah, Oozerah, Imam Bux of Khutary, Asmut, and Hunoman, a Brahmin of Jurrowah. Of these eight, Moradhun and myself are Sirdars. Mohur Singh has twenty-five men, and is a Sirdar. All the men were in these expeditions; but I cannot remember their names. We do not go armed: perhaps two may be armed. We strangle our victims generally; and never use a weapon, excepting in case of necessity. No wounds were inflicted on any of the victims of this district. Those who strangle receive an additional rupee.'

"The third witness, Goplah, son of Dyar, of the Lode caste, inhabitant of Muteepurwa, Zillah Cawnpore, aged twenty-six years said:—'A year ago, I left home alone, on a Thuggee expedition towards the east. When I reached Bhaugur Mow, in the Oude country, I met Kisseree Singh with twenty-five Thugs, and Bekram and Muhadut Jemadars with Mukdoom Bux and others. After travelling fifteen cose, we fell in with three travellers, whom Bekram, Mukdoom and Chudu strangled, and took their property. The bodies were thrown into a well. I had my share. Going by Meean Gunge and Hussun Gunge to Noel Gunge, we strangled five travellers. On arriving on Burount near Choby Bazar, Moradhun, Kadir, and Mohur Singh, Jemadars of Thugs, joined us with twenty-five men. Bekram and the other Oude Thugs returned thence. On the road from Mirza Mourad to Rajah-ka-Tullao, we met a Mussulman, who went with us to the latter place, where we rested at the Buneah's house near the temple, and, after taking some food, passed the night there. When the night was nearly over, we resumed our march towards Benares; and leaving the high road in a northern direction, struck into a pathway for a mile, until we came on a plain at some distance from a village. Mohur Singh strangled the traveller, and I and another threw the body into a well: we found on him seven rupees, a sword, two or four brass pots, and four or five cloths. In the division, my share was a turban. The cloths and pots were divided amongst us, and the rupees soon spent. We then came to Benares, and passed a day at the Serai Aurungabad. We crossed the Sepoy lines, and entered the Orderly Bazar, where we met two travellers with three bullocks. We inquired whence they came, and where they were going. They said from Hansy to Gorruckpore. Mohur Singh said, " I am on my way to Gorruckpore; come with us." We proceeded to Kupuldara, and put up at the Dhurm Salah for the evening. At the sixth hour of the night we renewed our journey. When we reached the Ganges east from Kupuldara, some of us seized the hands, and others the feet, of the travellers, whom Chutu and Imam Bux strangled: we then threw them into the river. Five rupees, a lotah, a sword, and a pair of pyjamahs, were taken. Mohur Singh took the three bullocks. We travelled afterwards to Sydpore, Kytee, and Rajghât, putting up at the Luckah Serai. The next day we went towards Sheopore; and stopping at Shunkur Talao, we drank some toddy. We saw two Sepoys and a Bearer sitting there; whom Mohur Singh asked where they were going, and whence they came. Their reply was, from Cuttack, and their destination Lucknow. We all went on to Sheopore; and from that place to Hurooah, where we rested at a Buneah's shop. In the latter part of the night we continued our march; and after walking a mile on the Punch Cossy road, Beeka, Bheegoo, and Moradhun, threw the travellers down, when Imam Bux, Mohur Singh, and Goury, strangled them. The others remained on the watch. Twenty-five rupees, a gold mohur, fifteen pieces of cloths, and twenty brass pots, were gained. Six men and a

Jemadar threw the bodies into a well. In the division of the plunder, a lotah, a merzai, and a rupee, were my share.'—The witness mentioned, that all the prisoners were Thugs, and concerned in the three expeditions that took place in the Benares division, with the exception of Asmut.

" The prisoner, Shumsherah, is an inhabitant of Purneah, Pergunnah Moneah, Zillah Patna, twenty-five years of age, of the weaver caste. Moradhun supported and protected him whilst a child: and whenever he went on a Thuggee excursion, the prisoner accompanied him.

" The deposition before the magistrate is as follows :—' In the month of Aghun, 1240 Fuslee, Moradhun, Kader Khan, Bukus, Oozerah, Meher Ali, Asmut, Imam Bux, and myself, proceeded on a Thuggee expedition. We strangled several persons in Oude, remaining there until the month of Maug; and then went to Allahabad, from whence we travelled, in an eastern direction, until we came to Burount. We found Goplah and Beeka there; and further on the road, Mohur Singh, with four other Thugs. We met a traveller as we proceeded. Mohur Sing, and his party, went on with him. We rested in the evening at Hunoman Chokey. When the night was nearly spent, we went on, and Huna strangled the traveller. Seventeen rupees, some cloths, and brass pots, were found on him, and the body was thrown into a well. I being the adopted pupil of Moradhun, he took my share. He gave me food only, and I was his follower. Proceeding on our march, we met a Mussulman travelling: Imam Bux attached himself to him. We halted for the night at Rajah-ka-Tullao; and towards morning recommenced our journey. Leaving the high road at Serai Mohun to the right, we followed a small pathway. After walking a mile, we came near a garden, where Imam Bux strangled the traveller. Ten rupees, a sword, two dhotees, a lotah, and some old cloths, were the plunder. Two or three men took the corpse, and threw it into a well. Near Benares we met two travellers, with three bullocks. Moradhun, Kadir Khan, Goplah, and Beeka, joined them; and in the evening we made Kupuldhara our resting-place, stopping at the Dhurm Salah. When one quarter of the night only remained, the march was resumed; and near the banks of the Ganges, about a mile off, Beeka and Unna strangled the travellers. I do not remember what plunder was obtained. Meher Ali, Moradhun, Kader Khan, and Beeka, threw the corpses into the river. We then went to Sydpore. A Burkundaz, Salaroo, recognised Mohur Singh, who, in consequence, gave him four rupees; and Moradhun sent the three bullocks, by Bukus, to his house. We afterwards returned to the village of Bettree; and, going by Chundwuk, arrived at Rajghât. Remaining there all night, we marched very early the next morning, in a western direction. After leaving the city, we met two Sepoys and a Bearer. Beeka entered into conversation with them, and they came on in our company. We halted at Hurooah Bazar. Towards day-break we resumed our route; and going about two miles on the Punch Cossy road, where there is a pucka well, with two mangoe-trees, Mohur Singh, Ramsuhoy, and Selwunt Rai, strangled the three travellers. They gained thirty-two rupees, some cloths and brass pots. The bodies were thrown into the well. The travellers had a horse and a mare with them: Kadir took the first, and Goplah the latter. We afterwards went to Burogong, where we divided the plunder; and separated, going to our respective homes. I have never strangled any one, but have aided in throwing bodies into wells. Eight annas is a very good remuneration for murdering a man. We often strangle a victim who is suspected of having two pice. We are unrestrained by any fears, in pursuing our vocation. We do not sell our plunder; but, when there is a large quantity, send it to our homes.'

"Bukus once accompanied Moradhun and others on a Thuggee expedition in Oude, and was with them two years; but has never practised in the Benares district, and is unjustly accused.

"Oozerah declares that he is innocent. He once found himself with Moradhun, &c., in Oude;

but ran away the moment he could, when he discovered his companions were Thugs.

" Meher Ali served Moradhun, as a grass-cutter, for five or six months. He acknowledged, before the magistrate at Patna, to having been his servant for the above number of years, and to having accompanied him in his Thuggee expeditions.

" Asmut was formerly called Dubery, alias Neeamut Ali, at present Asmut. He attributes his name being mentioned to a family dispute he had with the two brothers, Kadir Khan and Moradhun, with whom he is connected by marriage; and, of course, asserts his innocence. The depositions of Nanuk, Ramphul, Rujoo Singh, Balukgur, Purshad, Juggernat, Thakooree, Kudoo, Isseredyeal, Uchalall, and Matadyel, point out the halting-places of the Thugs in these expeditions; and the wells, &c. where the bones and other remains of the murdered persons were discovered."

The Court of Nizamut Adawlut sentenced four of the persons engaged in this transaction to be transported for life.

'The Thugs; or, Secret Murderers of India', Review of *Ramaseeana*, by W.H. Sleeman, *The Edinburgh Review*, or *Critical Journal* 64 (January 1837): 357–395.

Art. IV.—*Ramaseeana; or, a Vocabulary of the peculiar language used by the Thugs. With an Introduction and Appendix, descriptive of the system pursued by that Fraternity; and of the measures which have been adopted by the Supreme Government of India for its suppression.* 8vo. Calcutta: 1836.

It has often been said, and we fear with too much truth, that Indian subjects do not excite, in this country, an interest at all proportioned to their importance. We shall, however, be much surprised if what we now have to relate should fail to rouse the attention of the most sluggish reader.

We have to introduce to the knowledge of our countrymen a moral and political phenomenon, which is, perhaps, the most extraordinary that has ever existed in the world,—a phenomenon more striking than any thing that romancers have feigned touching the Old Man of the Mountain, or the Secret Tribunals of Germany;—a phenomenon, of which strange and appalling glimpses have been occasionally obtained, but of which the nature and extent have never, till the present time, been fully understood.

It appears, then, from the most overwhelming evidence, that there exists in India a vast fraternity of murderers, consisting of many thousands of persons;—that this fraternity has existed for many ages, and through many political revolutions;—that it has spread its ramifications over the whole of that vast country, from Cape Comorin to the Himalayas;—that it has flourished alike under Hindu, Mahomedan, and British rulers;—that it has every year destroyed multitudes of victims; and yet that its constitution —we may say its very being—have been quite unknown to the most active and vigilant English functionaries, and very imperfectly understood even by the native governments. It was indeed notorious, that gangs of thieves sometimes strangled travellers. It was notorious, that the members of these gangs were unusually expert at the operation of strangling; but that these gangs were merely small detached portions of a vast organized community, the members of which recognised each other as brethren in the remotest parts of India;—that these murders were all committed according to certain ancient and solemn forms, and were regarded by those who committed them, not as crimes, but as solemn rites, which it would have been sinful to omit—all this it was reserved for the present generation to discover. One of the many obligations which India owes to Lord William Bentinck, is the complete unveiling of this horrible and portentous system. The book now before us, is a collection of official papers, printed by the Indian Government for the information of its officers. No attempt has been made to digest into one connected statement the many interesting facts which these papers disclose. The book has not been published, and is, therefore, inaccessible to common readers; and even were it accessible to them, they would probably be repelled by the obscurity which is the effect of an utter want of arrangement. We think, therefore, that we shall certainly amuse them, and that we may perhaps instruct them, if we undertake to sum up the evidence on this extraordinary subject. We shall confine ourselves at present almost entirely to facts, and put off to another opportunity most of those curious speculations on human nature and on the frame of Indian society, to which the recent discoveries naturally lead.

The most interesting of the papers consists of a series of conversations with the captains of gangs, who have been admitted as king's evidence, from which we shall make liberal extracts.

These extraordinary people are known by the name of Thugs, and their profession is called Thuggee. They are divided into Burkas, or persons fully instructed in the art, and Kuboolas or novices. 'They consider a Burka as capable of forming a gang 'of Thugs out of the rude materials around him in any part of 'India; and a Thug who has arrived at this degree of proficiency 'in the art, ought not therefore to be left at large. A Kuboola, 'or Novice, they think, could do nothing if left to himself, and 'he might, therefore, be left at large without much danger to 'society, if he had no leader to join.'

These are by no means nominal distinctions. No Thug is allowed to take his degree as a Burka, or to assume the office of strangler, until he has been on many expeditions, and acquired the requisite courage and insensibility by slow degrees.

'They are first employed as scouts; then as sextons; then as shumseeas or holders of hands; and lastly as Bhurtotes or stranglers. When a man feels that he has sufficient courage and insensibility for the purpose, he solicits the oldest and most renowned Thug of the gang to make him his cheyla, or disciple. The Thug agrees to become his gooroo, or spiritual preceptor; and when the gang falls in with a man of respectability but not much strength, fitted for the purpose, he tells the gooroo that he is prepared, with his permission, to try his hands upon him. While the traveller is asleep with the gang at their quarters, the gooroo takes his disciple into a neighbouring field, followed by three or four old members of the gang. On reaching the spot chosen, they all face to the direction the gang intends to move, and the gooroo says, "Oh Kalee, Kunkalee, Bhudkalee. Oh Kalee, Mahakalee, Calcutta Walee. If it seemeth to thee fit that the traveller now at our lodging should die by the hands of this thy slave, vouchsafe us the Thibaoo." If they get the auspice on the right, within a certain time (half an hour), it signifies her sanction; but if they have no sign, or the pilhaoo (or sign on the left), some other Thug must put the traveller to death, and the candidate for honour wait for another time.

'Davey's sanction having been conveyed in the Thibaoo, they return to their quarters, and the gooroo takes a handkerchief, and facing to the west, ties the knot at one end of it with a rupee or other piece of silver inserted. This knot they call the Goor-knat, or classic knot, and no man who has not been thus ordained by the high priest, is permitted to tie it. The disciple receives it respectfully from the high priest in his right hand, and stands over the victim, with a shumseea, or holder of hands by his side. The traveller is roused on some pretence or other, and the disciple passes the handkerchief over his neck, at the signal given by the leader of the gang, and strangles him with the aid of his shumseea. Having finished his work, he bows down before his gooroo, and touches his feet with both hands, and does the same to all his relations and friends present, in gratitude for the honour he has attained. He opens the knot after he has heard or seen the Thibaoo, or auspice on the right, takes out the rupee and gives it, with all the other silver he has, to his gooroo, as a nuzur; and the gooroo adding what money he has at the time, purchases a rupee and a quarter's worth of sugar for the Tuponee, and lays out the rest in sweetmeats. The Tuponee sacrifice is then performed under the neem, the mango, or the byr, if they are available, and if not, under any other tree, except the babul, the sirsa (mimosa seris), and the reonja. The new disciple now takes his seat among the Bhurtotes around the carpet, and receives his share of the consecrated sugar; and the sweetmeats are distributed to all the members of the gang, of whatever grade. On his return home after the expedition, he gives a feast to his gooroo and his family, and, if he has the means, to all his relations; and he presents his gooroo with an entire new suit of clothes for himself, and one for his wife, and others for his relations, if he can afford it. The gooroo, after a certain interval, returns the compliment to him and his family, and the relation between them is ever after respected as the most sacred that can be formed. A Thug will often rather betray his father than the gooroo by whom he has been knighted.'

The Thugs travel along the roads under various assumed characters, in parties varying from ten or twelve to several hundreds. They appear as traders, as pilgrims, as sepoys seeking or returning from service; and sometimes one of their number figures as a Raja, with all the necessary equipments of tents, carriage, &c., and the rest act the part of his obsequious followers. If the gang is numerous, they are divided into separate parties, who follow each other at some distance, or, taking different routes, rendezvous at an appointed place in advance. Their victims are almost always travellers. The most expert members of the gang are employed to collect information, and insinuate themselves into the confidence of the travellers whom they find at the resting places, or overtake on the road. They usually propose to them to join company for mutual safety; and if the traveller suspects one party, he soon falls in with another, who pretend to enter into his feelings of distrust. A person is sent before to select a proper place for the murder, and scouts are employed to prevent intrusion. The travellers are generally induced to sit down under pretence of resting themselves, and they are strangled at once on a given signal. The bodies are then buried, after having been mangled to expedite dissolution, and to prevent their swelling and causing cracks in the ground. Two Thugs are employed in the murder of each individual, one of whom holds his legs or hands, while the other applies the noose. If a traveller have a dog, it is also killed, lest the faithful animal should cause the discovery of the body of its murdered master.

The best way, however, of conveying an adequate idea of the mode in which the murders are committed, will be to select some of the most striking instances before us. The first we shall extract will show the confidence the Thugs repose in the power of concealment which belongs to their system. 'There is darkness under the lamp,' says the Hindustani proverb; and such would, indeed, appear to be the case, when a whole family with their servants could be murdered under the circumstances about to be detailed, without any discovery taking place.

'We fell in,' said Chutter, a leading Thug, 'with the Moonshee and his family at Chupara, between Nagpore and Jubulpore; and they came on with us to Lucknadown, where we found that some companies of a native regiment under European officers were expected the next morning. It was determined to put them all to death that evening, as the Moonshee seemed likely to keep with the companies. Our encampment was near the village, and the Moonshee's tent was pitched close to us. In the afternoon some of the officers' tents came on in advance, and were pitched on the other side, leaving us between them and the village. The servants were all busily occupied in pitching them. Noor Khan and his son Sadee Khan and a few others, went, as soon as it became dark, to the Moonshee's tent, and began to sing and play upon a guitar, as they had been accustomed to do. During this time some of them took up the Moonshee's sword on pretence of wishing to look at it. His wife and children were inside listening to the music. The Jhirnee or signal was given, but at this moment the Moonshee saw his danger, called out murder, and attempted to rush through, but was seized and strangled. His wife hearing him, ran out with the infant in her arms, but was seized by Ghubboo Khan, who strangled her and took the infant. The other daughter was strangled in the tent. The grooms were at the time cleaning their horses, and one of them seeing his danger, ran under the belly of his horse, and called out murder; but he was soon seized and strangled, as well as all the rest.

'Q.—How, did not the servants and others, who were pitching the tents close by, hear these calls for help?

'*Chutter*.—As soon as the signal was given, those of the gang who were idle, began to play and sing as loud as they could; and two vicious horses were let loose, and many ran after them calling out as loud as they could; so that the calls of the Moonshee and his party were drowned.'

The next is the murder of an open-hearted old soldier, and the contrast is so striking between his easy simplicity and the wily villany of his Thug companions, as to excite our sympathy strongly on his behalf.

'It was on my return,' said Sheik Inaent, another noted Thug, 'from the first expedition which I made with my father to the Duckun, when I was fifteen years of age, and about thirty-five years ago. We were a gang of about eighty or ninety Thugs, under my father, Hinga, and some of the Deccan chiefs, lodged in the Mausoleum outside of the town of Elichpore. Two of our leaders, Gumboo and Laljoo, on going into the bazar, fell in with the grooms of the Nawab Subjee Khan, the uncle of the Nawab of Bhopaul, Wuzeer Muhommud Khan, who told them that their master had been with his son and his two hundred horse in the service of the Nizam at Hydrabad; and having had a quarrel with his son, he was now on his way home to Bhopaul. They came back and reported; and Dulele Khan and Khuleel Khan, and other leaders of fame, went and introduced themselves to the Nawab, pretending that they had been to the Deccan with horses for sale, and were now on their way back to Hindostan. He was pleased with their address and appearance, and invited them to return the next day, which they did; and the following day he set out with as many of our gang as it was thought safe to exhibit. He had two grooms, two troopers, and a slave girl, two horses, and a mare with a wound in the neck, and a pony. The slave girl's duty was to prepare for him his daily portion of subzee, and he told us that he had got the name of Subzee Khan, from the quantity of that intoxicating drug which he was accustomed to drink.

'We came on together three stages, and during the fourth stage we came to an extensive jungle this side of Dhoba, and in the Baitool district; and on reaching a water course at about nine o'clock, Khuleel said, "Khan Sahib, we have had a fatiguing journey, and we had better rest here, and take some refreshment." "By all means," said the Nawab, "I feel a little fatigued, and will take my subzee here." He dismounted, laid his sword and shield upon the ground, spread his carpet, and sat down. Dulele and Khuleel sat down by his side, while the girl was preparing his potion, of which he invited these two men, as our supposed chiefs, to partake; and the grooms were engaged with the horses, and the troopers were smoking their pipes at a distance. It had been determined that the Nawab should be first secured, as he was a powerful man, and if he had a moment's warning he would certainly have cut down some of the gang before they could secure him. Laljoo also went and sat near him, while Gomanee stood behind, and seemed to be much interested in the conversation. All being now ready, the signal was given, and the Nawab was strangled by Gomanee, while Laljoo and Dulele held his legs. As soon as the others saw the Nawab secured, they fell upon his attendants, and all were strangled, and their bodies were buried in the bed of the water course. On going back to Ellichpore, Gomanee sold the Nawab's shield for eight rupees, but it was worth so much more that the people suspected him, and came to our camp to search for him. Our spies brought us timely notice, and we concealed him under the housings of our horses.'

The last instance we shall give is, the Sutrooh, or sixty soul* affair, which, besides the surprising number of people who were instantaneously put to death, furnishes a good illustration of the patience with which the Thugs follow up their victims, until they find a fit opportunity to execute their abominable purpose.

'*Dorgha.*—After the capture of Gawilgur by General Wellesley (Duke of Wellington), it was restored to the Nagpore Rajah, who appointed Ghureeb Sing to the command of the fortress. Anxious to get some good soldiers from Hindostan to garrison it, he sent his younger brother, Ghyan Sing, with a number of followers, and a large sum of money, to raise them in the Oude country and districts between the Ganges and Jumna rivers.

'Ghyan Sing and his party passed through Nagpore, and came to Jubulpore in the month of June, while we were there concentrated from the different parts into which we had extended our expeditions that season. His party consisted of fifty-two men, seven women, and a Brahman boy, then about four years of age. Some of our gangs lodged in the town, some in the cantonments among the troops, and some were encamped at the tank of Adhar, two or three miles from the town, on the road to Mirzapore. As soon as we heard of the arrival of this party from the Deccan, every party of Thugs deputed some of its most respectable members to mix with them in the town and win their confidence. At first they tried to separate them into different parties to proceed by different roads, but though they had collected together at different times and places on the road, it was found impossible to separate any part of them from Ghyan Sing; and we agreed to unite all our gangs, and to lead the party by the most unfrequented roads till we might find a place convenient for the murder of the whole at once.

'On reaching Sehora, we persuaded them to quit the high-road through Belehree and Myhere, and take that through Chundeea and the old fort Bundoogur, which leads through very extensive tracts of jungle and uninhabited country. We went with them through all this country, however, without finding what we considered a fitting time and place, and reached Rewah, winning more and more upon their confidence every day. From Rewah we went to Simareea, and from that place to a small village half way to Chitterkote, called by us the Burwala Gow, from a large Indian fig-tree (Bur) that stood near it. Thence we sent on people, as usual, to select a place for the murder, and they found one about two coss and a half distant, in a very extensive jungle, without a human habitation for many miles on either side. We persuaded the party to set out soon after midnight; and as they went along, we mana-

* The Thugs designate remarkable affairs by the number of persons killed. The Chaleesrooh, or forty-soul affair, is also famous.

ged to take our appointed places, two Thugs by every traveller, and the rest in parties of reserve at different intervals along the line, every two managing to keep the person they were appointed to kill, in conversation. On reaching the place chosen, the signal was given at several different places, beginning with the rear party, and passing on to that in front; and all were seized and strangled except the boy. It was now near morning, and too late to admit of the bodies being securely buried; we made a temporary grave for them in the bed of the river, covered them over with sand, and went on with the boy and the booty to Chitterkote, intending to send back a large party the next night, and have the bodies securely buried. The rains had begun to set in, and after the murders it rained very heavily all the day. The party, however, went back, but found that the river had risen and washed away all the bodies except two or three, which they found exposed, and pushed into the stream to follow the rest.

'Q.—What became of the boy?

'*Dorgha.*—He was brought up by Mungul Brahmun, brother of Laljoo, and having taken to the trade of Thuggee, he was last year sent to the black water from Saugor.'

There is another tragedy connected with Gawilgur, which is of old date, and has not been equally well investigated. Still, the features of it are so extraordinary, that we cannot forbear mentioning it.

'In making the above inquiry,' Captain Robertson observes, 'I was informed of a still more frightful murder, which took place under Gawilgur, a very few years before, of five hundred recruits, that had come from some place for Gawilgur, and were pitched in tents for some reason or other below the fort. Somehow or other a quantity of treasure for the fort, for the night halted in this camp, and shortly after about one thousand, of apparently discharged sipahees, came up, said they were from Hindostan, and wanted service, and encamped at night in the same place, but in the morning there were none to be found of the latter. The rest were all laying strangled, and the treasure gone. People were sent all over the country, but none of the Thugs were caught.'

Sometimes, but very rarely, the Thugs are obliged to depart from their rule of putting their victims to death by strangling. This was the case in an affair in which they obtained a booty of £20,000 sterling. The circumstances are thus narrated by them.

'*Moklal.*—It gave us a great deal of trouble, as the dollars were laden on camels. They went fast, and afraid to appear near to them in a body, we several times lost all trace of them. We first fell in with them at Burhanpore. Ours was only one of three great parties that went from Bundlecund, Gwalior, and Saugor, that year to Kandeish; and it consisted of about one hundred and sixty Thugs, concentrating upon the treasure party. At Burwaha ghat on the Nerbudda river, we found them disputing with the custom-house officers about the payment of duties; and stating the hardship of being obliged to expose the value of their charge in an unsettled country. We paid duties for ourselves and our six ponies; and, leaving a few scouts, passed over the river, and went on to the small deserted village of Naen, in the midst of a jungly waste. Here we waited till the treasure party came up, consisting of eight men, mounted on camels, and armed with matchlocks, and a merchant, by name Futteh Alee, who had joined them on the road, in the hope of being more secure in their company than alone. It was about nine o'clock in the morning when they reached the place. The signal was given—we rushed in upon the camels, seized them by their bridles, and made them sit down by beating them with sticks. The men were seized and killed; some strangled, some stabbed with spears, and some cut down with swords. Futteh Alee was pulled off his pony and strangled. We transferred the treasure to our ponies; threw the bodies into a ravine, and went on for three days without halting anywhere, as we knew we should be immediately pursued. After we had got beyond danger, we rested and divided the booty, setting aside the proper share for the temple of Davey at Bindachul, near Mirzapore.'

In Bengal, which is much intersected by rivers, the plan is modified to suit the circumstances of the country. The practice there is to inveigle travellers on board pretended passage-boats, which are manned entirely by Thugs, and then to strangle them and throw the bodies into the river. Several of these boats follow each other at short intervals, so that if the traveller escapes one snare, he may fall into another. But as every body knows his own trade best, we shall leave the Thugs to tell their own story.

'The principal men of the gang, or the shrewdest of them, go along the roads, each having a servant carrying his bundle, and proceeding towards the ghat where his boat is to be found, whether going up or down the river. When a traveller overtakes him, he learns whither he is going, pretends to be ignorant of the road, to be going to the same place with the traveller, but to be entirely unacquainted with it, and anxious to have somebody to instruct him. If the traveller had not intended to go by water, the Thug soon pretends to be much tired, and wishes that he were near a boat. The traveller expresses the same wish, and they agree to diverge from the road to the river. Coming to the ghat, the Thug pretends that he is a good hand at a bargain, and is allowed to agree for a passage for both. He beats down the master of his own boat, after a good deal of disputing, to half-price, and the traveller is much pleased, and expresses his gratitude; they embark, and the traveller is killed as soon as they get away from other boats. If the traveller suspects or dislikes the first man, he soon falls in with the inveigler of another boat, who learns it by a sign, and pretends to enter into the traveller's feelings, and anxiety to throw off the first, who on some pretence remains behind, while his friend takes on the traveller to the other boat, further on than his own, where he is disposed of. They are much more numerous than we are. I have not heard of more than about thirty families of Mooteeas, and the Lodahas are not much above two hundred men, but the Bongoos are very numerous I have heard.'

The following may be taken as a fair specimen of this kind of Thuggee.

'We joined Jypaul at the Mormakeya ghat, where he had two boats at the different ghats, three or four miles from each other. Jhoulee Khan brought two travellers to the boat which Jypaul commanded in person, and Bhowur Khan and I embarked with them. As soon as we had all got on board, Jypaul said in Ramasee, "Let the Boras (Thugs) separate themselves from the Beetoos (travellers);" and we did so, leaving the two travellers together. Four men were on the bank, pulling along the boat, one was at the helm, acting at the same time as the Bykureea or spy, and seven of the gang were below with us and the travellers. 'We had got on about a coss, when the Bykureea at the helm seeing all clear, called out "Bhugna ko pawn do;" "give my sister's son pawn." This was their mode of giving the signal, and the two travellers were strangled. After strangling them, they broke their spinal bones *thus*, by putting their knees upon their backs, and pulling up their heads and shoulders. After doing this, they pushed them out of a kind of window in the side. Every boat has two of these windows, one on each side, and they put the bodies out of that towards the river. They break the spinal bones to prevent all chance of the people recovering and giving evidence against them. We generally stab the dead bodies through on both sides under the arm pits; but they are afraid to cut or stab the body, lest there should be signs of blood upon the water, as the corpses pass other boats that are following them on the river.'

The Thugs are forbidden by their rules to kill women of any description, and either men or women of the following classes—fukeers, bards, musicians by profession, dancing men or women, washerwomen, sweepers, oil-venders, blacksmiths, and carpenters, when found together, maimed or leprous persons, men with cows, and Ganges water-carriers, while they have the Ganges water actually with them; but if their pots are empty they are not exempted. These exceptions, however, are not made, as has been supposed, out of compassion, but from a feeling which we shall explain hereafter, and which is the strangest part of this strange system. The Thugs date all their misfortunes from their murder of a native lady, whom they call the Kalee Beebee, or black lady, who was proceeding to Hyderabad with a sheet of cloth of gold, for the tomb of a brother of Sulabut Khan. Since that, the northern Thugs have murdered women as well as men; but those south of the Nerbudda adhere to their primitive usage in this respect.

The extent to which the natural feelings of humanity have been extinguished in these miscreants, is perfectly astonishing. A party of them accompanied Newal Singh, a Jemadar in the Nizam's service, and his family, more than two hundred miles,—were on the most intimate terms with them for about twenty days,—and received essential favours from them. Once Newal Singh, not knowing them to be Thugs, procured their release, when they were imprisoned on a charge of setting a house on fire, in which they had lodged; and on another occasion his two daughters of eleven and thirteen years of age, saved them from detection by sitting upon some plundered silk, whilst they were searched by the police. The whole gang hesitated; and one party separated from the main body rather than be present at the murder. But will it be believed what was the cause of their demur? Not any dislike to sacrifice people to whom they owed so much, and with whom they had consorted on such friendly terms—that never entered into their minds—but the circumstance of Newal Singh having but one arm. He and all his family were put to death.

The Thugs also occasionally preserve young children of both sexes, and adopt them as their own; and sometimes young women of a riper age are saved to become the wives of the murderers of their parents. This practice often gives occasion to lamentable scenes, of which the following may be mentioned as examples.

'The signal was given, and all, except the two boys, were seized and strangled by the people who had been appointed for the purpose, and were now at their posts ready for action. The boys were taken by Jowahir and Kehree, who intended to adopt them as their sons: and the bodies of the twenty-five persons were all thrown into a ditch, and covered over with earth and bushes. On seeing the bodies thrown into the ditch, Jowahir's boy began to cry bitterly; and finding it impossible to pacify or keep him quiet, Jowahir took him by the legs, dashed his brains against a stone, and left him on the ground, while the rest were busily occupied in collecting the booty.'

* * * * * * * *

'By the time we reached the appointed place, the Bhurtotes and Shumseeas had all on some pretext or other got close by the side of the persons whom they were appointed to strangle; and on reaching the spot, the signal was given in several places at the same time, and thirty-eight out of forty were seized and strangled. The daughter of Gunga Tewarree was a very handsome young woman, and Punchum, one of our Jemadars, wished to preserve her as a wife for his son Buckholee. But when she saw her mother and father strangled, she screamed, and beat her head against the stony ground, and tried to kill herself. Punchum tried in vain to quiet her, and promised to take great care of her, and marry her to his own son who would be a great chief; but all was in vain. She continued to scream, and at last Punchum put the handkerchief round her neck and strangled her. The widow of Alfie's brother was strangled, but her daughter, a girl about three years of age, was preserved by Kosul Jemadar, who married her to his own son Hunnee Rae Brahmun, by whom she had two sons, one of whom is still living, and about ten or eleven years of age. Since the death of Kosul and Hunee Rae she has lived with her husband's mother.'

* * * * * * * *

'*Chutter*. Ghubboo Khan strangled the mother while her infant was in her arms, and he determined to keep and adopt the child; but after the bodies had all been put into the grave, Dhunnee Khan urged him to kill the child also, or we should be seized on crossing the Nerbudda valley. He threw the child living in upon the dead bodies, and the grave was filled up over it.

'Q. And the child was buried alive?

'*Chutter*. Yes.'

As the existence of Thuggee has been discovered at different times and in different parts of India, efforts have been made for its suppression. Mr Wright, magistrate of Chittoor, formerly made great exertions for this purpose in the south, and Messrs Halhed and Stockwell in the north of India. A very interesting paper was even published by Dr Sherwood of the Madras establishment, in the thirteenth volume of the *Asiatic Researches* on the subject, of which we have made occasional use. The full extent of the evil, however, was not then known; and whilst our active magistrates flattered themselves that they had put a stop to the practice, it was really only temporarily suspended in their own neighbourhood. A system which embraced the whole of India could not be suppressed by a few partial inroads upon it. The dispersion of the gangs had the usual effect of a persecution which does not go the length of entire eradication. The scattered Thugs formed numerous separate gangs; and, although the number of raw recruits whom they enlisted contributed in the end to their downfall, yet its immediate effect was greatly to increase the number of victims.

At last, the disclosures which were made on the occasion of the apprehension of a large gang of Thugs by Major Borthwick, in Malwa, in 1831, attracted Lord William Bentinck's attention; and a system was organised by him for the general suppression of this monstrous evil. Jubbulpoor was fixed as the centre of operations. Captain Sleeman was appointed superintendent, with a number of European assistants, and the co-operation of the native states was engaged. The plan of proceeding is founded on an accumulation of evidence given by Thug approvers. Two or three of the members of every gang which is seized, are admitted as king's evidence, and they are immediately called on to dictate a narrative of all the expeditions in which they have ever served,—mentioning the individuals with whom they were associated; and their authentic testimony is then considered as closed. The trials depend upon the concurrence of a number of depositions, the originals of which were taken in different parts of India, from different persons, without a possibility of previous intercommunication;—upon the recognition of the prisoner by the witnesses, to each of whom he is shown in a crowd of other people;—and upon the confirmation of the evidence by the discovery of the bodies in the places indicated. Each of the assistants has a section of India allotted to him, within which he is responsible for the apprehension of these miscreants, with the help of the approvers and of the accumulated evidence; and as the mass of information is rapidly becoming more and more complete, we may hope that every professional Thug in India will soon be known and secured. Up to October 1835, 1562 persons had been committed on the charge of Thuggee; of whom 382 had been hanged, and 986 transported or imprisoned for life.

In 1834 these operations were threatened with a severe check, which was happily averted by Lord William Bentinck's firmness. Maun Singh, the Rajah of Joudpoor, pleaded the right of granting asylum, and refused to give up the Thugs who had taken refuge in his territory; but he was informed that he could not be permitted to make his country the headquarters, whence these bands of assassins might carry on their attacks against all the neighbouring states. On his persisting, an army was assembled against him, and he quietly submitted. The power which put down the Pindaree system was alone equal to the suppression of Thuggee. Occasions like these afford the best illustrations of the advantages of our supremacy in India. Even if the requisite public spirit and intelligence were not wanting, the native states are incapable, from mutual jealousy and distrust, of combining together for the accomplishment of any object of general interest. At this point, the supreme power steps in;—explains to subordinate allies the extent of the evil, and the nature of the remedies which ought to be applied;— collects for one common effort the resources of the whole of India, and directs that effort by European intelligence, energy, and perseverance.

This is, indeed, a noble instrument of beneficence, but much credit is also due to the hand which has so effectually applied it. The grand characteristic of Lord William Bentinck's measures is, that they were directed to the permanent benefit of the *mass of the people.* Hence the dislike with which he is regarded by the privileged few, and the veneration in which his name is held by the people of India. No renown was likely to attend the suppression of Thuggee. There were no mounted hordes to be subdued by brilliant military achievements. The work could be performed only by the silent operation of uninteresting judicial proceedings. The ruling class in India, who are the dispensers of European fame, were not concerned in the matter. The Thugs had never molested them. They once held a consultation on the subject, and resolved against ever attacking Europeans, for three reasons; one of which was, that Europeans generally carry pistols when on a journey; the second, that they seldom carry money; and the third, that if they were molested, such a storm would be raised as must end in the destruction of the association. In this they judged quite correctly. If a single civilian or military man had been thugged, thuggee would have been abolished long ago; and the Governor-general who accomplished it would have had his praises sung from John O'Groat's House to Land's End.

This is one of the evils of our anomalous position in India. The character of a ruler is principally determined by the way in which the interests of the European residents are affected by his measures. Hence a Governor-general may be held up to reprobation in Europe for the very reason for which he is entitled to praise,—because he consults the interest of the many in preference to that of the few. The remedy for this state of things, as far as it admits of a remedy, is to unite all interests by subjecting the natives and the European settlers to common laws. Indian governors will then no longer be distracted between the interests of the powerless many, and the powerful few; and European energy will unite with native acuteness and local knowledge in improving institutions in which the welfare of all will be equally concerned.

We think it likely that our readers are by this time sufficiently interested in the Thugs to wish to know something about their origin. Seneca, who had himself been in Egypt, mentions 'those 'robbers whom the Egyptians call Philetas (fondlers), who em-'brace merely with a view to strangle.'

> '——— Under fair pretence of friendly ends,
> Baited with reasons not unplausible,
> Wind them into the easy hearted man,
> And *hug* them into snares.'

It is not, however, our intention to commence a disquisition upon the striking points of resemblance between ancient Egypt and India; or to trace a supposed emigration of the Philetæ from the banks of the Nile to the shores of Western India. All we mean to suggest is, that as a system nearly allied to Thuggee prevailed at an early period in a country closely connected with India, it is not improbable that Thuggee itself has an equally remote origin.

Thevenot is the first European author who notices the Thugs. He says—

'Though the road I have been speaking of from Delhi to Agra be tolerable, yet hath it many inconveniences. One may meet with tigers, panthers, and lions upon it, and one had best also have a care of robbers, and above all things not to suffer any body to come near one upon the road. The cunningest robbers in the world are in that country. They use a certain slip with a running noose, which they can cast with so much sleight about a man's neck, when they are within reach of him, that they never fail, so that they strangle him in a trice. They have another cunning trick also to catch travellers with. They send out a handsome woman upon the road, who with her hair dishevelled seems to be all in tears, sighing and complaining of some misfortunes which she pretends has befallen her. Now, as she takes the same way that the traveller goes, he easily falls into conversation with her, and finding her beautiful, offers her his assistance, which he accepts; but he hath no sooner taken her up behind him on horseback, but she throws the snare about his neck and strangles him, or at least stuns him, until the robbers (who lie hid) come running in to her assistance, and complete what she hath begun. But besides that, there are men in those quarters so skilful in casting the snare, that they succeed as well at a distance as near at hand; and if an ox or any other beast belonging to a caravan run away, as sometimes it happens, they fail not to catch it by the neck.'

This may have been all true in the 16th century; but if so, a considerable change has since taken place in the habits of the order. The sash has been substituted for the noose, as being less open to detection; and the Thugs who have settled habitations, seldom permit their wives to accompany them on their expeditions. The substitution of a more secret method of strangling for the lasso, is what might have been expected in the progress of improvement.

The Thugs themselves arrogate very high antiquity for their profession; and one proof which they allege in confirmation of their claim is too remarkable to be passed over. We shall give it in their own words:—

'Q.—You told Mr Johnstone the traveller, while he was at Saugor, that the operations of your trade were to be seen in the caves of Ellora?

'*Feringeea.*—All! every one of the operations is to be seen there: in one place you see men strangling: in another burying the bodies: in another carrying them off to the graves. There is not an operation in Thuggee that is not exhibited in the caves of Ellora.

'*Dorgha.*—In those caves are to be seen the operations of every trade in the world.

'*Chotee.*—Whenever we passed near, we used to go and see these caves. Every man will there find his trade described, however secret he may think it; and they were all made in one night.

'Q.—Does any person besides yourselves consider that any of these figures represent Thugs?

'*Feringeea.*—Nobody else; but all Thugs know that they do. We never told anybody else what we thought about them. Every body there can see the secret operations of his trade, but he does not tell others of them; and no other person can understand what they mean. They are the works of God. No human hands were employed upon them. That every body admits.

'Q.—What particular operations are there described in figures?

'*Sahib Khan.*—I have seen the Sotha (inveigler) sitting upon the same carpet with the traveller, and in close conversation with him, just as we are when we are worming out their secrets. In another place the strangler has got his handkerchief over his neck, and is strangling him; while another, the Chumochee, is holding him by the legs. These are the only two operations that I have seen described.

'*Nasir.*—These I have also seen, and there is no mistaking them. The Chumochee has close hold of the legs, and is pulling at them thus, while the Bhurtote is tightening the handkerchief round his neck, thus!

'Q.—Have you seen no others?

'*Feringeea.*—I have seen these two, and also the Lughas carrying away the bodies to the grave, in this manner, and the sextons digging the grave with the sacred pick-axe; all is done just as if we had ourselves done it; nothing could be more exact.

'Q.—And who do you think could have executed this work?

'*Feringeea.*—It could not have been done by Thugs, because they would never have exposed the secrets of their trade; and no other human being could have done it. It must be the work of the gods: human hands could never have performed it.

'Q.—And supposing so, you go and worship it?

'*Sahib Khan.*—No. We go to gratify curiosity, and not to worship; we look upon it as a Mausoleum; a collection of curious figures cut by some Demons, who knew the secrets of all mankind, and amused themselves here in describing them.

'*Hurnagur.*—We Hindoos go for the same purpose. We never go to worship. We consider it as a Pantheon of unknown gods.'

Notwithstanding the alleged antiquity of the profession, the Thugs to the north of the Nerbudda cannot trace their own pedigree higher than the era of the first race of Mahomedan kings of Dehli. Their tradition is, that their ancestors, who were then divided into seven clans, as their descendants still are, used to infest the roads in the neighbourhood of the capital, until they drew upon themselves the anger of an emperor of the house of Ghoree, by murdering one of his domestics, who was in league with them, and who threatened to betray them with a view to extort more money than they thought reasonable. On this, they were expelled from Dehli. The majority of them retired to Agra; and ultimately to the strong country at the junction of the Jumna, the Chumbul and the Kalee Sinde, which continued to be their headquarters until they were driven away by Mr Halhed in the year 1812. These seven clans are the original trunk upon which all the Thug associations to the north of the Nerbudda have been grafted. They were originally all Mahomedans; but for a long time past Mahomedans and Hindus have been indiscriminately associated in the gangs; the former class, however, still predominating. Their numbers are kept up by descent (the profession being, as is usual in India, hereditary), by adoption, and occasionally, but not often, by the admission of qualified adults.

The Thugs to the south of the Nerbudda boast a purer descent. They can trace back the trade of Thuggee in their families for more generations, and have adhered with greater strictness to the rules of their profession than those who are of Dehli origin. They also refuse to intermarry with the famlies of the latter,—saying, they are of lower caste, and formerly 'drove 'bullocks and were itinerant tradesmen.' This point was warmly disputed by the northern and southern Thugs before Captain Sleeman. It was admitted by some of the northern men that, at their funerals, the women who bring the water, chant the occupations of the ancestors of the deceased, in a manner which shows that they were originally descended from gangs of wandering Mussulmans, who followed armies, and lived in the suburbs of cities and in the wild wastes, and that their pretensions to higher descent were unfounded. Others acknowledged, that at marriages an old matron will sometimes repeat as she throws down the toolsee—* 'Here's to the spirits of those who once led bears and monkeys; 'to those who drove bullocks, and marked with the godnee;† and 'those who made baskets for the head;' but others, who were more zealous for the honour of their tribe, insisted that these were only disguises assumed by their ancestors to enable them to practise their trade in greater safety.

It is admitted on all hands, that two of the original seven clans of northern Thugs, which did not, like the others, settle at Agra after their expulsion from Dehli, retain their wandering habits to this day; and there seems reason to suspect, that most of the Gipsy tribes who are to be found in all parts of India, but are most numerous to the north and west, practise Thuggee as occasion offers. On this part of the subject we may refer to the following remarkable passages in the conversations.

'Q.—Do not the Brinjaras often perpetrate murder in their encampments?

'*Feringeea.*—Just before the twenty-six of my gang were taken by you at Bhilsa, and before Zolfukar joined us, we were cooking our dinner in the afternoon at a village three coss this side of Sehore, when five travellers came up on their way to Bhilsa. We tried to prevail upon them to wait for us, but they went on, saying they should spend the night at Hirora, a village four coss further on. We made sure of securing them at Hirora, and remained where we were to dine. We

---

* Ocymum sanctum. Tulsee was a nymph beloved by Krishna, and by him turned into this plant.

† Needle used in tattooing.

reached Hirora about nine at night, and searched all the village in vain for the travellers. We knew that they must either have suspected our designs, or been disposed of by other Thugs on the road; and I recollected that about three miles from Hirora we had passed a Brinjara encampment. In the morning I went back with a few followers, and there found a horse and a pony that we had seen with the five travellers. "What have you done with the five travellers, my good friends? You have taken from us our merchandise, Bunij," said I, in Rumasee. They apologized for what they had done; said they did not know we were after them, and offered to share the booty with us; but I said we had no fair claim to a share, since none of our party were present at the loading (killing). We left them and came on to Bhilsa, where we met your party of Nujeebs.

'*Q.*—And these Brinjaree Thugs are rarely seized or punished?

'*Sahib Khan, of Telinggana.*—How can their deeds be known? They do all their work themselves. They live in the desert, and work in the desert. We live in villages, and cannot do our work without the connivance and support of the farmers who hold, and the influential men who occupy them. Local authorities of all kinds and degrees must be conciliated by us; but these men are relieved from all this cost and trouble by foregoing the pleasure of other men's society, and the comforts of a fixed habitation. They are wiser men than we are!

'*Morlee.*—I was one day walking with some of our party near Jeypore by an encampment of wealthy merchants from the westward, who wore very high turbans. I observed to my friends as we passed, "what enormous turbans these men wear!" using our mystic term Aghasee. The most respectable among them came up immediately and invited us to sit down with them, saying, "my good friends, we are of your fraternity, though our Aghasee are not the same." They told us that they were now opulent merchants, and independent of Thuggee, the trade by which they had chiefly acquired their wealth; but that they still did a little occasionally when they found in a suitable place a Bunij worth taking: but that they were now beyond speculating in trifles! We were kindly entertained, and much pleased with our new friends, but left them the same day, and I have never met any men of the kind since. The common Moltanee Thugs, who strangle men with the thongs which they use in driving their bullocks, we have often met. They are to be found all over India, but abound most to the north-west.'

No system of secret murder has ever existed so extensive, so completely organised, or so successfully pursued as that of Thuggee. The self-devoted Assassins were mere bunglers compared with the Thugs. Our *Burkers*, with their sneaking, solitary, midnight murders, do not deserve to be named in the same day with the members of a confederacy who traversed every part of India in gangs of hundreds, and throttled sometimes as many as threescore victims at once. Besides, the Assassins and the Burkers flourished for a time, and passed away: both their beginning and their end are known; but the commencement of Thuggee is lost in the remotest antiquity, and it has been practised generation after generation down to our own times. Even now, it is by no means suppressed; and if the efforts now making for that purpose were only for a short time to be relaxed, it would overspread the whole of India as heretofore. It is therefore worth enquiring, what are the causes which have secured such unexampled success to this terrible confederacy; and above all, what is it which has silenced the voice of conscience in the minds of the Thugs, and infused into them a spirit and a love for their profession which would do credit to any cause.

The principle of Assassination was religion. The principle of Burking was gain. In Thuggee they are both united. Gain sanctioned by religion; human rapacity exercised under the supposed approbation of the Deity, is its principle.

'There are Thugs,' Captain Sleeman observes, 'at Jubulpore from all quarters of India; from Lodheeana to the Carnatic, and from the Indus to the Ganges. Some of them have been in the habit of holding, what I may fairly call unreserved communication with European gentlemen for more than twelve years; and yet there is not among them one who doubts *the Divine origin of the system of Thuggee*—not one who doubts, that he and all who have followed the trade of murder with the prescribed rites and observances, were acting under the immediate orders and auspices of the goddess Devee, Durga, Kalee, or Bhuwanee, as she is indifferently called, and consequently there is not one who feels the slightest remorse for the murders which he may, in the course of his vocation, have perpetrated or assisted in perpetrating. A Thug considers the persons murdered precisely in the light of victims offered up to the goddess; and he remembers them, as a Priest of Jupiter remembered the oxen, and a Priest of Saturn the children sacrificed upon their altars. He meditates his murders without any misgivings; he perpetrates them without any emotion of pity; and he remembers them without any feelings of remorse. They trouble not his dreams, nor does their recollection ever cause him inquietude in darkness, in solitude, or in the hour of death.'

The account which the Thugs give of the first establishment of their profession will explain the nature of its pretentions to a Divine origin.

'The Thugs have a tradition that a demon, by name Rukut Beej Dana, infested the world, and devoured mankind as often as they were born or created; and to enable the world to be peopled, Kalee Davey determined to put him to death. This demon, they say, was so tall that the deepest ocean never reached above his waist; and he could, consequently, walk over the world at his ease. Kalee Davey attacked him, and cut him down; but from every drop of his blood another demon arose, and as she cut them down, from every drop of their blood another demon sprung up, and the numbers increased at this geometrical rate, until she became fatigued with the labour. On this she formed two men from the sweat brushed off from one of her arms; and giving them each a handkerchief, told them to put all these demons to death, without allowing one drop of their blood to fall on the ground.

'After their labour was over, they offered to return to the goddess the handkerchiefs with which they had done their work; but she desired them to keep them as the instruments of a trade by which their posterity were to earn their subsistence, and to strangle men with these handkerchiefs, as they had strangled the demons, and live by the plunder they acquired; and having been the means of enabling the world to get provided with men by the destruction of the demons, their posterity would be entitled to take a few for their own use.'

The goddess also told them that they might leave the bodies of their victims on the ground, and she would take care that they should be removed, provided they never looked back to see how she disposed of them. On one occasion, however, a slave had the audacity to look back, and saw the goddess without any clothes on, devouring the bodies and throwing them about in the air. Her modesty and dignity were naturally offended, and she told them, that in future, they must bury the bodies themselves; but from some remains of compassion for her ancient followers, she bestowed on them a pick-axe endowed with various supernatural qualities.

A pick-axe is consecrated by each gang before setting out on an expedition, and is regarded by a Thug much in the same light as his sword is by a soldier. It is the mark of his profession;—he swears by it, and under such an awful sanction, that the person who forswears himself will, within two or three days, 'die a 'horrid death; his head will turn round, his face towards his 'back, and he will writhe in tortures till he dies.' The sound of the consecrated pick-axe is never heard in digging a grave by any except a Thug. It is carried by the shrewedest, cleanest, and most sober and careful man of the party in his waist-belt. While in camp, he buries it in a secure place with its point in the direction they intend to go; and if another direction is better, its point will be found changed. Formerly it used to be thrown into a well, whence it would come up of itself, when summoned with the appropriate ceremonies; but since the northern Thugs have begun to do what is forbidden, and neglected what is enjoined, it has lost that virtue, as far as they are concerned. In the Deccan, where the primitive spirit of Thuggee has not been departed from, this is still the case. 'During a whole ex-'pedition that I made with them,' says a northern Thug, who served a campaign with the people of his own profession, in the south, 'Imam Khan and his brother carried the pick-axe, 'and I heard them repeatedly in the morning call them from the

' well into which they had thrown them overnight, and saw ' the pick-axes come of themselves from the well, and fall into ' their aprons, which they held open *thus*—Here he described the ' mode.'

The most ordinary and effectual mode, however, in which the goddess interferes in behalf of her votaries, is by means of omens. These are considered by the Thugs as signs expressly appointed to guide them to their prey, or to warn them of approaching danger; and no member of the fraternity doubts, that if these omens had been attended to and the other prescribed rules observed, the system of Thuggee must have flourished under the auspices of its divine patroness, in spite of all our efforts for its suppression.

All the different kinds of omens are too numerous to be specified, but the following may be taken as specimens. The striking coincidence between the rules of augury observed by the Thugs, and those of ancient Greece and Rome, will not fail to be perceived.

' *Pilhaoo.*—The appearance or voice of the animals from which omens are taken, on the left. The reverse of the Thibaoo. If the Pilhaoo promises good according to their rules of augury, it is always the better from being followed by the Thibaoo soon after. If it threatens evil, that evil is mitigated by the Thibaoo.

' The Pilhaoo, or omen on the left, must be observed first on opening an expedition, and it must be followed by the Thibaoo immediately after, or the expedition cannot be entered upon. It signifies that the Deity has taken the gang by the left arm, to lead them on; but she must give them the Thibaoo, to signify that she has taken them by the right arm also, or the party appointed to take the auspices returns home, and the gang waits till the omens are unexceptionable.

' The Pilhaoo perceived on leaving any stage during the expedition or preparing to leave it, promises good. The Thibaoo threatens evil, and the gang halts. On reaching any stage, the Pilhaoo threatens evil, and they must move on without resting. The Thibaoo promises good, and they rest securely.'

' *Burauk.*—The omen of the wolf or wolves crossing their road. If from left to right, it threatens great evil. If from right to left, it is a good omen. If its call be heard during the day, the gang must immediately quit the country in which they hear it. If between midnight and daylight, it is bad; if between evening and midnight, indifferent; between mid-day and sunset, it is not so bad as between sunrise and mid-day. They call it the weeping (Chimmama) of the wolf, and consider the sound mournful. The single wolf portends more than a pair; and the Burauk is, whether for good or for bad, one of the most important omens.'

' *Chirriya.*—A chirping of the small owlet, which Thugs consider a bad omen, whether made while the bird is sitting or flying; it is said to be a melancholy and low sound, seldom repeated. Judæ, Jemadar, who was considered to be one of the best augurers of his day, lived at Murnae, a celebrated Thug village, and it is said that, returning one morning from a walk in the fields, he told his friend that he had heard the Chirriya in a manner that indicated some great calamity at hand. That night, or the night after, Mr Halhed is said to have attacked the village, and Lieutenant Monsel was killed. It was, I believe, in November, 1812.'

'*Duheea.*—The call or cry of the hare. They will perish in the jungles, they say, after hearing it, if they do not make sacrifices; and the hare or some other animal of the forest will drink water out of their skulls: if they kill any one whom they have with them at the time, they will find no booty on him, or what they find will tend to their ruin.'

The efficacy of this omen is illustrated in the conversations:—

'*Q.*—Do you ever recollect any misfortune arising from going on when a hare crossed the road before you?

'*Nasir of Singhapore.*—Yes; when General Doveton commanded the troops at Jhalna, we were advancing towards his camp: a hare crossed the road; we disregarded the omen, though the hare actually screamed in crossing, and went on. The very next day I, with seventeen of our gang, were seized; and it was with great difficulty and delay that we got our release. We had killed some people belonging to the troops, but fortunately none of their property was found upon us.'

'*Dunteroo.*—The ass. The Thugs think the omen of the ass the most important of all, whether it threatens evil or promises good. "Sou pukheroo ek Dunteroo."—"The ass is equal to a hundred birds," is a maxim in augury. The omen of the ass is also superior to that of all quadrupeds! If they hear it bray on the left on opening an expedition (Pilhaoo), and it is soon after repeated on the right (Thibaoo), they believe that nothing on earth can prevent their success during that expedition, though it should last for years.'

'"Even the most sensible approvers," Captain Sleeman observes, "who have been with me for years, as well Musulmans as Hindus, believe that their good or ill success always depended upon the skill with which the omens were discovered and interpreted, and the strictness with which they were observed and obeyed. One of the old Sindouse stock told me yesterday (May 30, 1835), in presence of twelve others from Hydrabad, Behar, the Dooab, Oude, Rajpootana, and Bundlecund, assembled for the purpose of revising this vocabulary, that had they not attended to these omens, they could never have thrived as they did, and that in ordinary cases of murder a man seldom escaped after one of them, while they and their families had for ten generations thrived, though they had murdered hundreds of people. "This," said he, "could never have been the case, had we not attended to omens, and had not omens been intended for us. There were always signs around us to guide us to rich booty and warn us of danger, had we been always wise enough to discern them, and religious enough to attend to them." Every Thug present concurred with him from his soul.'

Besides her ordinary interference in their behalf by means of omens, and the supernatural virtues of the sacred pick-axe, the goddess interposes in a special manner to protect or revenge her followers when the occasion requires. Of this several striking instances are given.

'Q.—Above the Nurbudda, chiefs have never had the same dread of punishing Thugs as below it; have they?

'*Feringeea.*—They had formerly, and have still in many parts.

'Q.—Why should they fear; have there been any instances of suffering from it?

'*Feringeea.*—A great many. Was not Nanha, the Raja of Jhalone, made leprous by Davey for putting to death Bodhoo and his brother Khumolee, two of the most noted Thugs of their day. He had them trampled under the feet of elephants, but the leprosy broke out upon his body the very next day.

'Q.—Did he believe that this punishment was inflicted by Davey for putting them to death?

'*Dorgha Musulman*—He was quite sensible of it.

'Q.—Did he do any thing to appease her?

'*Dorgha.*—Every thing. Bodhoo had began a well in Jhalone; the Raja built it up in a magnificent style; he had a tomb raised to their name, fed Brahmuns, and consecrated it, had worship instituted upon it, but all in vain; the disease was incurable, and the Raja died in a few months a miserable death. The tomb and well are both kept up and visited by hundreds to this day, and no one doubts that the Raja was punished for putting these two Thugs to death.

'Q.—But Bodhoo had his nose and hands cut off before, and could have been no favourite of Davey's?

'*Feringeea.*—But he was a Thug of great repute; for sagacity we have never seen his equal; people who had been robbed used to go to him as an oracle.

'Q.—But he had turned informer, and was sent to Jhalone by Mr Stockwell to arrest his associates?

'*Dorgha.*—He went to Mr Stockwell in a passion; his heart was not fully turned away from us then.

'Q.—Have you any other instances?

'*Inaent.*—Hundreds! When Madhajee Scindheea caused seventy Thugs to be executed at Muthura, was he not warned in a dream by Davey that he should release them? and did he not the very day after their execution begin to spit blood? and did he not die within three months?

'*Feringeea.*—When Dureear the Rahtore, and Komere and Patore, the Kuchwaha Rajpoots, Zumeendars, arrested eighty of the Thugs who had settled at Nodha after the murder of Lieutenant Monsel, they had many warnings to let them go; but they persisted, and kept them till some thirty died. They collected fourteen thousand rupees at the rate of one hundred and twenty-five rupees from every Thug. What became of their families? Have they not all perished? They have not a child left. Rae Sing Havildar, the Gwalior Subha of Nodha, took the money, but that very day his only son and the best horse in his stable died, and he was himself taken ill, and died soon after a miserable death.

'*Nasir.*—Ah, Davey took care of you then, and why? Was it not because you were more attentive to her orders?

'*Zulfukar*.—Yes; we had then some regard for religion. We have lost it since. All kinds of men have been made Thugs, and all classes of people murdered, without distinction, and little attention has been paid to omens. How after this could we expect to escape?

'*Nasir*.—Be assured that Davey never forsook us till we neglected her.

'Q.—Do you know of any instance of her punishing a man for annoying Thugs in the Deccan?

'*Sahib Khan*.—A great many. The Raja of Kundul, some ninety coss east from Hyerabad, arrested all the Thugs in his raj for some murders they had committed. For three successive nights the voice of Davey was heard from the top of every temple in the capital, warning the Raja to release them. The whole town heard her, and urged the Raja to comply. He was obstinate, and the third night the bed on which he and his Ranee were sleeping was taken up by Davey, and dashed violently against the ground.

'Q.—Were they killed?

'*Nasir*.—They were not killed, but they were dreadfully bruised; and had they not released the Thugs, they would certainly have been killed the next night.

'Q.—Were any of you present?

'*Sahib Khan*.—Our fathers were, and we heard it from them. It occurred sixty years ago.

'Q.—And do you think that the chiefs have still the same dread of punishing Thugs in all parts of India?

'*Sahib*.—Certainly not in all parts; because in many they have been suffered to punish them with impunity, on account of their neglectof rules and omens.

'*Morlee*.—There is no fear now. They are every where seized and punished with impunity; there is no resisting your good fortune.

'*Durgha*.—The Company's good fortune is such, that before the sound of your drums, sorcerers, witches and demons take flight, and how can Thuggee stand?'

Notwithstanding their recent backsliding, the Thugs are not wanting in gratitude to their divine patroness for all these favours. A choice portion of each spoil is set aside for her, previous to the division, and numerous rites are observed in her honour, of which the following will serve for an example.

'*Tupounee*. A sacrifice of sugar to Bhowanee. This sacrifice is offered at the first convenient place after every murder. One rupee and four annas worth of coarse sugar is purchased and put upon a blanket or sheet spread upon the cleanest place they can select. Near the pile of sugar and on the blanket they place the consecrated pick-axe, and a piece of silver, as a "Roop Dursun," or silver offering. The most esteemed leader of the gang, who is supposed to be most in favour with the goddess, and best acquainted with the modes of propitiating her, is placed on the blanket, with his face to the west. As many noted stranglers as it can conveniently contain, sit on each side of this leader, with their faces in the same direction. They must be, including the leader, an even number. The rest of the gang sit outside the blanket. The leader now makes a hole in the ground, and having put into it a little of the sugar, he lifts his clasped hands and eyes towards heaven, and with his mind fixed upon the goddess, he says, " Great goddess ! as you vouchsafed one lack and sixty-two thousand rupees to Joora Naik, and Koduk Bunwaree* in their need, so we pray thee, fulfil our desires." In this prayer all the Thugs fervently join, repeating the words after the leader. He then sprinkles some water over the pit and pick-axe, and places a little sugar upon the extended hands of every Thug seated upon the blanket with him. One of the gang now gives the signal for strangling in the same manner as if they were going to commit murder, and the Thugs upon the carpet eat their sugar in solemn silence. Not a word is spoken till they have eaten the whole, and drunk some water. The pile of sugar is now distributed, as consecrated food, to the whole of the gang entitled from their rank to partake of it. They eat it all with silent reverence, so that no part may fall to the ground ; and if any fall, it is put into the pit, that it may not be soiled by the foot of any one. The silver is then given back to the person who lent it for the purpose.

'No one but a man who has strangled with his own hands, and is at the same time a free man, is suffered to partake of the sugar thus consecrated. For those who have not yet strangled a victim, or are not free men, sugar is set apart from the pile before consecration, and they eat it at the same time as the others on the signal given. If any thing improper, or indecorous in language, manner, or conduct, takes place during this ceremony, they consider it an evident sign of the displeasure of the deity, and despair of further success during the expedition.

'If any particle of the consecrated sugar should be left on the ground, and eaten by a dog or any other animal, they would, they believe, suffer under the displeasure of the deity for years. If any other human being should taste the sugar, they are persuaded that he would immediately take to the trade of Thuggee, and never be able to leave it off, whatever may have been his rank or condition in life. If they have any young disciple about whose advancement they are very solicitous, they try to get for him a little of the consecrated sugar, assured that he will advance rapidly in his profession after eating it.'

It will now, we think, be apparent, in what the principle of Thuggee consists ; what it was which gave rise to the phenomenon of several thousand persons pursuing murder as a trade,—generation after generation, not one of whom entertained the least suspicion that he was doing wrong. The Thugs are the

---

* Joora Naik was a celebrated leader of Multan Thugs. He and his slave Khoduk Bunwaree are said to have killed a man who had, in jewels and other articles, property to the value of L.16,000, laden upon a mule. They brought home the booty, assembled all the members of their fraternity within reach, and honestly divided the whole, as if all had been present. Joora Naik, his wife, and slave, were all canonised in consequence.

followers of a deity who delights in blood. Thuggee is by no means the only horror which is patronised by her. Every murderer looks to her as his protectress. She is the goddess of destruction, and of all the Hindu Pantheon, she alone is appeased by human sacrifices. Till lately there was a petty state, called Jaintia, on the eastern frontier of Bengal, the Chiefs of which had long been notorious for kidnapping our subjects and offering them up on her shrine. In 1821, a shepherd boy was rescued from their servants while they were dragging him away from the Sylhet district for this purpose; and the Raja was then solemnly warned of the consequences which would follow a repetition of the act. After this, in 1831, as three of our subjects were passing along the high-road in our own district of Assam, the Jaintia people rushed out upon them, and carried them up into the hills. They were adorned for sacrifice, and separately conveyed to three temples on the peaks of the hill, where they were left, bound and guarded, to await the appointed hour. Fortunately, a storm arose, in the darkness and confusion caused by which, one of the victims succeeded in untying the cords with which he was bound. He rushed down the hill, and next morning at break of day he reached the nearest British police station more dead than alive, —the sacrificial garments and jewels still upon him. The murder was completed, as regarded the other two victims. After many vain attempts to obtain redress, the Raja and his Chiefs were punished, and the only effectual security was obtained against a recurrence of the practice, by the incorporation of the petty state with the British dominions. This is only one of many similar horrors which we might relate. It is no uncommon thing to hear of persons cutting their own throats, or decapitating their children at the shrine of this bloodthirsty deity.

To the Thugs, therefore, murder is an act of religion, just as much as the practice of charity is to a Christian. When, by according favourable omens, their patroness is supposed to have revealed her will for the sacrifice of travellers, those of the stricter sort dare not disobey.

'Q.—How' (asks Captain Sleeman) 'can you murder old men and young children without some emotions of pity—calmly and deliberately as they sit with you and converse with you,—and tell you of their private affairs,—of their hopes and fears,—and of their wives and children whom they are going to meet after years of absence, toil, and suffering?

'*A.*—From the time that the omens have been favourable, we consider them as victims thrown into our hands by the deity to be killed; and that we are a mere instrument in her hands to destroy them: that if we do not kill them, she will never be again propitious to us, and we and our families shall be involved in misery and want.

'Q.—And you can sleep as soundly by the bodies or over the graves of those you have murdered, and eat your meals with as much appetite as ever?

'*Sahib.*—Just the same; we sleep and eat just the same, unless we are afraid of being discovered.

'Q.—And when you see or hear a bad omen, you think it is the order of the deity not to kill the travellers you have with you, or are in pursuit of?

'*Sahib.*—Yes; it is the order not to kill them, and we dare not disobey.'

It is, however, still a controverted point of Thug theology, whether, when a traveller falls into their hands under favourable omens, they are bound by their religion to kill him, or are only permitted to do so, if it happens to suit their convenience. The orthodox divines of the south are, as usual, for the unsparing use of the sash. The heretics of the north recommend that mercy should be shown in such cases; and are, in consequence, looked upon by their brethren of the Deccan in much the same light in which a Baptist is regarded at Oxford.

'Q.—When you have a poor traveller with you, or a party of travellers, who appear to have little property about them, and you hear or see a very good omen, do you not let them go, in the hope that the virtue of the omen will guide you to better prey?

'*Durgha Musulman.*—Let them go!—never, never—kubhee nuheen, kubhee nuheen.

'*Nasar Musulman, of Telingana.*—How could we let them go? Is not the good omen the order from Heaven to kill them, and would it not be disobedience to let them go? If we did not kill them, should we ever get any more travellers?

'*Feringeea Brahmun.*—I have known the experiment tried with good effect.—I have known travellers who promised little let go, and the virtue of the omen brought better.

'*Inaent Musulman.*—Yes, the virtue of the omen remains, and the traveller who has little should be let go, for you are sure to get a better.

'*Sahib Khan, of Telingana.*—Never! never! This is one of your northern heresies. You could never let him go without losing all the fruits of your expedition. You might get property, but it could never do you any good. No success could result from your disobedience.

'*Morlee Rajpoot.*—Certainly not! The travellers who are in our hands when we have a good omen must never be let go, whether they promise little or much; the omen is unquestionably the order, as Nasir says.

'*Nasir.*—The idea of securing the good will of Davey by disobeying her orders is quite monstrous. We Deccan Thugs do not understand how you got hold of it. Our ancestors were never guilty of such folly.

'*Feringeea.*—You do not mean to say that we of Murnæ and Sindouse were not as well instructed as you of Telingana?

'*Nasir and Sahib Khan.*—We only mean to say that you have clearly mistaken the nature of a good omen in this case. It is the order of Davey to take what she has put in our way: at least so we, in the Deccan, understand it.'

As the Thugs have a religion of their own, they are regarded among themselves as religious or otherwise according to the degree of strictness with which they observe the rules of their peculiar faith. In England it may appear odd to classify professional murderers as religious or otherwise; but this distinction is not unknown to the more refined morality of India. 'His 'father (a noted Thug) used to drink very hard, and in his fits 'of intoxication he used to neglect his *prayers* and his *days of fast*. 'All days were the same with him. This lad, Shumsheera (also 'a Thug) was always sober, and *religiously disposed*, and separated 'from his father, living always with his uncle Dondee (another 'Thug) who was a *very worthy and good man*.'

Another consequence of the peculiar religious belief of the Thugs is, that they draw a distinction between Thuggee and murder. In our eyes, all killing is wrong which is not sanctioned by the laws of the country: in the opinion of the Thugs, it is wrong when it is not sanctioned by the municipal law of the country, or the divine law of their patroness Kalee. They add to the cases in which the destruction of human life is permitted, that of travellers who fall into their hands when the omens are favourable.

'Q.—And you believe that if you were to murder without the observance of the omens and regulations, you would be punished both in this world and the next like other men?

'*Sahib.*—Certainly; no man's family ever survives a murder: it becomes extinct. A Thug who murders in this way loses the children he has, and is never blessed with more.

'Q.—In the same manner as if a Thug had murdered a Thug?

'*Sahib.*—Precisely; he cannot escape punishment.

'Q.—And when you observe the omens and rules, you neither feel a dread of punishment here nor hereafter?

'*Sahib.*—Never.'

The superiority which the Thugs assume over ordinary murderers is in the highest degree amusing. They even lay claim to the title of public benefactors, on the ground of their having opened the shortest, and, if they are to be trusted, by far the most certain road to heaven.

'Q.—Are you never afraid of the spirits of the persons you murder?

'*Nasir.*—Never; they cannot trouble us.

'Q.—Why? Do they not trouble other men when they commit murder?

'*Nasir.*—Of course they do. The man who commits a murder is always haunted by spirits. He has sometimes fifty at a time upon him, and they drive him mad.

'Q.—And how do they not trouble you?

'*Nasir.*—Are not the people we kill, killed by the orders of Davey?

'*Kuleean.*—Yes, it is by the blessing of Davey that we escape that evil.

'*Durgha.*—Do not all whom we kill go to Paradise, and why should their spirits stay to trouble us?'

There is no end to the new and singular results of this distorted state of morals. In every respect in which their peculiar tenets do not clash with the ordinary rules of morality, these professional murderers are not only blameless, but even exemplary in the performance of the various duties of life.

'No men,' remarks Capt. Sleeman, 'observe more strictly in domestic life all that is enjoined by their priests or demanded by their respective castes; nor do any men cultivate with more care the esteem of their neighbours, or court with more assiduity the good-will of all constituted local authorities. In short, to men who do not know them, the principal members of these associations will always appear to be among the most amiable, most respectable, and most intelligent members of the lower, and sometimes the middle and higher classes of native society; and it is by no means to be inferred that every man who attempts to screen them from justice knows them to be murderers.'

The most hardened Thugs not unfrequently gain the esteem of the European officers employed in seizing them, by the propriety of their conduct and the mild decorum of their manner.

'Bhimmee,' observes Mr Macleod, 'is a mild respectable kind of man, who would certainly not appear born for a gallows, and I hope you will let him remain with me. I feel interested, too, for the whole of Laek's family, among whom I do not think there is naturally any vice; and shocking as their proceedings would appear at home, very many palliating circumstances evidently exist here, and we must be guided by what is expedient. To Laek the sentence of any of his brothers would be most disheartening. When he heard of their arrest, he repeated with great feeling a Hindostanee verse to this effect: "I was a pearl once residing in comfort in the ocean. I surrendered myself, believing I should repose in peace in the bosom of some fair damsel—but, alas! they have pierced me, and passed a string through my body, and have left me to dangle in constant pain as an ornament to her nose." Another officer, speaking of another Thug, says, "He has one of the most benevolent countenances that I have ever seen. He looks as though he would rather commit suicide than common and cold-blooded murder." And a third officer, speaking of another, says, "He is one of the best men I have ever known! and I believe that Makeem may be trusted in any relation of life save that between a Thug who has taken the auspices, and a traveller with something worth taking upon him. They all look upon travellers as sportsmen look upon hares and pheasants; and they recollect their favourite Beles, or places for murder, as sportsmen recollect their best sporting grounds, and talk of them, when they can, with the same kind of glee."'

It is certainly part of the business of a Thug to cultivate a mild and conciliatory deportment, both with a view to inveigle travellers and secure to himself protectors; but we conceive that this is not of itself sufficient to account for the facts before us. In Europe, hardened criminals are seldom distinguished even for having 'benevolent countenances;' and if we examine into the details of their domestic life, the traces of their ferocious occupation become still more apparent. Such persons are by no means remarkable for being good husbands, good fathers, or good neighbours. Neither do they almost invariably abstain from wanton cruelty, or from offering any outrage either to mind or body beyond what is necessary for depriving their victims of life, which is the case with the Thugs. 'No Thug,' Captain Sleeman observes, 'was ever known to offer insult, either in act or in 'speech, to the women they were to murder. No gang would 'ever dare to murder a woman with whom one of its members 'should be suspected of having had connexion.' Whence, then, is this difference? How does it happen that crime has lost its brutalizing influence in the case of the Thugs? The real explanation seems to be this. No man's moral feeling is offended by doing what he does not consider to be wrong. The Thugs are not hardened by the practice of murder, because they do not believe it to be murder in the way in which they commit it. Soldiers fighting in their country's cause could not be less conscious of doing wrong than the Thugs are. Both entertain an implicit belief, that an exception has been made in their favour in the general law for the preservation of human life; and, therefore, both are satisfied that they are doing nothing more than their duty in putting their fellow-creatures to death.

But although conscience may be silenced by false religion, human nature cannot be brought at once to view human suffering with indifference. Children are trained to the practice of Thuggee by a gradual process; and great care is taken not to shock them by too sudden an introduction to scenes of actual murder.

'*Sahib.*—The first expedition they neither see nor hear any thing of murder. They know not our trade;—they get presents, purchased out of their share, and become fond of the wandering life, as they are always mounted upon ponies. Before the end of the journey they know that we rob. The next expedition they suspect that we commit murder, and some of them even know it; and in the third expedition they see all.'

A striking instance is afterwards given of the danger of too abruptly exposing to children the mysteries of this horrid craft,

'*Feringeea.*—About twelve years ago my cousin Aman Subahdar took out with us my cousin Kurhora, brother of Omrow approver, a lad of fourteen, for the first time. He was mounted upon a pretty pony, and Hursooka, an adopted son of Aman's, was appointed to take charge of the boy.

'We fell in with five Sikhs, and when we set out before daylight in the morning, Hursooka, who had been already on three expeditions, was ordered to take the bridle and keep the boy in the rear out of sight and hearing. The boy became alarmed, and impatient, got away from Hursooka, and galloped up at the instant the signal for murder was given. He heard the screams of the men, and saw them all strangled. He was seized with a trembling, and fell from his pony; he became immediately delirious, was dreadfully alarmed at the sight of the turbans of the murdered men, and when any one touched or spoke to him, talked about the murders, and screamed exactly like a boy who talks in his sleep, and trembled violently if any one spoke to him or touched him. We could not get him on; and after burying the bodies, Aman and I, and a few others, sat by him while the gang went on: we were very fond of him, and tried all we could to tranquillize him, but he never recovered his senses, and before evening he died. I have seen many instances of feelings greatly shocked at the sight of the first murder, but never one so strong as this. Kurhora was a very fine boy, and Hursooka took his death much to heart, and turned Fukeer; he is now at some temple on the bank of the Nurbudda river.'

Instances also are not wanting of the amiable dispositions of human nature breaking through the restraints which have been placed upon them by a mistaken system, even in the case of the most practised Thugs.

'Q.—And you are worse than the Duckun Thugs, for you murder handsome young women as well as the old and ugly?

'*Feringeea.*—Not always. I and my cousin Aman Subahdar were with a gang of one hundred and fifty Thugs on an expedition through Rajpootana about thirteen years ago, when we met a handmaid of the Peshwa, Bajee Row's, on her way from Poona to Cawnpore. We intended to kill her and her followers, but we found her very beautiful, and after having her and her party three days within our grasp, and knowing that they had a lakh and a half of rupees worth of property in jewels and other things with them, we let her and all her party go: we had talked to her and felt love towards her, for she was very beautiful.

'Q.—And how came you to kill the Moghulanee? She also is said to have been very handsome.

'*Feringeea.*—We none of us ventured near her palankeen. The Musulmans were the only men that approached her before the murder. Madar Buksh approver strangled her.

'Q.—What did you get from them?

'*Durgha.*—Six hundred rupees worth of property.

'Q.—And was this enough to tempt so large a gang to murder a beautiful young woman?

'*Durgha*.—We were very averse to it, and often said that we should not get two rupees a-piece, and that she ought to be let go; but Feringeea insisted upon our taking her.

'Q.—How did you advise the murder of a young woman like this?

'*Feringeea*. It was her fate to die by our hands. I had several times tried to shake them off before we met the Musulmans, and when we came to Lalsont, I told her that she must go on, as I had joined some old friends, and should be delayed. She then told me that I must go to her home with her near Agra, or she would get me into trouble; and being a Brahmun while she was a Musulman, I was afraid that I should be accused of improper intercourse, and turned out of caste.'

A singular reason is assigned by the Thugs for their general indifference to the pangs of their victims.

'*Feringeea*.—"We all feel pity sometimes," observed a Thug leader, "but the sugar of the Tuponee sacrifice changes our nature. It would change the nature of a horse. Let any man once taste of that sugar, and he will be a Thug though he know all the trades and have all the wealth in the world. I never wanted food; my mother's family was opulent, her relations high in office. I have been high in office myself, and became so great a favourite wherever I went, that I was sure of promotion: yet I was always miserable while absent from my gang, and obliged to return to Thuggee. My father made me taste of that fatal sugar when I was yet a mere boy; and if I were to live a thousand years I should never be able to follow any other trade.'

There can be no doubt that Thugs 'become strongly attached 'to their detestable occupation. They rarely, if ever, abandon 'it. Those who, narrowly escaping the merited vengeance of 'the law, are released from prison on security, are seldom able 'to refrain from resuming their old employment; and those who, 'bending under the weight of years and infirmities, are no longer 'able to bear an active or principal part, continue to aid the cause 'by keeping watch, procuring intelligence, or dressing the food 'of their younger confederates.' This attachment to their profession may, however, be accounted for without attributing any miraculous influence to the 'sacred sugar.' Their calling is, in their esteem, both honourable and holy;—by a long course of education it has become habitual; and it is recommended to them both by its lucrativeness and by the intervals of leisure which it affords. Persons who have been accustomed to a life of mixed idleness and adventure are not easily reconciled to quiet and regular habits. It is well known, that scarcely any thing is so difficult to reclaim as a Gipsy, or an American Indian.

Some of the most curious passages in the dialogues are those in which an attempt is made by the Thug approvers to reconcile the supposed divine origin of Thuggee with our success against it. The system is under the special protection of deity, and yet unbelieving men have made serious inroads upon it. Nay, the more intelligent of the Thugs do not pretend to deny the probability even of its entire subversion. Here then is a problem of which we have the solution afforded us in the following conversations :—

'Q.—But if there was such a deity as Bhowanee, and she were your patroness, how could she allow me and others to seize and punish so many Thugs?

'*Nasir.*—I have a hundred times heard my father and other old and wise men say, when we had killed a sweeper, and otherwise infringed their rules, that we should be some day punished for it; that the European rulers would be made the instruments to chastise us for our disregard of omens, and neglect of the rules laid down for our guidance.'

* * * * * * *

'Q.—You think an institution formed by Davey, the goddess, cannot be suppressed by the hand of man?

'*Nasir.*—Certainly, I think so.

'Q.—But you think that no man is killed by man's killing, "adme ke marne se koee murta nuheen;" that all who are strangled, are strangled in effect by God?

'*Nasir.*—Certainly.

'Q—Then by whose killing have all the Thugs who have been hung at Saugor and Jubulpore been killed?

'*Nasir.*—God's, of course.

'Q.—You think that we could never have caught and executed them but by the aid of God?

'*Nasir.*—Certainly not.

'Q.—Then you think that so far we have been assisted by God in what we have done?

'*Nasir.*—Yes.

'Q.—And you are satisfied that we should not have ventured to do what we have done, unless we were assured that our God was working with us, or rather that we were the mere instruments in his hands?

'*Nasir.*—Yes, I am.

'Q.—Then do you not think that we may go on with the same assurance till the work we have in hand is done; till, in short, the system of Thuggee is suppressed?

'*Nasir.*—God is almighty.

'Q.—And there is but one God?

'*Nasir.*—One God above all gods.

'Q.—And if that God above all gods supports us, we shall succeed?

'*Nasir.*—Certainly.

'Q.—Then we are all satisfied that he is assisting us, and therefore hope to succeed even in the Deccan?

'*Nasir.*—God only knows.'

It is clear that, whatever the event may be, both parties will retain their own opinion to the last.

'*Moradun.*—We see God is assisting you, and that Davey has withdrawn her protection on account of our transgressions. We have sadly neglected her worship. God knows in what it will all end.

'Q.—True, God only knows: but we hope it will end in the entire suppression of this wicked and foolish system; and in the conviction on your part, that Davey has really had nothing to do with it.

'*Nasir.*—That Davey instituted Thuggee, and supported it as long as we attended to her omens, and observed the rules framed by the wisdom of our ancestors, nothing in the world can ever make us doubt.'

The association of Mahomedans with Hindus in the worship of Kalee must have attracted attention. This is the more remarkable, as the rules of the Mahomedan religion are especially directed to maintain, in the minds of its followers, the belief in the unity of the Godhead. No carved image, no painted representation of man or beast, is allowed either in their mosques or houses. The perpetual exclusion of idolatry from their religious system has always been their peculiar boast. Since the fourth century, Christianity has been more or less debased by idol worship; but, as far as we know, this is the first instance of its introduction into Mahomedanism. The Hindus have, in some respects, particularly in the South of India, adopted the religious practices of the Mahomedans; but we never before heard that the Mahomedans had fallen into the idolatry of the Hindus. We shall leave the Mahomedan Thugs to furnish their own explanation of this departure from the first doctrine of their faith.

'Q.—You are a Musulman?

'*Sahib.*—Yes, and the greater part of the Thugs of the south are Musulmans.

'Q.—And you still marry, inherit, pray, eat and drink, according to the Koran; and your paradise is to be the paradise promised by Mahommud?

'*Sahib.*—Yes, all, all.

'Q.—Has Bhowanee been any where named in the Koran?

'*Sahib.*—No where.

'Here a Musulman Thug from Hindostan interposed, and said, he thought Bhowanee and Fatima, the daughter of Mahommud, and wife of Alee, were one and the same person; and that it was Fatima who invented the use of the handkerchief to strangle the great demon Rukut-beej-dana; which led to a discussion between him and some of my Musulman native officers, who did not like to find the amiable Fatima converted into a goddess of Thuggee—an "Iphigenia in Tauris." The Thug was a sturdy wrangler, and, in the estimation of his associate Thugs, had, I think, the best of the argument.

'Q.—Then has Bhowanee any thing to do with your paradise?

'*Sahib.*—Nothing.

'Q.—She has no influence upon your future state?

'*Sahib.*—None.

'Q.—Does Mahommud, your prophet, any where sanction crimes like yours, the murder in cold blood of your fellow-creatures, for the sake of their money?

'*Sahib.*—No.

'Q.—Does he not say that such crimes will be punished by God in the next world?

'*Sahib.*—Yes.

'Q.—Then do you never feel any dread of punishment hereafter?

'*Sahib.*—Never; we never murder unless the omens are favourable; and we consider favourable omens as the mandates of the deity.

'Q.—What deity?

'*Sahib.*—Bhowanee.

'Q.—But Bhowanee, you say, has no influence upon the welfare, or otherwise, of your soul hereafter?

'*Sahib.*—None, we believe; but she influences our fates in this world, and what she orders in this world, we believe that God will not punish in the next.'

Deprecatory offerings to Kalee as the goddess of destruction, appear to be very general among the Mahomedans.

'*Feringeea.*—'Of course,' observed a Thug leader to Capt. Sleeman, 'all men worship at her temples.'

'Q.—No.—We Sahib log (Europeans) never do.

'*Feringeea.*—I mean all Hindus and Musulmans.

'Here my Mahomedan officers again interposed, and declared that they never did; and that it was only the very lowest order of Musulmans that did. But, unfortunately, these keen observers of passing events had seen the wives of some very respectable Musulmans at Jubulpore, during the time that the small-pox was raging, take their children to her temples, and prostrate them before the images of the goddess of Destruction. The officers admitted this to be sometimes the case, but pretended that it was unknown to their husbands.

'*Sahib Khan* and *Nasir.*—In the Deccan the greatest Nawabs and Officers of State worship at the temples, and prostrate themselves and their children before the image of the goddess when the small-pox or the cholera morbus rages. We have ourselves seen them do it often.

'Q.—And do they believe you Thugs to be under her special protection?

'*Sahib* and *Nasir.*—Some of them do, and though they often try to dissuade us from our trade, they are afraid to punish us. Bura Sahib Jemadar, of Madura, had several hundred followers, and used to make valuable presents to Nawab Dollee Khan, who knew how he got them, and offered him a high post with rent-free lands if he would leave off the trade. He would not.

'Q.—What became of him at last?

'*Sahib* and *Nasir.*—There was a great Decoit leader of the same name, who had been committing great ravages, and orders were sent by the Nawab to the local officers to blow him away from a gun as soon as they could seize him. They seized Sahib Khan Thug, and blew him away by mistake, before the Nawab got information of the arrest. In a few hours after his death a message came from the Nawab to say that he feared there might be a mistake, and when he heard that Sahib Khan Thug had been blown away, he was much grieved, but said that God must have ordained it, and the fault was not his.'

It is even asserted that we have ourselves contributed to the general delusion of this impious worship.

'The Thugs,' observes Capt. Sleeman, 'and I understand all other Hindus, believe Kalee to have first appeared upon the earth in Calcutta. They believe also that after she had, through the means of the Thugs created by her for the special purpose, destroyed the great Demon Rukut-beej-dana at Bindachul, on the eastern extremity of the Vindeya range, she carried the body to Calcutta, and there buried it where her temple now stands. That place they consider to be her favourite seat, where she works more miracles than in all the rest of India. They have got a notion that, in Calcutta, even the Christians attend her worship, and make offerings to her temple; and I believe the priests have always actually made offerings to her image on great occasions in the name of the Honourable Company, out of the rents of the land with which Government has endowed the temple. European gentlemen and ladies frequently attend the nautches and feasts of her great days in the Durga Pooja; and as these feasts are part of the religious ceremonies, this innocent curiosity is very liable to be misconstrued by people at a distance from the scene, and should not therefore be indulged. The Hindus have a verse which they often repeat in their invocations. "Kalee! Calcutta walee! tera buchun na jawe khalee." "Oh Kalee, great goddess of Calcutta, may thy promise never be made in vain." She is said to delight in the name of Kunkalee, or man-eater, and to be always drinking the blood of men and of demons. They all believe Kalee to have been extremely black, and to have had features so terrifically hideous that no mortal man could dare to look upon them.'

The system of Thuggee is made for secrecy. Acting upon the maxim, 'dead man tell no tales,' they never rob without first murdering. They never shed blood. In speaking of matters relating to their profession, they use a slang which is understood only by themselves. They never put their victims to death till they have a safe opportunity, even if it should be necessary to follow them hundreds of miles before they obtain one. There are also circumstances peculiar to India, which enable them to carry on the practice with much greater facility there than would be the case in most other countries. These circumstances are thus summed up by Captain Sleeman:—

'The practice all over India of sending remittances in the precious metals and jewels, whenever the rate of exchange makes it in the smallest degree profitable to do so, by men on foot and in disguise, without any guard or arms to defend themselves—the necessity of drawing recruits for our armies from distant provinces, and of granting a certain portion of leave to revisit their homes every year during the hot season, when they set out every morning before daylight in order to avoid the heat of the sun during the day—the custom of travelling on foot or on small ponies, almost universal among those who have occasion to make long journeys, of whatever rank or condition—their mode of providing and dressing their own food under the shade of trees by the wayside, without that communication with the people of the towns through which they pass, which would enable their friends to trace them when they disappear—the long tracts of grass and wood jungle through which all the roads pass—the little appearance of road that is any where to be found, and the consequent facility with which they are led aside by bye-paths into places suited for murder—the number of such places in wood and grass jungles, rivers, ravines, and water-courses by which every road is intersected or bordered—the unreserved manner in which travellers of the same caste mix and communicate, and the facility with which men can feign different castes—the right of search every where assumed by custom-house officers, which obliges travellers to display the nature and value of the property they carry—the paucity of commercial intercourse between towns along any of the great lines of road leading from and to the great seats of our civil and military establishments, in a country where every village produces what its population demands, and consumes almost all that it produces save its raw agricultural produce—the slow rate of transit where all produce is carried upon bullocks, and, consequently, the little chance the assassin has of being overtaken and interrupted in his operations;—all these and many other circumstances peculiar to the country, favoured the growth of this system, and caused it to spread from one end of India to the other.'

These causes, however, do not lie beneath the surface. If any practice at all approaching in atrocity to that of Thuggee, were to be discovered in England, it would be immediately put down by an united effort of the whole people. Those who heard the shout of exultation which ran from street to street in the neighbourhood of the Old Bailey on the evening of the conviction of Bishop and his associates, will be able to form some idea of the way in which a Thug association would be dealt with in England. In India, however, the state of moral feeling is quite different. The Thugs have nothing to fear from public opinion. Instead of being denounced by their neighbours, they are generally the most popular members of society, owing to their conciliatory manners and the freedom with which they spend their money. The native governments, instead of rooting them out, recognised them as a regular profession, protected them, and levied a fixed tax from them. 'Into whosesoever hands the principal Thug settlement at the junction of the Chumbul and Jumna 'fell, viz. the Nawab Wazeer, the Rana of Gohud, the Rohilla 'Chieftains, the Bhudorea Raja, the Raja of Bhurtpoor, and the 'Gualior State, from time immemorial, has a tax of Rs. 24-8 on 'every house inhabited by the Thugs been levied, and paid to the 'respective Amils.' What would be thought if the Chancellor of the Exchequer, on opening his next budget, was to announce a poll-tax upon *Burkers* as part of his ways and means! The truth is, that the same religious feeling which leads the Thugs to believe that they are performing a laudable action in murdering travellers who are thrown in their way, while the auspices are favourable, causes them to be regarded without horror by other Hindus. They are supposed only to be doing their duty in that state of life to which God has called them. All Hindus, as well as the Thugs, believe in Kalee; and regarding them as her followers, they respect them, and dread the consequences of being instrumental in their punishment.

Captain Sleeman observes, that 'the want of sympathy between men of different castes, or different places of abode, is, unhappily, the grand characteristic of Indian society; and as long as these assassins forbear to murder in and about the places where they reside, and conciliate or keep in ignorance the local police authorities, they are sure of being cherished as among the dearest members of society.'* This is perfectly true. In India an universal selfishness prevails. There is no mutual dependence,—no disposition to unite for the accomplishment of objects of common advantage. The 'royal law of love' has no prevalence there: nobody thinks of 'doing unto others as he would be done by.' The difference between ourselves and the natives in these respects is a constant theme of admiration to them. Great as our intellectual superiority is, it does not make nearly the same impression upon them as our moral superiority does. In regard to natural powers of mind, the natives and ourselves may be much on a level. Even in point of intellectual acquirements, the majority of the English in India have not much to boast of; but the superiority of our moral qualities,—our veracity, our trustworthiness, our mutual dependence, our disposition to unite for the attainment of objects of public interest, even though we may not be ourselves immediately concerned,—is fully admitted by them. Europeans, on their first arrival in India, are often surprised, and somewhat disappointed, at hearing such frequent praise of what appear to them the commonplace qualities of veracity and public spirit.

---

* The indifference with which the destruction of human life is regarded in India, when it does not affect a member of the same family or village community, is truly astonishing. 'In Oude,' Capt. Sleeman observes, 'where the fields are almost all irrigated from wells, the bodies were generally thrown into them; and when the cultivators discovered them, they hardly ever thought it worth while to ask how they got there, so accustomed were they to find them.'

He rather expects to hear our eminence in science and the arts, or our proficiency in war or government, made the subject of eulogy. Experience only can teach, that nothing is so truly astonishing to a morally depraved people as the phenomenon of a race of men, in whose word perfect confidence may be placed, and who are often ardent in the pursuit of objects in which their own interest is not directly concerned. The natives are conscious of their inferiority in nothing so much as in this. They require to be taught rectitude of conduct much more than literature and science.

In conclusion, we venture to affirm, that nothing which the missionaries have ever alleged against Hinduism is half so damning as the evidence which this book contains. We have here the extraordinary spectacle of a religion which is professedly directed to promote, not the peace and happiness, but the destruction of the human race. Other religions have had their abuses; but the essence of the religion of Kalee is pure, unmixed evil. She presides over a system of murder; and is represented as having made a grant of half the human race to her votaries the Thugs, to be slaughtered by them according to certain prescribed forms.

We should merely weaken the effect of such a disclosure as that which we have made, were we to go through the long catalogue of Hindu gods or goddesses, and to mention the vices which are under the special patronage of each. To what an extent such a mythology must operate to taint the morals of the people, it is hardly necessary to say. Almost every false religion has paid court to some of the bad passions of mankind. But neither in Greece, in Carthage, nor in Scandinavia, was superstition ever so diametrically opposed to morality as in India, at the present day. If we were to form a graduated scale of religions, that of Christ and that of Kalee would be the opposite extremes.

It must be perfectly obvious, that the application of force can only be a temporary and partial remedy for Thuggee, and the other evils which spring from a false belief. Some are not cognisable by the laws, and those which are, can be kept down only whilst the law is vigorously executed; which cannot be always depended on. If the noxious seed is left in the ground, it will spring up again whenever circumstances are favourable. Happily a more efficacious remedy is not wanting. Some time ago a young Hindu who had received a liberal English education was persecuted by his friends for neglecting idol worship. Having been forced to the shrine of Kalee, he took off his cap, made a low bow to 'Madam Kalee,' and said he 'hoped her ladyship 'was well.' An Indian boy educated as we are, can no more believe in Kalee than we can ourselves. Minds which have been imbued from childhood with the literature and science of Europe, cannot return to the absurdities which Bishop Heber found the Professors of the Government Sanscrit College at Benares engaged in teaching, in 1824. Since that time, we are happy to say, a salutary change has taken place. The upper and middle classes are now generally anxious for European instruction. Many new seminaries have been opened by the Government at the principal stations; and several thousand youths are actively engaged in the study of English. As an instance of the prevailing taste, we may mention, that when a new College was lately opened at Hoogly, in which means of instruction in Oriental and Western learning were provided in equal proportions, 1100 students flocked to the English, while only 300 applied for admission to the Oriental department. Under such circumstances may we not look forward with confidence to that national regeneration which the gradual infusion of English literature, English science, and English morals into the mass of Indian society, must produce at no distant period?

Review of *Ramaseeana*, by W.H. Sleeman, *The Foreign Quarterly Review* 21 (April 1838): 1–32.

THE

FOREIGN

QUARTERLY REVIEW.

ART. I.—*Ramaseeana, or a Vocabulary of the peculiar Language used by the Thugs, with an Introduction and Appendix descriptive of the System pursued by that Fraternity and of the Measures which have been adopted by the Supreme Government of India for its suppression.* Calcutta. 1836.

WE have perused this work with the greatest interest; for the subject is one which must excite the most acute feelings in the mind of every friend to humanity. We have here an account of probably the most extraordinary organized society of ruthless villains that ever existed on the face of the globe. Robbers, bandits, pirates are all influenced by the same incitement—the hope of plunder: in the course of their pursuit outrages, murder, and even wanton cruelty are often committed; but this is usually in the moment of triumph, when brutal passion is inflamed, and seldom results from any preconceived plan. The Thugs, on the contrary, systematically and invariably preface every robbery with deliberate murder, sparing neither age, sex, or class.

We have however, in some respects, been much disappointed with the work. It seems to be almost without plan, and the materials thrown together in so heterogeneous a manner, that information on any one portion of the subject must be sought for sometimes in a dozen different places, and is occasionally found in a part of the work where it would be least expected; while what should have formed valuable information is very indistinctly indicated—viz. how the plans now in force for the suppression of this horrible system of assassination were originally adopted, and brought to their present perfection. These deficiencies however are in a great degree to be attributed to want of leisure from official duties on the part of the author, Captain W. H. Sleeman of the Indian military service, who has long been employed on civil duty, and superadded ill health. His modesty has also prevented him from sufficiently bringing into view his own exertions in the cause.

To our conception the work should have been arranged on somewhat of the following plan. First, a description of the origin of the Thugs, their system and mode of proceeding in their vocation; how they were enabled to increase their numbers and extend their sphere of operations; and likewise their superstitions. Secondly, an account of the first notice of these associations by the British government; and of the successive steps which were taken, until the completely organized Thug police, which now exists, was established. Under this head would have been included a statement of the difficulties, amounting, in fact, to impossibilities, under which the ordinary tribunals laboured in their attempts to bring the Thugs to punishment: to conclude with some notices of their tempers, dispositions, and habits. To this might have been added, thirdly, an appendix, containing a vocabulary of their peculiar phraseology and slang terms; together with any documents, private or official, which threw light on the subject, or might be deemed useful to those employed in the suppression of the crime.

Instead therefore of merely reviewing the work, we shall attempt, as far as our limits will allow, to lay before our readers a summary of information upon the above plan, drawn not only from Captain Sleeman's book, but also from some official documents to which the kindness of a friend has allowed us access. And here, *in limine*, we beg to assure our readers that we shall avoid, as much as possible, introducing Oriental words and terms: and that of those which are unavoidably mentioned, the meaning will be given either in a parenthesis immediately following, or in a note.

The Thugs,* or Phansigars, for they are known by both names, and by other designations in the south of India, appear to be of remote origin. Herodotus, in his Polymnia, mentions as a part of the army with which Xerxes invaded Greece, a pastoral people of Persian descent, whose only offensive weapons were a dagger and a cord, made of twisted leather, with a noose at one end. With this cord they entangled their enemies or their horses, and, when they got them down, easily put them to death. Theve-

* The actual meaning of the word T-hug, is Cunning; in which sense alone it is still used in the Himalayah and other remote parts of India. P-hansigar signifies a man with a noose; from P-hansi, a noose. The *th* and *ph* are not pronounced as commonly in English, but with the *p* and *t* aspirated, like the *t-h* of pot-hook.

Neither of the foregoing, however, can be considered as an *original* derivation, any more than the *Tatar* of our last Number (p. 410). These points will be explained on a future occasion, when it will be shown that much of the imputed *Slang* of the Thugs is, in reality, the corrupted relics of an ancient tongue.—*Ed.*

not, who published his travels in 1787, speaking of the road between Agra and Delhi, observes,

" The cunningest robbers in the world are in that country. They use a certain rope with a running nooze, which they can cast with so much sleight about a man's neck when they are within reach of him, that they never fail, so that they strangle him in a trice, &c. &c. But, besides that, there are men in those quarters so skilful in casting the snare that they succeed as well at a distance as near at hand; and if an ox or any other beast belonging to a caravan run away, they fail not to catch it by the neck."—Quoted by Capt. Sleeman, p. 10.

On this our author remarks :—

" Now, though there is a vast interval of time between the Persian invasion of Greece and the travels of Thevenot; and of space between the seat of the Sagartii and that of the ancient capital of India, I am inclined to think that the vagrant bands who, in the sixteenth century, infested the roads as above described, between Delhi and Agra, came from some wild tribe and country of the kind; and I feel, myself, no doubt that from these vagrant bands are descended the seven clans of Mohammedan Thugs, Bhys, Bursote, Kachunee, Huttar, Ganoo, and Tundell, who by the common consent of all Thugs throughout India, whether Hindoos or Mohammedans, are admitted to be the most ancient, and the great original trunk upon which all the others have at different times and in different places been grafted. Bands of these vagrants, under various denominations, are to be found in all parts of India, but are most numerous, I believe, to the north and west. They all retain, in some degree, their pristine habits and usages; and taking their families with them, they allow their women to assist in the murders which they perpetrate in their encampments; but they have always some other ostensible employment; and as the other Thugs, who live amongst, and cannot be distinguished from other men, say " they live in the desert, and their deeds are not known.' "—p. 11.

The people mentioned both by Herodotus and Thevenot must have been very different from the present race of Thugs, and more resembling the Guachos with their lassos in South America, whom Captain Head so well describes. In the south of India there is a class of Thugs, who claim to have sprung up in that part, and profess neither to be descended from nor instructed by those of Delhi, whom they consider as an inferior race; and with whom they will not intermarry. These Thugs are divided into various tribes; but as it would be of little use to trouble our readers with a long list of hard and foreign names, we shall only mention one or two who may have any peculiar characteristic.

" Of these are the Mooltaneas, a class of Thugs, all Moossulmans, who are said to have emigrated direct from Delhi, and not through Agra, and therefore not among the *Agureeas*. They are said to call themselves Naiks, and to travel and trade as Brinjaras, (corn-merchants). They kill the greater part of their female children, and never allow those who survive to marry out of their own class. They travel with their families, and strangle travellers with the cords with which they are accustomed to drive their bullocks, and not, like other Thugs, with the handkerchief. They are among the ancient Thugs, and are considered strict in their observances, and staunch to their oath of secrecy."—p. 117.

The Mooteeas, who reside chiefly about Rungpoor, Dinapoor, and Purnea, derive their name from their custom of giving their leaders a handful (mooteea,) out of every cash booty over and above what they receive in the general division.

" The Sooseas, a class of Thugs of the Dhanuk, or lowest Hindoo caste, who call themselves Naiks and Thories, and reside in various parts of Malwa and Rajpootana. They have been increasing in numbers for many generations, though they are not considered very ancient, and from their low caste are looked down upon by all the other classes of Thugs, who never eat with them, though often associated with them in their expeditions."—p. 132.

The seven original clans, who were all Mahommedans, and from whom all others are supposed to be derived, are called collectively Sat Ryut. Some say they derived their descent from seven brothers about Delhi. Mussulman Thugs all over India are found to trace their descent from one or other of these great stocks; to be able to do so being a mark of superiority. It is worth remark that there is near Delhi, the tomb of a great saint called Nizam Ooddeen Oulea, who died in October, 1325, A. D. This tomb is visited by Mahommedan pilgrims from all parts of India, as a place of great sanctity, from containing the remains of so holy a man; but the Thugs all make votive offerings to it, as being the tomb of the most renowned Thug of his day. His known lavish expenditure, so much beyond his ostensible means, seems to indicate a dishonest means of obtaining money; although he contrived to propagate the idea that he was supplied from heaven.

One strange circumstance, supposing the idea to be correct that the Thugs were originally Mahommedans, is, that their principal deity is of Hindoo origin; and that their superstitions and ceremonies are much more similar to those of the Hindoos than of the Mussulmans. But it is of little importance to discuss this point in the present paper. Although some classes greatly predominate, the Thugs now comprise men of almost every class and caste in India. This, however, is an infringement on their strict rules, which forbids the admission into the fraternity of low castes. Their habits and cant language are generally similar, as also their modes of proceeding; so that they may be described as one class. Any peculiarity of those of any part of the country, which may be worth mentioning, will be noted hereafter. Thugs are to be found in almost every province, from the Punjab and the foot of the Himalayah to Cape Comorin. They have nothing peculiar in appearance to distinguish them from ordinary inhabitants. In some villages, their profession is not avowedly known to the rest of the residents, but, as a blind, they cultivate a small portion of land, and when questioned as to their absence for months every year, pretend that they go out to service; it being very common for some classes to leave their homes for several months every year in search of employment. At other places, where they are well known to the inhabitants, the protection of the chief, which they have purchased, enables them to be less scrupulous.

Generally speaking, they do not carry on their trade near home, but make long journeys to a distant country. To this, however, there are some exceptions, as observed by Captain Sleeman in the following note.

" In the districts between the Ganges and the Jumna, there were some associations of Thugs that seldom went far from home, and who made short and frequent excursions. So the Jumaldesee Thugs of Oude and the neighbouring districts; so some of the Thug families in Bundelcund. Generally, however, the Thugs north of the Nerbudda have been in the habit of making long expeditions, and remaining absent from six to eight months on each."—App. p. 331.

They are usually found in gangs of from ten to fifty; sometimes in much larger numbers, even to five or six hundred, but this is rare; and even when the gangs are so large, they very rarely remain together, except for a day or two, at a rendezvous. They divide into different parties, who either follow each other at intervals, or take different routes; each party following its prey, as far as it can singly, and collecting together when any work is to be done which requires a larger force. They assume a variety of disguises, and appear in various characters. Sometimes that of ordinary inoffensive travellers; at others, that of people going to seek for service; at others, that of native soldiers, either going on, or returning from, leave; to make which story more plausible, the leaders would even take the trouble to learn the English drill, while their associates passed for recruits. Occasionally, the head of the gang would assume the appearance of a wealthy merchant, the rest passing for his servants and attendants. In such cases, the very horses, bullocks, and carts, belonging to those who were murdered, were added to his establishment, both to increase his consequence and carry his plunder. But a small portion of them carry arms, the less to excite suspicion.

They sometimes assume the appearance of natives of rank, or of government servants.

To enable our readers to understand how such proceedings exist, it may be necessary to explain, in a few words, the Indian mode of travelling. Such conveniences as stage coaches, public waggons, and boats, (excepting the Ganges steamers just established by government,) do not exist. There are not even any conveyances which a person may hire from stage to stage, unless in a very few parts of the country, where a traveller might, for a short distance, be supplied at each stage with a pony which would go at the rate of about three miles an hour; and he could hire a few porters to carry his baggage. The only attempt at any thing like travelling post is by going in a palkee (*Anglicè*, palanquin) carried by bearers.

Travelling *dâk*, or in a palanquin, is a mode of conveyance only available to the rich. A palkee holds but one, and the charge is never less than one, sometimes two, shillings a mile, as dear as posting in England. The traveller is obliged to give from two to five days' notice to the postmaster, according to the distance; and the average rate of proceeding is about four miles an hour.

In ordinary journeying in India, the traveller is obliged to carry every thing with him. If a rich man accompanied by his family, his goings forth are like those of the patriarchs of old, with his "flocks and herds, his camels, and his beasts of burden, his menservants and his maidservants;" he travels on his own horses, or on an elephant, while his tents, beds, cooking vessels, &c., &c., are carried on camels or in carts. Some of his attendants accompany him on horseback, or on ponies; and the rest walk, at the rate of ten or twelve miles a day. Should he travel by water, he hires a comfortable boat for himself and his family, with as many more as he requires for his kitchen and baggage, and embarks with all his retinue. Individuals of less wealth convey their property in a few carts, and are content to sleep and eat under the shelter of trees, or of one of those magnificent groves, mango and other, which are found at a few miles interval in many parts of India. According to the rank or wealth of the individual, his mode of travelling and number of attendants varies; some have only a pony to carry their baggage, while they walk on foot; and the poorest not only walk, but carry their own stores, consisting of a blanket or quilt for a bed, a pot of brass or copper tinned* to boil pulse in or make a curry, a smaller one to drink out of, and a round plate of sheet-iron, on which, supported by two

* It is a curious distinction between the Hindoos and Mussulmans, that the former all use brass vessels, the latter those made of copper tinned.

stones or lumps of earth, and with a few sticks or a little cow-dung underneath for fuel, he bakes his cakes of unleavened bread, which is merely flour and water, kneaded for a few minutes. Merchants who have goods to dispatch hire either boats, carts, camels, pack-horses, or bullocks, to convey their wares to their destination; and the same conveyances, and the same drivers or conductors, proceed the whole distance, although it may be five hundred or even a thousand miles. Large sums of treasure or jewellery, amounting sometimes to several thousand pounds at a time, are constantly dispatched by the bankers of one town to their correspondents at several hundred miles distance, by the hands of common porters. These men, instead of going in large parties well armed, usually travel in small numbers, without any arms whatever; trusting for protection to the appearance of utmost poverty which they assume. They, however, often fall victims to the ruthless vigilance of the Thugs.

There are but few inns or serais in India; the best of them consist but of a quadrangle of arches or arcades. Some of these, raised under the Mahommedan princes, are beautiful specimens of Oriental architecture, with lofty gateways and battlements; but the greater part are more like what are built on the foundation of a new street in London, to be afterwards converted into cellars. Under the native rulers, these buildings were rather numerous and kept in tolerable order; a regular establishment of guards and servants was maintained at them; and there were private doors and apartments for women. Our readers, who are familiar with Oriental tales and the Arabian Nights, will remember them, under the name of caravanserais or khans, as the scene of so many of the adventures therein described. Under the extortion of the earlier English government in India, however, and the consequent impoverishment of the country, all have suffered, more or less, and many of the most splendid are gone entirely to ruin. There are generally a few shops within the square; and, in places of considerable thoroughfare, a few people of a class called Buttearas, who cook dinners for travellers. Where there are no serais, travellers sleep in the verandahs of houses or in any open sheds they can find; but the climate of India is such as not to render shelter necessary for nine months in the year; and none but single travellers or very small parties care for serais or houses. All who are rich enough to carry tents, or those who travel in tolerable numbers, usually prefer encamping under the shade of trees, at some distance from the dirty serais or villages; and when one party is so encamped under a shady grove, a single traveller, or even several together, will easily be induced to join them, and often ask permission to do so, for the sake of protection.

It is the existence of such customs which renders the operations of the Thugs so practicable. They often wait at or near serais or towns where travellers usually rest, and some of the gang enter the serais, and the towns and villages, to ascertain if any travellers are there, or if any persons are about to take a journey. The Sothaees, or inveiglers, then proceed to induce the travellers to accompany them, on pretence of affording protection; or if the travellers be numerous, the Thugs will, by small parties, ask permission to join them, alleging the same reason. "Skilled in the art of deception, they enter into conversation, and insinuate themselves by obsequious attentions into the confidence of travellers of all descriptions, to learn from them whence they come; whither, and for what purpose, they are journeying; and of what property they are possessed."* When they think a traveller worth robbing, the next point is to carry their operations into effect. Should their place of encampment be deemed a convenient and sufficiently retired spot, the murder is usually perpetrated just before dusk. While all are employed, either in cooking their evening meal or preparing for their night's rest upon the ground, the stranglers and assistant-stranglers, called Bhurtote and Shumshea, take up their positions respectively near each traveller; scouts are sent out to watch at a little distance from the encampment, that no one approaches; the signal is given, the twisted cloth is thrown by the strangler round the neck of each victim, who is held by the assistant, and in a few seconds all is over! Others dig the grave; and the bodies are deposited, after being cut open, which, they say, prevents them from swelling and cracking the earth above; for in this case the smell, by attracting the jackals to dig up the body, might lead to detection. Should it be in a frequented place, they light fires over the spot to hide the appearance of the earth being newly moved; if it is lonely and retired, they will perhaps leave the bodies as they lie, or hide them loosely under a heap of stones; sometimes the limbs are disjointed, in order to pack the bodies closer, when they have several to dispose of.

The mode of proceeding occasionally varies, and they not unfrequently murder the travellers as they are walking along the road, i. e. when the encamping place is not considered convenient. In this case, one or more of the gang are sent on overnight to select a fit spot for the murder, and often to dig the graves beforehand. The travellers are then induced to set off before daybreak, either to avoid the heat, or on some other pretence: as they walk along, the stranglers and their assistants attach themselves to their respective victims, generally chatting

* See Appendix, p. 332.

with them in the most friendly way. At the proper spot the signal is given; the unfortunate travellers are strangled, stripped of whatever they possess, and disposed of in the ready-made graves. So admirably arranged is their system, that they will simultaneously murder thirty or forty travellers at once! On one occasion, a party of sixty people, consisting of fifty-two men, seven women, and a boy of four years old, were, all but the child, simultaneously strangled, as they were travelling along the road, although many of them were on horseback, and well armed.—See Text, p. 209, and Appendix, p. 107.

The Thugs have a cant or slang language, understood by themselves alone; and a variety of signs and signals, by which they can discover members of the fraternity, although personally strangers to each other. Their mode of salutation would pass with the uninitiated for the ordinary expression, but a Thug immediately understands it as coming from a brother: and as the very use of cant language, called by the Hindostannee Thugs "Ramasee," might sometimes excite suspicion in the intended victims, to obviate this the Thugs have attached their own peculiar meanings to certain phrases of hourly use. The signal for murder, for instance, is usually, " Give me some tobacco." " Go and clean the cooking pots," is the word to search for a *bail*, or proper spot for the murder. They have also signs, consisting of mere ordinary motions of the head or hand; coughing in a peculiar way, &c.

" Drawing the back of the hand along the chin, from the throat outwards, implies that caution is requisite—that some stranger is approaching. Putting the open hand over the mouth, and drawing it gently down, implies that there is no longer cause for alarm. If an advanced party of Phansigars overtake any travellers whom they design to destroy, but have need of more assistance, they make certain marks on the roads, by which those of the gang who follow understand that they are required to hasten forwards. A party in advance also leaves certain marks where a road branches off, as intimations to those who follow of the route their comrades have taken."—See *App*. p. 345.

In some instances, they will actually make their destined victims carry the message and signal which occasions their own destruction. When a party of Thugs, in advance, have got with them some travellers whom they intend to murder, but who are as many as they can manage, should they meet with others worth robbing, they will request these to carry a message to Bajeed Khan (a common name), and others of the party, who are behind, requesting them to hasten on. The Thugs in the rear, on receiving this message, understand by it that the coast is clear in advance, and the travellers who deliver it are worth plundering: they immediately attach themselves to them for that purpose.

The confidence which these miscreants exhibit in the course of their infernal vocation, is not one of their least remarkable features: they will sometimes murder travellers who had been persuaded to join their party, when encamped within a few yards of a village, or of another encampment of travellers. A remarkable instance of this occurred at the village of Lucknadown, between Nagpoor and Jubulpoor. A moonshee (secretary to a native chief) was travelling with his wife and children, several servants and attendants, besides horses, and was joined by a party of Thugs, who accompanied him for several days, treating him with attention, and some of them every evening singing and playing on the guitar for his amusement. The whole party were encamped close to the above village; and within a few yards of them, on the other side, quite within hearing, were some officers' servants, employed in pitching the advance-tents of a native regiment, which was expected next morning. Although it was not a very convenient spot for the murder, the Thugs determined to perpetrate it, fearing the moonshee might escape them by accompanying the regiment; and, as described by the man who turned approver,

"The tent-pitchers were all busily occupied in pitching the tents. Noor Khan, and his son Sadee Khan, and a few others, went as soon as it became dark to the moonshee's tent, and began to sing and play upon the guitar, as they had been accustomed to do. During this time, some of them took up the moonshee's sword, on pretence of wishing to look at it. His wife and children were within, listening to the music. The Jhirnee, or signal, was given, but at this moment the moonshee saw his danger; called out 'murder!' and attempted to rush through, but was seized and strangled. His wife hearing him, ran out, with the infant in her arms, but was seized by Ghubboo Khan, who strangled her and took the infant. The other daughter was strangled in the tent. The grooms were at the time cleaning their horses, and one of them, taking the alarm, ran under the belly of his horse and called out 'murder!' but he was treated in like manner, as well as all the rest of his companions."

The murderer who took the infant had intended to adopt it, but on one of the gang urging that it might lead to discovery, it was thrown alive upon the other bodies, and the grave was closed.*

We have said that there is nothing in their appearance to distinguish Thugs from ordinary individuals. It might be expected that men who spend their whole lives in the commission of such atrocities, would acquire a peculiar or ferocious cast of countenance; but of the hundreds of Thugs it has been our lot to see we can recollect but one whose aspect exhibited any thing remarkable, and he had certainly an expression of mingled cun-

* They abhor bloodshed, (even in self-defence,) considering it Murder, and repel any imputations of this, or of Theft.

ning and ferocity, which would have attracted the notice even of a casual observer. They are adepts at various disguises, and it is the apparently gentle and winning manners of those who are employed on that part of the duty which enables them to entice travellers to join them; so much so, that they even frequently persuade people who have already taken up their abode for the night in a serai, to quit the shelter, and to join the Thug camp at a little distance. Some of the gangs are found in situations where they would never be suspected. One of the most noted of them in the south of India, opened a linen-draper's shop in the military cantonments of Hingotee, where he was considered one of the most respectable men of the place. A list of the most notorious Thugs in that part was sent to Captain Reynolds, with directions to arrest them, and approvers to point them out:

> "On hearing that the Huree Sing of the list sent to him of noted Thugs at large in the Duckun, was the Huree Sing of the Sudder Bazaar, Captain Reynolds was perfectly astounded; for so correct had he been in his deportment and all his dealings, that he had quite won the esteem of all the gentlemen of the station, who used to assist him in procuring passports for his goods on their way to Bombay; and yet he had, as he has himself since shown, been carrying on his trade of murder up to the very day of his arrest, with the gangs of Hindustan and the Duckun, on all the roads around, and close to, the cantonments of Hingoke; and leading out his gangs of assassins, while he pretended to be on his way to Bombay for a supply of Irish linens and broad-cloth."—*Ibid.* p. 35.
>
> "Captain Reynolds had for several years, up to this time, had the civil charge of the district of Hingotee, without having had the slightest suspicion of the numerous murders that he has now discovered to have been every year perpetrated within his jurisdiction. Yet nothing was more true, as this man's own confession, besides the evidence against him, afterwards fully proved."—*Ibid.*

The noted approver Ferringhea, was for several years in the service of Sir David Ochterlony as a jemadar; a sort of sergeant in command of the armed attendants of a great man: but a more remarkable instance we are enabled to adduce from the official documents already alluded to. A man, named Dhunnee Khan, had for a while been a sergeant of police in the district of Mynpoorie. So high was the opinion entertained of him by the magistrates, that in 1822, on the occasion of Soorawun, a noted Thug, and several others, having escaped from gaol, Dhunnee Khan, assisted by two constables, was selected to trace and apprehend the fugitives. He was furnished with a general warrant and letter, addressed to all British authorities, and ordered to proceed through Bundelcund and Central India. This man, as it afterwards appeared, had been in league with a numerous body of Thugs who resided in that part, but had contrived to obtain the high estimation in which he was held by the magistrate, by apparent zeal, and by occasionally arresting insulated Thugs, who were for some reason or other obnoxious to his own gang. On receiving the warrant, he immediately collected this gang and many others, increasing his numbers as he proceeded until they amounted to a hundred and fifteen, and started on a Thug expedition. In the course of it they murdered thirty-two people and collected considerable plunder. The sergeant had apprehended Soorawun, and put him in irons as a blind, in the event of being questioned on the road. Near Jubulpoor they were arrested upon the charge of an informer; but the sergeant and constables showed their badges of office, warrants, and other documents, pointed to the prisoner in irons, explained that some of those who accompanied him were relations and friends, anxious to distinguish themselves and obtain service, (a common custom in India when police are ordered on a hazardous duty,) while the rest passed for travellers; and, in short, so far deceived Mr. Molony, the Commissioner at Jubulpoor, that he ordered their release. They were, however, subsequently retaken, and eventually punished, as will be hereafter mentioned. It was this gang that murdered the moonshee's party, as already detailed.

It would be supposed a mockery to mention religion in connection with such atrocities, but the demon of superstition has perhaps the principal share in their commission: in this instance it is clothed in a female form, the goddess Bhawanee, whom they believe to preside over their proceedings, and to be pleased with the sacrifice of the victims.

> "Of Thugs from all quarters of India, from Lodheeana to the Carnatic, and from the Indus to the Ganges, there is not one among them who doubts the *divine origin of the system of Thugghee;* not one who doubts that he and all who have followed the trade of murder with the prescribed rites and observances, were acting under the immediate orders and auspices of the goddess Devee, Doorgah, Kalee, or Bhawanee, as she is indifferently called; and, consequently, there is not one who feels the slightest remorse for the murders which he may, in the course of his vocation, have perpetrated or assisted in perpetrating. A Thug considers the persons murdered precisely in the light of victims offered up to the goddess; and he remembers them as a priest of Jupiter remembered the oxen, and a priest of Saturn the children sacrificed upon their altars. He meditates his murders without any misgivings; he commits them without any emotions of pity; and he remembers them without any feelings of remorse. They trouble not his dreams, nor does their recollection ever cause him inquietude in darkness, in solitude, or in the hour of death."—p. 7.

They have a variety of ceremonies and omens, which they observe both on setting out on an expedition and during its continuance. They believe these to have been dictated by Bhawanee, and that on their observance or non-observance depends their success. Although these ceremonies are in some measure varied by Thugs in different parts of India, there does not appear to be any distinction between those two opposite classes, the Mahommedans and the Hindoos of the same provinces. Both worship the same deity, and observe the same rites. The Mussulman Thugs explain it by asserting that Bowanee (or Bhawanee) and Fatima, the daughter of Mahommed and the wife of Ali, were one and the same person. Of their ceremonies the most essential is the consecration of the Pickaxe before setting out on an expedition, accompanied by a variety of forms too tedious to relate: but there is not—

" a Thug by birth, or one who had been fully initiated into its mysteries, who doubted the *inspiration* of the pick-axe, when consecrated in due form;—not one who doubted that the omens described in this work were all-sufficient to guide them to their prey, or to warn them of their danger; or that they were the signs ordained by the goddess expressly for these purposes;—not one who doubted that if these omens were attended to, and the prescribed rules observed, the system of Thugghee must have flourished under the auspices of its divine patroness, in spite of all our efforts for its suppression."—p. 9.

Their superstitions and omens are very numerous, and are drawn from the most trivial and even childish circumstances. They are taken principally from the flight of birds and motions of different animals, or from the cries and calls of various creatures. The call of a partridge, for instance, if heard on the left, promises good; if on the right, it threatens evil. The rest are much of the same nature, or even more absurd.

" Different castes and clans of Thugs have, in some few instances, different rules for interpreting these sounds and appearances; and what is considered to threaten evil by some, is thought to promise good by others; but, on such occasions, they all follow the leader who opens the expedition, or leads the greatest number of Thugs associated together in any expedition."—p. 123.

Sometimes the omen is thought so bad that the expedition is altogether abandoned; at others, broken up and re-opened with fresh ceremonies: sometimes the evil omen is averted by performing certain rites upon the spot. Instances have occurred where travellers, who were upon the point of being murdered, have been allowed to pass on unmolested, in consequence of an unfavourable omen, such as the scream of a hare. Many of them believe, that if the omens are favourable, they would feel the anger of their deity, if they were not to murder the travellers; while that to allow the first traveller met with, in going on an expedition, to escape, *provided he has but little property,* will bring good luck. It is asserted positively by them, that in the caves at Ellora are to be found sculptures representing every operation of Thugghee.

According to the strict rules of the Thugs, they were never to murder any of the following classes :—A sweeper, a carrier, oil seller, washerman, goldsmith, dancing-girl, bard ;—two descriptions of religious mendicants called Nanuk-puntee and Jattadarree; carriers of grain, elephant drivers, travellers who had a cow with them, a woman, or a married person. By some the list of exemptions was extended; by others it was more confined. There were also restrictions regarding some other classes, who were not to be the first victims upon the opening of an expedition: but these have been disregarded by the majority of the Thugs in the north-west, and in Central India, and for some years whoever has fallen into their hands has been murdered without regard to class, age, or sex. It is to this cause, and to the neglect of proper attention to their omens and rites, that they attribute the anger of their goddess, and the consequent success of the British Government in exterminating them. One remarkable feature in this association of murderers is, that no instance has yet been discovered of *wanton cruelty;* by which is meant pain inflicted beyond what was necessary to destroy life—pain either to mind or body.—"No Thug was ever known to offer insult, either in act or speech, to any woman they were to murder." They let off poor travellers sometimes, and even beautiful women. Considerable restriction was formerly adopted as to the classes who could be admitted into the association of Thugs, but latterly some gangs have received all castes into the fraternity.

The different bodies of Thugs form a complete division of labour in appointing the duties of the respective members of the gang, each of which has its peculiar name. These are the jemadar or leader, who usually gives the signal for the murder; the sothaees or inveiglers of travellers; the stranglers; the assistant stranglers; those who carry the body to the grave; the grave-diggers; those who cut up the bodies to render them more compact; and the belhæ, who go on before to search for a proper place of murder during the next day's journey, when the present encampment is not deemed convenient for the purpose. Others keep watch at the time of the murder to obviate any danger of interruption; and those who go out for the first time, or who are dull and slow in learning their business, are employed in menial offices, such as sweeping the encamping ground, or tending the horses and bullocks which belong to the camp. Children are initiated at ten or twelve years old. During

—"the first expedition they neither see nor hear any thing of murder. They know not our trade; they get presents, purchased out of their share, and become fond of the wandering life, as they are always mounted upon ponies. Before the end of the journey they always know that we rob: the next expedition they suspect that we commit murder, and some of them even know it; and in the third expedition they see all.

"*Q*. Do they not become frightened?

"*A*. Not after the first expedition."

But some extraordinary cases to the contrary have occurred.

"About twelve years ago, my cousin Aman Subadur took out with us my cousin Kuhora, a lad of fourteen, for the first time. He was mounted on a pretty pony, and Hursooka, an adopted son of Aman's, was appointed to take charge of the boy.

"We fell in with five Sikhs,* and when we set out before daylight in the morning, Hursooka, who had been already on three expeditions, was ordered to take the bridle and keep the boy in the rear out of sight and hearing. The boy got alarmed and impatient; got away from Hursooka, and gallopped up at the instant the signal for murder was given. He heard the screams of the men, and saw them all strangled. He was seized with a trembling, and fell from his pony;—he became immediately delirious; was dreadfully alarmed at the turbans of the murdered men: and when any one touched him or spoke to him, talked about the murders, and screamed exactly like a boy talks in his sleep; and trembled violently if any one touched or spoke to him. We could not get him on, after burying the bodies. Aman and I, and a few others, sat by him while the gang went on: we were very fond of him, and tried all we could to tranquillize him; but he never recovered his senses, and before evening he died. I have seen many instances of feelings greatly shocked at the sight of the first murder, but never one so strong as this. Kuhora was a very fine boy, and Hursooka took his death much to heart, and turned religious mendicant: he is now at some temple on the bank of the Nerbudda river."—(See pp. 148, 149.)

A discovery has been more recently made of an extensive combination of river Thugs on the Ganges. Their plan of operation is to have many boats at various landing-places on the river, which are kept extremely neat and inviting for travellers. From fourteen to sixteen Thugs are on board each boat, of whom some are disguised as, and perform the work of, ordinary boatmen; while the others assume the appearance of well-drest, respectable travellers, who profess to be either going or returning from pilgrimage to Benares, or some of the holy places on the river. The inveiglers are sent out on the roads which lead from or run parallel to it, where they fall in with parties whose destination is either up or down the stream. Having acquired the necessary information, the inveiglers pretend to be bound to the same place; talk of the

* Sikhs or Singhs, the nation inhabiting the Punjab.

delay and fatigue of a land journey, and propose to proceed by water. The travellers are then taken to the spot where one of the Thug boats is waiting, and, after some bargaining, are taken on board. Often, to lull suspicion, much difficulty is made about receiving them; the captain of the boat objects on the pretence of having been already hired by others; and the Thugs, who figure as passengers, declare that there is no room to spare. When at length the travellers are received, the boat pushes off, the Thugs familiarly chatting with them: all being at length prepared and no other boat near, the steersman above gives the signal by three taps, and the victims are strangled. The bodies are then stripped and thrown into the river.

The difficulty of eradicating the river Thugghee will be far greater than has been found in dealing with this crime by land, on account of circumstantial evidence not being forthcoming. In the land Thugghee, the depositions of the approvers are corroborated by digging up the bodies, hundreds of which have been brought to light; but this resource fails in the river Thugghee, where the bodies are carried away by the stream; and there the sight of corpses floating excites no observation, because thousands of the poorer classes, not being able to afford the expense of burning their dead, merely throw them into the river. Plundered property also is sometimes found on the land Thugs, or proved to have been in their possession; but the custom houses on the river were so numerous, and the fear of search so great,* that the miscreants there never retained about them any article at all likely to lead to suspicion. Nevertheless, by a proper system of Thug police, this, as well as Thugghee by land, will be eradicated. The superstition of the Thugs themselves will assist in this end; as many of them now believe that, owing to their neglect of the rites and ceremonies prescribed by their deity, she has ordained that the British Government shall eradicate Thugghee. They are appalled at the numbers that have been hanged or transported; and of late no sooner is a gang arrested on suspicion than some of them offer to become approvers to save themselves; so much so, that many more approvers can be obtained than are required.

Our readers will almost deem it impossible that such organized gangs of murderers, amounting to several thousands, could carry on their villainy almost undiscovered so long;—for two or three centuries at least. The difficulty, however, nearly vanishes when we reflect on the mode of travelling in India, described at the head of this article, and on the peculiar system of the Thugs. In the first place they seldom murder near their own homes: but

* These custom houses have since been abolished to the great benefit of trade.

even this would be a point of little importance when we consider, secondly, that travellers, and generally from a distant part of the country, are their victims: thirdly, that they invariably murder before they rob.

"It is a maxim with these assassins that 'dead men tell no tales,' and upon this maxim they invariably act. They permit no living witness to their crimes to escape, and therefore never attempt the murder of any party, until they can feel secure of being able to murder the whole. They will travel with a party of unsuspecting travellers for days, and even weeks together; eat with them, sleep with them; attend worship with them at the holy shrines on the road; and live with them on the closest terms of intimacy, till they find time and place suitable for the murder of the whole."—(p. 53.)

Lastly, they avoid exciting suspicion by being careful to leave behind them no marks even of a crime having been committed. The travellers who become their victims were men seeking for service; or returning home with the savings of years; merchants going on business to a distant town; or others journeying either from business or pleasure. They might be murdered in the morning twilight within half a mile of the serai or village in which they had passed the night; while the Thugs who watched and had marked them for their prey were encamped at a short distance. No one missed them: the people of the serai or village which they had left took it for granted that they had proceeded on their way; and those of the next halting-place in advance were ignorant of their approach. It is not till days, weeks, months, or even years had passed away that their relations, hearing nothing of their arrival at their intended destinations, make inquiries, and it is seldom that they can ascertain even the place about which the travellers were probably murdered. Unless the inquiry be made within a short time, and there may have been something in the appearance or equipage of the travellers to attract attention, the villagers and others who reside along the road would not recollect whether those inquired for had passed or not. But even supposing (as has occasionally occurred) that the relations succeed in tracing the travellers to a certain spot, beyond which all clue is lost; this gives a moral certainty that they have been murdered at no great distance, that is, within a few miles adjacent.—But how, within such a space, are they to pitch upon the spot where the bodies are interred?—and more,—where are the murderers? probably hundreds of miles away; and even should they by chance be again encamped on the very spot, what means are there of detection? In ordinary thefts, and by local thieves, the tracing and discovery of stolen property affords a very powerful means of bringing the matter home to the perpetrators; but this has but little effect against Thugs. They contrive to obtain full knowledge of the persons, residence, and destination of those they murder, and are careful not to dispose of any recognizable articles where they might by chance be perceived. Such as have any peculiar marks are destroyed.

Considering all these circumstances, it is not astonishing that so little has been done towards suppressing this association of miscreants. The fact is, that until this five or six years, no one had any correct notion of its extent: all that was known up to that period was, that travellers were occasionally enticed and murdered by people called Thugs, who assumed the garb of inoffensive way-farers. By some extraordinary chance, such as one of the victims having made his escape, or some of the stolen property being unexpectedly recognized, or one of the gang having turned informer in consequence of a quarrel for the division of the spoil, a few of these miscreants were occasionally discovered and punished. Even had the various governments into which India is divided, been aware of the extent of the evil and anxious to destroy it, they would have been unable to do so: insulated efforts would have produced little or no benefit; the jealousies which existed would have prevented their combining for the purpose; and for a century and half or more, there has not existed any paramount power which could devise a general plan of operations, and compel the rest to submit to it.

Other causes are not wanting which tended to prevent any attempts being made, even in detail, to arrest the proceedings of the different gangs of Thugs. Some of the native chiefs knowingly harboured and protected them as a source of revenue from which they derived considerable sums annually, out of the profits of their plunder. The Thugs lived in villages like other people, and generally cultivated small portions of ground to maintain appearances: so that the native chiefs, if questioned, pretended of course to know nothing of their real character; asserting that these people lived, cultivated, and paid their rent like others, and accounting for the absence of most of the male population during several months, by saying that they went for service and returned periodically with the amount of their earnings. In other cases, native chiefs who would have readily punished a gang of thieves when apprehended, were deterred from doing so by a superstitious dread. The Thugs always endeavoured to impress the belief that they were acting according to the injunctions of their deity Bowanee, and that all who opposed them would feel the vengeance of their goddess. The few instances in which Thugs were put to death by native chiefs were generally cases of personal vengeance, because these villains had murdered some relation or dependant of the chief, and were by good fortune apprehended immediately, " in the red-hand." It has unfortunately in several instances occurred that after punishing Thugs, the chief himself, his son, or some relation has died within a short time : whether some of the Thug fraternity took secret means to ensure such an occurrence, cannot be ascertained ; but they seized all such opportunities to substantiate the belief which they endeavoured to inculcate. In general, a native chief would merely extort a sum of money from the Thugs, or keep them in confinement for a time, after which they were released ; and not unfrequently they were discharged at once. Their own superstition however, as has just been explained, is now beginning to operate against them.

The following will show what extraordinary proceedings occur sometimes in India. A dispatch of dollars to the value of four thousand pounds sterling, made on account of a rich merchant of Indoor, Dhun Raj, was carried off by Thugs, who murdered the attendant guards, near a place called Burwaba Ghaut, on the Nerbudda. He contrived to ascertain who the Thugs were, and, being a man of considerable influence, to occasion their arrest and detention in gaol by the native chiefs in whose jurisdiction they lived : after some time an agreement was made with the Thugs to release them if they would refund the money or its amount.

" Some paid out of the fruits of former expeditions, others borrowed in anticipation of future success; and those who had neither money nor credit, pledged themselves to pay part of their future earnings."—p.190.

The Thugs durst not break their engagements for fear of Dhun Raj, and after some time he realized the full sum of which he had been plundered. Finding, however, that he could turn his power and influence to so good an account, he began to assume the character of a patron of Thugs : he had always some of the principal leaders about his person, and yearly exacted large sums of money from the principal gangs in return for his protection, threatening those who refused with arrest and punishment : and such was his influence, that he could procure the release of a gang from almost any gaol in central India.

Though the British Indian government was free from the superstitions or the corruption which prevented the native chiefs from punishing Thugs, it was not the less hampered by prejudices of its own, and by real difficulties which lay in the way of the object desired. Regarding the prejudices alluded to, it is necessary to explain a little of the secret springs that actuated the government. The members at the head of the administration have always had a tolerably correct idea of the oppressive nature of our rule in India, and of the light in which it is held by the natives; but it has always been a primary object to prevent this knowledge from reaching the English public. To effect this, the reports forwarded to the Court of Directors have always descanted on the admirable system of internal government which we have established in our territories; the blessings which our native subjects enjoy; and their consequent gratitude. The feeling descends through the various ranks of government servants, who generally take their cue accordingly. It may be observed too, that the majority of the officers of government, civil or military, are extremely ignorant of the natives of India, and of their real sentiments; and are therefore easily misled by a few designing favourites, who alone possess their ear, and have their own ends to serve.

To acknowledge, even had they been fully aware of it, the existence of such an evil as Thugghee over the whole of our provinces, was by no means agreeable to our government: it would have contradicted their repeated assertions and representations. If an evil could be suppressed quietly and without incurring any additional expense, it would have been a source of deep satisfaction; but the proceedings of government have almost warranted a belief that they would prefer the existence of an evil, provided it were not generally known, even to the discovery of a remedy, if this should tend to produce a considerable sensation and excite inquiry. We could at least instance several public officers who have brought considerable annoyance upon themselves by too broadly bringing to notice the existence of evils, or the enormous extent to which crimes of the deepest dye, such as murders, gang robbery, and others, are perpetrated. Appearances are, however, kept up. The zeal and ability of the officer are praised, and his praiseworthy motives duly appreciated;—but then come certain remarks indicating an "apprehension of his being misinformed;" doubts that "the evil is not so bad as he has represented;" with a concluding observation that copies of the correspondence will be sent to the superintendent of police, judge of circuit, or some superior officer, who will be desired to report on the subject. This individual, if he have any tact, or any thing to hope or fear from the favour of government, frames his report according to what he sees is wished or expected from him: states the district to be not in worse order than others (which perhaps is true enough, owing to the vigorous measures of the magistrate in question, by which crime has been abated); and, by a careful adjustment of words and phrases, contrives to do away entirely with the impression which, in accordance with truth, ought to have been received. Occasionally, where the magistrate has persisted in his representations, the affair has actually ended by his removal, while his successor has reaped the full benefit of his exertions, and gained the entire credit of them.

A strong instance of the way in which the ends of justice may be defeated by a mistaken anxiety in public officers to gain a good name with the government by making it appear that crime does not exist, occurred in the district of Chupra in 1827. Two men were murdered by a gang of Thugs, who, almost immediately after, got drunk and quarrelled. Four of them in consequence gave information against the others, who were arrested with the property of the murdered men in their possession: these were committed for trial, and the four first allowed to turn king's evidence. The state of the case was as follows:—There was, first, the evidence of the approvers; second, the deposition of the wives of the men, who swore to the property found; and, thirdly, the men accused of being Thugs could give no satisfactory account of themselves. The defence was merely a denial, and an assertion that the property claimed by the widows was their (the prisoners') own. The judgment given will scarce be credited by our readers. The prisoners were released; the approvers and the police were severely punished for perjury and for oppression; government was led to believe that no such crime as Thugghee existed in that part of the country; and the magistrate, Mr. Pringle, who had been active in apprehending many Thugs, and had reported the same, received a severe reprimand.

One fact yet remains to be mentioned, which will show the difficulties of the case. The judge, Mr. Elliot, ordered the property which was claimed by the widows to be retained in court, while all the rest of the property found on the prisoners was returned to them. Now, for whom was the above to be retained? It could not belong to any third person, but either to the prisoners or to the murdered men. If the judge disbelieved the whole story for the prosecution, and deemed the prisoners innocent, he should have restored to them this property along with the rest that was found upon them, and which they claimed as their own. If he believed the statement of the widows, that those things belonged to their husbands, then must the prisoners have been punished as the murderers, and the property would have been given to the widows. This little fact is one of those which either show a strange perversion of judgment, or denote a vacillation of mind indicating that the judge himself felt that all was not right in the orders he gave.* The truth of all that was stated on

* No mention of this order to retain that portion of the property is to be found in Captain Sleeman's book. We derive it from a statement publicly made by Mr. Pringle.

the part of the prosecution has since been fully proved by depositions of other Thug approvers; and not only so, but that Thugghee existed to a great extent in those districts, at the very time that Mr. Elliot was assuring government that no such crime occurred.—(p. 244 of Appendix.)

Many of the English magistrates were actuated by the same feelings. Some would not allow that Thugghee could exist in their districts, and even within this year were excessively indignant at such statements being made by the officers employed in the suppression of this crime: they were perfectly astounded, when men dispatched by those officers proceeded to dig up the bodies of persons recently murdered in various places, sometimes within a short distance of the police functionary's residence. Others admitted that such a thing might occur occasionally; while a few boldly and openly stated what they had discovered, and gave much valuable information. Our limits do not permit us to add extracts from the official papers: we must, therefore, refer our readers to various letters from Mr. Wright, a Madras magistrate. —(See Appendix V. in Captain Sleeman's book.)

But even if all the English magistrates in India had been aware of and cordially co-operated with each other, they would have effected little towards the suppression of Thugghee. The ordinary tribunals and modes of proceeding, which answered in some degree for the detection and punishment of ordinary offenders, were of little avail against Thugs. Except in the rare instance of a gang being apprehended with stolen property in possession, which the relations of the murdered persons were there to identify, the only witnesses who could ever be brought against them were some of their own fraternity; and the evidence of men whose preliminary step must be to confess themselves the most ruthless villains in existence, is naturally received with distrust, of which the case commemorated by Mr. Pringle is a memorable example, and doubtless may plead for the judge. For further particulars we refer our readers to pages 200, 221, 257, 262, of the text of our author; and to Appendixes K. and L., in some of which they will find that the informers were punished, though not to the same extent as in Mr. Pringle's case.

Such being the English mode of proceeding, it is no wonder that approvers and informers were slow to come forward; for no sooner did they lose the protection of our functionaries, than they were murdered by their accomplices. The dilatoriness and inefficiency of our courts; the great power which the subordinate police and court officers possess to disguise the real merits of a case; the influence which the Thugs contrived to obtain over these by means of bribes; the few instances in which stolen property or bodies were discovered; all conspired to increase the difficulty under which the ordinary magistrates laboured in detecting the perpetrators of this crime. But even where the bodies were found in wells, which was a common mode of disposing of them when in a hurry or likely to be disturbed, in the Doab, Oude, and other parts, the owner of the ground and his neighbours generally buried them as quickly as possible that the police officers might know nothing of the matter; and if these did become acquainted with the circumstance, a bribe would usually prevent their reporting it to the magistrate. The farmers and others had just grounds for what they did, owing to the strange mode in which the English government conducts its police affairs. In such cases as those now mentioned the common practice is to summon to court the owners of the neighbouring lands, and many of the neighbours;—at a distance, perhaps, of from ten to eighty miles, and to fine them severely as a matter of course, if they could not produce the perpetrators of the murders.

But even when an insulated gang was actually brought to justice, it was but a drop in the ocean towards the suppression of Thugghee;—nor would, nor will any thing effect this, but a general system, which shall be in operation all over India. Different magistrates might receive information which, if it were combined and compared together, might prove of the greatest value, but which becomes useless when frittered away among separate officers, who have no communication with each other. The whole business too was so little understood, that few could bring themselves to credit the extent of such an organized system of murder. Although sufficient was known, so far back as 1810, to induce the commander-in-chief to issue a general order to the native soldiery who went on leave, urging them to take bills on the different treasuries for the amount of their savings, instead of carrying cash, for fear of being robbed on the road, yet year after year passed, and men did not join their corps: but it was always supposed they had deserted, and little suspicion apparently was entertained of their being murdered, which however, was since discovered to have been the case in almost every instance. The scattered residences of the Thugs was another obstacle, and rendered them much more difficult to deal with than ordinary criminals, who inhabit the same locality. The members of a single gang often came from different parts of the country, some of which were hundreds of miles asunder. Numbers of them, perhaps the greater part, were residents of foreign states over which our magistrates had no control; and, although the British government might have requested the co-operation of the different princes, little or no good would have been effected. Even a system of Thug police, such as has been now established, if confined to our own provinces, could have been of no permanent use. The Thugs would have emigrated for the time to the native states, and although the crime might for a while cease in our own territories, as soon as the special Thug police was abolished, those miscreants would all have returned and prosecuted their trade as vigorously as ever.

Occasionally when a gang, residents of a foreign territory, were arrested, and moral proof against them was strong, but legal proof, according to our own system, failing; if the government made them over to their own native chief in the hope that he would punish them, this usually ended in their being released by paying a sum of money—sometimes without. On the other hand, when our subjects were apprehended on a Thug expedition in a native state, they sometimes contrived, by flattering English prejudices, to obtain the protection of our functionaries. The established creed of the government is the superior excellence of their own administration, and the blessings enjoyed by their native subjects; and they descant largely on the tyranny and oppression which exists in all native states. This is well known to our native dependants and officials, who play their part accordingly. With many of them the Thugs maintained a good understanding, and when any of those wretches, residents of our territories, were arrested by a native chief, a pitiable story was presented to some English functionary of "poor innocent British subjects on a trading expedition," or something of the sort, having been confined by a tyrannical chief, in order to extort money from them. Of course, a due proportion of compliments and flattery of the English was mixed up with the representation, and this would produce, often without the slightest inquiry, a strong letter from the English functionary to the native chief on the injustice of his proceedings, and generally ensured the release of the Thugs.—(See Appendix, p. 417.)

Things had gone on in this way for years, chequered occasionally by the vigorous attempt of some individual functionary to eradicate the evil, but without any solid benefit. The most notorious of these efforts was an attack made by Messrs. Halhed and Stockwell, in the year 1812, on the strong-hold of a large body of Thugs, in the province of Sindouse, in the Gualior territory. They had formed a large village there, whence they issued annually on their excursions, and paid a regular tribute to that state for their protection. Many were killed; but the greater part, being driven away, scattered themselves all over India, joining other gangs or forming new ones wherever they went: so that the enterprize, from not being followed up on a system of information derived from some of those who were captured, actually in its results produced more evil than good.

The next event which occurred, and which ultimately laid the foundation of the successful measures that have been since pursued, was the arrest of a gang of a hundred and fifteen, near Jubulpoor, in 1823: it was accomplished by the following means. A noted leader of Thugs, named Kulian, was in the Jubulpoor gaol. Seeing the proof strong against him, he offered to turn informer to save himself; and was promised his life in the event of his doing good service. He accordingly desired his brother, Motee, to accompany the first large gang he should meet, travelling in that direction; to note well the murders and places where the bodies should be buried; and, as the gang approached Jubulpoor, to give information to Mr. Molony, agent to the governor-general. The gang which Motee joined was that of Dhunnee Khan: he strictly fulfilled his instructions, and caused the apprehension of the whole: this has been already related; and also how Dhunnee Khan contrived to persuade Mr. Molony to order their release. In despair at this, Motee followed the gang, and, by dint of frightening some of them with assurances of speedy re-apprehension, persuaded a few to return with him to Mr. Molony, and declare what they really were. On this additional evidence, a large police force was sent after the gang, and succeeded in capturing a hundred and three, who were safely lodged in gaol. Mr. Molony unfortunately died soon after this: his successors apparently did not know how to proceed in the case, until Mr. F. C. Smith took it up in 1830, shortly after his appointment as governor-general's agent at Jubulpoor: seventy-five were convicted; the others having died in gaol, excepting some who were made informers.

Another considerable gang was apprehended in the same territories in 1826 by Captain Wardlow, employed there as a civil officer; a third by Captain Sleeman, in Bhopal, in the beginning of 1830; and a fourth by Major Borthwick, political agent of Mahidpoor:—

> "These arrests were attended by a combination of circumstances, so fortunate, that a man might consider them as providential without exposing himself to the charge of superstition. The feelings of every one whose feelings were of any importance to the cause, from the Governor-General Lord William Bentinck, and Sir Charles Metcalfe, Vice-President in Council, to the humblest individual, seemed to be deeply and simultaneously interested in promoting its success."—See p. 46.

Of all these gangs, some of the members, frightened at what had already occurred, turned approvers, in order to save themselves; but the evidence of these men, in particular of a Brahmin approver, named Ferringhea, was perfectly astounding, and laid open a scene of barefaced villainy which could scarcely be credited: nevertheless, every statement hitherto made by them, and by others, has been corroborated.

Captain Sleeman observes :—

" When I was in civil charge of the district of Nursingpoor, in the valley of the Nerbuddah, in the years 1822, 1823, and 1824, no ordinary robbery or theft could be committed without my becoming acquainted with it; nor was there a robber or a thief of the ordinary kind in the district, with whose character I had not become acquainted in the discharge of my duty as magistrate; and if any man had then told me that a gang of assassins by profession resided in the village of Kundelee, not four hundred yards from my court; and that the extensive groves of the village of Mundesur, only one step from me on the road to Saugor and Bhopal, was one of the greatest *beles*, or places of murder in all India; and that large gangs from Hindustan and the Deccan used to rendezvous in these groves; remain in them for many days together every year, and carry on their dreadful trade along all the lines of road that pass by and branch off from them, with the knowledge and connivance of the two landholders by whose ancestors these groves had been planted; I should have thought him a fool or a madman: and yet, nothing could have been more true. The bodies of a hundred travellers lie buried in and around the groves of Mundesur; and a gang of assassins lived in and about the village of Kundelee while I was magistrate of the district, and extended their depredations to the cities of Poona and Hyderabad."—See p. 22.

" When Feringhea, a Thug leader of some note, for whose arrest government paid 500 rupees, was brought in to me at Saugor, in December, 1830, he told me, that, if his life were spared, he could procure the arrest of several large gangs, who were in February to rendezvous at Jeypoor, and proceed into Guzerat and Candeish. Seeing me disposed to doubt his authority upon a point of so much importance, he requested me to put him to the proof;—to take him through the village of Seloda, which lay two stages from Saugor on the road to Seronge, and through which I was to pass in my tour of the distriot, of which I had received the civil charge, and he would show me his ability and inclination to give me correct information. I did so, and my tents were pitched, where tents usually are, in the small mango grove. I reached them in the evening; and, when I got up in the morning, he pointed out three places, in which he and his gang had deposited, at different intervals, the bodies of three parties of travellers. A pundit (priest) and six attendants, murdered in 1818, lay among the ropes of my sleeping-tent; a serjeant and four seapoys, murdered in 1824, lay under my horses; and four Brahmin carriers of Ganges-water, and a woman, murdered soon after the pundit, lay within my sleeping-tent. The sward had grown over the whole, and not the slightest sign of its ever having been broken was to be seen. The thing seemed to me incredible; but after examining attentively a small brick terrace close by, and the different trees around, he declared himself prepared to stake his life upon the accuracy of his information. My wife was still sleeping over the grave of the water-carriers, unconscious of what was doing or to be done. I assembled the people of the surrounding villages, and the police officer and his men, who resided in the village of Korac, close by, and put the people to work over the grave of the serjeant. They dug down five feet, without perceiving the slightest signs of the bodies or of a grave. All the people seemed delighted to think that I was become weary like themselves, and satisfied that the man was deranged; but there was a calm and quiet confidence about him that made me insist upon their going on; and at last we came upon the bodies of the whole five, laid out precisely as he had described. My wife, still unconscious of our object in digging, had repaired to the breakfast tent, which was pitched at some distance from the grove; and I now had the ropes of the tent removed, and the bodies of the pundit and his six companions in a much greater state of decay were exhumed from about the same depth, and from the exact spot pointed out. The water-carriers were afterwards disinterred, and he offered to point out others in the neighbouring groves; but I was sick of the horrid work, and satisfied with what he had already done. The gangs which were concentrating upon Jeypoor were pursued, and the greater part of them taken, and Feringhea's life was spared for his services.

The disclosures made by these different approvers, and the information given, threw open so fine a field for a general plan of operations, that the matter was warmly taken up by Mr. Smith, agent to the governor-general, and Captain Sleeman, district officer of Nursingpoor, each zealously cooperating with the other. On the 21st September, 1830, Mr. Smith wrote to government, and intimated the necessity of some such plan: but the eyes of the latter had been opened, and before the receipt of Mr. Smith's dispatch, a letter from government, dated 8th October, was addressed to him, requesting his opinion on the subject. In reply, he submitted a plan, of which the following is an outline.

1st. That an officer, to be termed superintendent of operations against Thugghee, should be appointed, with power to send out parties to apprehend those against whom he might have information in any part of the country.

2nd. The superintendent to commit all whom he deems guilty for trial, before the governor-general's agent in the Saugor and Nerbudda territories.

3rd. Lists to be made out against all upon whom suspicion rests, and sent to the different English functionaries.

4th. The residents at native courts also to give their assistance.

The draught likewise contains several minor provisions regarding the search for dead bodies; rewards to those who deserve such a mark of approbation; penalties for harbouring Thugs;

prevention of abuses by approvers; and other clauses not worth enumerating here, although highly useful in practice.

The suggestions were, however, but partially adopted by government, for unfortunately Lord William Bentinck, at that time at the head of affairs, was not in the habit of indulging in a general or comprehensive view of any question; and his mind, while in India, was chiefly occupied in the minor details of government and the consideration of petty economical retrenchments. Captain Sleeman was, in January, 1831, removed to the Saugor district, authorized to act as superintendent, to send out parties for the arrest of Thugs, and proceed as above proposed; but he was still expected to perform all his duties as civil officer of the Saugor district, without any additional pay, such being Lord William Bentinck's system. Still under so able and indefatigable an officer as Captain Sleeman much benefit occurred, and numerous arrests were made; but it soon became evident, from the extensive nature of the Thug operations, that more aid must be granted. Accordingly, in January, 1832, another officer was appointed to take charge of the revenue and civil duties of the Saugor district, over which Captain Sleeman then presided, leaving to the latter only the magistracy department; thus allowing him more leisure to devote to Thug affairs. Three junior officers were appointed his assistants, and detached to apprehend such Thugs as they could obtain information of.

Still, the more that was done the more seemed requisite to do. Every arrest brought to light new combinations and associations of these professed assassins, and discovered new scenes in which their dreadful trade was at work. It was obvious that nothing but a general system, undertaken by a paramount power, strong enough to bear down all opposition by interested native chiefs, could ever eradicate such well-organized villainy; and the other members of government at length succeeded in persuading Lord William Bentinck that it was incumbent upon a government calling itself enlightened to take the lead in so good a work; and that a moderate expense would be well bestowed in suppressing an association which was causing the annual murder of some thousands of his fellow creatures. In prosecution of the extended system of operations, Captain Sleeman was, in January, 1835, relieved altogether from ordinary civil duties, and appointed superintendent; and several additional officers were nominated to act under him in various parts of the country.

Jubulpoor, the residence of the agent to the governor-general in the Saugor and Nerbudda territories, was appointed Captain Sleeman's head-quarters. All Thugs apprehended within those territories, Jeypoor, Hyderabad, Nagpoor, and other contiguous native states are tried by the agent at Jubulpoor. Those of Oude and Indore by the residents of those courts; and such as have committed crimes in what are called our regulation provinces, are tried by the officers who are there stationed. Operations have lately extended into Bombay, Madras, the eastern parts of Bengal, and the north westernmost parts of the Indian continent; and there is no doubt that, to ensure complete success, it will be necessary to nominate additional superintendents as well as subordinate officers for each of these divisions: to which should be added functionaries specially appointed for the trial of those committed.

The success of the combined operations has been beyond hope; and if properly followed up, it will be almost impossible for a Thug to remain at large. The mode of proceeding is, to take the deposition of those who turn approvers, wherever this may happen to be. These men are then required to give, to the best of their recollection, a full account of every expedition on which they have been, mentioning the dates of every one, and the detail of every murder; together with the names of those who had formed the gangs, their residence, caste, &c., &c. All this is registered in the office of the general-superintendent, and lists of those to be apprehended are sent to the different subordinate officers, who are all provided with approvers and guards. These officers also take the depositions in full of all whom they may apprehend, copies of which are sent to the general-superintendent. It is obvious that when depositions, thus taken almost simultaneously from different people hundreds of miles apart, who have had no means of collusion, and none of them expecting to be apprehended, agree in describing the same scenes and the same actors, it is obviously next to impossible to refuse belief. But another test is applied. When a Thug is arrested, he is brought direct to the officers' residence, and placed in a row between unconcerned people. The approvers, who have been detained at the stations, are then sent for singly, and required to point out any individual of the party whom they may know. If they all fix upon the same individual, and their statements also agree with those previously made by others, it is impossible that better evidence can be had.

We mention this, because we are aware that a prejudice has gone forth against the mode of conducting both the previous investigations and the sessions part of the business in Thug trials. That a man who has only seen or heard the latter should have some suspicions is not surprising; for the whole evidence of events long past is given so glibly, that it appears to bear strong marks of fabrication. But in fact the sessions part of the business is the least to be relied on: if that were all a man had before him to enable him to form his judgment, few Thugs would have been punished: before the trials come on, the approvers have all been brought together; have had opportunities of seeing the prisoners, and of fabricating what tales they please. But this they dare not do; they know well that what passes in the sessions, though the actual trial, yet serves chiefly to inspect the papers and operations of the subordinate officers, in order to ascertain that all has been correctly couducted; and that in reality, the previous proceedings form the evidence mainly relied upon. The whole association of Thugs is, in fact, different from that of any other known villains in existence. Their system is such, that they are beyond the reach of the ordinary tribunals of the country, and a special system must be put in force against them. That some petty abuses have been committed, we allow. Money has occasionally been extorted from people, under threat of accusing them of being Thugs; and others, though innocent, have suffered a temporary imprisonment. But there is no system, however well organized, that may not be open to imperfections; and what are such evils as the above, which are the sum total of all that has occurred, to ridding the world of some hundreds of professed assassins.

We are fully convinced, after taking every thing into consideration, that there are no trials in which a man may with so safe a conscience pronounce sentence, as those of the Thugs; in proof of which we have only to refer to the table in p. 38 of Captain Sleeman's work. No less than eleven different functionaries, judicial and political, are there mentioned as having held Thug trials; yet the general result is the same in all, as to the proportion found guilty and acquitted. We could mention many individual instances in proof of the correctness of the information obtained and evidence brought forward, but will content ourselves with one very striking case from Hyderabad. About eighty Thugs had been arrested in various parts of that kingdom by different parties of our approvers; they were collected into a gang and sent off to Jubulpoor under a guard. As they were passing the residence of the local governor of one of the Hyderabad provinces, he gave in charge to the guard eleven men whom he had apprehended on suspicion. The whole were safely brought to Jubulpoor; but it so happened that the papers and documents relating to their arrest had not been received by the time of their arrival; and the officer commanding the guard made no report as to whence the different men who composed the gang under his charge had been received: they were, therefore, as a matter of course, supposed to be all Thugs who had been arrested by our approvers. Nevertheless the usual form was proceeded in, *i.e.* the approvers who remained at Jubulpoor were sent for singly to inspect the gang: all were recognized to be Thugs excepting eleven men, of whom the approvers said they knew nothing. On the receipt of the documents a few days afterwards, these eleven proved to be the party given in charge to the guard by the local governor, with whose arrest our approvers had no concern.

The success which has attended the exertions of the officers employed to suppress this crime, has hitherto equalled our most sanguine expectations. In most parts of Central India, Bundlecund, Bogelcund, and from Allahabad to the Himalayah, Thugghee now scarcely exists: the great proof of which is, that the servants of English gentlemen, and Sepahees, who go on leave into those parts of the country, have, during the last three years, all returned in safety; whereas previously, not a year passed without many of them being missed. We mention these two classes, for their movements only can we correctly ascertain; but it is a fair inference that other natives have travelled in equal safety. There can be no doubt that if the British government will pursue vigorous measures for a few years, the system will, with proper supervision on the part of the ordinary police, be completely eradicated, never again to arise; but if exertions are slackened, and any fully initiated Thugs left at large, they would infallibly raise new gangs, and Thugghee would again flourish all over India. It is certainly incumbent on a government which assumes to itself the character of enlightened, and which is now paramount in India, to exert itself for the suppression of such an atrocious system. It is impossible to ascertain with accuracy the extent to which it has been carried annually, and, could it be done, the statement would scarcely be credited. Reckoning the number of Thugs in all India to be ten thousand, and that, on the average, each Thug murders three victims a year, this will give an amount of thirty thousand murders annually committed for many years past, of which, till lately, scarcely any thing was known. Frightfully enormous as this may appear, it is probable that both estimates are under the mark, which is warranted by what appears on the trials, where, of course, but a small portion of the crimes actually committed are proved.

"These men are commonly tried for one particular case of murder, perpetrated on one occasion, in which case all the gang may have participated, and of which the evidence is most complete. On the average, more than ten of these cases have been found to occur on every expedition; and every man has, on the average, been on ten of these expeditions. The murders for which they are tried are not, therefore, commonly more than a hundredth part of the murders they have perpetrated in the course of their career of crime. In the last sessions held at Jubulpoor by Mr. Smith, for 1834-5, thirty-six cases from Hyderabad, committed by Captain Reynolds, and forty-two cases from other parts, committed by myself, were tried, and two hundred and six prisoners convicted of the murder of four hundred and forty persons. Of these the bodies of three hundred and ninety had been disinterred, and inquests held over them, leaving only fifty unaccounted for."—p. 38.

In the sessions of 1836, lately held by the Honourable F. I. Shore at Jubulpoor, two hundred and forty-one prisoners were convicted of the murder of four hundred and seventy-four individuals, of whose corpses three hundred and fourteen were disinterred, and inquests held upon them.

The results have been hitherto highly satisfactory. Within these few years more than two thousand Thugs have been arrested by the officers attached to the Jubulpoor and Central India establishment alone. Of these about three hundred have been made approvers; taking in the sessions of 1836 first mentioned, the abstract of which is not included in the table at p. 38 of Captain Sleeman's book, which was printed just before the sessions were held, eighteen hundred and three were committed for trial. Of these four hundred and nineteen were sentenced to death; one thousand and eighty to transportation for life;* ninety-five to imprisonment for life; leaving two hundred and nine, who were either sentenced to limited imprisonment, allowed to turn approvers, died in gaol, or were otherwise disposed of. Only twenty-one of the whole have been acquitted; and this proves the extraordinary care with which the cases are prepared by the officers to whom this duty has been intrusted, and the strong nature of the evidence adduced. We cannot but wish them every success in exterminating a system which spares neither sex nor age; whose members never abandon their profession as long as they possess the power to engage in an expedition; who watch for their prey like wild beasts or vultures; and talk of the principal scenes of their crimes as a sportsman would of his favourite preserves. We trust also that no miserable fit of economy on the part of government may arise to thwart the measures in progress, but that every co-operation will be given to those praiseworthy exertions.

---

* These sentences are at once carried into execution, and not commuted, as is so common in England.

F. Hollick

Murder Made Moral; or, An Account of the Thugs, and Other Secret Murderers of India.

Manchester: A. Heywood, 1840.

MURDER MADE MORAL, ETC.

AMONG the many examples which may be given, of the change produced in the characters of men, by a change in the circumstances by which they are surrounded, none are so striking as that of the Secret Murderers in India. In this country, we have been induced by our early training, to consider, that man has implanted within him, an innate moral sense of right and wrong, commonly called *conscience*, which acts as a kind of monitor, to deter him from crime; or, to punish him with the sting of remorse, if he is not guided by its warnings. And further, that, in addition to this *conscience*, we have also a religious sentiment, which, however it may be perverted, always leads us to admiration of the Deity, and to love and reverence of his wisdom and goodness. From these peculiar notions on Religion and Morality, we have been led to imagine that such a crime as *Murder*, is necessarily so repugnant to man, that *every one*, upon committing it, must *feel* that he has done wrong, and that his conduct cannot but be highly displeasing to the Almighty. But, how forcibly are we convinced, that these feelings are simply the results of our peculiar education, when we find whole tribes of individuals, who pursue *Murder* as their avocation; who perpetrate it not only without *remorse*, but with the *positive approval of their consciences*; and, who believe further, that it is one of the most essential, and most acceptable *religious duties* they can perform!!

We see at once, from such an instance, that our *Conscience* and our *Religion*, both result from the peculiar local influences to which we are subject, exactly the same as do our peculiarities of speech and manner.

In the following pages will be found an account, extracted from good authorities, of a singular people, who are thus made, by their peculiar education, to believe that Murder and Robbery, are MORAL AND RELIGIOUS DUTIES, highly commendable, and particularly grateful to the Divinity.

Hindoostan, it is well known, is more subject to the domination of Priestcraft, and exhibits more religious insanity, and that too of the most ferocious and detestable kind, than any other country in the world. With *three hundred and thirty millions of Gods*, and countless hordes of Priests and Devotees, we can scarcely be surprised at any moral or mental monstrosity exhibited among her benighted population. Nevertheless, so hideous and revolting are the characteristics we are going to pourtray, and so different to what we have ever seen, that we are struck with astonishment and horror, when they are submitted to our contemplation.

In order to fully understand how it is, that this monstrous abortion of human character can be produced, it will be necessary to give a brief sketch of the general condition of the people, in that portion of the world. The great number of their Gods and Priests has already been adverted to; but, it must also be understood, that the Priesthood are a *class* quite seperate and distinct from the rest of the people, who regard them with the most abject fear, and the most slavish veneration. It is esteemed a disgrace for a priest, or any one possessing any degree of *sanctity*, to do any thing useful, so that they subsist almost entirely upon charity; this, it will be seen, from their immense numbers, and the poverty of the country, is no slight burden to the people; who, however, bear it all willingly, and seem to adore these holy men, in proportion to their filth, idleness and debauchery. The condition of the main body of the Brahmins, and their influence over the people, is forcibly shown in the following extract, from an article in the "Polytechnic Journal," for October, 1840, entitled "The Phansigars of Hindoostan;" from which these statements are mainly taken. "This revered caste in some parts of Bengal, is in a state of awful moral degradation. The women pursue a course of revolting licentiousness, unequalled by any thing in Europe, though even here it is sufficiently bad. The extreme profligacy of the Brahminée women in India, arises from their early marriages; female children of two or three years old, being contracted to old men, and the marriage is consummated when the girl is about *nine years old!* As a matter of course, their tyrants soon become odious to these youthful wives, and they almost invariably choose some paramour of a more congenial age."

Brahmins are constantly brought before the British tribunals in Bengal, charged with the blackest crimes. Ward observes, in his *View of the History and Literature of the Hindoos*, vol. i. p. 83. that a great portion of the Dacoits, (plunderers,) are Brahmins. "I am informed," he says, "that in one day, ten Brahmins were hanged at Dinagepore, for robberies committed by them; and, I doubt not, the well known remark of Governor Holwell, is in substance true. 'During almost five years that we presided in the Judicial Cutchery Court of Calcutta, never any murder, or other atrocious crime came before us, but it was proved in the end, that a Brahmin was at the bottom of it.' *—And yet, these very men, even when covered with the grossest taint of moral infamy, are still objects of the profoundest veneration. To drink water into which *a Brahmin's toe has been dipped*, is considered a very great privilege. When inquiring into this circumstance, I was informed that vast numbers of Sudras, while fasting, thus purify themselves daily; that others make a

* Holwell's Historical Events, vol. ii.

vow to attend to this duty for a length of time, *to remove some disease.* Indeed Sudras may be frequently seen, carrying water in a cup, and intreating the first Brahmin they meet to put his toe in it; after which, they *drink the water and bow to, or prostrate themselves before the Brahmin,* who bestows his blessing on them!! Others preserve some of this consecrated water in their houses. Persons are found, who endeavour to collect the dust from the feet of a hundred thousand Brahmins. One mode of doing this is by spreading a cloth before the door of a house where many are assembled at a feast; as each Brahmin comes out, he shakes the dust from his feet upon this cloth. Many miraculous cures are said to have been performed upon persons *swallowing this dust!!"*

The religious creed of this people, is as singular as their veneration for their Priests is slavish. They have, like the Christians of this country, an "Holy Trinity"—or three principal Deities, from whom all the rest seem derived. Not *three in one,* but three separate and independent Divinties, each having followers, and being worshipped with rites and ceremonies peculiar to himself. These Deities are named Brahma, Vishnu, and Siva. The first being the *creating* power, the second the *preserving* power, and the third the *destroyer.* Each of these Gods is likewise married, and their consorts frequently partake of the adoration which is paid their husbands. The spouse of Siva, the destroyer, named KALI, is the being worshipped by the Phansigars, or secret murderers, with such horrid rites.

In the *Polytechnic Journal,* for September, 1840, article, "Hindoo Mythology," I find the following account of this terrible Goddess. "She has several names, but the murderers worship her under the name of *Kali,* which signifies any thing black, or dreadful. She is always represented under this designation, as ruthless to the last degree; and her votaries, the Phansigars, are among the most atrocious of human monsters. Murder is their avocation. They commit it *in the name of their Divinity;* and thus hold the perpetation of it to be, *not only justifiable, but commendable*! The power, to which they offer their homage, is represented under the image of a monstrous woman, deformed and hideous.— It is often dragged through their towns and villages, on certain Festival days, amid a din and uproar perfectly deafening. The image presents a most revolting aspect, which it is said to assume, in order to *frighten sinners into repentance.* Her attitude is one of fearful threatening, calculated to inspire terror, and this even to the most obsequious of her worshippers. The expression of her countenance is, to the last degree, horrible. Her eyes are large and projecting; her nose thin, with nostrils greatly dilated, as if under the immediate influence of intense passion. The mouth extends nearly the whole width of the face, being armed with a row of immense teeth, like small hatchets; and from the upper jaw, at each corner of the extended gums, projects a short, thick tusk, curling towards the ear on either side, which it nearly touches. From her mouth, a large rough tongue protrudes, and descends to her waist; under it and round her scraggy neck, is twined a *Cobra di Capello* snake, a deadly reptile, which supports this monstrous member upon its snaky folds. Beneath each ear is one of those deadly serpents, hanging from it, as an ornamental pendent to this monstrous head. The hood of the snake is expanded, as in the act of attack. The ears of the idol are large, pendulous, and project considerably from the head, greatly increasing its hideousness of aspect. The body is gaunt and macerated; but the limbs are extremely robust, and are all bent, to express great energy of action. The hands are gigantic, the fingers, long, and armed with thick pointed nails, like claws. A serpent encircles the waist, with the hood extended. No lips cover her teeth, and the mouth, therefore, grins horribly. Her bloated cheeks and fierce goggle eyes are fixed, with an appalling stare upon the beholder. Her hair is erect, and stiffened out upon her unsightly head, forming a frightful glory round it, diverging to meet a wider glory, which rises from a flower on each side, forming a support to the figure, which is altogether disgusting to behold; and to this, besotted millions kneel in idolatrous adoration!!"

Such is a picture of the personal appearance of the patron Goddess of the Phansigars;—and horrible as this idol is, the worship that is paid to it is still more so. They imagine that the Murder of a human being, is one of the most acceptable sacrifices which can be offered to Kali, and they accordingly take every opportunity which offers for its perpetration.

It is now an invariable custom with them to mutilate the bodies of their victims before burying them, in order that they may not be recognized. But it appears it was not always so; for their Goddess, according to tradition, used to accompany them and devour the bodies; thus saving them all trouble about them whatever.—It seems however, that she was very particular about enjoying her banquet in private; and one day, when a victim had been left for her to feast upon, one of the Murderers happened to look back, and saw her busy picking the bones. This so offended the Goddess, that she vowed never to eat another body murdered by the Phansigars; and, therefore, they have since had the trouble of burying and mutilating them. In order, however, to make up a little for the loss of such assistance, she presented them with one of her Tusks for a *Pickaxe*, which was to last for ever; with one of her ribs for a *knife*, the edge of which, nothing would turn; and with the hem of her Petticoat, for a *noose to strangle her victims with.** Thus

* See Polytechnic Journal, for September, 1840, Article, "Hindoo Mythology."

equipped and sanctioned, they sallied forth, and plied their fearful trade with the most consummate skill, and the most untiring perseverance.

It is not possible, with the scanty materials we possess, to say any thing with certainty, as to the origin of this fiendish superstition; but it is very possible that, like many others, it originated in the perversion or misunderstanding of some symbol or allegory, used in former times, to convey information to the people. Indeed their three Deities, and the offices assigned them, may very probably be part of a grand mystical illustration of the phenomena of nature; and, in this way, the whole system becomes very sublime and philosophical. The Priests in ancient times may have better understood, or more honestly interpreted these things than they do now. Be that as it may, it is certain, that at the present time, they lend their influence, and give religious sanction to such practices, besides taking their share of the plunder gained by such detestable means. "It is a remarkable fact," says the article in the *Polytechnic Journal*, for October, "that these tribes of plunderers belong to no particular caste, but are made up of all; being composed of Hindoos, Mahommedans, Pariahs, Chandellahs, nay, even *Brahmins*, are frequently found among them. This arrises from the circumstance of their never destroying the children of those persons whom they rob and murder. The children they take care of, *and bring up to their own horrible mode of life*, which at once accounts for the strange mixture of castes in their societies."

What a lesson does this teach us; these very children thus made to look on murder with savage delight, might, under other arrangements, be made to shudder at the idea of taking the life of a fellow being.

Imperfect legislation, and other vitiating surrounding circumstances, seem to have long made robbery a common, and even an honourable pursuit in Hindoostan. Sir

John Malcolm, in a paper published by him in the first volume of the *Transactions of the Asiatic Society*,—thus speaks of a large body of plunderers, called *Bhills*, who are found in several of the hilly districts of the country.* "Existing, as they have hitherto done, under despotic governments, which placed them beyond the pale of civil society; and, which not only gave them neither encouragement nor protection, but authorised the lowest of the fiscal officers to take their lives without a trial; considering themselves a proscribed and contemned race; ignorant to a deplorable degree; believing in witchcraft; blindly obedient to the orders of their chiefs; subject to extraordinary privations; and constantly exposed to dangers from their fellow creatures, and from the ferocity of wild beasts, with whom they shared the forests; the Bhills have, *in consequence*, become the enemies of order and peace. They have cherished predatory habits as the means of subsistence; and, receiving no mercy or consideration, they have sought, from natural impulse, to revenge the wrongs they sustained. Time has interwoven their habits of life and feelings with their superstitions, until they *actually believe that they were created to prey upon their neighbours!!*—'I am *Mahadeva's* Thief,' is *the common answer* of a Bhill detected in a crime; and his promise of amendment is usually so qualified as to period, that it seems more like a truce than a pact of permanent good conduct. * * * * Encouraged by the general apathy of the native princes, tolerated desperadoes commit their depredations with comparative security; and, in many instances, their extraordinary dexterity is equalled only by the savage *hilarity* with which they perpetrate their deeds of blood. Ferocity is their *pride*, brutality their *pastime!!* Despised, but dreaded by every class of the community, save that outcast tribe, the Pariahs, with whom alone, they maintain any intercourse; though these

* See Polytechnic, for October.

they commonly treat with the grossest indignity, they look upon themselves to be the common enemies of mankind, detested by all, pitied by none; and act generally therefore, upon a system of fierce retaliation, whenever they make their base reprisals, for the general odium in which they are held."

It will readily be imagined, that when men were thus trained to plunder, and made callous to any thing like compunction on the matter, they would not be long in arriving at the conclusion, that it was even meritorious. Nor would their Priests, who always lived upon them, under any circumstances, be long in persuading them that it was also *Religious*. For when these holy men saw that they must either take plunder for their subsistence, or else be content with nothing, they would not be long in making their choice. And, accordingly, we find that they are ever ready to give their holy sanction to robbery, and the violence attendant upon it, providing that a due share of the proceeds are awarded them for their acquiescence.

To this state we find the Phansigars have long since arrived. In the words of the article already quoted from,* they are "probably unequalled in any part of the world, for cold-blooded and heartless depravity. They pretend to a religious sanction for their crimes; and, the greater these are, *the more vain are they of their achievements in their abominable calling!!* They delight in blood, and *venerate the hand that spills it.* Even when brought before the English tribunals, they have been often known to hear the sentence of death passed upon them with a smile of ferocious triumph, at the number of victims they have offered to their vindictive Deity, *and to die with a murmur of exultation upon their lips!!* Their system of plunder is as peculiar as it is horrible. The record might well make the sternest humanity shudder. With them the

* Polytechnic for October.

destruction of their fellow creatures, is *an obligation* imposed by *the Deity whom they affect to adore*! It is a covenant of blood. When these ferocious robbers plunder, they invariably murder. No adult is ever spared. Escape is the only chance for the victim; and, this is a forlorn one, for escape from these monsters, when once in their power, is a rare exception in their black calendar of events. * * * * Phansigar signifies a *strangler*; and these assassins employ a *Phansi*, or noose, which they suddenly cast over the heads of those whom they intend to plunder, and strangle them. By this method of murderous precaution, their victims are unable to raise an outcry, for the compression of the noose upon the throat, effectually prevents the voice from rising to the lips. They thus secure their booty without resistance, and with little chance of detection; acting invariably upon the maxim, that dead men tell no tales. They calculate the chances of discovery with Geometrical precision; and, considering the frequency of their crimes, detection has been comparatively very rare. So true are they to each other, that a Phansigar can seldom be induced to betray his brethren, even by the offer of pardon; indeed, were he to escape the gallows, in consequence of such betrayal, he would not long survive his escape. He would be dogged until full retribution were visited upon him; for Phansigars are always fatal in their revenge. * * * *

"Among the Phansigars, as I have said, Brahmins are frequently found; and, notwithstanding, continue to receive the monstrous veneration paid to this influential class. They, however, exercise none of their exclusive privileges among the robbers with whom they associate; but conform themselves with rigid subserviency, to the laws of that sanguinary association; committing murder with as little scruple as those of the basest caste.

A gang of these persons, varies from a dozen to sixty or seventy persons. Occasionally they amount to two or three hundred; but these are exceptions to the general order of their legislative economy. They are governed by very strict laws, which are severely vindicated when violated; and, though their licentiousness is excessive when dismissed to their homes, after an excursion of plunder, they are seldom known to commit a breach of their rules. Their discipline is observed with an exactness worthy of a better constitution; and, they are singularly faithful to each other, when it is considered of what baneful elements their confederacy is composed. They never vary, except in extreme cases, from their ordinary practice, which experience has taught them to be the safest; always committing their depredations at a distance from their place of common resort, being frequently absent for several months, during which they oftentimes amass considerable plunder; and return to their homes to spend the produce of their ill-gotten booty, in the lowest debauchery. In this their wives and children participate without restriction; and, in fact, *glory in the degradation.*

Upon these occasions of plunder they are not particularly choice in their objects. They will occasionally murder the poorest Pariah, though it is certain that no more than a few pice, (the pice being about the third of a penny, English money,) will be the reward of their crime. Their victims, however, are generally travellers, whom they happen to fall in with on the road. Assuming the garb of pilgrims, or appearing as families removing to a distant part of the country, by their apparently peaceable and homely guise, they beguile the unwary; who, when thus lulled into security, become an easy prey. By affecting great sanctity—they commonly pretend to be on their way to visit some celebrated shrine—they generally contrive to draw out of the persons whom they thus insiduously engage in conversation, whether they have money or other valuables; and the information thus obtained, proves invariably, fatal, to those who communicate it.

So wary are they in their approaches towards stangers, that they are seldom or never suspected; and, they are so well practised in disguise, that, though their hearts are to the last degree, hardened by the savage butcheries almost daily committed by them, their countenances are commonly wreathed in bland smiles, while their tongues give utterance to the sweetest sentiments of humanity.

Each company of these plunderers has a chief, to whom they scrupulously defer; and so completely is his ascendancy over them, that they submit to any restraint, however arbitrary, which he may think fit to impose; and, in the very wantonness of power, he often treats those under his immediate control with extreme severity. He directs all their operations; but, in general, is not actively employed, except in obtaining intelligence, which is a very important trust, requiring too, not only great caution, but much prudent management; and, in those less hazardous offices, demanding more acuteness than courage or manual promptitude.

These chiefs are generally selected from among the aged robbers, who have signalised themselves by their determination and dexterity, during the more youthful part of their lives. These, when steeped to the very crown, in the engrained dye of murder, are considered the more fit to direct the operations of less practised members of their atrocious trade, whom they fail not soon to render complete adepts in their sanguinary art. The approbation of their chief, is always held to be the greatest stimulus to exertion.

When upon active service, the Phansigars usually separate into small parties, of from eight to twelve, for the day's duty. These again subdivide into small sections, of two and three, according to circumstances, following each other within sight, in order to take immediate advantage of any casualty that may occur, favourable to their brutal purposes. They then instantly unite; and, from their numbers, easily hush their victim, or victims, in everlasting silence. None of the parties, into which the main body divides on these occasions, ever keep far asunder; thus, if one division requires a reinforcement, it is quickly obtained; and, they have a sort of telegraphic mode of communication, known only to themselves, by which their chief is soon apprised how they are going on. He distributes his orders accordingly, to the various divisions under his superintendence. So punctually are these orders executed, that it seldom happens he has to complain, either of the alacrity, or skill, exhibited by those subject to his commands. In appearance, these chiefs are not to be distinguished from the general members of the association, being generally habited in the most homely attire; this consisting of a piece of dirty cloth, resembling coarse calico, rolled round their loins; their temples being encircled with a turban, of the same material. Their wrists and ankles are usually encompassed with annular ornaments of buffalo's horn.

The parties of these robbers, when assembled for an excursion of plunder, frequently meet in small towns and villages, as if by accident, pretending to be in pilgrimages to different temples. There they unite as occasion may require, and form their diabolical plans, for they are never known to exercise their murderous craft in localities where the amount of population would greatly reduce their chances of escape, should detection follow. Their murders are almost invariably committed at a distance from places of public intercourse, where they are much less likely to be interrupted; and where, even if discovered, they can by their numerical strength, awe the inhabitants into silence. Having with them a number of children, of different ages, whenever they appear abroad upon their enterprises of robbery, they seldom awaken suspicion. The children by whom the are accompanied, being ignorant of their practices, can never betray them by any unguarded prattle, and their artlessness is always a presumptive guarrantee to the traveller of his own safety. Before a party of Phansigars commit a murder they remove their youthful companions from the scene.

Two or three of these robbers will sometimes take up their station in a choultry, which is a building erected by the wayside for the convenience of travellers; and when a victim appears, their companions are immediately apprised. These latter then drop in under the guise of ordinary wayfarers, engage in casual conversation, as if strangers to their own party, and having lulled the unsuspecting traveller into perfect, but fatal security, accomplish their purpose while he sleeps; or rather, they violently rouse him, and when he starts from his recumbent position in sudden surprise, they cast the noose over his head and strangle him. They then drag his body from the choultry and bring it upon the borders of the jungle, having first secured the effects of the unfortunate stranger. So secretly is this effected, and with such dispatch, that the spot where so foul a crime was perpetrated is never suspected to have been the scene of murder, unless when the fact happens to be divulged by some wretched Phansigar, about to forfeit his life to the outraged laws of his country. Other victims arise, and are subjected to the same melancholy fate; while their distant friends probably imagine them to have become the prey of wild beasts, not suspecting that there are beings of their own kind far more savage.

A single person is never attacked by less than two Phansigars. To deviate from this rule would be a breach of the laws of their order, and subject them, for a time, to the forfeiture of the privilege of which they are *so proud*—the privilege of *throwing the noose over the head of the traveller!* If, at any time, there should appear the least chance of resistance, the two murderers are always joined by a third, who never fails to secure the issue. But such is the skill which these desperate wretches employ in thei deadly trade, that they are scarcely ever frustrated in the accomplishment of their inhuman purposes. *Delighting* as they do, to see the death-struggles of the unhappy stranger who falls into their power, when a member of their own community dies, their lamentations are loud and bitter. They manifest the deepest sympathies of grief, and consign his body to the earth or to the funeral pile—for they do both, according to convenience or caprice—with numerous rites, declaring their expectations of rejoining him in *a world of future bliss*. Though some of them appear to have little or no apprehension of a future state, yet many, if not the large majority of them, have such an expectation, and imagine that their reward will be *precisely in proportion to the dexterity they have manifested in their office of human mactation* *; for any one whom they succeed in strangling they look upon as *an offering to their odious divinity*—Kali, the destroyer!!

The usual mode of perpetrating their murders is as follows:—when their victim is lulled into perfect security, one of the party suddenly passes the noose or phansi, formed of a twisted handkerchief, or a strip of thin but strong muslin, over his head, and drawing it dexterously round the neck, instantly tightens it with all his strength. The moment this is accomplished a companion strikes the suffering man upon the joints of the knees behind, which causes him to fall forward, and thus to accelerate this summary process of strangulation.

When he is prostrate, they kick him violently on the temples until his sufferings terminate, which is generally within the space of a minute. The whole thing is at once so rapidly and adroitly performed, that the sufferer has little or no power to make resistance; in fact he is overpowered before he can command the oppurtunity of exerting his strength; and whatever that strength may be, it is

* Mactation, killing for sacrifice.

seldom or never of any avail against these practised adepts in murder.

Such is the plan commonly pursued, but of course their operations must, in some degree, be suited to the occasion; although, therefore, there may be an occasional deviation in the details of the process, yet the method of killing by strangulation is never departed from. This, in fact, is with them *a religious obligation,* and were a Phansigar to destroy a victim in any other way, Kali would never be propitiated, and an eternal stigma would attach to his name.

Thus it is that, under the presumed sanction of religion, they perpetrate, with unblushing confidence, the foulest crimes to be found in the blackest registers of human actions. They consider themselves *pledged* to their perpetration; and, under the frightful delusion of being rewarded for assassination, they render themselves the most dangerous enemies of their fellow men.

The existence of such a demoniacal race, a race let it be remembered, of RELIGIOUS ENTHUSIASTS, shows us to what shocking results false views in religion may unhappily lead. The Phansigars of Hindoostan, are, at this moment, a living proof that religion, if improperly inculcated, may be made the vehicle of the most detestable abominations which sin has introduced into the world. It is clear, that if a man can be brought to the conviction that God is to be propitiated by murder, there is nothing too monstrous for his belief. What will not his credulity swallow?

So cautious are these sanguinary miscreants, that they do not venture to attempt a robbery, which is *invariably* accompanied with murder, until they have taken every practicable precaution against surprise, and secured themselves, so far as human foresight can extend, against the probability of a failure. They have been known to follow their intended victim for weeks, when they have ascertained that he is possessed of valuable baggage, before the desired opportunity of putting him to death and making themselves masters of his property has occurred ; and their patience in waiting for this, is only equalled by the heartless ferocity with which they finally accomplish their diabolical purpose. They are deterred by no consideration either divine or human, from the atrocities of their profession ; and so lightly do they value the life of a fellow citizen, that they will often take it for the few rags which cover the body of the poorest traveller. The smallest sum of money is, in their minds, a sufficient provocative to murder. After they have committed one of these monstrous outrages against the laws both of God and man, should any person unexpectedly pass upon the road before the body of their victim has been removed, they throw a cloth over it, making doleful lamentations as if for a departed relative ; or one of them will fall down and writhe in apparent agony, in order to divert the attention of the unwelcome passengers from the object of their pretended sorrow. This farce is always successful, as all orders of Hindoos have a natural repugnance to approach the dead ; and consider themselves defiled if they even accidentally touch a corpse. Thus, the native passengers keep as far from the body as they conveniently can, being repelled by the strong prejudice of caste, from seeking to interfere with the obsequies of any belonging to a class of which they do not claim to be social members.

If the opportunity presents itself, the Phansigars usually perpetrate their deed of blood near some jungle ; and, as has been already stated, at a distance from the frequented track of travellers. They prefer the proximity of a Nullah as the body is more easily disposed of ; but they always bury it, if possible, in some remote spot, where the soil is light or sandy ; as this favours the necessary expedition of all their proceedings. Here a grave is quickly prepared by some of their party, who are always at hand with the necessary implements; and, after having barbarously mutilated the corpse, they cast it into the hastily formed receptacle, with the head downwards. It is gashed all over to prevent its swelling, and thus raising a tumulus, or causing cracks, which might attract jackalls, and other beasts of prey, and so lay open their guilt to the casual passenger. Sometimes the legs are disjointed at the knees and hips, and turned back upon the body, when haste obliges them to dig too small, or two shallow a hole, which is then hastily filled. But if there should appear no chance of interruption, the murderers sometimes *pitch a tent upon the spot, and regale themselves over the dead body*, which they have consigned to so melancholy and succinct a burial. During these revels, they drink arrack to excess, until the greater portion of them become senselessly intoxicated. There are, however, a certain number on the watch, who always keep their heads sufficiently clear, to give timely alarm should danger threaten; though this is very rarely the case, as the scenes of these brutal debaucheries are always at a distance from any populous district, and upon the borders of some unfrequented forest.

The calculating caution of these people, under circumstances so revolting to our common nature, is a distinguishing feature in their system of plunder. They seem to leave unconsidered no circumstance that can, in the slightest degree, tend to wrap their crimes in concealment. Every thing appears to be calculated with almost philosophic foresight; and, the provision made against the chance of detection is so perfect, that it is all but impossible to track them in their career of blood. It is astonishing how few of these robbers have been convicted, in proportion to their numbers, and the extreme heinousness of their guilt; though of late years, in consequence of the extraordinary activity of the British functionaries, in localities where they have the power to act, many hordes of Phansigars have been entirely exterminated; and, it is hoped that these successes will infuse a better spirit into the native tribunals.

When a party of Phansigars has committed a murder, in a place unfavourable for the burial of their victim, they inclose the body in a sack, and cast it into a well, or hide it in some secluded part of a neighbouring jungle, secure from the ravages of vultures, jackalls, and other beasts of prey, until a favourable place is discovered, whither it may be safely deposited. Here it is at once removed, and disposed of as already described. Should a dog happen to accompany the person whose life has been taken, it is always killed, lest the faithful animal should lead to the discovery of its master's mangled remains. So systematic are these inhuman butchers, in their detestable vocation of slaughter, that if they fail in the performance of a single particular in the regulations established among them, for putting to death the object of their plunder, they consider they have committed an offence against the sanguinary Deity, to whom they present their daily homage, and make an oblation as a propitiatory offering. They esteem it a meritorious act, to present to their Dumb Divinty, a portion of the gains obtained by the death of a fellow being; and, in truth, it is not surprising that they should be so perfectly reconciled to the shedding of human blood, if they can really persuade themselves that the Divinity, whom they are taught to worship as the one great source of all things, can accept, as an act of grateful adoration, such abominable offerings.

Thus we see that Religion is made a sanction for the blackest crimes. With such perversion of mind, we can scarcely wonder at the extent of human depravity.

The Phansigars, though they most commonly attack single travellers, have been known to destroy a whole party of eight or ten persons; and, when such an instance of wholesale murder is successfully executed, *their rejoicing knows no bounds!* It is succeeded by several days' revelry, during which, their savage exploits are boasted of, as if these exhibited the highest degree of magnanimity. In some secluded locality, they erect their tents, and abandon themselves to the foulest excesses, rejoicing like demons, *at the mischief they have committed, and the probable misery they have caused!* Sometimes the booty they obtain during their excursions is very large, though at others it is so trifling as scarcely to supply them, during these predatory journeys, with the common necessaries of life. When this is the case, they work at their own trades, for most of them have some occupation to which they resort, during the intervals of repose from their murderous expeditions; and, though much is not obtained in this way, they cheerfully submit to the necessity, which a want of success imposes; encouraged by the hope of a speedy reward. When this does not follow, under the excitement of baffled expectation, they utter the fiercest abuse against the hideous divinity whom they serve, without any apparent apprehensions of punishment for their irreverence.

After a successful expedition, when these Stranglers have collected their plunder, a division is regularly made; the most valuable portion being set apart for the Polygars, or petty chiefs, who connive at their depredations, and are thus liberally remunerated for their protection. This connivance, on the part of these selfish princes, is the chief canse of the remarkable increase of the Phansigars, in those parts of Hindoostan, over which the preventive influence of the laws of England, have not yet extended. Another portion is appropriated to the expenses of *Religious offerings*, which they never fail to make, after their return from a journey, in which their criminal wishes have been fully realised; while the PRIESTS, with a heartlessness of purpose, only second to that of their tributaries, make large demands upon them, *for the benefit of their spiritually kind offices with the Goddess, whom they are desirous to propitiate!!*

Inured as these people are, to the most appalling crimes, they are rigidly scrupulous in performing the rites of their abominable worship ; and, willingly devote a large portion of their gains, to the shrine of their idol divinity. After these two important portions are taken from their booty, the remainder is divided among them in certain proportions, according to their admitted claims.

To their chief is appropriated a double share, he being considered the animating spirit of the society. The person who casts the Phansi, and actually strangles the victim, receives *a share and a half*, so does he who *mutilates the body*, for in this, considerable dexterity is shown, and none but an experienced hand is able to perform it properly. All who were present, but not actually engaged, have each one share, and they who were not present, half a share. These divisions are made with such regularity, and with such a strict adherence to the rules of their order, that there is neither bickering or dissatisfaction. Each person disposes of his share as he pleases. It is usually sold to the readiest purchaser for the twentieth part of its value, and there are numerous such purchasers, who feel no remorse at obtaining in this manner, the fruits of murder. They do not consider it criminal thus to reap the harvest of crime. To obviate suspicion, their plunder is always disposed of at a distance from the scene of assassination.

Considerable difficulty it seems is felt in detecting these Phansigars, scattered as they are through various communities, and carrying on their operations so secretly. But it appears they abound among the numerous hordes of mendicants which infest Hindoostan ; among whom many Brahmins are constantly to be found.

" In the province of Bengal alone, it has been computed that there is a population of at least *two millions* who subsist entirely by begging, when they are not occupied by other modes of plunder. Thus, supposing each person to obtain no more than eighteen-pence per week, the sum so obtained would amount to upwards of *seven millions annually*, and this too extracted, for the most part, from the labouring classes, who are extremely poor." Indeed it appears that *begging*, like *murder*, "holds a conspicuous place among the *religious duties* of the Hindoos;" and none among their community can attain to the *extreme rank* of *spiritual distinction*, except through one or other of these honourable occupations.

Such is a brief sketch of this horridly peculiar people, the circumstance of whose singular belief and practice, is a convincing proof that man is like "clay in the hands of the potter," and that he may have given to him any one of ten thousand different modifications of character, according to the nature of the circumstances by which he is surrounded. The very individuals who now shudder at reading this narration, if they had been, like the Phansigars, trained to it from infancy, might have thought it an honourable and proud distinction to be allowed to twist the fatal noose. And, on the contrary, the worshippers of Kali might have been made as easily to regard their dreadful occupation with detestation and abhorrence as they now are to look upon it as being very meritorious.

The *material* of human nature is the same in Hindoostan as in England—the difference which is found in the characters of the population of the countries is simply owing to the different manner in which that *material* has been operated upon, or *worked up*.

Other accounts of similar fraternities, differently denominated, and modified in their mode of procedure, hav been laid before the public at different times; among which may be mentioned an article in the *Edinburgh Review*, for January, 1837, written upon a volume published at Calcutta, in 1836, and entitled *Ramaseeana, or a*

Vocabulary of the Peculiar Language used by the Thugs; with an Introduction and Appendix, descriptive of the System pursued by that Fraternity; and of the Measures which have been adopted by the Supreme Government of India for its suppression. From the subjoined extract it will be perceived that if the *Thugs* and *Phansigars* are not identical, there is no essential difference.

From the statements in the *Edinburgh Review*, it appears that the Thugs are of ancient date, and that they are abundantly diffused over the greater part of Hindoostan. Much the same account is given of the general proceedings as that already detailed respecting the Phansigars. Some particulars however, are new, and of a very striking character. Their occupation is that of murdering and plundering travellers, with certain rites and ceremonies, and in the name of the Goddess Kalee, or Bhudkalee. They are regularly divided, when out on an expedition, into the *scouts*, *sentries*, *stranglers*, and so forth, like a well organised army; and they travel, sometimes as merchants, sometimes as Rajas, with their followers; at others, as strangers, or boatmen, according as it will best suit the peculiar exigencies of the occasion. The leader of the band carries a pick-axe, which is esteemed sacred, and is the object of many strange religious ceremonies previous to being taken out on an expedition. It is, in fact, like a standard to them, under which they think themselves protected by their divinity, and which they think will be sure to ensure them success in their murderous undertaking.

The evidence of Captain Sleeman, who tried several Thugs at a place called *Jubbulpoor*, and obtained their confessions, is given in the Review; and from it may be gained many horrid particulars respecting their transactions. It seems, they remember, and speak of their deeds, according to the number of lives taken on each particular occasion. Thus, we hear of the "*sixty soul affair*," the "*twenty soul*," and so on!! It is stated as a general rule, that "the Thugs are forbidden by their rules, to kill women of any description, and either men or women of the following classes:—fukeers, bards, musicians by profession, dancing men or women, washerwomen, sweepers, oil venders, blacksmiths and carpenters, when found together, maimed or leprous persons, men with cows, and Ganges water carriers, while they have the Ganges water actually with them; but, if their pots are empty, they are not exempted." * Some of the Northern Thugs it seems, are not so rigid in their adherence to this rule, and women occasionally are their victims. In 1831, a gang of them were discovered in Malwa; and by October, 1835, *fifteen hundred and sixty-two*, had been committed, of whom three hundred and eighty-two were hanged, and nine hundred and eighty-six transported, or imprisoned for the whole term of their lives. The celebrated sculptures in the caves of Ellora are said by them to be representatives of *Thugee*, which they contend is of divine origin. The following legend is curious, as showing how they imagine this abominable custom obtained the sanction of heaven.

"They have a tradition that a demon, by name *Rukut Beej Dana*, infested the world, and devoured mankind as often as they were born, or created; and to enable the world to be peopled, Kalee Davee determined to put him to death. This demon, they say, was so tall that the deepest ocean never reached above his waist; and he could, consequently, walk over the world at his ease. Kalee Davee attacked him, and cut him down; but from every drop of his blood another demon arose; and as she cut them down, from every drop of their blood another demon sprang up; and the numbers increased at this geometrical rate, until she became fatigued with the labour. On this, she formed two men from the sweat brushed off from one of her arms; and giving them each a handkerchief, told

* Editor of the Review.

them to put all these demons to death without allowing one drop of their blood to fall on the ground. After their labour was over they offered to return to the Goddess the handkerchiefs with which they had done their work; but she desired them to keep them as the instruments of a trade by which their posterity were to earn their subsistence, and to strangle men with these handkerchiefs, as they had strangled the demons, and live by the plunder they acquired; and, having been the means of enabling the world to get provided with men by the destruction of the demons, their posterity would be entitled to take a few for their own use." With such a belief as this, it is not surprising that the Thugs should murder without thinking it wrong to do so, since it is evidently, with them, of sacred origin. We are told further on, that "a Thug considers the persons murdered precisely in the light of victims offered up to the Goddess; and, he remembers them, as a priest of Jupiter remembered the oxen, and a priest of Saturn the children, sacrificed upon their altars. He meditates his murders without any misgivings; he perpetrates them without any emotion of pity; and he remembers them without feelings of remorse; they trouble not his dreams, nor does their recollection ever cause him inquietude in darkness, in solitude, or in the hour of death."

They are, nevertheless, exceedingly superstitious; and are often put out of their way, by omens and prodigies, similar to what frighten ignorant people in other countries.

In Captain Sleeman's work, are numerous statements, respecting the time and place of several of the most dreadful murders; the number of Thugs employed; and the amount of treasure obtained. On one occasion, the booty obtained, was so considerable, that a tax was imposed upon the Thugs, of a certain amount annually, at Golund, in Central India. The following is the statement of what has been done towards the extinction of Thugee in India. "In nine years, more than 2000 Thugs have been arrested;

1470 have been tried and convicted, in 167 trials, for the murder of 947 persons. Of these, 382 have been hanged; 909 transported; 77 imprisoned for life; 92 imprisoned for certain periods; and 21 acquitted. Besides these, 11 have escaped; 31 died before sentence; and near 250 have, at different times, been admitted king's evidence, and exempted from death, or transportation. First, to secure the conviction of those already in custody; and, secondly, to aid in arresting their associates at large." It must also, be borne in mind, that almost every individual convicted, has been concerned in several *affairs;* so that the actual amount of murder, which has been committed, is very much greater than what they are charged with.

In the Review, many cases of great *land* murders are quoted; but, as the manner of proceeding, is similar to that adopted by the Phansigars, already given, it is not necessary to extract any. Some of the Thugs, however, ply their trade more particularly on the *water;* and, the following statement of an affair on the the Ganges, will give a tolerable notion of the plan adopted on that element. It is from the evidence of one of the murderers on trial:—

"*Q.* I understand you have served with the river Thugs of Bengal?—*Shumshera.* On one occasion only. I had been on one expedition with Dilawur Khan, and one with Futteh Khan; and, after these, I went with Bhowur Khan and Moradun, two Lodaba Thugs, and joined Jhoulee Khan the fair, and Gholamun. Jhoulee Khan had a man to carry his bundle, by name Nathoo, as he was to act this season with Jypaul Kaet, a Jamadar of the Bongoos, or river Thugs. He acted as their sotha, or inveigler, this season. We joined Jypaul at the Mormakeya Ghat, where he had two boats at the different Ghats, two and three cose from each other. Jhoulee Khan brought two *beetoos* to the boat, which Jypaul commanded in person, and Bhowur Khan and I embarked with them. As soon as we had all got on board, Jypaul said, in Rumasee, 'Let the Boras (Thugs) separate themselves from the beetoos,' and we did so, leaving the two travellers together. Four men were on the bank, pulling along the boat; one was at the helm, acting at the same time as the *bykureea*, or spy, and seven of the gang were below with us and the travellers. We had got on about a cose, when the bykureeu at the helm, seeing all clear, called out, 'Bhugna ko pawn do,'—'Give my sister's son pawn.' This was their mode of giving the *jhirnee*, or signal, and the two beetoos were strangled. After strangling them, they broke their spinal bones thus, by putting their knees upon their backs, and pulling up their heads and shoulders. After doing this, they pushed them out of a kind of window in the side. Every boat has two of these windows, one on each side, and they put the bodies out of that towards the river. They break the spinal bones to prevent all chance of the people recovering and giving evidence against them. We generally stab the dead bodies through on both sides, under the arm pits; but they are afraid to cut or stab the body, lest there should be signs of blood upon the water, as the corpses pass other boats that are following them on the river. * * * *

"*Q.* How are the river Thugs not suspected by the people who live on the banks of the river?—*Shumshera.* They are very well known by the goreyts (policemen), and some other people of the small villages along the banks of the Ganges; they sometimes keep their boats near these villages for several days together. The two lotahs taken from the two men, whose murder I have described, were given to the goreyt of the village of More, whom Jypaul, after the murder, sent off for eight annas worth of spirits. These Thugs never keep any part of the booty but the money, lest it should bring them into trouble. The clothes of the two men were thrown into the river. The principal men of the gang, or the shrewdest of them, go along the roads, each having a servant carrying his bundle, and proceeding towards the ghat, where his boat is to be found, whether going up or down the river. When a traveller overtakes him, he learns whither he is going, pretends to be ignorant of the road, to be going to the same place with the traveller, but to be entirely unacquainted with it, and anxious to have somebody to instruct him. If the traveller had not intended to go by water, the Thug soon pretends to be much tired, and wishes that he was near a boat. The traveller expresses the same wish, and they agree to diverge from the road to the river. Coming to the ghat, the Thug pretends that he is a good hand at a bargain, and is allowed to agree for a passage for both. He bates down the master of his own boat, after a good deal of disputing, to half-price, and the beetoo is much pleased, and expresses his gratitude; they embark, and the beetoo is killed as soon as they get away from other boats. If the beetoo suspects or dislikes the first man, he soon falls in with the inveigler of another boat, who learns it by a sign, and pretends to enter into the beetoo's feelings and anxiety to throw off the first, who, on some pretence, remains behind, while his friend takes on the traveller to the other boat, further on than his own, where he is disposed of. They are much more numerous than we are. I have not heard of more than about thirty families of Moteeas; and the Lodahas are not much above two hundred men: but the Bongoos are very numerous, I have heard.

"*Q.* What do they consider the best season for their work?—*Shumshera.* The months of November, December, January, and February. In March it becomes too hot, and in the rains the river is considered to be too rapid, and the boats cannot be pulled along the banks.

"*Q.* This lad says the Bongoos are known to the villagers on the bank of the river?—*Bukhtawur.* He is a mere boy; if they were known to the villagers, how could they escape so well? They rarely keep their boats near villages; but when they do so, they conciliate the goreyts, and other policemen, that they may not ask questions.

" *Q.* They never keep any thing but money, he says?—*Bukhtawur.* Rarely. They throw every thing else away, in order to keep clear of the custom-house searchers, who are very numerous in that quarter."

Many more quotations might be given, from works, which have appeared at different times; but, as the statements in all are similar, and all show the same results, it would be useless to carry our readers further.

One peculiar modification of Thugism, however, we must allude to, as it tends to show the extensive ramifications of this system, and the modifications it undergoes, to suit peculiar circumstances.

The following extract from *The Friend of India,* will give a fair view of this branch of the great body of the Secret Murderers of India.

MAJOR SLEEMAN'S REPORT ON MEGPUNNAISM.

" We now redeem our pledge of giving an abstract of the valuable Report which has just been sent in to Government, on the subject of Megpunnaism. This barbarous term refers to a division of the crime of Thugee, out of which it grew, after the siege of Bhurtpore, in 1826. While the Thugs murder their victims to obtain their wealth, the Megpunnas immolate travellers to obtain their children, whom they afterwards sell into slavery. The great founder of this system, Kheama Jemadar, was considered so holy a man, that after his arrest he was entreated by the villagers to extinguish a fire which had broken out in a village; and by a singular coincidence, the fire ceased as his hands were extended to heaven in supplication. The greater part of the gangs who have engaged in this revolting system of murder sustain the character of religious mendicants; and the system itself is firmly believed to be under the potronage of the goddess Kalee. In common with the Thugs, they have a slang language, common to all the initiated. Unlike the Thugs, however, they always take their families with them on these murderous expeditions; the females assist in inveigling travellers, and in taking charge of the children, till they can be disposed of. Their victims are generally chosen from the more indigent classes, the disappearance of whom is less likely to excite suspicion than that of more wealthy individuals; and they find that it is more lucrative, as well as more safe, to murder the poor for the sake of their children, than the opulent for their wealth. The Brinjarras, who are widely scattered throughout the upper provinces, are ever ready to receive the children of the murdered parents; and they enjoy many facilities for subsequently distributing them among the brothels of the principal cities, or disposing of them to men of wealth and consideration. Suspicion may be at once lulled by the declaration, that the children were purchased from indigent parents, who had no longer the means of supporting them. The system is of so recent an origin, that it has not as yet spread farther than the Upper Dooah, the Delhi territories, and the Rajpootana and Alwar States; and the number of the initiated does not exceed three or four hundred. The conviction of offenders is rendered difficult, by the custom they adopt of throwing the bodies of their victims into the nearest river; and, by the distance to which the children are carried, and the obstacles which are found in tracing and identifying them.

"The present report consists of the confessions of some of the principal offenders, and the depositions which were taken in cases brought to light by the exertions of the officers in the Thugee department.

"The report closes with a list of *two hundred and twenty-three* Thugs, employed in the system of murdering indigent parents for the sake of their children, who are still at large; together with their age, caste, connexions, and their respective districts: and a note appended to it says—'A gang of forty-four of the above prisoners has been arrested by Lieutenant Mills since this list was preferred; and with them, seven more children of murdered parents, have been recovered.'"

There is however, one distinction between the river Thugs, and those who carry on their occupation by land. They always throw the noose *before* the victim, while the others cast it behind.

The extreme secrecy of these murderers has already been alluded to; but, to such an extent is this necessary quality carried, that we are assured, that "wives have been frequently known to pass long lives with husbands who have been in the yearly practice of Phansigaree, and to have died ignorant of their alliance with such human monsters. Some of the most respected merchants in the bazaars of the native towns,—men, whose honour has been trusted for years, and whose just dealings have obtained for them the confidence of their fellow citizens.—have been discovered, not only to have lived in habitual connexion with Phansigars, but frequently to have joined their gangs, and to have strangled travellers."

Nor is it any thing unusual, to find men possessed of more than an ordinary share of social and domestic virtues, who are held in high esteem, and who are loud in their condemnation of the failings of others, still practised adepts in secret strangulation. Sometimes their children are brought up ignorant of the practices of their parents, receiving good educations, and parental endearments; and, occasionally marrying into the highest families, without its ever being suspected from what a polluted source they sprung.

It is the general practice, to bring up the children to their parents' profession; and admirably adapted is the plan of education they adopt, to form their characters in the proper mould. They commence when very young, and gradually accustom the young Phansigar to his horrid trade,—inciting him on by their praise, and by assurances that he is pursuing a course of conduct which is certain to gain him eternal happiness hereafter. The consequence is, he is eager to begin, and try his hand. He is first employed as a sort of servant by some old and experienced hand, till the proper time, denoted by certain *omens*, and auguries, for his complete initiation has arrived. When he is supposed to be sufficiently educated, he is made the object of many religious ceremonies,—among the rest, bathing in a tank of *dirty water*, which is supposed to be peculiarly *sanctifying*; he is then clothed in a new robe, and conducted to a confederacy of the chiefs; where, with the emblems of the Sacred *Pick-axe* and noose before him, after a *prayer* from the priest, he is solemnly installed in his profession; and receives a piece of coarse sugar to eat, consecrated to Kâlee, whose faithful worshipper he promises to become for evermore.

The next important step in his education is the commission of his first act of *Strangulation*; an event looked forward to, with as much anxiety and impatience, and which, if he succeed well, brings as much honour and pleasure to the hopeful pupil, as the gaining of a prize at Oxford and Cambridge, does to our future professors of Law and Theology.

Before he begins, many prayers are said over him, and many sacrifices offered to the *holy Pick-axe*. He is then bathed, anointed with sweet-scented oil, a patch of red paint put upon his forehead, and the work of preparation is complete. They generally provide some poor Pariah for him to experiment upon,—sometimes several are required; and if he succeed well in this his first essay, he is admitted at once into the band, receives the title of Chuttote, and thus obtains the object of his highest ambition.

Thus early practised in every art necessary to make

their vile trade successful; and taught to consider it as the most meritorious course of life they could pursue, we need not wonder at the callousness and brutality of these people, any more than we do at their manual dexterity, since both are the natural results of the training they receive.*

From the above sketch, it is evident that man may have given to him a Moral and Religious character, totally different to what we see him ordinarily possess. We see the Thug esteeming Murder and Robbery to be both Moral and Religious. And, therefore, committing them, with the perfect approval of his conscience, and with a firm belief that they are acceptable to God. While, in this country, men are so trained, that their consciences tell them just the contrary. It is evident then from this, as we before remarked, that we have no "*innate sense of right and wrong;*" but that our "*Conscience*" may be so *manufactured*, as to approve, or disapprove of any course of conduct whatever.

And equally evident is it, that men may be made to imbibe the most opposite opinions, respecting what is acceptable to God, or in accordance with his commands. So that our *Religion* is thus shown to be equally forced upon us, by the circumstances in which we are placed.

And though we cannot but feel sorrow and regret, when we see men so brutalised as the Secret Murderers of India, yet, the very fact of their existence, is a pleasing confirmation of the truth of that great principle—"*The Formation of Character,*" which only requires to be generally acted upon, under wise regulations, to make the world a Paradise.

The very fact that these men are made to be the characters they are, proves that we can make man *what we please!!* Our course then is plain,—we have simply to discover what arrangements will make him

* See the Polytechnic for December for the above particulars.

VIRTUOUS and HAPPY, and immediately put them in operation.

May we profit by the lesson we have thus learned,—and may it soon enable us to change the world from the Pandemonium it now is, to a brighter heaven than ever yet has been imagined, is the sincere wish of

Your Friend and Brother,

F. HOLLICK.

Much more curious information (not here quoted) is given in the articles referred to, respecting the mann[illegible] and customs of the Thugs, and the probable origin of their singular superstition. This was not needed in the present work; and, we therefore merely give directions for those to find it, who wish to push their inquiries further.

THE END.

Edward P. Eddrup

The Thugs; or, Secret Murderers of India.

London: Society for Promoting Christian Knowledge, 1853.

It is not improbable that under an Eastern Government Feringea would have been tortured and then put to death after giving evidence, which would have effectually deterred any others

[1] Ramaseeana, p. 28.

from coming forward; indeed, nothing but their confidence in British good faith would have induced these men to confess as they did, and this may teach us the many advantages (not to speak of the obligation of duty) which result from keeping engagements even towards enemies. Had not every promise been held sacred and inviolable it would have been hopeless to expect success in this undertaking. Indeed, few things cause greater admiration to the Hindoos than finding that they can, as a rule, depend on the word of an Englishman, falsehood and treachery being, among themselves, the prevailing and almost universal vice. We may notice also the benefits arising from British energy and mutual co-operation. On the arrest of some of the Thugs it might happen that there was no local evidence against them, but then there was in possession of the officers a mass of depositions, descriptions of person, lists of names, and other particulars, collected from all parts of India; so that if the party arrested were really guilty, it was very unlikely that evidence would be wanting sufficient for his conviction. The native governments could never have put down the Thugs, from their want of union and a common plan of operations. If one state had roused itself they might easily have taken refuge in another; even our own system of suppressing them was seriously threatened in 1834 by the Rajah of Joudpoor, who refused to give up the Thugs who had found an asylum in his territories; but Lord William Bentinck informed him that he could not be permitted to make his country the head-quarters whence these assassins might carry on their attacks against all the neighbouring states. On his still persisting, a large force was assembled to march against him, upon which he quietly submitted.[1]

We will conclude this division of our subject by citing a few cases out of the large collection before us, giving them in the words of the Thugs, as taken down at the time of confession. The following murder is remarkable for having been perpetrated almost in public without any discovery taking place. "We fell in," said Chutter, "with the moonshee (teacher) and his family at Chupara, between Nagpoor and Jubulpore, and they came on with us to Lucknadown, where we found that some companies of a native regiment, under European officers, were expected the next morning. It was determined to put them all to death that evening, as the moonshee

[1] See *Edinburgh Review,* vol. lxiv. p. 368.

seemed likely to keep with the companies. Our encampment was near the village, and the moonshee's tent was pitched close to us. In the afternoon some of the officers' tents came on in advance, and were pitched on the other side, leaving us between them and the village. The servants were all busily occupied in pitching them. Noor Khan, and his son Sadee Khan, and a few others, went, as soon as it became dark, to the moonshee's tent, and began to sing and play upon a guitar, as they had been accustomed to do. During this time some of them took up the moonshee's sword on pretence of wishing to look at it. His wife and children were inside listening to the music. The jhirnee, or signal, was given; but at this moment the moonshee saw his danger, called out murder, and attempted to rush through, but was seized and strangled. His wife hearing him, ran out with the infant in her arms, but was seized by Ghubboo Khan, who strangled her and took the infant. The other daughter was strangled in the tent. The grooms were at the time cleaning their horses, and one of them seeing his danger ran under the belly of his horse and called out murder, but was seized and strangled, as well as all the rest.

Q. "How did not the servants and others, who were pitching the tents close by, hear these calls for help?

Chutter:—"As soon as the signal was given, those of the gang who were idle began to play and sing as loud as they could; and two vicious horses were let loose, and many ran after them, calling out as loud as they could, so that the calls of the moonshee and his party were drowned."[1]

The following instance, which took place in 1805, is remarkable, among other things, for the number of persons, no less than sixty, who were put to death at once. The relator is a Thug named Dorgha. "After the capture of Gawilgur (in 1803) by General Wellesley (Duke of Wellington), it was restored to the Nagpoor Rajah, who appointed Ghureeb Sing to the command of the fortress. Anxious to get some good soldiers from Hindostan to garrison it, he sent his younger brother, Ghyan Sing, with a number of followers, and a large sum of money, to raise them in the Oude country, and districts between the Ganges and Jumma rivers. Ghyan Sing and his party passed through Nagpore, and came to Jubulpore in the month of June, while

[1] Ramaseeana, p. 170.

we were there concentrated from the different parts into which we had extended our expeditions that season. His party consisted of fifty-two men, seven women, and a Brahman boy, then about four years of age. Some of our gangs lodged in the town, some in the cantonments among the troops, and some were encamped at the tank of Adhar, two or three miles from the town, on the road to Mirzapore. As soon as we heard of the arrival of this party from the Deccan, every party of Thugs deputed some of its most respectable members to mix with them in the town and win their confidence. At first, they tried to separate them into different parties to proceed by different roads, but though they had collected together at different times and places on the road it was found impossible to separate any part of them from Ghyan Sing; and we agreed to unite all our gangs, and to lead the party by the most unfrequented roads till we might find a place convenient for the murder of the whole at once. On reaching Sehora we persuaded them to quit the high road through Belehree and Myhere, and take that through Chundeca and the old fort Bundoogur, which leads through very extensive tracts of jungle and uninhabited country. We went with them through all this country, however, without finding, what we considered, a fitting time and place, and reached Rewah, winning more and more upon their confidence every day. From Rewah we went to Simareea, and from that place to a small village half way to Chitterkote, called by us Burwala Gow, from a large Indian fig-tree (Bur) that stood near it; thence we sent on people, as usual, to select a place for the murder, and they found one about two coss and a half (five miles) distant, in a very extensive jungle, without a human habitation for many miles on either side. We persuaded the party to set out soon after midnight; and as they went along we managed to take our appointed places, two Thugs by every traveller, and the rest in parties of reserve at different intervals along the line, every two managing to keep the person they were appointed to kill in conversation. On reaching the place chosen, the signal was given at several different places, beginning with the rear party and passing on to that in front, and all were seized and strangled except the boy. It was now near morning, and too late to admit of the bodies being securely buried, and we made a temporary grave for them in the bed of the river, covered them over with sand, and went on with the boy and the booty to Chitterkote, intending to send back a large party the next night and have the bodies securely buried. The rains had begun to set in, and after the murders it rained very heavily all the day. The party, however, went back, but found that the river had risen and washed away all the bodies except two or three, which they found exposed, and pushed into the stream to follow the rest."

The following confession, taken by Captain Paton in 1837, may serve to show both the cool treachery with which these murders are accompanied, and the freedom from remorse, or rather complacency, with which they are looked back upon afterwards. The relator is Dhoosoo, the leader of a band of thirteen Thugs, and speaking of a locality not far from Allahabad. He says: "Here I saw a traveller whom I inveigled thus —he was a sowar, or horseman, rode a very large horse, and was armed with two swords, a shield, pistols, &c. While he sat cooking his dinner in the serai I was in search of some spices for my food, and was asking the bhuttearee, or keeper of the serai, if she could supply me. She said no. The horseman hearing this, said he would give me some, and immediately supplied me; this led to a friendly conversation, before which I had no thought of murdering him. I asked him whence he came and whither he was going. He said he was going to Fyzabad. I said I was also going there. "Then, let us go together," said he. I agreed, and we proposed starting in the morning. I then went and communicated to all the Thugs that there was a traveller from a great distance, upon whom we should find much money. They all agreed that he would be a good man to thug. I proposed we should take him on a day's journey to Ashruf Gunge, and in advance of that to murder him. (The villain Dhoosoo relates all this with a smile upon his face as if he had been doing a kindness to the traveller, whom, in return for an act of kindness and confidence, he was thus deliberately planning to murder in cold blood.) In the morning we set out and reached Ashruf Gunge, where we halted during the day. I sent from thence the old man to look for a good place for the perpetration of the murder. He returned, and told us that he had selected a good place. As the traveller was a powerful armed man I selected two staunch stranglers—Adhar, approver, and Rujub. We started in the morning, and when we reached the appointed spot, I, and others of the gang, induced him to dismount and wait for us. He did so. Khan Mahomed had a small carpet spread, and invited the traveller to sit with him; he did so, and in an instant both stranglers seized and strangled him."

In one of the cases brought to light it was discovered that no less than five hundred sepoy recruits were cut off at once. Sometimes they obtain an immense booty; on one occasion, as much as £20,000, by the murder of a treasure-party mounted on camels. After dividing the spoil a proper share was set apart for one of the temples of their goddess. At other times, however, people are put to death for the sake of the most trifling gains; in one instance a turban only fell to the share of one member of the gang. "We often," confesses one of them, "strangle a victim who is suspected of having two pice (about ¾*d.*). Eight annas (about 1*s.*) is a very good remuneration for murdering a man." Near Baroda they once dispatched some travellers whom their spies had reported to be carrying treasure, but "to the great disappointment and chagrin of us all, no property was found upon them, for they turned out to be common stone-cutters, and their tools tied in bundles and carried over their shoulders deceived the spies."

In these various murders sad scenes are sometimes witnessed, as might be expected; on an occasion when twenty-five had been put to death, two boys were reserved by the robbers, when one of them beginning to cry very bitterly, and refusing to be pacified, was seized by the legs and his brains dashed out against a stone. At another time, a mother with her infant in her arms having been among the victims strangled, the Thug determined to keep and adopt the child, but after the bodies had been put in the grave, one of his companions urged him to kill the child also for fear of detection; the child was thrown into the grave upon the dead bodies and buried alive.

There are also River Thugs, who chiefly prevail in Bengal, where the system is altered in order to suit the circumstances of the country, which is much intersected with rivers. The leader, disguised as a traveller, with a servant to carry his bundle, stations himself on the road towards the ghât, or landing-place, where his boat is waiting, and falling in with a traveller persuades him to join company. He pretends to be a good hand at a bargain, and is allowed to agree for a passage for both; he beats down the master of his own boat after a great deal of disputing, to half-price, and the traveller, much pleased, gives him many thanks, and readily embarks, never to come out alive. If it should happen that the traveller suspects or dislikes the first man, he soon falls in with the inveigler (sotha) of another boat, who, learning by a sign what has happened, pretends to enter into his fear and anxiety to throw off the first, who, at length, finds occasion to remain behind, while his confederate takes the wayfarer into his own boat where he is soon destroyed. They usually break the spine across the knee in order to prevent any chance of their victims recovering, and having stripped the body, drop it into the river.

Two other cases only need be mentioned as bearing on the branch of the subject we are next to speak about—the religious system of the Thugs. The first, however, affords also a striking instance of the power of their unhappy superstition to destroy in the heart all common feelings of gratitude and friendship. They accompanied an officer in the Nizam's service, named Newal Sing, and his family, among whom were two little girls of eleven and thirteen years, for two hundred miles, and were on intimate terms with them for twenty days, during which time they received several substantial acts of kindness from them, on one occasion being released by their means from an imprisonment into which their mal-practices had got them, and yet, on the first favourable opportunity, they were all murdered. This time there was much hesitation on the part of the whole gang, and some separated from the main body rather than be present at the murder; but the cause of this hesitation was no awakened scruple of remorse or tenderness, but the mere fact that Newal Sing had one arm; maimed or leprous persons being, it seems, among those whose sacrifice is unacceptable to their goddess. They are also forbidden to kill musicians, dancing men or women, and some others; Ganges water carriers, while they have the sacred water with them, but if their vessels are empty their immunity ceases. The sacred animal, the cow, is also a protection. A Thug, whose deposition was taken in 1837, attributed a fever which confined him for ten months, to strangling a man who had with him a cow and her calf; all the band agreed that it arose from the displeasure of the goddess at the deed. In illustration of this point of their belief we will cite the last case of assassination with which we think it necessary to trouble the reader. "A party of Thugs projected the murder of fourteen persons, including several women; but the design could not be carried into effect because the victims had a cow with them. With some difficulty they were prevailed upon to sell the cow to the Thugs, who, to induce the travellers to consent to the sale, pretended that they had to make an offering of a cow at Shaphore, and were in want of one. The cow was actually presented to them at Shaphore, and the obstacle being removed, the whole of the unsuspecting travellers were two or three hours afterwards strangled."

We will now direct the reader's attention to the religious principles of the Thugs and the goddess they worship, confining ourselves here to the Hindoos; for though there are Mahommedan Thugs, the differences are not so important as to require to be separately noticed. This is a point full of interest as a moral phenomenon, a striking instance of the power of a false worship in depraving natural conscience, and perverting the common instincts of humanity. Men, indeed, rob and murder everywhere, but we know not that we have ever heard of any others who thought it *right* to do so; and even these men think that common murders and thefts are wicked—murders done without their peculiar ceremonies, or accompanied with the infringement of any of their appointed rules. They distinguish, a subtle distinction truly, between Thuggee and murder. No doubt there is much self-deceit in the matter, as is evident from their selecting as victims those who have about their persons something worth taking; so that very often their real motives are the love of plunder and lawless adventure, which they disguise to themselves by the pretence and formality of religion. But, in order to explain how it is possible that there can be a connexion between such evil deeds and even the mere profession of any kind of piety, it will be necessary to say a few words on part of the religious system of India, a land overshadowed by the dark cloud of idolatry, whose boast is to worship, they say, 2,000,000 of gods. Among these is Kâli, the wife of Sîva, the destroyer; her names are nearly one hundred—Parbatti and Davey are two of the most common; and as she has many names, so, like other idols, is she worshipped under many forms. They believe her to be extremely black, and to have features so hideous that no mortal man could dare to look upon them. She is represented sometimes with four hands, in which she holds a drum, a trident, a serpent, and a vessel for begging. She is said to rejoice in drinking the blood of men and demons, whence is derived one of her names—Kunkalee, or man-eater. In her honour, people sometimes sacrifice themselves or their children. Human sacrifices are even at the present day being discovered in India,[1] and have for a long time, more or less, prevailed there, and in other lands; and were it not beside our present purpose, it would not be uninteresting to give some account of them, and to connect this worship of Kâli with that of Moloch or Saturn (or Chronus as the Greeks called him), which prevailed among the Canaanites both in Phœnicia, and Palestine, and in their colony of Carthage. It was a branch of this horrible worship which the Israelites learned from them, and, in spite of the warnings and denunciations of the Prophets, persisted in practising, burning their children in the fire in sacrifice to Moloch.[2]

[1] See a letter from India on the Meriah sacrifices, in the *Colonial Church Chronicle* for August, 1851, vol. v. p. 64. It was shown to me by a friend who had just received it from his son, and, judging it to be of general interest, I forwarded it, with his permission, for publication.

[2] See, for instance, Ps. cvi. 35, 37; 2 Chron. xxviii. 2, 3; Jerem. xix. 5, xxxii. 35; (which place also shows that Baal and Moloch were the same deity; the words are of kindred meaning, Baal signifying Lord, Moloch

Of this goddess, Kâli, the Thugs consider themselves the priests and ministers. Their murders are acts of devotion; their victims are offered in her honour, the goddess permitting them, in reward for their labours, to take to themselves the property of the slain. They have ancient legends which relate the rise and origin of their occupation, and declare that Kâli gave the twisted handkerchief used in strangling as a gift to the first two Thugs whom she herself had created. They believe themselves to be under her especial protection; and tales circulate among them which tell of the sicknesses and calamities which have befallen some of the native princes who have endeavoured to suppress them. Thus, while murderers elsewhere are looked upon as the outcasts of society, these men consider themselves, and are esteemed by others, according to their position in life, as among the most respectable members of their village communities: intelligent, agreeable, and most careful in observing all the regulations of their caste. Neither public opinion nor their own conscience condemns them, these murders being with them lawful and religious acts, such

king.) Micah vi. 7. These sacrifices of children to Baal may be traced at Carthage down to the time of our Lord's crucifixion.

as deeds of charity or following a profession would be with a Christian. The following extracts from conversations are of considerable interest :—

Q. " How (asks Captain Sleeman) can you murder old men and young children without some emotions of pity ; calmly and deliberately as they sit with you and converse with you, and tell you of their private affairs, of their hopes and fears, and of their wives and children, whom they are going to meet after years of absence, toil, and suffering ?

A. " From the time that the omens have been favourable, we consider them as victims thrown into our hands by the deity to be killed, and that we are a mere instrument in her hands to destroy them : that if we do not kill them she will never be again propitious to us, and we and our families shall be involved in misery and want.

Q. " And can you sleep as soundly by the bodies or over the graves of those you have murdered, and eat your meals with as much appetite as ever ?

A. " Just the same : we sleep and eat just the same, unless we are afraid of being discovered.

Q. " And when you see or hear a bad omen you think it is the order of the deity not to kill the travellers you have with you, or are in pursuit of?

A. " Yes: it is the order not to kill them; and we dare not disobey."[1]

And again:—

Q. " Are you never afraid of the spirits of the persons you murder?

A. " Never: they cannot trouble us.

Q. " Why? do not they trouble other men when they commit murder?

A. " Of course they do. The man who commits a murder is always haunted by spirits. He has sometimes fifty at a time upon him, and they drive him mad.

Q. " And how do they not trouble you?

A. " Are not the people we kill killed by the orders of Davey?"

" Yes," added another Thug; " it is by the blessing of Davey that we escape that evil."

Upon which this remark was added by a third, " Do not all whom we kill go to Paradise? and why should their spirits stay to trouble us?"

In connexion with this idea, of their being instruments in the hands of their goddess, may

[1] Ramaseeana, p. 147.

be mentioned the opinion which they entertain, in common with many Hindoos, that all things are predestined, and driven forwards by a fixed and unalterable fate. "A Thug leader," says Captain Sleeman, "of most polished manners and great eloquence, being asked one day in my presence by a native gentleman, whether he never felt compunction in murdering innocent people, replied with a smile, 'Does any man feel compunction in following his trade? and are not all our trades assigned us by Providence?' The native gentleman said, 'How many people have you in the course of your life killed with your own hands, at a rough guess?' 'I have killed none.' 'Have you not just been describing to me a number of murders?' 'Yes; but do you suppose I could have committed them? Is any man killed from man's killing? is it not the hand of God that kills him, and are not we mere instruments in the hand of God?"[1] Feringea, mentioned above, feeling some remorse for the murder of a young woman who had followed him, having fallen in love with his beauty, consoled himself with the reflection, "It was her fate to die by our hands."

Among their religious ceremonies we may

[1] Ramaseeana, p. 75.

notice the regard which they pay to omens, which are supposed to be intimations of the will of their deity, and to convey warnings as to the failure or success of their expeditions. We are here reminded of classical times; and though the system of divination practised by the Thugs, by which they think to foretel the future by the voice and passing of certain animals and birds, is not so grand and elaborate as the auguries of ancient Greece and Rome, to which it bears in many points a close resemblance, it is sufficiently complicated and perplexing to the uninitiated. An omen on the left at starting, or on the course of a journey, promises good; it must be followed by an omen on the right, or the expedition is put off; for though the first predicts its successful result, it is the latter only which also promises a safe return. If they hear an omen on the left when about to halt it threatens evil, and they must pass on till they hear one on the right. Omens are taken in various ways, according as they are heard in the day or night, or according as they cross their path from right to left or from left to right, from wolves, from the low melancholy note of the small owlet, from the cry of hares, from the braying of an ass. If a hare run across the road by which they are travelling, it is looked upon as portending great misfortune, and, singular as it seems, the omen of the ass is judged to be superior to that of all others; if they hear it bray on the left when setting out, and soon after it is repeated on the right, they believe nothing on earth can prevent their success during that expedition, though it should last for years.

They also pay veneration to a consecrated pickaxe, which is entrusted to the most watchful and careful of the gang. When they halt it is buried with its point in the direction they wish to go; and they assert that, if another route is better for them, its point will be found to have changed its position. By this they swear, and conceive that dreadful tortures will fall on any of them who ventures to break this oath. It is used in digging the graves of their victims, and, according to their mythology, Kâli herself presented one in by-gone ages to the founders of their sect. When displeased at their turning round to look at her while devouring the slain, she left them henceforth to bury in the earth the bodies of those whom they sacrificed in her name. This legend of the goddess, eating the corpses of the murdered, is interpreted, reasonably enough it would seem, to be an allegory referring to the good old times of Thuggee, when the unsettled state of the country rendered it needless for them to use any precaution to escape detection, and they could leave their victims unburied on the highway.

After every murder a sacrifice of thanksgiving, called Tupounee, is offered. A blanket is spread upon the ground, on which is placed a pile of sugar, the consecrated pickaxe, and a piece of silver; the leader of the gang then sits upon the blanket, with his face to the west, and as many of the stranglers as conveniently can, sit on each side of him. They must be an even number. The leader, having buried a portion of the sugar, offers a prayer to Kâli, in which the rest fervently join: he then sprinkles some water on the pickaxe and on the little pit containing the sugar, and places some sugar on the hands of those sitting with him: the signal for strangling is then given, as though they were going to commit a murder, and the sugar is eaten in solemn silence. The remainder of the pile of sugar is distributed to the rest of the Thugs who are sitting outside the blanket, and none may partake of it who has not strangled a man with his own hands.

It remains briefly to notice some particulars

in Indian manners and opinions, which have greatly facilitated the operations of the Thugs, and enabled them for so long a time to escape with comparative impunity.

In the first place we may notice a point which has been already touched upon: public opinion is not particularly shocked by these murders. Kâli is worshipped by other Hindoos, though not in exactly the same way. In many parts goats and fowls are sacrificed, and their blood poured forth as a libation before her shrine; and all destructive things are looked upon as her ministers, and in many villages they would dread her vengeance if they were to interfere to check their working: thus, to destroy a wolf, even though it had carried off a child a week, would be regarded in some districts as likely to entail terrible calamities; and when the cholera was raging it was considered flying in the face of God, and utterly impious, to prescribe or take medicine for it; for was it not the means which Kâli had appointed for the destruction of a certain portion of the human race?

Secondly, we might remind the reader of the selfishness and indifference to the sufferings of others, which has prevailed, indeed, in every place where the royal law of loving one's neighbour as oneself has not been proclaimed in its fulness and majesty, but which is peculiarly aggravated in India by the institution of castes, and the isolation between different classes which this has so great a tendency to produce. Thus, in addition to the superstitious fear of consequences from the vengeance of Kâli which many would feel if they became instrumental in the punishment of the Thugs, they have no sufficient motive to induce them to run this risk, so long as the Thugs conciliate the police and people of their own district, and confine their depredations to strangers. Thus, in Oude, where the fields are almost all irrigated from wells, the bodies were usually thrown into them; and when the cultivators discovered them, they hardly ever thought it worth while even to ask how they came there, and became at last quite accustomed to it. The officers reckon, among the difficulties of suppressing them, this unwillingness on the part of the villagers, the authorities, and even sometimes of the relatives, to put themselves to the trouble of coming forward to give evidence. Bankers, whose treasure-bearers had been murdered, refused to acknowledge their losses, or allow reference to be made to their books until they received an assurance that they should not be called upon to appear publicly in court. Incredible as it may seem, some of the native governments recognised Thuggee as one of the lawful professions; and, so far from endeavouring to extirpate the Thugs, levied a regular tax upon them, and a list of the families who paid it may be found in Captain Sleeman's appendix. Just imagine parties in England applying to the Secretary of State for a licence to rob and murder by the year. When to all this we add the indolence and apathy which are such general traits of native character, and the deadening effects of the belief in an irresistible fate which prevails among others besides the Thugs, we need not be surprised that their evil deeds should have failed to rouse any deep feelings of indignation: most are content to let things go on as they have done, and consider the Thugs, as they consider themselves, instruments in the hands of God. Individuals may be vexed when their relatives have suffered, but they have no energy to unite together for their suppression, or to take the trouble and make the sacrifices necessary to promote the ends of justice. "If similar losses are predestined, they will take place in spite of all sacrifices; and if not predestined, no sacri-

maxim, and it falls in exactly with the notions of the selfish, the idle, and the feeble-minded. It is worthy of remark that the Thugs never attack Europeans; they are reported to have held a consultation on the subject, and to have resolved against it for three reasons:—the first, that Europeans generally carried pistols on a journey; the second, that they seldom carried money; but thirdly and chiefly, that they held so together, that, if one were molested, such a storm would be raised as must end in the destruction of the association.[1]

In the last place, we may mention a few points relating to Indian customs and habits, which have enabled the Thugs to carry out their purposes much more easily than they could have done elsewhere. Such as the practice of sending remittances in the precious metals and jewels by men on foot and in disguise without any guard; the necessity of starting in the dark before day-break in order to avoid the heat of the sun; the custom of travellers of providing and dressing their own food under the shade of trees by the wayside, without that communication with the people of the towns through which

[1] See Edinburgh Review, vol. lxiv. p. 368.

they pass, which would enable their friends to trace them when they disappear ; the long tracks of grass and wood jungle, through which all the roads pass, and the many ravines and water courses which intersect or run parallel to them affording every opportunity for hiding the bodies so that they shall not be discovered ; the little appearance of road that is found in many parts, and the consequent facility with which travellers are led aside by bye-paths into places suited for murder; the unreserved manner in which travellers of the same caste mix and communicate, and the ease with which men can feign different castes ; the little commercial intercourse between the different towns, on the great roads in a country where each village produces what its population demands, and consumes almost all that it produces save its raw agricultural produce ; the slow rate of transit where all produce is carried upon bullocks, and consequently the little chance which the assassin has of being overtaken and interrupted ; these may be noticed as among the circumstances which have favoured the growth of this terrible system, enabling it to last for hundreds of years, and to spread from one end of India to the other.

It is difficult for those who have been brought

up under the shelter of Christ's most holy Faith, which in a thousand unperceived and indirect ways has influenced all things around, has moulded to a very considerable extent the opinions even of those who make no direct profession of religion, and has sanctified in some degree the general tone of society, giving stability to law, and a better direction to public feeling; it is difficult, I say, for those who have enjoyed this great blessing to picture to themselves what heathenism is.

Let us, then, in order to assist some of our readers to realize this, offer by way of conclusion a few remarks on the facts which we have had before us, and recapitulate some of the reflections which they have suggested—

1. We have seen human life held cheap: none can have any true conception of the value of life, who do not know that there is a great day of reckoning for all things done in this present life, and that death is the end of the time allotted for man's probation. Thus in heathen lands there is no sufficient conception of the vast importance of life, or of the purposes for which it is given. The Hindoos, moreover, have lost or greatly obscured that other great truth which is the foundation of

human responsibility, that the soul of man has a distinct personality. All things they conceive to be part of God; the trees, and stones, and meanest insect, as well as men, are manifestations of the Deity who filleth all things. Man departing this life changes into some other form of bird or beast, or it may be at last some new human shape, or is absorbed back again into the essence of God, and yet, during all these changes, still remains a portion of Deity. How, then, can they look on life and death as we have been taught to do?

2. We have seen in addition to this what man may become when destitute of the Spirit of God, and misguided by a false worship, and the evil passions of his own heart; how the most dreadful crimes have been performed under the notion that they were religious services. We have seen something of demon worship, and men at last become assimilated to the deities whom they revere; and sad is it to behold conscience, the only guide left to those who have no revelation of the true God, so utterly perverted, and steeled, by a deadly superstition, and the fearful doctrine of fatalism, against the common instincts of nature, and the entrance of remorse.

3. We learn the importance of a healthy state of public feeling with respect to the commission of crimes: with ourselves happily such iniquities as we have been relating, or anything even approaching to them, would arouse a righteous indignation, and all would conceive themselves bound, if it were in their power, to aid in bringing the offenders to justice. Whatever may be said of the sins and neglects of British rule in India—and I for one have no wish to excuse or defend them—this at least is something to be urged in its favour; that as soon as it came to our knowledge, we suppressed infanticide, we suppressed Thuggee, and even now have sent detachments of troops to put down the lingering remains of human sacrifices. But with the Hindoos public feeling or unity of purpose is unknown; the blight of heathendom has fallen on all things; not only do they look upon these murderers as following a legitimate profession, and a justifiable mode of worship, but their intense selfishness renders them indifferent to any misfortunes that may befal others: too often are they found to be at once indolent and hard-hearted.

It would be a long tale were we to record the abominations and unhappiness which have sprung rom the worship of false gods throughout all ıeathendom, from the beginning of idolatry, that s, alas, almost from the beginning of the world; the superstitions and miseries of India alone would fill a volume. We have seen something of what one branch of heathen-worship has been able to inflict on that fair land, so rich and fertile, blessed by such abundant gifts of nature, but accursed by the presence of sin. We have in this sketch, lifted up, as it were, one little corner of the veil which distance and imperfect knowledge has hung before that dark scene, and surely it has been an evil and revolting prospect which has opened on our view.—But these few pages will not have been written in vain if they enable some of their readers to see to some extent the force of those places of Holy Scripture, which tell us that the heathen world was lying in wickedness, under the power of the devil; that the strong man armed was keeping his goods in peace, the souls and bodies of men in a miserable thraldom; that they were aliens and strangers, having no hope and without God in the world; walking in darkness and in the valley of the shadow of death. When we call to mind, that before the coming of Christ, the world had been groaning under the burden of heathenism for nearly 4,000 years, these expressions will no longer appear to us metaphors, but stern realities; I had almost said, hardly adequate descriptions of a plain and simple fact. Let me add that we must show our value for Christianity, not by contrasting our state with theirs, in an indolent and self complacent spirit, but by leading ourselves in very deed Christian and holy lives, and by doing all in our power to advance the great cause of Missions, and to rescue heathen men from the servitude and error in which Satan holds them bound, and to spread far and wide that Gospel to which we owe so great a part of our national greatness, and all our own personal hopes and consolations.

THE END.

R. CLAY, PRINTER, BREAD STREET HILL.

John William Kaye

The Administration of the East India Company.

London: Richard Bentley, 1853. 2nd ed.

CHAPTER II.

Thuggee—Increased Knowledge of the Habits of the People—Its Results—Antiquity of Thuggee—Its Progress—Manners and Customs of the Thugs—Thuggee Expeditions—Efforts for the Suppression of Thuggee—The Thuggee Department—Colonel Sleeman and his Associates—Complicity of the Zemindars—Success of our Efforts—Decrease of the Crime.

THERE is nothing more remarkable in our recent connexion with the East than our increased knowledge of the manners and customs, the literature and the religion, the vices and the virtues, of the people. We had been nearly two centuries connected with them, by ties at least of commerce, before we knew very much more about the natives of India than that they were a race of black people, with bare legs, carrying the greater amount of their apparel piled up on the top of their heads. We looked upon them for a great number of years simply as a people to be trafficked with—a people with whom it was our mission to drive hard bargains for muslin or silk. In time we came to look upon them as a people to be subdued; and then, having subdued them, we began to regard our dusky subjects as so many millions of revenue-payers—people from whom it was our duty to extract so much in the shape of rent or taxes in recognition of their subjection. Then, after another lapse of years, we looked upon them as a people to be governed. We invented, as has been seen, new codes of laws for their restraint and correction, and we did our best, whilst keeping them in order, to protect their properties and their lives. But it is only within very recent times that we have thought it worth our while to *know* anything about the natives of India, and to turn our knowledge to profitable account.

The study of books in India preceded the study of men. Learned orientalists, at the close of the last century, took counsel with the Pundits and Moulavees, and wrote elaborate dissertations upon the Hindoo and Mahomedan codes and scriptures, which they diligently translated for the benefit of the Christian world. From these ancient authorities they derived a vast deal of very recondite information, which did not, however, in our commerce with the people, prove to be of much use. That which, perhaps, we most required to know was not set down in these books. It was not, indeed, set down anywhere in written characters; but it was stamped, broadly and deeply—seemingly, indeed, ineffaceably—upon the heart of Indian society. It was not, however, of that kind which he who runs may read. It was not blazoned upon the mosques or inscribed upon the pagodas. An English traveller might make his way from one end of the country to the other and see nothing of the things with which it was so profitable to make permanent acquaintance. He acquired the scantiest possible knowledge of the habits and customs of the people. He passed through them, perhaps lived amongst them, but he only saw the surface of society. Perhaps he did not desire to look beneath the outer shell. Perhaps he beheld feebly some indications of hidden mysteries which he did not care to fathom. Certain it is, that he left much for his successors to drag into the clear light of day. We have much to learn even now. But honor is still due to our cotemporaries for what they have revealed—for what, by stubborn inquiries, by deep probings and subtle anatomisations, they have mastered, and comprehended, and exposed. Little was it that we could do for India until we knew something of the people whom Providence had committed to our care. How could we address ourselves to the remedy of the evils which were preying upon the vitals of Indian society, whilst we had no distinct understanding of what those corrosive evils were?

I do not write this in condemnation or reprehension of our predecessors on Indian soil. It was natural—almost necessary, indeed—that there should have been such short-comings as these. There are truths not to be arrived at except by long and patient induction. There are secrets buried deep beneath the surface which it is a work of time and toil to extricate from the deceptive clay which clings around them. Institutions, purposely veiled in darkness, of a strange, mysterious, almost incredible character, were likely to have escaped the notice of the European eye. It was long before we suspected the systematic war against life and property which had been carried on for years in almost every part of the country from Oude to the Carnatic. It was long before we could bring ourselves to understand that organised bands of professional and hereditary murderers and depredators, recognised, and indeed, to a certain extent tolerated by their fellow-men, were preying upon the uninitiated and unwary sections of society, and committing the most monstrous crimes with as much forethought and ingenuity as though murder were one of the fine arts, and robbery a becoming effort of human skill; nay, indeed, glorying in such achievements, as acts welcome to the deity, and bringing them to perfection with a due observance of all the ceremonial formalities of a cherished religious faith.

But in time we began to understand these things. We obtained a clue and we followed it up, until the hideous mystery was brought out into the clear light of day. There is not an intelligent reader at the present time who does not know what a *Thug* is. The word, indeed, has been adopted into our own language, and has been applied to other depredators than those who worship the Goddess Davee. It is well known that a Thug is a professional murderer. We found the Thugs carrying on their fearful trade, and as soon as we came to understand them we made war upon, and struck them down. The servants of the East India Company have extirpated Thuggee. It is an exploit worthy to be celebrated by every writer who undertakes to chronicle the achievements of the English in the East—one which it is impossible to dwell upon without pleasure and pride.

Of the antiquity of Thuggee there is no doubt. In the creed of its votaries it had, of course, a divine origin. Everything monstrous and abominable in India has the sanction of some puerile or obscene legend to recommend it to the superstitious and the depraved. The legend which declares the divinity of Thuggee is preposterous even for an Oriental tradition. I do not know a more absurd chapter in all that monstrous farrago of absurdities, the Hindoo mythology, than that which sets forth how the Goddess Kalee made war upon a gigantic monster, every drop of whose blood became a destructive demon; how the blood of these demons generated other demons, until the earth was in a fair way to be overrun by the noxious brood; how, at length, the goddess hit upon the notable expedient of creating from the celestial ichor which exuded from her trenchant arm two men, to whom she gave handkerchiefs, or waistbands, with orders to destroy the demons by strangulation without shedding a drop of blood; and how, the demons having been so destroyed, the grateful goddess gave the handkerchiefs to her myrmidons, and told them that thenceforth they and their descendants might carry on a profitable trade by exercising the destroying implements upon the human race. The Thugs, of course, claim to be descended from these unbegotten heroes, and are very proud of the descent. "I am a Thug of the royal records," said one of these professional stranglers; "I and my fathers have been Thugs for twenty generations."*

And what was this royal profession of which the members were so proud? It was simply the cowardly strangling of unsuspecting travellers in remote places, generally committed under circumstances of falsehood and treachery of the deepest dye. These Thugs, leagued together in a great brotherhood of crime, having taken the sacrament with all possible solemnity,† went about the country murdering in their cold bloodless style all the unwary wayfarers whom they could seduce into their toils. There was nothing to distinguish these artists from ordinary travellers. They assumed many different disguises, and played many different parts. They separated on the road, straggled into the towns and villages in little parties of three and four, and met as though they were strangers to each other. Perhaps one of the gang

* Thevenot, who travelled in India in the seventeenth century, has given an account of the Thugs, from which it appears that in those days they employed female decoys :—"Though the road I have been speaking of, from Delhi to Agra, be tolerable, yet hath it many inconveniences. One may meet with tigers, panthers, and lions upon it; and one had best also have a care of robbers, and above all things not to suffer anybody to come near one upon the road. The cunningest robbers in the world are in that country. They use a certain slip, with a running noose, which they can cast with so much sleight about a man's neck, when they are within reach of him, that they never fail, so that they strangle him in a trice. They have another cunning trick also to catch travellers: they send out a handsome woman upon the road, who, with her hair dishevelled, seems to be all in tears, sighing and complaining of some misfortune which she pretends has befallen her. Now, as she takes the same way that the traveller goes, he easily falls into conversation with her, and finding her beautiful, offers her his assistance, which she accepts; but he hath no sooner taken her up behind him on horseback than she throws the snare about his neck and strangles him, or at least stuns him, until the robbers, who lie hid, come running to her assistance, and complete what she hath begun."

† The sacred element was a kind of coarse sugar. According to the Thugs the deity entered largely into it, and there was a kind of transubstantiation, which wrought mightily upon the communicants. At all events, they declared that the sacred sugar changed their whole nature. "It would change the nature of a horse," they said. "Let any one once taste of that sugar and he will be a *Thug*, though he know all the trades and have all the wealth in the world." "My father made me taste of that fatal sugar," said a *Thug* to Colonel Sleeman, "when I was yet a mere boy; and if I were to live a thousand years, I should never be able to follow any other trade."

travelled in some state, as a man of rank, accompanied by numerous attendants, and a few palanquins or doolies, in which were said to be the ladies of his family, though in reality they contained little but the implements of their profession. On the road, so disguised, with nothing about them to awaken suspicion, these traders in death would fall, as though by accident, into the company of other wayfarers, and watching a favorable opportunity on the skirts of some jungle, or in some secluded place bordering upon a convenient watercourse, would throw the murderous waistband or turban-cloth round the neck of their victim, and scientifically do him to death. One man threw the fatal noose, another, seizing the other end of the rope or cloth, drew it tightly round the helpless wretch's neck, the two together pressing his head forward with their disengaged hands, whilst a third seized him by the legs and threw him to the ground. There could be no resistance. The work was quickly done. The body was then stripped, the property secured, and very soon the corpse was buried. The consecrated pickaxe, plied with miraculous silence, soon dug a grave for the body.* If a stranger approached whilst they were thus engaged, they laid a cloth decently and reverently over the carcase of the murdered man, and kneeling down beside it, lifted up their voices and wept, over the death of a beloved comrade.

Various were their artifices—great their cleverness. They were, indeed, consummate actors. If the locality were a dangerous one, the country much frequented,

* The pickaxe, forged with due solemnity, and then consecrated with certain prescribed formalities, was held in especial veneration by the Thugs. It was forbidden to bury the dead with any other instrument; for it was the symbol of their profession, and a legacy left, it was believed, by the goddess herself. "Do we not worship it," said a *Thug* to Colonel Sleeman, "every seventh day? Is it not our standard? Is its sound ever heard, when digging the grave, by any but a *Thug*? And can any man ever swear to a falsehood upon it?" Another asked, "How could we dig with any other instrument? This is the one appointed by Davee and consecrated; and we should never have survived the attempt to use any other."

they would throw up a slight enclosure of canvas, pretending that their women were behind the screens, and bury the body within it. Or, warned of the approach of travellers by one of their scouts, some clever member of the gang would throw himself down by the wayside, and simulate the spasms and convulsions, or the exhaustion and prostration of a dying man; and whilst the sympathising travellers were gathering round him and administering such simple remedies as were within their reach, his companions would conceal the body of their victim, and clear away the traces of their guilt. Sometimes the locality favored a readier and easier mode of disposing of the corpse, which was flung into a neighbouring river, or dropped into a convenient well.

Thus were these murders—systematically, artistically—perpetrated, with an adroit avoidance of detection which seldom or never failed. Human life in India is not of much account. A corpse by the wayside in England fills nearly a whole county with horror and astonishment. In India, even a humane English gentleman passes it by on the other side, and is only so far concerned at the spectacle, that probably his horse has shied at it, as it would at the trunk of a tree. Every one is accustomed to the sight of human bodies drifting down the river—floating islands inhabited by gorging birds of prey; or if you should chance to reside in a villa on the river-side, you are not concerned by the knowledge that the round white balls which dot your lawn like snow-flakes, or with which your little children are playing, are so many human skulls. Still less do the natives of India, by whom the European gentleman is infected, in due time, with this apathy, bestir themselves, body or soul, about these indications of our frail mortality. Death in India comes in many sudden shapes. If a certain Moodoo-sooden, or Rungoo-Lal, is missing from his accustomed place, or does not reach the end of a journey (should any one expect him), his anxious relatives take it for granted that he has been bitten by a serpent—that the cholera has preyed upon his vitals, or a wild beast has eaten him up. No descriptions of the missing one are inserted in the newspapers, and no members of the detective police are employed to discover the cause of his disappearance. Somehow or other he has been absorbed. "*Mur-gya*"—He has gone dead.

And so it happens that hundreds of natives of India disappear;* and their disappearance is either hardly noted, or it creates no astonishment or alarm. A journey in India is an affair of many months; and numerous are the perils which beset the path of the unprotected pedestrian. Hence it is that whole hecatombs were sacrificed to the Goddess Davee, and no one took account of the victims. Travellers likely to be missed were not especial objects of regard with the Thugs. They suffered such noticeable personages to pass on their way unheeded. Or, if tempted by the largeness of the spoil which glittered before them, they were betrayed into a departure from their ordinary cautious mode of procedure, they summoned to their aid something more than the common artifices of their profession, and surpassed themselves in cunning and skill. Sometimes the very envi-

* I ought rather to have written thousands. A correspondent in the Thuggee Department wrote me a few years ago: "In India hundreds of thousands disappear in a year or two, without the most distant clue but Thannadar's reports, to ascertain whether they have not been foully murdered. Villagers have assured me that to their own certain knowledge scores of men murdered by robbers, or in affrays, have been reported dead of cholera, snakebites," &c. It is not easy to arrive at a correct estimate of the number of people murdered annually by the Thugs. A native newspaper (the *Sumachar Durpan*) of great respectability, in 1833 declared that "one hundred *Thugs* slaughter, on an average, *eight hundred persons in a month*. It is not, therefore," added the writer, "going beyond the truth to affirm that, between the Nerbudda and the Sutlej, the number murdered every year is not less than ten thousand." The writer calculates that within these limits a hundred Thugs were always out on their murderous expeditions—probably many more were so employed. And this calculation only relates to a certain tract of country. I am inclined, however, to think that the individual performances of the Thugs is here somewhat overrated.

ronments of the marked man favored the escape of his murderer. The Thugs always knew their men. They never threw the noose without previously acquainting themselves with the circumstances of their victim. If they murdered a Company's Sepoy, on leave to his native village, carrying his savings wrapped up in his waistband, they knew that it would be long before he would be missed, either by his own family, or the adjutant of his regiment; and that, if missed by the former, his disappearance would be attributed to ordinary death, or if by the latter, to desertion. If they murdered a confidential public or private servant, bearing treasure from one station to another, they knew that the absence of the man, or the party of men at the accustomed place, would be attributed to the dishonesty of the treasure-bearers; and that whilst the police, if set upon the track, were in search of him, they would be far away from the district through which his journey had lain. They took care to leave behind them no living witnesses of their guilt. If they hunted down a man of note, they destroyed all his attendants. They always went *forward;* they never presented themselves in a town or village through which one of their victims had passed. So that even if they went on, riding the horses or wearing the clothes of the men they had murdered, their appearance excited no mistrust. They had always a ready story at command. They had always a given character to assume. They understood each other thoroughly, and they acted in concert, though often they appeared to be strangers. They had a secret dialect of their own; but often more serviceable than this were the secret signs by which they silently communicated with each other. They played their parts, indeed, with consummate address; and they passed on unsuspected to pursue their dreadful trade in the next convenient locality. For such localities they had keen and disciplined eyes, as artists have for the picturesque or sportsmen for good covers; and their faces sparkled and their hearts swelled when they chanced on these good murder-grounds.

It might seem from this account of the depredational excursions of these professional robbers, that they were men without a local habitation or a name, flitting from place to place, and never establishing for themselves such social connexions as were likely to cause their migrations to be matter of observance, or, indeed, to attract any kind of continued notice. But such was not, by any means, the case. They belonged for the most part to particular villages, where they left their wives and children; and they outwardly followed some peaceful calling. They cultivated the fields—rented a few acres of ground—or, perhaps, embarked as agriculturists on a larger scale, and employed laboring men to work under them.* Their occasional absence from the village was necessarily remarked. Sometimes the real cause was not suspected; but often it was a matter of open notoriety. A Thug set out on his dreadful journey, and every one in the village knew the cause of his departure—except, perhaps, his own wife.

It was not, indeed, a matter of much concernment to the villagers that these migratory murderers should set out upon their journeys to remote places, and return richer than they went. They did not murder their neighbours. Indeed, the village directly benefited by the blood-money that was brought home. The Zemindar, or head man, had an immediate interest in the success

* Take from among many instances the following, from the evidence of Colonel Sleeman's approvers:—"I remained in my own house for about a year and a half at Guntoulee, working upon my own fields as a cultivator, for I rented 100 beegahs of land, and employed laborers; the villagers knew that I was a man who went from home occasionally, but they knew not that I was a murderer."—Again: "I remained in my own house for two months after this, cultivating in my fields, for I rented three or four beegahs of land, chiefly, however, as a blind to conceal that I was a Thug, and to make a show that I was a cultivator. I started again on Thuggee."

of the expedition. A certain amount of tribute, or hush-money, was always paid to him; and the police officials, in the same manner, were bribed into silence.* Often, indeed, the brothers, or other near relatives of the village police, were members of the Thug gangs; and Thugs themselves have been known to wear the official brass-plates on their breasts which stamped them as Government employés. The protection of the Zemindars often went the length, especially in the native states, of overt and violent interference, and pitched battles have been fought in defence of the tribute-paying criminals when extermination has threatened the gangs.† The payments made by the Thugs and other depredational leagues, of which I shall speak presently, formed no inconsiderable item of their revenue. They looked to it, indeed, as to a perennial source of income from which they could make good any deficiencies in the amount of the Government claim, and sometimes applied the screw with such freedom that the unhappy Thugs, alarmed by their increasing exactions, migrated altogether from the extortionate village, and sought a resting-place where they might dwell without disgorging so large a share of their murder-gotten wealth. At one time, it may be added, so openly was the traffic carried on, that merchants often came from a distance to purchase the plunder brought home by the migratory gangs; but it would seem that the extension of the Company's judicial machinery, and

* "I always," said one approver, "after my journey, was obliged to give the Zemindar, Ragonauth Sing, of my village, some present, for the whole village knew that I was a Thug, and the Zemindar would have had me put in irons but for these presents. All Thugs thus propitiate their Zemindars."

† "At last," said another approver, "being traced by the Saugor guards, the Gwalior Regent, Bayza Bhaee, was induced, at the suggestion of the British Agent, to send out a detachment of two companies of infantry to secure them. The head man of the village was determined to protect them, in consideration of the share of the booty they had always given him. An action took place, in which several lives were lost, while the camp of the Governor-General of India, Lord William Bentinck, and that of the Bayza Bhaee, were within hearing of the guns. The Thugs all made their escape, in disguise, with the women, but were soon after taken."

the greater vigilance of its officers, soon indicated the necessity of greater caution in the disposal of the spoil.*

It may be doubted whether any class of natives ever followed their peculiar avocations with a keener relish than these Thugs.† They were brought up from early youth to the dreadful trade. Thuggee was to them not merely a profession. It was a religion. They believed that the Goddess Davee smiled down upon their exploits, and communicated with them through the agency of certain recognised sights and sounds. They performed ceremonial rites in propitiation of the deity, and then looked eagerly for the anticipated omens. No augurs, in remote ages of classical antiquity, ever consulted the auspices with more solemn outward observances, or a firmer inward faith in the expected revelations. A larger range of deity-directed signals was, however, embraced in the code of these Eastern soothsayers. Men and women, of different kinds, and in different situations, were pressed into the service as omens, and various animals, wild and tame, were believed to have the same commission from the goddess. There seems to have been no harmony and consistency observed in the inter-

* The following, from a very interesting Report, by the late Captain Lowis, on River Thuggee, contains a very decided opinion on the subject of the complicity of all classes of the village communities: — "To conclude, there seems no doubt that this horrid crime has been fostered by nearly all classes of the community — the landholders, the native officers of our courts, the police, the village authorities—all, I think, have been more or less guilty. My meaning is not, of course, that every member of these classes, but that individuals, varying in number in each class, were concerned. The Foujdaree police gomastahs have, in many instances, been practising Thugs; and the chowkedars, or village watchmen, frequently so. It is much to be feared that men so respectable in position as to make it seem almost incredible that they should give protection to such criminals, have, in fact, done so, for it appears out of the question that the total population of a village should be Thugs engaged in the regular practice of Thuggee, and several of them frequently apprehended on the gravest suspicion of that crime, without the cognisance of the Zemindars."

† I have alighted upon only one statement which militates against this general assertion, and, perhaps "proves the rule." A Thug, named Dhosoo, examined by Captain Paton, at Lucknow, declared "we only thug from necessity, not from pleasure — it is fearful business." But I could pile up proofs of the relish with which they pursued their trade.

preting of these divine manifestations. Thus a lame man and a dancing-master—a potter and an oil-seller, were equally unpropitious. Of the brute creation, the donkey and the jackal were regarded as the most important members, and various were the sights or sounds of encouragement, or warning, eagerly looked for from the unconscious beasts. Certain months of the year, and certain days of the week, were proscribed as of ill omen; and it was necessary that they should regulate both their diet and their toilet in the manner of which Davee was supposed to approve. If they were fortunate, they ascribed all their good fortune to a due regard of these heavenly directions, and if misadventure befel them, they attributed it, with praiseworthy candor, to their own misinterpretations, or neglect of the omens through which the goddess had frequently vouchsafed to make known her wishes to her people. "Even the most sensible approvers," writes Colonel Sleeman, "who have been with me for many years, as well Mussulmans as Hindoos, believe that their good or ill success always depended upon the skill with which their omens were discovered and interpreted, and the strictness with which they were observed and obeyed. One of the old Sindouse stock told me in presence of twelve others, from Hyderabad, Behar, the Dooab, Oude, Rajpootana, and Bundelcund, that had they not attended to these omens they could never have thrived as they did; and that in ordinary cases of murder a man seldom escaped after one of them; while they and their families had for ten generations thriven, though they had murdered hundreds of people. 'This,' said he, 'could never have been the case had we not attended to omens, and had not omens been intended for us.' Every Thug present concurred with him from his soul."

When once the omens had shown themselves to be

propitious, and Davee had smiled down upon the enterprise, murder became not only a religious duty, but a pleasant task. No compunctions then visited the enlightened Thug. "And do you never feel sympathy for the persons murdered—never pity or compunction?" asked Colonel Sleeman of a Thug, who had turned approver. "Never," was the answer. "How can you," pursued the English officer, "murder old men and young children, without some emotions of pity—calmly and deliberately as they sit with you, and converse with you—and tell you of their private affairs—of their hopes and fears—and of the wives and children they are going to meet, after years of absence, toil, and suffering?" And the answer returned was: "From the time that the omens have been favorable, we consider them as victims thrown into our hands by the deity to be killed, and that we are the mere instrument in her hands to destroy them; that if we do not kill them, she will never be again propitious to us, and we and our families will be involved in misery and want." "And," questioned Colonel Sleeman, "you can sleep as soundly by the bodies, or over the graves of those you have murdered, and eat your meals with as much appetite as ever?" And still the answer was: "Just the same—we sleep and eat just the same—unless we are afraid of being discovered." These last words do not indicate the fulness of faith which we should have expected to find in such a worshipper of Davee; for it was the professed belief of the Thugs, that if the omens were properly observed and interpreted, they never could be discovered.

Indeed, such was their confidence in the protective power of the goddess, that they believed that she would not only, if religiously served, shield them from harm, but visit with her wrath all who injured them. Nor was this belief confined exclusively to the Thugs. Their ravages were regarded with something of superstitious awe even by influential chiefs. At least, such was the statement of the murderers themselves, and there is other evidence to support the supposition. When Colonel Sleeman asked an approver if he knew any instances of influential natives suffering for acts of enmity or opposition to the Thugs, he was answered: "A great many. Was not Nanha, the Rajah of Jhalone, made leprous by Davee for putting to death Bodhoo and his brother Khumoolee, two of the most noted Thugs of their day? He had them trampled under the feet of elephants, but the leprosy broke out upon his body the very next day." "Did he believe," asked Colonel Sleeman, "that this punishment was inflicted by Davee for putting them to death?" "He was quite sensible of it," was the answer. "Did he do anything to appease her?" was then asked. "Everything," replied the approver. "Bodhoo had begun a well in Jhalone; the Rajah built it up in magnificent style; he had a tomb raised to their name, fed Brahmins, and consecrated it; had worship instituted upon it—but all in vain; the disease was incurable, and the Rajah died in a few months a miserable death. The tomb and well are both kept up and visited by hundreds to this day, and no one doubts that the Rajah was punished for putting these two Thugs to death." This was but one of many instances which Colonel Sleeman's approvers were eager to relate. One man, when asked if he knew any other cases of the same kind, replied, "Hundreds! When Madhajee Scindiah caused seventy Thugs to be executed at Multoun, was he not warned in a dream by Davee that he should release them? and did he not the very day after their execution begin to spit blood? and did he not die within three months?" Then other witnesses were ready with other proofs of the omnipotence of Davee, and told how, when certain Rajpoot chiefs arrested eighty Thugs, all their families were afflicted, how they all perished, "not a child left;" and how one who had imposed certain fines upon the gang, the very day that he took the money lost his only son, "and the best horse in his stable; and was himself taken ill, and died soon after a miserable death." But they all acknowledged that even Davee could not withstand the good fortune of the Company. "The Company's good fortune is such," they said, "that before the sound of your drums, sorcerers, witches, and demons take flight—and how can Thuggee stand?"

Thuggee did not stand—it fell. The great work of rooting out these monstrous depredational leagues was accomplished in a few years by the energies of a few European officers. Up to the year 1829 but little had been done to suppress the abomination. Occasional evidences of the crime had presented themselves some years before, and a few gangs of professional murderers had been arrested. In 1810, General St. Leger, then Commander-in-Chief, issued an order cautioning the troops, especially the Sepoys, about to proceed on leave to their homes, against "a description of murderers denominated Thugs," who infested the districts of the Doab, and other parts of the Upper Provinces. About the same time some of the more active of our magistrates in Upper India had succeeded in securing the persons of a number of these murderers, but although several of them confessed, and the property of the murdered men was found in their houses, the higher judicial authorities did not consider that the evidence was sufficient to convict them. "Mr. Wright apprehended seventy-six, of whom seventeen made confessions which strongly criminated the remaining fifty-nine, who denied. Those who denied, and those who confessed, were alike released by one sweeping order from the Nizamut Adawlut without security or anything else;"* and sent back to carry

* *Letter from G. Stockwell, joint magistrate, Etawah, to T. Wauchope, magistrate, Bundelcund, December*, 1814.

on their old trade, emboldened by impunity and success.

These were but fitful efforts resulting in nothing. The subject excited little general interest, and no organised efforts, on an effective scale, were made to root out the enormous evil. Indeed, its extent was imperfectly known even to the best informed of our officers until about the time which I have indicated, under the government of Lord William Bentinck, operations were formally commenced, and a regular "Department" for the suppression of Thuggee instituted by that enlightened nobleman. And so vigorously was this great work prosecuted—with such remarkable intelligence, and such admirable perseverance were all our measures shaped, and all our projects executed—that, ten years afterwards, Colonel Sleeman, to whose benevolent energies we are, under Providence, mainly indebted for the success of the undertaking, was enabled to write:—"In 1830, Mr. George Swinton, who was then Chief Secretary to the Supreme Government of India, and our best support in the cause which Mr. F. C. Smith and I had undertaken, wrote to him to say that he feared success must be considered as altogether unattainable, for he had been given to understand by those who appeared to be well informed on the subject, that the evil had taken deep root in all parts of India, and extended itself to almost every village community. There were certainly at that time very few districts in India without these resident gangs of Thugs ; and in some, almost every village community was more or less tainted with the system, while there was not one district free from their depredations. No man aware of the fearful extent of the evil could ever have expected to see so much progress made in its suppression within so short a time ; because no man could have calculated on those many extraordinary combinations of circumstances upon which our success has chiefly depended—combinations which it behoves us gratefully to acknowledge, as Providential interpositions for the benefit of the people entrusted to our rule—interpositions which these people themselves firmly believe will never be wanting to rulers whose measures are honestly intended, and wisely designed for the good of their subjects."*

How this great work was accomplished is soon told. These vast criminal leagues had hitherto thriven upon the ignorance of the British authorities. We could do nothing to suppress them, for, indeed, we knew little or nothing about them. They were mighty secrets—hidden mysteries—dimly guessed at, not at all understood. But now Sleeman and his associates, resolved that this trade of Thuggee should no longer be any more a mystery than tailoring or carpentering, began to initiate themselves into all the secrets of the craft, and were soon, in their knowledge of the theory of the profession, little behind the professors themselves.

It need not be said that all this information was derived from frequent intercourse with the Thugs themselves. Our officers having apprehended some of these professional stranglers, selected the likeliest of the party, and by holding out to them promises, not only of pardon, but of employment, soon wormed their secrets out of them. In a little time Sleeman and his associates had learnt from these "approvers" all that was to be learnt from them—all the mysteries of their craft, the whole art of Thuggee—how the murder-gangs set out on their journey, how they propitiated the goddess, how they consulted the omens, how the victim was first beguiled, how the noose was thrown, how the body was buried—how they brought up their children to the trade, how generation after generation of Thugs lived prosperously and securely, and how it happened that the native chiefs

* *Sleeman.* Preface to published Report on the Depredations committed by the Thug gangs of Upper and Central India. Calcutta, 1840.

either protected or stood aloof from them, whilst the English were ignorant of their doings. Everything that these approvers, turning their backs for ever on Davee, and bowing down before the irresistible *ikbal* of the Company, now revealed—and they were tolerably loquacious in their revelations—was carefully noted down, and the statements of one informant collated with those of others. From these men Sleeman and his associates learnt not only the whole theory and practice of Thuggee, but gathered no small amount of knowledge concerning the gangs that were in actual operation, and the men who were connected with them. With such clues as the approvers afforded, it was now easy to hunt down the different gangs which were scattered over the country, and many large captures were made. New approvers were brought upon the lists of the "Department," and new gangs were hunted down. Many criminals were thus brought to trial, convicted, and sentenced either to be hanged, transported, or imprisoned.*

These captures struck terror into the hearts of the whole fraternity of Thugs. And far more terrible than the English officers, environed with the prestige of that irresistible ikbal of the Company, which was acknow-

* One or two extracts from Colonel Sleeman's Reports will suffice to convey an idea of the extent of these captures and their results:—"When they arrived at Dakhola, Captain Borthwick having heard of their proceedings, detached a party of horse to apprehend them. The horsemen came upon the gangs unawares, while encamped outside a village, and accused them of stealing opium; they were glad to have an opportunity of clearing themselves of this unfounded accusation, so accompanied the horsemen to the village for the purpose of being examined; immediately on their arrival they were secured and taken to Captain Borthwick, of whom seventy-nine were made prisoners—viz., five made approvers, seventy-four tried by Colonel Stewart (resident at Hyderabad), thirty-nine condemned to death, twenty-one to imprisonment for life, eleven to limited imprisonment, and three acquitted." Again: "Capt. Borthwick having received intelligence of the residence of these gangs, arranged for their apprehension as soon as a party of them returned from one of their excursions. He proceeded with Capt. Macmahon and about 200 of the Jhowrah cavalry, and came upon their villages before daylight, and so completely surrounded them that the capture of the whole gang was effected without the escape of a single individual—in all fifty-three Thugs; four of whom were made approvers, twenty-two executed, eleven transported, three sentenced to limited imprisonment, and thirteen released for want of evidence."

ledged to be too powerful for Davee to combat, and his well-armed, well-mounted followers, was the knowledge that their own brethren were turning against them, and that ever at the stirrup of the Thug-hunting Englishmen went one or more apostate members of their own murderous Guild. It was plain to them, now that all their secrets were revealed—that there was no safety any longer to be derived from the ignorance of the dominant power—that let them go where they might in the Company's territories, the Thug-led Thug-hunters would be upon their track. Some endeavouring to find in the neighbouring native states a fair field for their operations, or to obtain service under the native chiefs, fled hastily across the boundary-line; but there, too, the Philistines were upon them. English humanity was not brought to a stand at the confines of the country subject to our own regulations, and guarded by our own police. From Northern Oude to Southern Hyderabad our influence at the native Courts, and the labors of our political officers, produced the same results as in our own provinces; and even there some, hopeless of eventual escape, and weary of a life of unceasing anxiety, rushed into the presence of the English officer, flung themselves at his feet, and implored him to receive them as approvers.*

* Indeed the operations of our officers in the Deccan and in Oude do not constitute the least interesting chapter in the great history of Thuggee-suppression. There were greater difficulties to be overcome by those who operated in the native states—difficulties such as are here set forth by Captain Malcolm: "No analogy," he writes, "exists between the proceedings in the Thug Department within the territories of the Honorable Company, or any other well-regulated state, and those which are carried on in the Nizam's dominions, in which no system of police can be said to exist. In the former, the parties charged with this duty are armed with a warrant, before which the gates of every village are thrown open, and the police, if not aiding or furthering the object on which they are employed, dare not openly at any rate throw any obstacles in their way. In the Nizam's territory, however, the case is very different; a few of the principal Talookdars evince the greatest readiness to afford me prompt assistance whenever called on by Government to do so. Their authority, however, does not extend to the villages held on military and other rent-free tenures witu which their districts are studded, aph the Potails of which affect to attend to no orders but those emanating from their immediate superiors. The consequences frequently are, that when a Thug is traced into a village of this class, the gates are shut in the face of the pursuing party; or should they have been allowed to enter from igno-

But great as was the personal energy and ability brought to bear upon the suppression of the crime of Thuggee, it was hardly probable that our officers should have achieved complete success unless armed with peculiar powers—unless a certain relaxation of the law, warranted by the extraordinary character and the extreme enormity of the crime, had been legalised by the Supreme Government. For some years we had been trying men accused of Thuggee; but they had almost invariably escaped. It had been difficult, to a degree perhaps not readily appreciable by English lawyers or any other residents in this little island of Great Britain, to convict men, upon clear judicial evidence, of specific acts of Thuggee. The migratory character of the murder-gangs—the vast extent of country which they traversed—the number of local screens and fences—the difficulty of personal identification—the craft and subtlety of the offenders themselves—the unlimited amount of false swearing and of false impersonation which, at any time, they could bring into our criminal courts—were obstructions to the course of justice, under a strict interpretation of the existing law, which were seldom or never overcome. A timid or even a cautious—perhaps I ought to write a "conscientious" judge, would be sure to acquit even a notorious Thug for want of satisfactory evidence of the commission of a specific offence. Some of the causes which I have recited contributed largely, also, to the embarrassment of the question of jurisdiction. A murder was committed in one part of the country, and the murderers were apprehended in another, perhaps some hundreds of miles distant from the scene of the

rance of the object of their visit, the Government orders, when produced, are treated with the utmost contempt; and if the party do not quietly take their departure, they are generally forced to do so by the armed men stationed at the place on the part of the Jagheerdars, or by the armed villagers themselves. Serious collisions have in consequence arisen, in which several of my men have at times been severely wounded, and at others treated with the greatest indignity."—[*Captain Malcolm to Captain Reynolds. Preface to Captain Sleeman's Report.*]

atrocity. To limit the jurisdiction in such a case to the particular Zillah in which the crime was committed, was to throw up all sorts of difficulties and delays, and almost to ensure the prisoner's escape. These impediments to the strict and prompt administration of justice were wonderfully protective of Thuggee. The more complicated the machinery, and the more formal the procedure of our courts, the better for these professional stranglers. They throve upon the legal niceties and the judicial reserve of the English tribunals, and laughed our Regulations to scorn.

It was wisely determined, therefore, after due consideration by the supreme Government of India, to make the case of Thuggee an exceptional case, and to sanction a relaxed application of existing laws and regulations to members of the great fraternity of Thugs. Accordingly an Act was passed in 1836, by which a man convicted of belonging, or having belonged, to a gang of Thugs was rendered amenable to imprisonment for life, whilst at the same time, prisoners accused of Thuggee were made liable to the jurisdiction of any of the Company's Courts, without reference to the locality of the alleged offence, and the formality of the Mahomedan ***Futwah*** was dispensed with as a preliminary to the trial of this class of proscribed offenders.* The

* The act being conveniently short, I may as well give it in a note:

Act XXX., 1836. (1) "It is hereby enacted, that whatever shall be proved to have belonged, either before or after the passing of this Act, to any gang of Thugs, either within or without the territories of the East India Company, shall be punished with imprisonment for life with hard labor. (2) And it is hereby enacted, that every person accused of the offence made punishable by this Act, may be tried by any court, which would have been competent to try him, if his offence had been committed within the Zillah, where that court sits, anything to the contrary, in any Regulation contained, notwithstanding. (3) And it is hereby enacted, that no court shall, on a trial of any person accused of the offence made punishable by this Act, require any Futwah from any law officer."

A supplementary Act (No. XVIII. of 1837) decreed that "any person charged with murder by Thuggee, or with the offence of belonging to a gang of Thugs, made punishable by Act No. XXX. of 1836, may be committed by any magistrate, or joint magistrate, within the territories of the East India Company, for trial before any criminal court competent to try such person on such charge."

good effect of these enactments were soon felt. They were all that the Thuggee officers needed to enable them to carry out the great work which was placed in their hands. The strong defences of the Thug gangs were now struck down. They had no longer our ignorance on the one side, and our judicial over-scrupulousness on the other, to protect them. So the work of suppression went on bravely. The gangs were hunted down; our gaols were filled with Thugs; conviction and condemnation were no longer unattainable ends; and a great institution which had existed for centuries was broken up in a few years.

I do not say that there is no such thing as Thuggee, at the present time, in any part of the Company's dominions. It is probable that still an occasional traveller may, from time to time, be strangled by the wayside. But the cases are few in number, and comparatively insignificant in character. The system is destroyed; the profession is ruined; the Guild is scattered, never again to be associated into a great corporate body. The craft and the mystery of Thuggee will no longer be handed down from father to son. A few English officers, acting under the orders of the supreme administrative authorities, have purged India of this great pollution. If we have done nothing else for the country, we have done this one good thing. It was a great achievement—a great victory. And it is one to be contemplated without any abatement of satisfaction, or any reservation of praise.

It is a greater exploit than the conquest of Sindh or the Punjab, or the annexation of Pegu; and the names of the commander of that little army of Thug-hunters and of his unflinching lieutenants, ought, in every History of India, to have honorable mention, and by every student of that history to be held in grateful remembrance. I cannot conclude this chapter better than by the mention of them. They are Sleeman, Borthwick,* Ramsay, Reynolds, Malcolm, Etwall, Hollings,

* Two examples of gangs captured by Captain, now Colonel, Borthwick, are given in a note at page 372, from Colonel Sleeman's Report. But the first of these is so remarkable, not only for the interesting character of its details, but also from the circumstances of its being an account of the capture of, I believe, the first considerable gang of Dacoits convicted and punished in any part of India, that I am induced to give in this place an amplified version of the story almost in the words that it was related to me:—"Captain Borthwick was at the time Political Agent of the western division of the province of Malwa, in which the principality of Rutlam is comprehended. The chief of this state was then a minor—a circumstance which occasioned a more frequent and minute interference in the administration of its affairs than commonly characterised our political control over the native states of that province. So situated, the Political Officer was necessarily kept constantly informed of all that transpired, both by the Akhbar-Nowese, or news-writer, whom he had stationed in the principality for the purpose, and by the minister himself of the state. In the course of almost daily communications from these individuals, Borthwick received an account stating that five bodies of the Bunnyah or Sudookar class had been discovered in the jungle, a few paces from the high road, ten or twelve miles to the southward of Rutlam, the capital of the state. They were slightly covered with stones, and had the appearance of having been recently murdered. The part of the country where these bodies were stated to have been discovered, was much infested by predatory Bheels, and on reading the report, Borthwick's first impression was that the crime had been committed by them. The unusual atrocity of it, however, determined the British agent immediately to proceed to Rutlam and investigate the case. The inquiry was accordingly commenced; but it had not proceeded far before Borthwick saw that the Bheels were in no way concerned in the murders, but that the perpetrators were evidently Thugs. At the same time it transpired that six or eight days previously, about which time it was supposed that the murders must have been committed, a large body of travellers had passed through that part of the country along the highway towards Hindostan. They had the appearance, and, indeed, gave out that they were pilgrims returning to their homes, after having paid their devotions at a shrine of peculiar sanctity in the western part of Guzerat. All this tended so strongly to excite Borthwick's suspicions that these travellers were the authors of this atrocious deed, that he resolved upon taking immediate measures for arresting them. It was observed that they were travelling very leisurely, but, after the lapse of so many days, they could hardly have proceeded to a distance of less than 100 miles. Resolved, however, upon making the attempt to effect their seizure, and having obtained from different persons, who had well observed and even conversed with some of them, a full description of their appearance, he despatched a party of native horsemen, under the command of a smart and intelligent officer, in pursuit of them, with the strictest orders, when once he came up with them, not to lose sight of them until they were secured and brought in for examination. Furnished with a description of the supposed gang, and with requisitions on the local authorities of the villages and districts through which they would have to pass, calling upon them in the name of the British Government to afford him every assistance in their power to effect this object, the party set out in pursuit. It was only at the village of Dekhola, about 150 miles from Rutlam, whence they were despatched, that they came up with the gang. Having satisfied himself that they were the people of whom he was in pursuit, the officer went to the principal man of the place and presented his requisition for aid; but finding the latter was unable to give him the assistance he required (the village being a small and poor one), he had recourse to a piece of

Lowis, Graham, Paton, Riddell, Ludlow, Birch, Miles, Marsh, Whiteford, and others of good service and good

strategy, which is worthy to be held in remembrance for the sake of its own cleverness as well as for its excellent results. The Government of India had established a strict monopoly of opium over Malwa, which had then existed for some time, and these very horsemen formed a portion of the body of troops employed by Captain Borthwick, and posted at the different commanding outlets to prevent the unauthorised export of the drug. So it occurred to the officer, on finding the village could not supply him with means sufficient to use coercion, to take advantage of this circumstance—to denounce the gang as smugglers, and charge them with having contraband opium in their possession. Too glad to find there was not the slightest insinuation thrown out as to their real characters, they were eager with their offers to submit their luggage at once to the officer's inspection. This, however, not suiting his purpose, he pretended that no inspection at so paltry a village, where there were no authorities of sufficient importance to testify to the result, would be satisfactory to the British Agent, and signified his desire to have it made at a place where it could be effected in a more open and authoritative manner. After some hesitation on the part of the gang they agreed to go back with him to Bhulwâra, a stage to the southward of Dekhola, which they had passed a day or two before. At Bhulwâra there was a large body of Sebundies, or police soldiers, which, on arriving there, the authorities, in compliance with the requisition presented by the officer, placed at his disposal. He now considered he had sufficient means to make a capture of the gang, and thinking it no longer necessary to disguise his suspicions and intentions regarding them, openly charged them with being Thugs, and declared his determination to carry them before Captain Borthwick, to be subjected to a strict examination. Boldly and clamorously they attempted to repel the charge. They declared themselves to be innocent and inoffensive people returning from their pilgrimage to shrines in the west of Guzerat. To all this he paid no attention, but was not a little staggered on a paper being presented to him by one of the leaders, which was asserted to be a passport of the English Government, under the protection of which he (the leader) declared they were travelling. This caused doubt and anxiety to the officer, which, however, was in some measure appeased by considering the strictness of his orders, and in feeling assured that if it came to pass that a mistake had been made, every allowance would be shown to him. All his fears, however, were speedily dispelled by one of the gang, in a paroxysm of fear, coming to him and confessing that they were Thugs, and offering, if his life were assured to him, to make a full disclosure of all their proceedings. This was a contingency for which Captain Borthwick had fortunately prepared him, and he accordingly on the instant separated this proffered approver from the gang, and kept him from that moment away from all intercourse with his comrades. In the mean while Captain Borthwick himself, after despatching the officer and party from Rutlam, proceeded to Joura, a small town twenty miles to the north of the former, there to await the result of the measures he had taken. Shortly afterwards he received a report from the officer of the success that had attended him, which was speedily followed by his arrival at Joura with the gang in his custody. Borthwick immediately entered upon the examination of the approver. Of the information which was thereby elicited, that part which contained a full and particular account of the murders committed by the gang, from the time they passed Rutlam until they were overtaken at Dekhola, claimed his immediate attention. The approver gave an account of no less than eighteen different murders committed in that short interval; and in order to confirm this part of his evidence, Capt. Borthwick sent him the following day under a guard, and accompanied by a native writer, to note all that transpired along the line of road upon which the murders were stated by him to have been perpetrated. In every instance stated, the place where the body of the

repute. Many of these were afterwards distinguished as agents for the suppression of professional Dakoitee. But to this important subject I must devote another chapter.

This chapter, however, would hardly seem to be complete without some mention of a fact, more prominently noticed elsewhere, illustrative of the completeness of the efforts which were made for the entire suppression of Thuggee. Through the instrumentality of Colonel Sleeman and one of his assistants, Lieutenant Brown, Schools of Industry were established at Jubbulpore, with the view of affording employment to adult approvers, and of educating their children—so that the little ones, instead of being initiated into the fearful mysteries of Thuggee, were trained to the understanding and the practice of useful trades, and the rising generation of professional murderers turned into industrious artisans.*

murdered person was deposited was pointed out. The several bodies were disinterred, and each instance was verified by the village authorities nearest to the spots. Thus a complete corroboration of the approver's statements was obtained; and other approvers having come forward, the guilt of the gang, individually and collectively, was fully established by a mass of incontrovertible proof."

* See the Chapter on Education, and the papers in the Appendix, for a further account of these schools.

Selections from the Records of the Government of India (Foreign Department).
No. XXIV. Calcutta: John Gray, 'Calcutta Gazette' Office, 1858.

STATEMENT

SHOWING THE

NUMBER OF CRIMINALS

ARRESTED AND DISPOSED OF BY

OFFICERS OF THE THUGGEE DEPARTMENT

DURING 1856.

No. 29 OF 1857.

FROM

MAJOR J. SLEEMAN,

General Superintendent of Operations for the Suppression of Thuggee and Dacoity,

To

G. F. EDMONSTONE, ESQUIRE,

Secretary to the Government of India, Foreign Department,

FORT WILLIAM.

Dated Jubbulpore, the 20th March 1857.

SIR,

I HAVE the honor to forward, for submission to the Right Hon'ble the Governor General of India in Council, Tabular Statements* showing the number of professional criminals apprehended and disposed of by the Officers of the Department during the year 1856, and the number of each class still remaining at large on the Continent of India, against whom sufficient information has been recorded to warrant their arrest.

Establishments at Lahore how employed.

2. Forty-five Phansigar Thugs, fourteen Dhatooreea Thugs, and twenty-six Professional Dacoits, have been arrested by the Establishments in the Punjaub during the year.

3. No cases of Thug, Murder, or of Dacoity, by the Professional Dacoits of the Punjaub, were reported to have occurred within the Province during the period under review.

* Nos. 1, 2 and 3.

4. Strict search has been made for organized Gangs of Poisoners, who were supposed to exist in the Mooltan and Goozcerat Districts, but no trace of such gangs has been discovered, and the local Authorities are, I believe, now satisfied, that the cases of murder by poison occurring in the Punjaub are perpetrated by desultory offenders, who, as in the old Provinces, infest the great highways and depredate independently of each other.

No trace of organized Gangs of Poisoners discovered in the Punjaub.

5. Lieutenant E. D. R. Ross officiated for Captain Lawrence, Extra Assistant General Superintendent, from 18th April to 7th November 1856, and conducted the duties of the Office very satisfactorily.

6. The Establishments under Captain Chamberlain, Assistant General Superintendent at Etawah, have been actively engaged in efforts to break up the Bhudoureea Dacoit Gangs, which have been for many years located on both banks of the Chumbul River, and in the District of Kunawur, in the Gwalior Territory; and this very desirable consummation has, I am happy to say, been in a great measure effected by the arrest of sixty-two criminals, and among them many leaders of note and influence, some of whom have been admitted approvers.

The Establishments at Etawah how employed.

Nine of the Bhudoureea Dacoits admitted as approvers.

7. The Gwalior Durbar have evinced every disposition to assist Captain Chamberlain, by furnishing him with Perwannahs on the local Authorities; but the petty Officials are generally interested in protecting the leaders of Dacoit Gangs, who pay liberally for impunity, and Captain Chamberlain has found that, while pretending to assist, they in most instances thwarted his arrangements.

Local Authorities in the Gwalior Territory frequently thwart arrangements for the arrest of criminals.

8. The most notorious leader of Bhudoureea Dacoits, Pretum Singh, has up to this time managed to evade capture.

9. He has a great many friends and connexions among the landholders in Etawah and Mynpooree, who notoriously conceal and shelter him when pursuit grows warm in the Gwalior Territory, and yet manage it so cleverly as to avoid conviction.

Zemindars in Etawah and Mynpooree protect Dacoit leaders from arrest.

10. If this man were arrested, I should have no fear of a reorganization of the Bhudoureea Dacoit Gangs, as he is the only leader still at large, in whose influence and skill the non-scattered members have unlimited confidence.

Pretum Singh, the only influential leader of Bhudoureea Dacoits, still at large.

11. The most strenuous efforts have been made for Pretum's capture, and as these will be sustained, I hope soon to be able to report his apprehension.

12. The Dacoity Statements for 1855-56 show that the operations against the Dacoits along the Gwalior frontier have had the effect of almost entirely suppressing the crime of Dacoity in those Districts most exposed to attack.

The crime of Dacoity almost entirely suppressed in the Dooab.

13. In the conterminous Districts of Etawah and Mynpooree, no case has occurred during the year 1855-56, and the information recorded regarding the Bhudonreea Gangs is now so extensive and complete, that the operations of another year will suffice to make this suppression permanent.

Information regarding the Bhudonreea Dacoit Gangs complete.

14. Captain Chamberlain was in charge of the Etawah Office throughout the year.

15. The Establishments under the Extra Assistant at Agra have been exclusively employed in the pursuit of the Meenah Dacoits of Ulwur and Rajpootana, and considering the very limited means at his disposal, and the difficult nature of the duty, I consider Major Williams's success has been considerable.

The Establishments at Agra how employed.

16. Of sixty-six Meenahs convicted and sentenced, several approvers have been made, and the information recorded will enable the Department to pursue to conviction some sixty or seventy of their accomplices still at large.

Seven Meenah Dacoits have been admitted as approvers.

17. Members of the Meenah class are found all over Rajpootana, in the Ulwur Rajah's Territory, and in that of Bhurtpore.

18. Fortunately for society, all Meenahs are not Dacoits; but they have all an unusually strong feeling of clanship, and never fail to sympathise with and support, by every means in their power, any members of the class how are pursued for offences against the Law.

Arrest of Meenah Dacoits rendered very difficult by the strong feeling of clanship common to the whole tribe.

19. This feeling, added to the absence of all zealous co-operation on the part of native officials in independent States, make the pursuit and arrest of Meenah Dacoits a most difficult duty, requiring the greatest tact and

Want of zealous cooperation on the part of native officials in independent States.

perseverance on the part of the Police Agents engaged in it, and sufficiently accounts for the limited success attained.

20. From information obtained by Major Williams, it appears that the famine of 1833 first induced the Meenahs to follow Dacoity as a profession, and the great success of two gangs, under Girdharee and Maneea Jemadars, who depredated, at that period, in our Provinces, with great impunity, has served to perpetuate their taste for plunder.

Meenah Dacoity first induced by the famine of 1833.

21. The rank of Jemadar is not hereditary among them, as it was among the Budhuk class: their leaders are chosen from among those who have displayed most enterprize and courage on former expeditions, and no leaders so selected find the smallest difficulty in filling their ranks with eager followers, whenever an expedition is proposed.

Among the Meenahs rank not hereditary, as among the Budhuks and Thugs.

22. The Meenahs have no exclusive language like the Thugs, the Budhuks, and some others of the criminal classes; but they resemble the former in their worship of "*Davee*" (the Goddess of Destruction) and in their respect for omens, without taking which they never proceed on an expedition.

Meenahs have no exclusive language; they worship "*Davee*," and respect omens.

23. Members of the class are very generally employed as Chowkeedars throughout Rajpootana and the Ulwur Territory, and the system which obtains in these, in common with most Native States, of fining the Chowkeedar of a village in which a robbery takes place, in the full amount of the property lost, obliges the party so fined to resort to Dacoity for means to meet the demand.

Native system of fining Chowkeedars encourages Dacoity.

24. In narrating the events of their life of crime, they frequently say, we undertook such an expedition to find means to meet a demand made upon us in consequence of a robbery which occurred in such and such a village, of which a relative of ours was the Chowkeedar.

25. This system, so evidently calculated to encourage crime, is a favorite one among native rulers, as it relieves them from the trouble of investigation and furnishes the means of reimbursing the plundered party, if the subject of a Government powerful enough to demand it, without expense to the State.

Fining Chowkeedars a very favorite system in Native States.

26. Major Williams is of opinion, that the Meenahs might readily be reclaimed by judicious management and extensive employment in the Police of Districts ; but my own experience leads me to a very different conclusion.

27. I consider them to be a race essentially criminial, and of a nature too false and treacherous to be trusted with any employment which would remove them from strict and constant supervision.

Meenah character false and treacherous.

28. Nothing but a conviction of the extreme probability of detection, and of the certainty of very severe punishment following it, will, in my opinion, deter Meenahs from violent crime, and the operations now in progress against them are best calculated to effect this object.

29. Major Williams, Extra Assistant General Superintendent, was in charge of the Agra Office throughout the year.

30. The Establishments at Lucknow have been engaged throughout the year in a search for the fugitive Phansigar and Dhatooreea Thugs, supposed to be still at large in Oudh, and in carrying out a system of Patrols on the great thoroughfares, which has the effect of deterring the Budhuks, who still haunt the Turaee, from leaving its fastnesses for the purpose of plunder.

Lucknow Office Establishments how employed.

31. Several murders by poison have occurred in the Province during the year ; but nothing has transpired to connect the few professional poisoners still at large with these cases, which appear to be the work of desultory offenders unknown to the approvers.

Cases of murder by poison in Oudh committed by offenders unknown to the present approvers.

32. Captain Weston was in charge of the Lucknow Office throughout the year.

33. The Establishments at Jubbulpore, Nagpore, and Indore, have been chiefly engaged in the pursuit of the Goar and Mooltanee Bunjarahs, the only classes of professional Dacoits which have lately been actively engaged in Southern India.

The Establishments at Jubbulpore, Nagpore, and Indore how employed.

34. These Bunjarahs are ostensibly engaged in carrying corn from the interior of the Saugor and Nerbudda Provinces to the Coast, and salt from the Coast to the interior ; but never fail to avail themselves of the opportunities their wandering life affords for the practice of Dacoity.

Bunjarahs ostensibly employed in carrying corn and salt.

List of thirty-six Tandahs and Table of Routes furnished to the local Authorities.

35. Conceiving that the depredations of these classes might at once be checked and eventually suppressed, by a system of escorts supplied from the Police of Districts, I furnished the Resident at Hyderabad, and the Commissioners at Nagpore and in the Saugor and Nerbudda Territories, in May last, with a list of thirty-six of the principal Bunjarah Tandahs (or Camps), and a Table showing the routes usually adopted by them in their progress through the country, and the sites of their encampments during the monsoon.

Arrangements for the escort of Tandahs suggested.

36. I at the same time suggested arrangements by which every Tandah might be kept under the surveillance of the Police from the time it entered North Berar, till it again crossed that frontier on its way to the Coast.

37. These arrangements have been generally adopted, and their effect has already been felt in the almost total cessation of Dacoities in the Saugor and Nerbudda Territories since that period.

Of 6,000 men attached to the Tandahs, only 487 are at present known to be Dacoits.

38. The thirty-six Tandahs here alluded to have about 6,000 men attached to them, and of this number only 487 are denounced and registered Dacoits; but as every new approver names fresh men as his accomplices, we must conclude that there are hundreds of Dacoits among them yet unknown to us.

39. While the Berar Province and the Nagpore Territory remained under native rule, it was impossible to arrange any combined plan of operations by which we could hope to suppress thoroughly this formidable system of depredation; and though the arrests and convictions were numerous, the system remained unshaken.

40. But now that these Provinces have come under British management, and a regular system of Police has been established, the great difficulties will vanish before well-sustained efforts, and in a few years a very great evil will, I hope, be completely eradicated.

Reform among the Paidees, Thakoonkars, and Koolhatees.

41. The work in the Hyderabad Office has been greatly reduced since the cession of Berar from the "Paidees," "Thakoonkars," and "Koolhatees" having in a great degree renounced their predatory habits and taken to tillage and other honest occupations.

Judicious treatment of these rude tribes by the Deputy Commissioners in Berar.

42. This happy change has been induced by the judicious measures adopted towards these rude tribes by the Deputy Commissioners in charge of Districts in Berar, who have employed them extensively in the Rural Police, and improved their self-respect by restoring them to their village rights, of which, under the Native Government, they had been deprived.

Belgaum Office Establishments how employed.

43. The Establishments at Belgaum in the Dekhun have been exclusively employed in the pursuit of Kaikaree Dacoits; but arrests have not been numerous, owing to the general alarm excited among the tribe by the successful pursuit of former years, and the consequent flight of the denounced members from their usual haunts to other parts of the country, where they are, with extreme difficulty, traced and apprehended.

System of registration projected.

44. A system of registration, similar to that applied to the Muzubbee class in the Punjaub, has been projected for this rude tribe within the last year, which will, when completed, enable Police Officers to check their wandering propensities, and thus assist the efforts now making to induce the Kaikarees to settle down to habits of industry.

45. Captain Hervey proceeded to England on Furlough in April 1856, and Captain Dickson, of the Bombay Army, officiated for him throughout the remainder of the year.

I have, &c.,

(Signed) J. SLEEMAN,

General Superintendent of Operations for the Suppression of Thuggee and Docoity.

JUBBULPORE;
General Superintendent's Office,
The 28th March 1857.

No. 2.

STATEMENT showing the number of Thugs arrested during the Year 1856 by the Officers of the Thuggee Department, and the number still remaining at large on the Continent of India.

Number.	Class of Criminals.	Remaining at large *vide* Report for 1855.	Denounced by Approvers admitted in 1856.	Total.	Arrested during the year.	Remaining at large on the 1st January 1857.	Remarks.
	Thugs.						
1	Punjabee Phansigar	559	0	559	45	514	
2	Punjabee Dhatooreea	0	14	14	14	0	Desultory offenders.
3	Hindoostanee Phansigar	400	0	400	1	399	A great many of these were men of advanced age when they first fled from justice in 1855, and a third of them may naturally be supposed to have died ere this.
4	Dhatooreea	38	8	46	8	38	The remnants of a Colony of professional poisoners, who were found located in several villages upon the Frontiers of Oudh and the Allahabad Districts.
	Total	997	22	1,019	68	951	

(Signed) J. SLEEMAN,

General Superintendent of Operations for the Suppression of Thuggee and Dacoity.

JUBBULPORE;
General Superintendent's Office,
The 28th March 1857.

Charles Hervey

Report on the Crime of Thuggee by Means of Poisons in British Territory for the Years 1864, 1865, and 1866. Delhi: General Superintendent's Office Press, 1868.

No. 624.

From

COLONEL CHARLES HERVEY, C. B.,
General Superintendent of Operations for the Suppression of Thuggee and Dacoity.

To

E. C. BAYLEY, ESQUIRE,
Secretary to the Government of India, Home Department.

Dated Simla, 1st August 1868.

SIR,

In continuation of the Series of Statistical Papers (Dacoity Statements,) forwarded under my letter under date 30th April, No. 344, I have now the honor to submit Statements for the crime of Thuggee, whether by poison or by strangulation, for the same three years, 1864, 1865 and 1866, of occurrence in Districts under British Administration.

2. Owing to the absence of detailed reports in such cases, and to a general hesitation on the part of District Officers, or for want of definite instructions, in determining in what manner to mark them off in their Returns, I have not been enabled to give that statistical fulness to these Statements, which perhaps characterized the Dacoity Papers. For it will be observed in the body of the Remarks against the several Districts in which the crime occurred, that while some Officers properly recognized *as cases of Thuggee,* those instances of crime which manifested indications of their being the deed of adepts, although strangulation should not have been resorted to, there were others who did not do so except death had ensued,—some who returned some murders as Thuggee without reference to the means which were resorted to,—others who passed by poisoning cases altogether whether death ensued or not, even although they evidenced symptoms of being class crime,—others who noticed some cases of the crime and passed by others,—some who drew some kind of distinction between the different degrees of poisoning and endeavoured to draw a line of demarcation between cases of "murder by poison" (some calling this *Thuggee,* some not,) "attempts to murder by poison," "robbery by poison," "poisoning for the sake of robbery," "grievous hurt by poison," "poisoning with hurt" and so on,—others who massed offences of various kinds under lump figures and merely quoted against them the Sections of the Indian Penal Code under which they severally were tried, among which were Sections under which the criminal use of poisons as a means for committing an offence, might or might not be recognized—thus leaving to conjecture any decision on the subject on the part of a Statist—while some again left unnoticed even cases of death by strangling. Instances of this incongruence, are furnished in the Statements in the column of Remarks.

3. I might thus have avoided, without blame, the preparation of any Returns at all. But, as Government is aware, I have long been impressed with the seriousness of this crime of poisoning, of which I have so frequently submitted that the danger of its gaining head was in proportion with the difficulty of its detection,—and I therefore considered that it altogether belonged to me to place to view the extent of its *reported* existence in the different Governments and Administrations comprising the Government of India, that is to say, inasmuch as I was enabled to do so by the data at my disposal. For under the different views formed of the crime, I was not able to depend upon receiving any very steady reports of the occurrence of it, and experience too, had taught me, that in the majority of instances, perhaps no report of it would be made at all, *even to District Officers themselves* (as evidenced under Bengal,) except death should have been the unhappy result,—and that even then, death would often be attributed to anything but poisoning! In order, therefore, to prepare any Returns at all, I had

to search through the several Police Administration Reports, and these papers are the result of the examination.

4. I have to regret that the information at my disposal, should not have enabled me to draw up any Statistics of the crime such as I was able to submit with the Dacoity Statements. The reason for this is explained in the Column of Remarks,—and I would observe that although *every* case of poisoning or of strangling, has been embodied in these papers, I would by no means affirm, that all were cases of *Thuggee*;—for it has on the contrary, been shewn, which of them might (with the information obtained respecting them,) be classed as cases committed by the professional criminal and which not, whenever I have been able to arrive at such a discrimination.

5. But while every case of poisoning or of strangling which was to be noticed in the Reports from which all were gathered, has been entered in these Statements, those cases which were palpably *not* the deed of class criminals, have been excluded from the reckoning and have not been confounded with cases which either were or might reasonably be supposed to have been perpetrated by persons who committed the crime for the sake of robbery.—For this was no light question,—and I trust that the preparation of these Statements such as they are, will be approved of by Government.

6. The measure has, however, been one of experiment only. For I have supposed that Government, perceiving that it fell short of conveying the complete information which ought to be available, would issue some orders according to which *future* Statements should be fuller of details,—and this might perhaps be ensured by District Officers being required to keep a register of *every* act of poisoning or of strangulation, *whatever the attendant circumstances,* briefly narrating those circumstances and noticing the Police action in each case and its results. If it were further directed that the documents so prepared, should be forwarded every six months to this Office, for the information of the Government of India, that analyzed Statement might be prepared from them, which the heinousness of the crime altogether requires should be periodically placed before Government,—and in furtherance of this object, I would also propose that Inspectors General of Police be required to add to their crime Tables the Columns noted in the margin, shewing the number of each case of the classifications denoted therein.

POISONING.						
WITH MURDER.		With robbery.	For the sake of but without robbery.	THROUGH REVENGE OR MOTIVES OTHER THAN OF ROBBERY.		Total.
For the sake of robbery.	Otherwise.			With intent to murder.	Without intent to murder.	
1	2	3	4	5	6	7

N. B. The above does not contemplate any separate column for "attempt to commit murder,"—for the cases in which death did not ensue, would be entered either in columns 3 and 4, or in column 5, according to the circumstances attending them.

7. In stating that the occurrence of the crime was not always reported, I have instanced the cases in Bengal. Many acts of poisoning took place in that Province, of which the Police knew nothing, although some of them had resulted in the deaths of the victims. It was discovered early in 1865, that the crime was becoming serious in certain parts of Bengal, and at the recommendation of the Inspector General of Police, the late Colonel Bruce, an Officer was specially employed to investigate them, *and was placed in communication with myself.* Perceiving in Mr. Relly, the Gentleman appointed, a valuable coadjutor, I invited him to communicate with me without reserve, and tendered to him my advice and counsel as freely; and although the course pursued by me in considering him in a measure

under my personal directions and making use of him accordingly, did not for a special reason, meet with approval from the Lieutenant Governor of Bengal, the result of our connection was nevertheless most gratifying. A great deal *more* of the existence of the crime in Bengal, was discovered, than I had anticipated. Cases, *several attended with murder,* were brought to light in 1865, of occurrence in 1864 and preceding years, *of which sometimes not even a record existed!* Mr. Reily prosecuted them in person with great tact and intelligence, and even gained from the Judges of the High Court, a high encomium for detective ability. A great many of the criminals were arrested and convicted, and several of them were executed or transported for life or for shorter periods. This shewed the utility of extraneous pressure, little however my own part in it might have been. The subject has been noticed in the column of Remarks for Bengal in the Statement for 1865, and Mr. Reily's proceedings and success are recounted in two Appendices to the Statements for 1865 and 1866, both replete with painful interest. He was, I am happy to add, soon subsequently advanced to the grade of a Deputy Inspector General of Police.

8. In my Report in the Foreign Department, No. 794, dated 15th September 1863 (para. 20,) I submitted to notice some cases of poisoning by returned Emigrants from the Mauritius, and that it was believed that the crime was practised in that Island by fugitives from India. It was not at the time considered necessary to act upon my suggestion to ascertain from the Mauritius Government, whether this was really so. The recurrence, however, of similar cases in this Country, the deed of returned Emigrants, will be observed in the present Papers.*—According to the information of this Department, men from Oudh and the North Western Provinces, have from time to time, gone as Coolies to the Mauritius and other oceanic Colonies, who committed both Dacoity and Poisoning, and it is stated by some of our *Passee* Approvers of the poisoning class, that an Emigration Agent from Calcutta engaged at random, a few years ago at Lucknow, a great number of persons for shipment as Coolies beyond the Sea, among whom were several Dacoits and Dhatoora Thug Poisoners. We know that in India men who practised Dacoity, have, for want of opportunities to commit it, turned their hands to the more secret and less easily detected crime of Poisoning, of which probably some instances may be discernible in the present Statements, under Oudh.—*If the opportunity offers they will revert to Dacoity,* and some facilities for doing so, may have been presented in the Colonies, should the report be correct that both crimes have appeared in the Mauritius. The indiscriminate deportation of such or other criminals, might, however, be in some degree checked, were a system observed of instituting an enquiry through our local Magistrates, into the character of the persons who offered themselves as Coolies to Emigration Agents.

*Vide especially, cases 3 and 5 under Benares in the Statement for 1864, and a case under Behar in that for 1866.

9. It will be further perceived, that these Statements also present some cases of the crime of Poisoning, in which the accused escaped conviction, although the poison reasonably believed to have been employed by him for criminal purposes, was found in his possession.—Of this a remarkable instance will be found in the Statement for 1866, under the District of Etah, in the North Western Provinces. The Prisoner in that case, declared he used the substance (which was *Dhatoorah) as medicine for sick Cattle.* Others have similarly asserted that *they were themselves in the habit of taking that drug.*—The device is a very common one.—When those "mysterious cases" as they were called, occurred in Oonao in Oudh, in 1860 and 1861, in which corpses were found on the high road, with knotted strings fastened round the neck,—of which I may here observe, there would seem to be a reappearance in the same neighbourhood as well as elsewhere,—under an impression that *poisoners* were probably the culprits, who first had drugged their victims and then had tied on the cords as above *in order to baffle detection*—or in other words, to induce a belief that Thug Stranglers had been at work in an unprofessional way, *and not expert Thug Poisoners*—I suggested to Magistrates to require the Police to look out for men, in the garb of religious mendicants, who should put up at *Serais* or other resting places, and to search their persons in view to the discovery of poison or other noxious substance, upon some at least of them. Upon this a *Byragee,* as he pretended

to be, was arrested on his return to Cawnpore, who had, after a very short stay at the ***Serai*** at that place, been perceived to go over into Oudh across the adjacent Ganges, leaving behind him, however, a bundle composed seemingly, of tattered clothes only, too miserable looking, he thought, to excite any suspicion.—Called upon to account for some seeds of the ***Dhatoora*** found tied up in a corner of one of the old garments, he unhesitatingly declared ***that he used the drug as medicine*** and at once raised his hand as if to eat some of it on the spot. In this he was prevented by the sitting Magistrate, by whom he was thereupon sent over to my Assistant, Major Chamberlain, at that time located at Lucknow, where, on his making the same proposal, he was in view to put him to the test, even permitted to do what he had offered. Nothing daunted, ***he forthwith swallowed some of the seeds*** to the dismay of the above Officer. Insensibility had already partially set in before the usual antidotes could be applied. On his being restored to consciousness, however, the further to disconcert beholders, he at once remonstrated at the measures taken for reviving him, declaring, as the Hasheesh Eater we may suppose would do, that " he was just getting into the glory of the thing!"—Transferred eventually to myself, he disclosed to me a long list of acts of Poisoning and of Dacoity both on land and river, in which he had taken part, and revealed too, among other like barbarities, that he was one of the infuriated band by whom Mr. St. George Tucker of the Bengal Civil Service, was beset and finally murdered in his Bungalow at Futtehpore on the outbreak of the Mutiny in 1857, and that he had even received a bullet in his leg, from the seldom erring Rifle of that brave Man. I here only revert to this anecdote, in connection with the subject of the expediency of a Law making it ***penal*** to be found to possess, without a license, the deleterious things commonly used by Poisoners, such as I had ventured to propose for enactment in my letter to your address, No. 930, under date 13th September 1865.—I believe an objection to such a Law was urged in the fact that ***Dhatoora***, for instance, was often used by Natives for medicinal purposes.—If justice should be defeated by these detestable criminals making use of the same argument in support of their innocence, it were weakness for us to urge it too, if through it they should be saved from punishment! It is the well known character of the Thug, to make that null which would be evidence in our Courts of Law,—and for him to advance that in his defence, which he knows we are ourselves so tenacious about,—for him to declare that he kept poison by him ***to use it as medicine***, because we say that it ***is*** used by Natives for such a purpose ***and may therefore be possessed by them***, is altogether to sustain that character and to overreach us. As submitted, however, in my letter under advertence, the inconvenience of a prohibitory Law of the scope advocated by me, to those who really used drugs for curative purposes, would affect a very few in comparison with the very many whom the restriction would protect. They who required such things for honest aims, would suffer little from the mere trouble of having to seek permission to possess them, while the effect upon those who wanted them for criminal ends, would at least be that they would in some measure be deterred from too readily using them, lest they should be discovered ***unlawfully*** to have them.

10. That the old crime of Thuggee by strangulation, has been superseded by that of ***poisoning***, is, I believe, now generally admitted,—or it would be admitted from the information presented by these Statements alone, if former Reports had not sufficiently established the fact,—and it is only in continuation of my very earnest efforts for the suppression of the dreadful evil, that I have ventured to come up to Government with these proposals,—an evil accomplished by secret means at once diabolical and cowardly, and which if it should not be attended with the destruction of life in every case, the destruction thereof is so far contemplated, that the purpose being effected, namely, the robbery of the victim, it is of no concern to the criminal whether the man dies or not,—his recovery being on the other hand, often attended with the sacrifice of his intellect or of his bodily health,—and under these conditions I humbly commend these Statements to the consideration of Government.

I have the honor to be,
SIR,
Your Most Obedient Servant,

CHAS. HERVEY, *Colonel*,
General Superintendent.

STATEMENT of reported Cases of Thuggee by means of Poison in British Districts during the year 1864.

Governments or Administrations.	Number of Districts in which no Cases were reported.	Number and Names of Districts in which Cases were reported.	Number of Cases.	Remarks.
BENGAL.		(1) Bhaugulpore ...	4	Police Administration Report:—"There were *four* cases of administering stupifying drugs, three of which were successfully dealt with by Police, and convictions obtained. This is one bright spot in the whole Return." Memo:—(No account of the number of persons arrested and convicted in these cases, or of the other usual details, is to be perceived in the Police Administration Report.)
	51	(2) Monghyr ...	5	Police Administration Report:—"There were 4 cases of administering poisonous drugs for the purpose of robbery, and another case in which two bodies were found in a state which leaves little doubt of a similar crime having been committed. A special Officer of the Detective Department has been deputed to investigate this crime and has met with great success. His proceedings, however, belong to the present year (1865.)"—No details given of the persons arrested, convicted, &c. Three of these cases, 8th July, 31st August and 10th October 1864, were worked out by Mr. Reily, Superintendent of the Detective Agency, in communication with the General Superintendent of the Thuggee and Dacoity Department, *viz*:— (1) Mr Reily to Colonel Hervey, General Superintendent.—Case 8th July 1864 at Ranee Godoh:—"Four persons poisoned, who recovered: Plundered Rs. 225-0-0: Concerned 2 persons: Arrested 2. This case occurred in July 1864, *the Police could make nothing of the case.* A Head Constable was punished for attempting to conceal the case. The District Superintendent was requested by me to send for all persons who had been drugged in his district for the last year or two. The two first named (plaintiffs Rajjub Sing and Munrotè Sing) were produced. On their being taken to the Magistrate's *Hajut* (Lock up,) they readily recognized Soodin and Beharee as the two men who had drugged them. This case was also mentioned at the Sessions." (2) Mr. Reily to ditto.—Case 31st August 1864 at Mahadabah:—"Two persons poisoned, who recovered: Plundered Rs. 15-0-0: Concerned 2 persons: Arrested two. This case occurred in August 1864, *the Police failed altogether in tracing the criminals.* On my arrival at Monghyr, I requested the District Superintendent of Monghyr to send for all of the men who had been drugged during the last year or two. Kenoo (one of the plaintiffs in this case) was produced, and was taken by me to the Magistrate's *Hajut*, where at least 40 or 50 prisoners were under confinement. He examined every one and at once picked out Soodin and Beharee as the two men who had drugged him. The description he gave at the time, which is in the record in the case, corresponds exactly with Soodin and Beharee. Kenoo appeared as a witness in the Sessions Trial against Soodin and Beharee." Memo:—(These two criminals were sentenced to death for a similar case of poisoning in April 1865, at the Bahir Chowkee, in the district of Monghyr, in which two persons died of the drugs administered to them—*Vide* Statement for 1865.) (3). Mr. Reily to ditto.—Case 10th October 1864 at Burriarpore:—"Two persons poisoned, who died: Plundered Rs. 50: Concerned 4 persons: Arrested 3. Two men, Rajbullub and Sookreeh, have confessed to this case, and in their confession the record has been traced which corroborates their statements completely. It appears 4 or 6 men belonging to the Koomargunge gang were out on a poisoning expedition. Gurboo Sha drugged two travellers near the bridge at Burriarpore. The travellers went about a mile and fell down. On robbing them they found cash and some *attar of roses* in a flask, &c. The Record shows that 2 travellers were found dead at Burriarpore on the 10th October 1864, evidently poisoned. On enquiry it turned out that they were the servants of a Scent Merchant at Ghazeepore, and one of them *had a flask of attar of roses* when he left the boat. This is a singular corroboration of a confession. Gurboo Sha has been arrested, and in his house has been found a flask of attar of roses, with a small quantity still in it. The case is still under investigation and promises well. The merchant from Ghazeepore and the boatmen have been sent for. *The local Police failed entirely at the time.*" Memo:—(Of the three prisoners in this case, one named *Gurboo Sha* was hanged, another *Dwaree* was transported for life, and the third *Sook Lall* was sentenced to 3 years' imprisonment.)
Crd. over	51	2 Districts ...	9	

Governments or Administrations.	Number of Districts in which no Cases were reported.	Number and Names of Districts in which Cases were reported.	Number of Cases.	Remarks.
Brt. over	51	2 Districts	9	
BENGAL.		(3) Patna	3	Police Administration Report:—"Three cases of administering poisonous drugs for the purpose of robbery, occurred during the end of the year. The Head of the Detective Department has been specially deputed to investigate these cases, and his efforts have been crowned with remarkable success." Memo:—The Report does not give any account of the number of persons arrested in these cases, or of how they were disposed of. There was no mention of these cases in the Reports received in this Office from Mr. Reily of the special Detective Agency.
		(4) Bogra	2	Police Administration Report:—"In the remaining 3 cases of murder (*two of* which were cases of poisoning,) defendants were arrested, but the cases fell through, owing to defective evidence." Memo:—These two cases do not appear among those reported to this Office by the Superintendent of the Detective Agency.
		(5) Town and Suburbs of Calcutta ...	7	Taken from Table C of Police Report for 1865, in which the cases for that year (9 in number) are compared with the number in 1864, and in which the crime is classed as "causing hurt by means of poison with intent to commit offence." Fourteen persons were arrested in these seven cases, of whom 3 were convicted and 11 were released. Memo:—No Police Report for Calcutta for 1864 was received in this Office. The following is the only account received in this Office of any of the above cases, *viz*:— October 1864 at Kolah Bagan in Calcutta:—Name of the victim Goolab prostitute, who recovered: Implicated 1 person: Arrested 1. "*Peero* arrested, who has been identified by Goolab." No further notice of the case was communicated.
Total	51	5 Districts	21	In a General Annual Return of Crime for the whole of the districts of Bengal (Assam excepted,) for the year ending on the 31st December 1864, "two cases of Thuggee, &c., are given, in which Rs. 30-4-0 were "stolen," but without any other details. Whether they are identical with any of the cases above noticed, or are additional cases, does not appear, no separate mention of them being made anywhere else throughout the Police Administration Report for 1864. (*End of Bengal for* 1864.)
NORTH-WESTERN PROVINCES.	16	(1) Agra	3	Taken from the Police Administration Report for the North-Western Provinces for 1864, but which contains no account of these cases or of the Police action in them. In reference however to Ajmere, the District Superintendent of Police had reported: "During 1864, there were no cases of robbery by the administration of poisonous drugs."(!)
		(2) Etah	1	
		(3) Muttra	2	
		(4) Ajmere	1	
		(5) Allahabad ...	2	
		(6) Banda	1	
		(7) Cawnpore ...	6	
Crd. over	16	7 Districts	16	

Governments or Administrations.	Number of Districts in which no Cases were reported.	Number and Names of Districts in which Cases were reported.	Number of Cases.	Remarks.
Brt. over	16	7 Districts ...	16	
NORTH-WESTERN PROVINCES.		(8) Jounpore ...	1	This case terminated fatally. "On the 16th May, the Gorait of Sikrora, in the Buxsha Division, brought a body to the Station, accompanied by a young woman, Murreum, daughter of deceased, whose name was Zeenut-Huzzeel. It appears that mother and daughter had been on a pilgrimage to Mecca and on their return they were joined at Bhopal Tal by a man named *Girdharee Kewut*, who mentioned he was a resident of Jounpoor, and was on his way there. They proceeded in company as far as Muchlee Shahur where they put up at a serai. During the night, Girdharee cooked food and asked the deceased to partake of it. He also gave the daughter something in a *chillum*, which made her giddy and sick; the mother, too, shortly after, became insensible, when Girdharee robbed her of Rs. 9-5-3 and decamped. Early next morning the daughter finding her mother still in a precarious state, got alarmed, and hired an *Ekka* for the purpose of taking her into Jounpoor. The *Ekka* driver, however, probably from fright, seeing the mother's state, did not take them the whole way but left them under a tope of trees at Sikrora and drove off. The same evening the mother died. *Although every endeavour has been made to trace the culprit, he has not yet been heard of.* From enquiries instituted, it appears that Girdharee is unconnected with any similar undetected cases in the division (Benares.) He is, however, an absconded offender from the Jounpoor district, in a case of theft." (Police Administration Report for 1864.)
		(9) Mooradabad ...	3	No account of these cases in the Police Administration Report for 1864, nor of the police action in them.
		(10) Shajehanpore ...	1	
		(11) Benares ...	5	(1) 18th August 1864:—"A Constable found two young *Chumarin* girls insensible in Bissasurgunje in the city, and having removed them to his station, it was discovered, and also confessed to by the defendant, that they had *bhang* mixed in *goor* given to them by a chumar lad named Bundhoowa, in view to his having criminal connection with them. After they had become intoxicated. The young women, on reaching the Superintendent's house shortly after, had quite recovered their senses, and recognized the defendant as the person who had been in their company and gave them the *goor*, and the whole story was confirmed by three other lads who were with Bundhoowa when he purchased the *bhang* and administered it to the plaintiffs. The prisoner was duly forwarded for trial, under Section 328 of the Code, and committed to the Sessions, and sentenced to five years' imprisonment." (2) "As there is no robbery in this case, nor apparently any intention of such, perhaps it should not have found entry in this report; but as it has been shown in the Benares statements, I have also deemed it advisable to mention it, *viz*:— 12th November 1864:—"It appears that three travellers, Sheokurn, Khooseeram, and Sookram Dass, residents of the Meerut District, were travelling towards Juggurnath. At Allahabad they were joined by one Girwur, who made himself exceedingly agreeable on the journey. On arrival at Benares they put up at a Dhurumshalah, when Girwur went and purchased *poorees* and sweetmeats, and the whole party eat their meals together. In the evening, the said Girwur brought some *choora* and *goor*, of which Khooseeram and Sookram Dass partook, but Sheokurn declined. Soon after, the two former got stupified, and about midnight Sookram Dass began to vomit; on this Sheokurn got frightened, and suspecting foul play on the part of Girwur, searched his brother Khooseeram to see whether his purse which contained Rs. 8 was safe; not finding it he at once suspected Girwur of the theft and complained to the Police. Rs. 11 were found on Girwur, but Khooseerams' purse was not forthcoming. On being questioned, he confessed to the theft, but denied having tampered with the evening meal. However, from the condition of the two men and the Medical Officer's report, there was no doubt that something deleterious had been mixed with the food. The case being strong against Girwur, he was arrested and forwarded for trial, committed to the Sessions, and sentenced to fourteen years' imprisonment." (3) 17th November 1864:—"An insensible traveller was found by the chowkeedar of village Shoojabad, lying close to a jowar field near the river bank, and was brought by him to the Rajghat out-post. The Sub-Inspector of Ramnugger happened to be there at the time, and, imagining the
Crd. over	16	11 Districts ...	26	

Governments or Administrations.	Number of Districts in which no Cases were reported.	Number and Names of Districts in which Cases were reported.	Number of Cases.	Remarks.
Brt. over	16	11 Districts ...	26	
North-Western Provinces.		Benares, —*continued.*		man had an epileptic fit, sprinkled his face with water, &c. After two or three hours the man came to his senses and told his tale—that he was travelling from the Upper Provinces towards Gya, and on reaching Mohun Serai (about eight miles from Benares) was accosted by a man calling himself an Aheer, who said he was going to Patna where he had a brother; they walked on in company, crossing during the afternoon the bridge-of-boats at Rajghat, where they pulled up and seated themselves by the river bank. Ramasur (the plaintiff) then told his companion to get some *suttoo*, which he brought tied up in two bundles: one portion he gave to Ramasur, and eat the other himself. After taking a little, he detected a bitter taste in the *suttoo*, and threw the remainder away into the river, asking his friend what sort of *suttoo* he had brought; he replied that it was the best to be had. Shortly after, Ramasur became giddy,—the Aheer then led him along the bank of the river for about half a mile when he became insensible. He had a *lota*, a *ruzzai*, and Rs. two in cash with him; these must have been taken from him by the Aheer, who had disappeared. The search after the defendant was unsuccessful at the time, but shortly after he was engaged in a similar crime and arrested—*Vide* case 5." (4) 5th December 1864:—"The fourth case occurred in the Dussasoomade Division of the city of Benares. About 5 P. M. two men, one calling himself Gokul, the other (name unknown), apparently his servant, visited a prostitute by name Chunder Monee. The former gave her a Rupee and proposed remaining the night. Two other women who lived close by happened to be there at the time, but went away soon after. Gokul then sent his servant for *poorees*, sweetmeats, and cream, and they all partook; soon after Chunder Monee became insensible, and remembered nothing till seven the following morning. When she awoke she found she had vomited all over the floor, and that the two men had disappeared. On looking about, she discovered a box of her's had been broken open, and the contents consisting of clothes and jewels valued at Rs. 114-8-0 stolen." "The first intimation to the Police was at 10 A. M. on the 6th, when the Sub-Inspector proceeded to the plaintiff's house, and having collected the substance vomited forwarded it to the Civil Surgeon. He then obtained a descriptive roll of the culprits, and after a few hours' search found Gokul in another prostitute's house. When brought before the plaintiff he was at once recognized by her, as also by the two women who were visiting her the previous evening, and was duly forwarded for trial; but the fact of his having given any drug not being properly established, he was released on that charge. However, on further enquiry on the part of the Magistrate, he was disposed of under Section 280 of Act XXV. of 1861. Although every endeavour was made to trace the second culprit, the efforts of the Police were unsuccessful, and he is still at large." (5) 5th December 1864:—"The fifth and last case in this district occurred near Rajah talao. The Sub-Inspector of the Mirza Moorad Station had been in that direction enquiring into a case, and returning about noon, saw a man lying down about a stone's throw from the tank. On being called, he raised his head for a moment. The Sub-Inspector then went close to him, when he informed him that his name was Hookmee Hujjam, and that he had come from Allahabad; that some three koss back he had met a man, calling himself an Aheer, who had given him some *suttoo* whilst seated at a tank; and that, on arrival at Rajah talao, feeling himself heated and dizzy, he had laid down, and that his companion had gone on a-head." "The Sub-Inspector, suspecting foul play, at once obtained a description of the supposed Aheer and started in pursuit. Immediately after, seeing a man going in the direction of Hookmee, and his appearance tallying with the descriptive roll, he arrested him, when the plaintiff at once recognized him as the person who had given him the *suttoo*. The defendant on being questioned was found to be a *Passee;* his name was Shewdeen. He confessed to having given Hookmee some bhang to drink mixed with a small quantity of opium, then the *suttoo*, and concluded by making him a ganja *chillum* mixed with two dhuttoora seeds, and that it was his intention to rob his victim when quite insensible. Hookmee was at once sent in to the Medical Officer, and sufficient evidence in support of the confession being forthcoming, Shewdeen was forwarded for trial." "When first seen by the Superintendent of Police, he was identified as the person who had escaped in the Ramnuggur case (No. 3 *supra)*, and on him were discovered the articles stolen on that occasion. He acknowledged his guilt, and mentioned that he had been initiated into the system by the professional poisoner Bishoondyal, who was arrested, convicted, and hanged at Benares in 1863. Shewdeen was duly tried and convicted, and is now undergoing 10 years' imprisonment. The first case against the
Crd. over	16	11 Districts ...	26	

Governments or Administrations.	Number of Districts in which no Cases were reported.	Number and Names of Districts in which Cases were reported.	Number of Cases.	Remarks.
Brt. over	16	11 Districts ...	26	
North-Western Provinces.		Benares,—*continued.*		defendant was not gone into, owing to the absence of the plaintiff, and to there being no other direct evidence against him." Memo:—This case was reported to this Office, and Shewdeen Passee was found to be in the rolls of the Thuggee and Dacoity Department as a registered Thug poisoner. For Bishendyal's case, *who was a returned emigrant from the Mauritius, vide* General Superintendent's Annual Report for 1862, No. 794, dated 15 September 1863, Para. XX.
		(12) Mirzapore ...	4	(1) 10th May 1864:—"A man was found lying insensible near a liquor-shop, a short distance from the Kuchwa bazar, by the Head Constable of that Station when out patrolling. The Police Officer learnt that the man had been there since 12 o'clock, and that he had shown signs of intoxication when he arrived, and had remained so up to the hour (6 P. M.) of the Head Constable's coming up. The Officer tried to move him, but failed, and, thinking his appearance different from that of a drunken man, forwarded him for medical examination, when it was ascertained to be a case of drugging. The man did not recover his senses sufficiently for twenty-four hours after his arrival at Mirzapore, when he stated that he was proceeding from Allahabad to Benares, and at Gopeegunj was joined by a man, who, after administering some drug (discovered to be *dhutoora*) in his food, decoyed him off the main road. Soon after they must have reached the above-mentioned liquor-shop, when the prisoner, finding his companion getting worse and worse, decamped, after relieving his victim of property valued at Rs. 5-8-0. From the time of the first discovery, the Kuchwa Police did their best in the case, but without any good result. The culprit, however, was subsequently arrested in another case (3) when the commission of this one was traced to him." (2) 16th May 1864:—"A party of ten *beparees* came into the bazar with grain for sale; six of them were in one partnership, and four in another. They all put up at one Fukeer Hulwaee's house, where they were always in the habit of lodging. Having disposed of their goods, the former party returned to their homes on the following morning, leaving the four others behind, three of whom had during the night become insensible, the fourth man, Ram Koomar by name, being all right. From the statement of the chowkeedar, who reported the case, it appears the said Ram Koomar had done his utmost to keep the other three from the public gaze and the Police the evening before, and apparently succeeded until the report was made. It was ascertained that the victims had sold their grain for Rs. 65-8, and the money made over to Ram Koomar, who wishing to appropriate the whole amount, mixed some *dhutoora* seed into the food of his partners, in view to make off when the drug had taken proper effect. The money had for some time been made over to one Oujoodhia, in whose house it was found tied up in a jacket belonging to the said Ram Koomar, who was duly committed to Sessions, convicted, and sentenced to five years' imprisonment." (3) 24th June 1864:—"A little girl, Dilbahar, informed the Police that her mother (a prostitute) named Budma was lying insensible at her house, and that a man had been there at 8 A. M., who shortly after asked her (Dilbahar) to go out and purchase a little sugar; when brought, he made a shurbut, of which the mother partook. He then sent her again for *pan.* On her return, half an hour after, she found her mother insensible, and the man gone off with jewellery valued at Rs. 28-6. The report was made at 1 P. M., and at 4 P. M., from the description obtained from Dilbahar, the man was arrested at the Railway station, and on being brought to Budma's house was at once recognized by the girl and a neighbour. His name was Mungur, and on further enquiry he turned out to be the individual who drugged the man in case (1). He was committed to the Sessions, convicted, and sentenced to 20 years' imprisonment." (4) 31st October 1864:—"A woman calling herself Kutree, went to the house of Bechoo Kulwar in Bhudoee and claimed relationship with the family through Debee Kulwar of Gopeegunj, and said she had come to talk about some marriage in the family, which she was anxious to prevent. She then proposed having some food with Bechoo and his family consisting of his wife and two or three other persons. The chupatees were ready cooked, and preparations were made for cooking some vegetables, when one of Bechoo's children, about eleven years old, began to grind spices to flavor them. The stranger talked about family matters, and presently suggested to the little girl that she should help her to grind the spices; shortly after, the little girl and her mother went out for natural purposes. When the food was ready, Bechoo and his father partook, but another daughter who joined them in the meal, *thinking it tasted nasty,* spat it
Crd. over	16	12 Districts ...	30	

Governments or Administrations.	Number of Districts in which no Cases were reported.	Numbers and Names of Districts in which Cases were reported.	Number of Cases.	Remarks.
Brt. over	16	12 Districts ...	30	
NORTH-WESTERN PROVINCES.		Mirzapore,—*continued.*		out. When the meal was over, Bechoo and his father became insensible. Bechoo's wife returned, and finding them in this state, tried to bring them round; and in the confusion the stranger decamped with her ornaments valued at Rs. 17. From the way in which she went to work, there is every reason to suppose that Kutree must be a professional poisoner. A woman answering to the description was subsequently arrested at Gopeegunj, but the plaintiff failed to recognize her as the culprit, and no report having been made to this Office of her capture, I conclude Mussamut Kutree must be still at large." Memo:—Cases of this kind have taken place in other parts of the country, and were fully reported upon in the General Superintendent's Annual Report in the Foreign Department for 1862. For a remarkable instance, *vide* para. XXI. of Col. Hervey's Report, No. 794, dated 15th September 1863.
		(13) Goruckpore ...	2	The Police Administration Report contains no separate account of these cases nor of the police action in them.
		(14) Allyghur ...	4	One case 31st January 1864:—"This case is one of the usual stamp. Bida Ram, Constable, while proceeding on duty from Chundose to Coel, observed a *bhylee* passing him, and being struck with the appearance of the driver (Dhokul), who looked intoxicated, he stopped him; a man, a woman and a girl were walking alongside. Dhokul was too ill to speak, but he made signs that the people with him had given him something to eat, upon this he took all three into custody, but being alone the man ran away. Some arsenic and *poorees* were found in the *bhylee.* On recovering, the *bhylee* driver gave evidence against the man and woman. The man was subsequently arrested and sentenced to ten years' and the woman to seven years' imprisonment." Memo:—The habit of a class of professional poisoners, of selecting *hackery and bhylee drivers* for their victims, was described in the General Superintendent's Report to the Government of India, Foreign Department, No. 794, dated 15th September 1863, paras. XIX and XXIV. The Police Administration Report for 1864 gives no account of the other three cases, or of any police action in them.
		(15) Boolundshahur ...	3	Inspector General of Police:—"During the year, the District Superintendent of Police (from information received,) discovered and prosecuted to conviction a poisoner named Kullooah who had committed two robberies by administration of *dhutoorah* in 1863. This man was a professional robber by poison, and his discovery, capture and conviction, are matters of congratulation." Memo:—This man Kulloo Kachee was in connection with one Mohun and other poisoners, implicated in several cases of Thuggee by means of poisons investigated by the Thuggee and Dacoity Department *before* its withdrawal from British Territory by the Resolution of 1863. He had poisoned a man in Budaon in July 1861, and a reward of Rs. 50 was offered for his arrest. No account of the 3 cases here returned for 1864, or of the action taken in them, was given in the Police Administration Report for 1864; but the following is the account of *one* of them as reported to the Thuggee and Dacoity Department, *viz*:— 20th September 1864:—"Goolzar Pathan had sold a horse and pony at Allyghur for Rs. 135, which he had with him. He put up one night at the serai at Soomna, and the next night at Khoorjah. A man from near the Railway station at Allyghur had accompanied him. He came with the complainant as far as Cholah, where the latter fell asleep, and this man went off with his money, &c. It appears that near Cholah, the thief had procured him some *poorees,* which he ate and proceeded on his way. When he got some little distance, he fell down and became insensible. When he recovered a little, he went to Secundrabad to report the theft. A Sub-Inspector had not proceeded with him very far, when he again began to feel the effects of the *dhutoora,* but he recovered shortly afterwards. He stated that the man had given his name as Buldeo, son of Nutho Jat, resident of Hatrass in the Allyghur District. From the complainant's account of the man, it would seem that he belonged to a gang of poisoners located at Hatrass where one of them had been previously seized for some similar cases of poisoning."
Crd. over	16	15 Districts ...	39	

Governments or Administrations.	Number of Districts in which no Cases were reported.	Number and Names of Districts in which Cases were reported	Number of Cases.	Remarks.
Brt. over	16	15 Districts ...	39	
NORTH-WESTERN PROVINCES.		(16) Meerut ...	4	No details of these cases, or of any police action in them, are given in the Police Administration Report for 1864; but from a statement received in this Office, it would seem that one of the number took place on the 17th March 1864, and that one person died from the effects of the drug administered, but no other details were communicated.
		(17) Moozuffurnuggur...	3	(1) 17th May 1864:—Kulloo, a sweeper, was travelling to Umballa accompanied by his wife and two children and by his brother Sufree, to visit some relations who were sweepers attached to the Horse Artillery at that station. He deposed: We reached a village in Meerut and not far from Sirdhunah, we met a man who partook of food with us. We came along to Boorbanah, eat some *chubeena* and started to Kurhur. We eat separately and came on to a place two *koss* from Shamlee where there was no habitation. He there fed us with some *mulleeda* (a cake of *goor*, flour and water.) Half an hour afterwards, I became quite insensible; my tongue became dry, and I could not speak; my head and body pained dreadfully. I was insensible one whole night and a day. I was purged and vomited, otherwise I should not have escaped. My brother died owing to the drug being administered to him in a large quantity. While insensible I was robbed of a silver chain 6 Rupees, necklace 4 Rupees, cloth and utensils (value not known,) and Rs. 2-8-0 in cash. I can recognize him if apprehended. He was of small stature, small beard, of middling complexion, aged about 40 years. He is a Mahomedan. The poisoner was with our party for two days. He did not accompany us from Meerut; we fell in with him on the Mozuffernuggur side of Sirdhuna." Memo:—The Police Administration Report contains no account of the above case. An unpartaken portion of the *mulleeda* was sent to Dr. Macnamara, the Chemical Examiner to Government, who reported, *viz*:— "As the physiological test only can be relied on for such poisons as *dhutoora*, I made an extract of a portion (about 2 ounces) of the bread, and gave a part of the extract to a cat. The pupils of the animal became in a very short time widely dilated, and continued so for several hours. No other symptoms showed themselves. I dropped some of the liquid extract into one eye of each of two other cats. The pupils of the eyes so treated became markedly dilated. From these experiments I have no doubt the bread contained *dhutoora* or some other poison." (2) 12th July 1864:—"Sireea went to Nuthun Jat's house, and told him he could recover his bullock which had been stolen; so Nuthun taking Rs. 11 started off with defendant. He did not return home, and his father and relatives being alarmed at his absence, commenced enquiries, and reported at Barote Police Station that his son had gone away with Sireea, and he feared he (Sireea) had murdered him. The Police commenced enquiry, and ascertained that Juga Ram, Nuthun's uncle, had gone to the Kurnaul District to look for Sireea, whom he had recognized when going with his nephew Nuthun, and that Sireea was arrested and made over to the Police by the zemindars of Sireea's village in the Kurnaul District on 25th July, charged with suspicion of having murdered Nuthun. At this time it was not known that Nuthun had been drugged, only that he was missing. Now comes the curious part: It so happened that, on the 10th July, a requisition came from the Superintendent of Police, Saharunpore, to search for a lunatic in this district (Mozuffernuggur), and on the 13th July, a man lying on a charpoy (who afterwards turned out to be Nuthun), and very like a lunatic, was taken to the Kyranah Police Station. The Sub-Inspector thought the man was the lunatic in question, and forwarded him to the Sudder Station. On arrival here he was forwarded on, by order of the Magistrate, to Saharunpore. On arrival at Saharunpore he turned out *not* to be the man that was required, and was accordingly sent back to this station, when he was released by the Magistrate and he returned to his village. On the 30th July Nuthun went to Barote, and *recognized Sireea as the man who had drugged him near Kyranah*. The case was transferred from the Meerut district to this. The Magistrate of the district has tried the case, and the crime has been clearly proved against 'Sireea.'" Memo:—This culprit had committed another case of poisoning by exactly the same device in the previous December, 1863. He was tried upon both charges and sentenced to 14 years' imprisonment. There is no account of the third case.
Crd. over	16	17 Districts ...	46	

Governments or Administrations.	Number of Districts in which no Cases were reported.	Number and Names of Districts in which Cases were reported.	Number of Cases.	Remarks.
Brt. over	16	17 Districts ...	46	
		(18) Saharunpore ...	1	No account of this case in the Police Administration Report, or of any Police action in it.
Total	16	In 18 Districts ...	47	In the Police Administration Report for 1865, it was stated that the cases in 1864 numbered 35 only, while in Appendix II. of the same Report, the number was 47. Inspector General, of Police :—"No case of Thuggee (by strangulation) has occurred within the year, and only *two* cases of old occurrence remain undetected." "There has been a sensible decrease in the offence of *robbery by administration of poison.* The conviction of Hurpershad and his gang in 1863 will probably have contributed a good deal to this, and the seizure and conviction of other professionals during 1864, will, I hope, together with measures now in progress at Allyghur, further reduce the number of these offences. During the year, 47 cases occurred : 40 cases were detected, leading to the conviction of 32 persons." Memo :—The number of persons arrested and other details, are not shown in the Police Administration Report. Hurpershad and his gang were brought to justice by Major Chamberlain, Assistant General Superintendent at Lucknow, for an account of whose proceedings in that remarkable case, *vide* the General Superintendent's Report to the Government of India, No. 794, dated 15th September 1863, Paras. XIX and XXIV. Deputy Inspector General of Police (*Major Tyrrwhitt*) :—*Professional poisoning by dhutoora, &c.*—"This atrocious crime, rendered so facile by the ease with which the vegetable poison is procured, and the difficulty of detection, owing to the victim being for so many hours in a state of *coma* before he can give information, is, I am glad to say, not much on the increase." "The course pursued by the professional *dhutoora* poisoner, in entrapping and drugging his victim, is so well known to the Police Officers of the North-Western Provinces, that it would be a work of supererogation for me to enter into it in this Report. To those who have lately joined the Police, I recommend the Report of Major Chamberlain, Assistant General Superintendent, for 1862. Suffice it to say, that the usual victims are travellers and men of the Native Army proceeding on leave, and that a large number of *bhylees* and cattle are stolen by the use of this drug, as evidenced in the case of Deesa of the Etah District and Sireea of Kurnaul, arrested in the Mozuffernuggur District. I have much reason to believe that this crime was in full swing in the Allyghur and Etah Districts during the cholera epidemic of 1861, *and that numbers of persons poisoned and found dead were entered in the Police diaries, as having died from cholera or starvation.* The drug is administered in various ways, but the *chillum* and sweetmeats are the favorite forms of professional poisoners. 23 cases remained undetected in the Meerut and Rohilcund Divisions from January 1861 to 1st January 1864 ; of these, 2 cases of 1863 were detected in 1864, *viz.*, 1 at Mozuffernuggur, and 1 at Boolundshuhur. During 1864, *thirteen* cases occurred (in those two Divisions), eight of which were detected during the year. In August, I examined at Agra, two life prisoners, Mohun and another. Mohun gave valuable information in the case of Kulloo, who was the perpetrator of the poisoning case at Bhoor in the Boolundshuhur district, and he is now at Allyghur working fairly under Mr. Williams, District Superintendent of Police." Memo :—The cases in this Division (Meerut and Rohilcund,) amounted to 19, it would seem, and not to 13 only. Mohun confessed to Major Chamberlain, to as many as 17 cases of poisoning in Etah, Agra, Muttra, Budaon, and Allygurh. He was sentenced for life in a case of poisoning in the Muttra District on the 22nd July 1861. Deputy Inspector General (*Major Davis*) :—"Robbery by administration of poison, whilst it numbered 22 cases in 1863 (in the Agra and Allahabad Division,) is reduced to 13 in 1864. Few of these present any serious features, such as would lead one to think them, as a rule, the work of organized and wide spread gangs. They are mostly cases of one man taking advantage of simple villagers, casually met, to stupify and then rob them of what little they possessed. The exception to this case, is the gang of poisoners convicted in the Banda District, (*i. e.* Hurpershad's Gang.)"

Governments or Administrations.	Number of Districts in which no Cases were reported.	Number and Names of Districts in which Cases were reported.	Number of Cases.	Remarks.
Total	16	In 18 Districts, —*contd.* MEMO.* Meerut and Rohilcund ... 19 cases. Agra and Allahabad ... 15 „ Benares ... ... 13 „ Jhansie ... ... nil. Ajmere ... ... 1 „ Total 47 cases	47*	"The amount stolen in this way in 1864 is Rs. 246-2-0 in the 13 cases *Out of 65 persons concerned in them*, 30 were brought to trial. Of these 21 may be said to be convicted, against 9 acquitted—an average which seems fair when the nature of the crime is considered, and that in most cases, *all* the party acted upon, are victims to the stupifaction caused by *dhutoorah*, and which prevents their giving much or any information to identify the poisoner." Memo:—The cases in this Division amounted, it would seem, to 15 and not 13 only. Deputy Inspector General *(Major Manning)*:—"Robberies by the administration of poison or other deleterious drugs. Of these, 10 cases occurred in this Division (Benares,) *viz*: 5 in the Benares District, 4 in Mirzapore, and 1 in Jounpore." Memo:—It would seem that the cases in this Division were 12 and not 10 only. Deputy Inspector General *(Major Dennehy)*:—"This Division (Jhansie) has been altogether free from dacoitee, *thuggee*, or robberies by the administration of poisonous drugs during the year 1864." "I have at present on my file 3 cases of administration of poisonous drugs, 1 of thuggee and 2 of dacoitee. They are all of 1861 and 1862, but the perpetrators of the two former crimes are birds of passage in this Division, Humeerpoor being the district which they favor most. They leave but little clue, and that little I have found it difficult, after such a long interval, to take up." Government North Western Provinces:—"It is satisfactory that no case of thuggee has occurred within the year, and that only two cases of old occurrence remain undetected." "There has been a sensible decrease in the offence of robbery by administration of poison, which is satisfactory." *(End of North-Western Provinces for 1864.)*
OUDH.	8	(1) Oonao	3	Police Administration Report:—"There were 5 cases of robbery *three of which were effected by administering poisonous drugs*. In only *one* of the drugging cases was an apprehension made, and that resulted in acquittal." (1) "A man named Jheryuk, caste Dhobee, was proceeding along the road in the Moraon jurisdiction, when a man came up to him, and after talking, they proceeded together. Towards evening the stranger offered some suttoo, which the Dhobee ate, and shortly afterwards became insensible. The officer in charge of the Police Station was on the spot as soon as possible, and every endeavour was made to trace the poisoner, *but to no purpose*. Descriptive Rolls were sent to the neighbouring district, and every effort made through the Police and Chowkeedars, but without avail. The small property of the Dhobee had of course been stolen." (2) "The second case occurred in October near the village of Passakheyra in the Poorwa jurisdiction. A man, Ram Buksh, was going along, when a stranger entered into conversation with him, and they proceeded together. At evening the stranger offered the Brahmin some suttoo which he greedily ate and became insensible; his small property was taken off. The Inspector and the Officer in charge of the Police Station were for a long time employed in searching all the villages round, in endeavoring to get the plaintiff to identify the culprit. This however was without success. The drugged man having said that the man who drugged him had stated he was a resident of Cawnpore, an intelligent Officer was despatched there with the plaintiff, and they remained several days watching the bazars, *but to no purpose*. There is very considerable doubt if the victim *could* recognize his drugger as will be seen by the next case." (3) "The third case occurred between the villages of Shewpore and Murroze in the Achulgunj jurisdiction. One case is the counterpart of the other. A man Shewdeen was going along towards Cawnpore, when he was overtaken by a man, calling himself an Aheer; they proceeded together. At nightfall, the stranger offered some suttoo which was eaten. Shortly afterwards, the victim became insensible, and his small belongings were stolen. The most strenuous efforts were made. The Inspector and Chief Constable went to almost every village on the route the man had taken through portions of the Roy Bareilly and Sultanpore Districts. The District Superintendent endeavoured through the Chowkeedars to find the man.
Crd. over	8	1 District ...	3	

GOVERNMENTS OR ADMINISTRATIONS.	NUMBER OF DISTRICTS IN WHICH NO CASES WERE REPORTED.	NUMBERS AND NAMES OF DISTRICTS IN WHICH CASES WERE REPORTED.	NUMBER OF CASES.	REMARKS.
Brt. over	8	1 DISTRICT ...	3	
OUDH.		OONAO,—*contd.*		The inspector patrolled the road with the drugged man, and went to watch the ghat at the Ganges. The victim pointed out a man who he said was the man who gave him the suttoo. He said he recognized his kummul and a little bag. On examination this broke down entirely. His witnesses could not identify the articles, and the man apprehended established an 'alibi' most clearly."
		(2) HURDUI	1	POLICE ADMINISTRATION REPORT:—All the 13 murders, *including one by poison*, are, however, ordinary for the sake of revenge, &c. The Police apprehended inevery case, but one." MEMO:— This leaves it doubtful whether the poisoning case was among the detected cases or not.)
		(3) FYZABAD ...	3	These cases were entered in a "Statement showing cases of Thuggee in the District of Fyzabad" received from the Deputy Commissioner under date 19th March 1866, as of occurrence (1) at Hajeepore on the 1st July 1864, persons implicated 25 arrested 8: (2) at Kuniapore on the 13th August 1864, persons implicated 16, arrested 9: (3) at Serai Raneepore on the 17th August 1864, persons implicated 20, arrested 1: total implicated 61, arrested 18: but no other details were given, and it seems probable that the occurrence of these cases only became known *after the date of the Police Administration Report for* 1864.
		(4) PERTABGHUR ...	1	POLICE ADMINISTRATION REPORT:—" Nine murders, *of which one was by poison* * * * The murder by poison was an ordinary murder for revenge."
TOTAL	8	4 DISTRICTS ...	8	INSPECTOR GENERAL OF POLICE:—" No perceptible effect on the crimes of the provinces has been produced by the abolition of the Thuggee Department." "There have been no cases of Thuggee." "*Robbery by administering intoxicating drugs*: During the year, only 4 crimes of this nature were reported and none ended fatally; three cases were reported in the Oonao District and one in Fyzabad." "The case (in Fyzabad) occurred at a bathing place on the road to Sultanpore among travellers returning from bathing at Ajoodhya; it was for robbery, but the poisoners were disturbed before they could complete the offence. It will be observed that the Fyzabad case was an unsuccessful attempt." MEMO:—No separate mention of this case was given in the Police Administration Report under the Fyzabad District unless it was alluded to in the following sentence, *viz*:—in one case of "attempt at murder," it was decided that the crime was not committed." It will be perceived from the date and place of this case, that it is not one of the three above entered against Fyzabad. Thus by rejecting this attempted case and the 2 revenge cases for Hurdui and Pertabghur, there remain 3 cases only for all *Oudh according to the Police Administration Report for* 1864, and those too, of occurrence only in Oonao! POLICE ADMINISTRATION REPORT, TABLES A AND B:—"*Murders by poison.* Three cases against 5 in 1863: arrested 6 persons, acquitted 1: convicted 2: 'died, transferred or escaped' 1: under trial at the close of the year 2 persons in 1 case." MEMO:—Whether these are the three cases for Oonao or not is not plain—the latter having been described above *not to have ended fatally*, whereas these are otherwise described. But it is possible that these 3 cases comprise two with murder in Hurdui and Pertabghur, and another "revenge case" by means of poison in some other not mentioned district *and not the Oonao cases*, the following remark appearing in para. 158 of the Police Administration Report for 1864, *viz*: "The remaining cases (of murder) were 101 in number, *and, including the* 3 *by poison*, were ordinary murders committed from jealousy, revenge or quarrels, &c." Without reference to classification, the number of reported cases of poisoning in Oudh in 1864, whether stated in the Police Administration Report or otherwise gathered as in the cases for Fyzabad, and the details to be collected regarding them, would seem to be summarized as follows:— RECAPITULATION:—Total cases 10 (including an *attempt* in Fyzabad, and a case *attended* with murder in some unmentioned district) against 6 in 1863: Concerned 61 persons in 3 cases in Fyzabad as reported by the Deputy Commissioner: Number concerned not stated in 7 cases: Arrested 25 persons in 7 cases: No one arrested in 3 cases: 1 man released in one case (in Oonao:) 2 persons convicted, 1 acquitted, 1 otherwise disposed of

Governments or Administrations.	Number of Districts in which no Cases were reported.	Number and Names of Districts in which Cases were reported.	Number of Cases.	Remarks.
Total	8	4 Districts,—*continued.*	8	in 2 cases (of revenge:) 20 persons pending in 4 cases (*viz:* 3 in Fyzabad and 1 a revenge case:) Property robbed not shown: Murder in 3 cases: No murder in 7 cases. Inspector General of Police:—"The Province, I am thankful to has been comparatively free from this horrible crime during the year under review." Chief Commissioner:—"In murder by poison there has been a decrease, and the Chief Commissioner understands that none of these crimes were for purposes of robbery." "The effect of the abolition of the Thuggee Department continues to be imperceptible as the Chief Commissioner expected." "Three of the 4 cases of robbery by administering intoxicating drugs occurred in Oonao. The reason probably is that three-fourths of the travellers who leave and enter Oudh cross the Ganges at Cawnpore." (*End of Oudh.*)
PUNJAB.	12	(1) Umballah ...	2	No details given.
		(2) Loodianah ...	1	Three persons convicted. Memo:—According to Appendix III of the Police Administration Report for 1864, the cases in Loodianah were *two.* No other details were given.
		(3) Delhi	5	Fourteen persons convicted. Memo:—According to Appendix III of the Police Administration Report for 1864, the cases in Delhi numbered *ten.* No other details given.)
		(4) Goorgaon ...	4	One only of these cases (11th August 1864,) was reported to this Office. Two travellers arrived at the serai at Sonah for the night. At 10 P. M. it was discovered that one lay stretched upon a cot quite dead, and that the other had gone off. The deceased had been poisoned and robbed of all his property. The culprit was not discovered. He had given his name as Cheytram. No account of the remaining cases was communicated. In addition to these cases, a report was received, in the Thuggee and Dacoity Department, of a dead body of a female having been found at a well near Delhi (15th December 1864,) with the hands fastened and a rope round the neck. The enquiry into this case resulted in its being ascertained (it was stated,) that this was not a case of thuggee or poisoning, but that the woman had been murdered by her son-in-law.
		(5) Hissar	1	No account or details of this case in the Police Administration Report.
		(6) Rohtuck ...	2	The Police Administration Report gives no account of these cases. One only of them was reported to this Office, *viz:*— "At 10 P. M. of the 5th December 1864, a cart driver name Hiddayut Oollah ran into the village of Kukrana with foam issuing from his mouth, and unable to give any utterance. He recovered his senses after 3 days, and stated that he had come from Delhi with his cart to the serai at Rohtuck where three persons engaged him for a sum of three rupees and a half, to take them to Nawur; that they were employés in the Canal Department at Kurnaul and were on leave; that when come a little beyond Kukrana, they gave him some *mulleeda* which had been drugged, which he ate; that a mile or two further on he became insensible, and in that condition wandered back to Kukrana; the strangers had taken away his cart and bullocks. No traces of the culprits or of the cart and bullocks were discovered." Memo:—This was a repetition of the hackery cases practised by Hurpershad's Gang—*Vide* remarks on the subject in the present Statement under the North-Western Provinces.)
		(7) Lahore... ...	2	No account of these cases in the Police Administration Report; but one case according to a report of it to the Thuggee and Dacoity Department, took place as follows (date not stated:) "This case, although not attended with the death of the victims, was no doubt perpetrated *by*
Crd. over	12	7 Districts ...	17	

Governments or Administrations.	Number of Districts in which no Cases were reported.	Numbers and Names of Districts in which Cases were reported.	Number of Cases.	Remarks.
Brt. over	12	7 Districts ...	17	
PUNJAB.		Lahore,—*continued.*		*professional thug poisoners;* both of the parties arrested for it (a man and a woman) having been suspected as accomplices in previous cases of robbery with drugging. On the present occasion they had established themselves in a village, *and after a residence of some weeks had entirely gained the confidence of the inhabitants.* After some weeks, the man persuaded some of the village people to accompany him for the purpose of buying cattle in the Malwa districts. On the road he persuaded them to appoint 2 men as *mooktyars* and consign to their care all the money requisite for the purpose. These two persons he contrived to separate, and then drugged one of them, carrying off all the money in his charge as well as his horse. The woman in the meantime decamped fro m the village with a large quantity of ornaments which she had borrowed on the plea of attending a marriage. Both were subsequently apprehended by the Lahore Police and the greater portion of the property was recovered. Both were sentenced to 7 years' transportation." Memo:—The conviction of these 2 persons was not, it seems, included in the Police Administration Report.
		(8) Umritsur ...	4	Two persons convicted. The Police Administration Report gives no further account of these cases. Police Administration Report—*Umritsur City*:—The increase in murders is remarkable. Of these cases, *two* were unfortunate prostitutes *strangled* for the sake of their ornaments. Major McAndrew (some time Assistant General Superintendent) points out that this is a kind of "Thuggee," though not what would be ordinarily understood by that name. The offender perpetrates the offence generally unaided, and hence the difficulty of discovery. Similar cases have occurred in Lahore and Jullunder in past years, *and in none have the Police been successful.* "During the past five years" Major McAndrew states "but one case has ever been detected, and in that the offender was a Pathan Sepoy marching with a detachment; he confessed to several other similar murders." Memo:—Some other cases of this kind, strangling prostitutes, occurred in the City of Agra and were similarly ascribed to thugs.
		(9) Goordaspore ...	1	No account of this case was given.
		(10) Jullundhur ...	1	Two persons convicted. According to Appendix III of the Police Administration Report there were *two* cases in Jullundhur, convicted 2 persons. No account of them was given.
		(11) Kangra ...	1	The Police Administration Report gave no account of this case, and the following report of it was obtained from a Statement of cases of Thuggee for 1864 received from the Commissioner of the Division:—"A man calling himself Goolam Nubbee (Sheik,) resident of Chutbunoor of Puttiala, administered *dhutoora* to two old persons (a man and his wife,) *Joolahas* or Weavers, of the village of Dook in the Budsur Ilaqua of the Khangra District (21st December 1864.) While these two persons were insensible, Goolam Nubbee stripped them of their jewels and made off. Meantime the old man and his wife quite recovered. The offender has been traced to Ropur in the Umballah District, and it is hoped will soon be arrested." Memo:—The above case was subsequently detailed in full in the Police Administration Report for 1866. The old couple were taken ill immediately after partaking of some *goor* which was given to them as *Neaz* or consecrated offering by the man Goolam Nubbee, who, in the garb of a Fucqueer, had been their guest for a fortnight. Some was also given to their daughter, but who spat it out by *on finding it bitter.* The village headmen at once administered the antidote of milk, which acted as an emetic and revived the old people. The culprit was very persistently tracked from place to place, and was eventually arrested in the Umballa Bazar and was there recognized as the man who had committed some other recent poisoning cases in the Umballa District. By some misapprehension he was tried for one of those offences only, and in accordance with the sentence passed (7 years) he had even been actually transported to the Andamans when the mistake of not trying him for the Khangra case was discovered. Whereupon he was recalled and placed on his trial for that offence also, on conviction whereof, he was sentenced to 7 years' additional transportation. His proper name was *Rahman.*
Crd. over	12	11 Districts ...	24	

Governments or Administrations.	Number of Districts in which no Cases were reported.	Number and Names of Districts in which Cases were reported.	Number of Cases.	Remarks.
Brt. over	12	11 Districts ...	24	
PUNJAB.		(12) Rawul Pindee ...	1	The Police Administration Report contained no account of this affair.
		(13) Jhelum ...	1	Two persons convicted. No account of this case is given in the Police Report for 1864.
		(14) Shahpore ...	1	One person convicted. No account given.
		(15) Goojrat ...	1	The Police Report gave no account of this case.
		(16) Sealkote ...	3	One man convicted. These cases are not included in the Police Administration Report for 1864. They were committed by a Thug Approver of the old Thuggee and Dacoity Department, named *Sobha*, who escaped from the custody of the Lahore Police in May 1864, and was recaptured near the City of Sealkote in the following August. On one occasion, he gave the poison of "dhutoora stramonium" to a man and a boy, on the 5th July, at Chukgilhana, a village in the Sealkote District. The poison was given in a dish of rice, mixed with coarse sugar. The boy died from the effects of the poison. The Civil Surgeon on a *post mortem* examination found *dhutoora* seed in the stomach of the deceased, mixed with rice. Sobha was hanged. He declared that between the time of his escape and capture, he had, joined by several associates, *committed as many as 13 cases of poisoning by dhutoora, many of which had terminated fatally.* Memo:—The seed found in the stomach was according to the medical officer "only a portion of it, much being partially digested, and life must have been destroyed with that quantity in the stomach. The stomach in contact with the seed was irritated. There was moreover, no appearance of disease or any other cause for death, and having ascertained the symptoms previous to death ensuing, I could come to no other conclusion." Police Administration Report for 1865:—"There were three Thuggee cases in 1864, in the Sealkote district, committed by one Sobha, a Thug Approver, who escaped from the Central Jail and who was soon after taken and hanged." Memo:—As there is no doubt of these cases "of Murder by Thugs," *three* is the number returned in the present Statement for Sealkote, and the above is the account of one of them, no account of the other two having reached this Office. In the Police Administration Report for 1864, however, only *one* was given.
		(17) Mooltan ...	1	This case, although included in Appendix I of Police Administration Report for 1864, was excluded from Appendix III: no account of it was given.
		(18) Peshawur ...	2	One person convicted: but according to Appendix III of Police Administration Report, there was only *one* case. No account of it was given.
		(19) Huzzara ...	1	This case was omitted from Appendix III of the Police Report. No account of it was given in the body of the Report.
		(20) Bunnoo ...	1	This case was also omitted from the list of cases given in Appendix III of the Police Administration Report for 1864.
Total	12	20 Districts ...	36	According to Table A and Appendix I of the Police Administration Report, the total number of cases was 33, but according to Appendix III they were 34. The number returned in the present Statement conforms with Appendix I, with the addition, however, of three cases in Sealkote which were not included in the series given in the Police Administration Report for 1864, and have been added, as will have been seen, from the mention made of them in the Police Administration Report for 1865. *Table A*:—Thirty-three cases against 34 in 1863. "The greatest number of these cases occurred in the following districts, Umritsur 4, Goorgaon 4, Delhi 5."

Governments or Administrations.	Number of Districts in which no Cases were reported.	Number and Names of Districts in which Cases were reported.	Number of Cases.	Remarks.
PUNJAB.				

	Appendix I. Cases.	Appendix III. Cases.	Appendix III. Persons convicted.
Umballah	2	2	0
Loodianah	1	2	3
Delhi	5	10	14
Goorgaon	4	4	0
Hissar	1	nil.	0
Rohtuck	2	2	0
Lahore	2	2	0
Umritsur	4	4	2
Goordaspore	1	nil.	0
Jullunder	1	2	2
Kangra	1	1	0
Rawul Pindee	1	1	0
Jhelum	1	1	2
Shahpore	1	1	1
Goojrat	1	1	0
Sealkote	nil.	nil.	
Mooltan	1	nil.	
Peshawur	2	1	1
Huzzara	1	nil.	
Bunnoo	1	nil.	
Total ...	33	34	25

Police Administration Report :—*Apendix IV* :—24 persons in Jail on the 31st December 1864, and 46 under Police surveillance *for administeriny poisonous drugs.*

The following is gathered from Appendix III of the Police Administration Report for 1864, *viz* :—65 cases of murder by thugs: convicted 125 persons. "Of these 3 were murders by a thug."

Memo :—Perhaps 2 of these murder cases are identical with those of the *strangled* prostitutes as entered in the remarks against Umritsur, and the third, the case under Sealkote, by the *Thug* Approver Sobha, which, although effected by means of poison, had not, it was then observed, been included in the series of the poisoning cases detailed as above in the Police Administration Report.

In respect to the above cases of murder "by thugs," the Lieutenant Governor observed to the Inspector General Police : "You intimated that whereas 29 cases of thuggee were entered in the Returns for 1863, as having occurred in that year, you had subsequently ascertained that in reality but one case had occurred, and there can be no doubt whatever, that the entry of 65 cases under the same heading for 1864 is yet more erroneous.

Recapitulation :—Total of poisoning cases 36 : Concerned 8 persons in 7 cases : Number concerned not shown in 29 cases : Number of persons arrested or released not stated : Convicted 28 persons in 25 cases including 1 man, *Sobha*, hanged : Number convicted or otherwise not shown in 11 cases : Died (it would seem) from the drug administered 4 persons in 4 cases, *viz :* 1 in Goorgaon and 3 in Sealkote : Number of persons died or otherwise not shown in 32 cases.

Strangling cases : Two in Umritsur City : Arrested none.

(*End of Punjab*)

Governments or Administrations.	Number of Districts in which no Cases were reported.	Number and Names of Districts in which Cases were reported.	Number of Cases.	Remarks.
CENTRAL PROVINCES.		(1) Saugor	1	Police Administration Report :—"One robbery was effected by administering poison, but it does not appear that the criminal, who was arrested and convicted, was a professional poisoner."
	13	(2) Jubbulpore ...	1	This case does not appear in the Police Administration Report in the Crime Account for Jubbulpore, but it is included under Table H. The following account of it is obtained from a report of it received in this Office :—"On the 7th January 1864, a Gosaen named Talapoorie, resident of Sehora, was poisoned; three persons were arrested for it, of whom one, Bhugwan, was acquitted, a woman named Kormsilla was sentenced to 5 years, and a Buniah named Ramdeen was fined in a sum of Rs. 25 for selling the poison."
Crd. over	13	2 Districts ...	2	

APPENDIX II.

***Accompanying Thuggee Statement for* 1866, *being Extract paras* 3 *to* 24 *from the Report on the Detective Department as contained in the Police Administration Report for Bengal for* 1866.**

"In the investigation of the poisoning cases, the Department worked chiefly on information obtained in 1865, with the object of detecting the accomplices of the men who had been successfully prosecuted in Monghyr and Bhaugulpore."

"Three men belonging to the Bhaugulpore gang, Boodhoo, Phooloo, and Nunkoo, were arrested by the Special Inspector, and sent up to the Magistrate of Bhaugulpore, who committed them for trial to the Court of Sessions, as they were implicated in the Colgong case, mentioned in page 189 of the Police Report for 1865. The Judge in that case recorded that 'the Assessors, after expressing their horror at the disclosures made by the confessing parties, 'gave their own opinion that Boodhoo, Phooloo, and Nunkoo were equally guilty of the 'charges.'"

"The two men, Rajbullub and Sookrun, who proved themselves so useful in bringing to light so many cases last year, were unable to restrain themselves this year. In endeavouring to enrich themselves they have met the punishment which they so richly deserved. They had confessed to having drugged and robbed two women in the bazaar of Toolsheepore;—when two of their gang, Bugbut and Lakha, were with them, and that Lakha had taken a fancy to a highly ornamented bamboo *lattee*, or stick, which he had appropriated to himself. The Special Inspector, finding Lakha's name mentioned in so many confessions, searched his house at Parthoo, in the Patna District, and found there a quantity of suspicious property; and, amongst them, a handsome stick, which Rajbullub declared was the one he had obtained at Toolsheepore. The Special Inspector then proceeded to Toolsheepore and ascertained that two women, Dhurshanee and Choonee, had been drugged and robbed about eight months ago. These two women stated that three travellers had put up in the house of Kharoo Moodee; they came to their house and proposed passing the night with them. In the evening, when the men came, Choonee was cooking; they sent her to purchase some liquor, and Dhurshanee had occasion to go out at the same time; and they believe the men must have taken this opportunity of poisoning their food; for shortly after they had eaten their dinner, they became insensible, and remained in this state for two or three days. When they recovered their senses, they found themselves robbed of every thing they possessed. These women, before the Magistrate, recognized Rajbullub, Sookrun, and Bhugbut, as the three travellers who had been to their house on the night in question; and also identified the stick found in Lakha's house, and stated that they had purchased the stick from Beerbul of the same village, who, in his evidence before the Magistrate, clearly recognized the stick, and described the ornamental work on it. He further stated that he had sold the stick to Dhurshanee. The Magistrate made Rajbullub and Sookrun Queen's Witnesses, sending up Bhugbut for trial. It appears, however, that Bhugbut had paid Sookrun and Rajbullub a hundred Rupees, and these men, without actually falsifying the case gave contradictory evidence, believing the Court would acquit the prisoner Bhugbut. But their conduct was brought to the notice of the Court, and the contradictions were so palpable and wilful, that the Judge convicted Rajbullub and Sookrun on their own confessions, corroborated by the facts ascertained on these confessions; and Bhugbut, on the evidence of the two women, which corroborated the evidence of Rajbullub and Sookrun. They were each sentenced to ten years' imprisonment. The lesson read in this case to Queen's Witnesses will, it is to be hoped, prove salutary."

"Lakha Doshad was subsequently arrested at Patna by the Police, on information furnished to the Superintendent by this Office. After his arrest, the District Superintendent sent him up on a charge of having drugged and robbed one Bhekah Passin; and the Magistrate of Patna committed him for trial to the Sessions. The Judge, however, discredited the evidence of Bhekah Passin, and the Jury released the prisoner."

"On learning that Lakha was about to be released, application was made to the Magistrate of Bhaugulpore, bringing to his notice that Lakha had been concerned in a case of Dacoity at Colgong, and had broken Jail; and also that there was evidence against him in the Toolsheepore case. Lakha was accordingly transferred from Patna to Bhaugulpore. The Magistrate of Bhaugulpore committed him for trial on a charge of Dacoity at Colgong; and of drugging and robbing the two women at Toolsheepore. At the trial, Lakha pleaded guilty to both charges, and was sentenced to seven years' rigorous imprisonment for the first, and seven years' for the second case."

"In paragraph 166 of the Police Report for 1865, Lakha is correctly described as one of the *Surdars* or Chiefs of the gang of Poisoners in the Patna District. The gangs in that District remained untouched, and several cases of Poisoning had been recently reported, in which the Police had failed to discover the perpetrators. Lakha, at the same time, offered to assist the Police in the detection of his gang. Application was accordingly made to the Government for permission to make Lakha over to the Police, for detective purposes in the Patna District. By Government letter No. 476, dated the 19th of January 1867, the proposal was sanctioned, and Lakha was sent to Patna in charge of the Special Inspector. The prisoner was taken before the Joint Magistrate, where he detailed the circumstances connected with eight cases of robbery by means of Drugging, some of which were attended with murder."

"It may be here remarked, that investigations founded on information furnished by *prisoners* are attended with great difficulty. First, there is a strong prejudice against acting on statements made by a convicted felon;—inexperienced Magistrates, who have no *practical* knowledge of the Criminal class, are unreasonably sensitive on this point. In every country in the world, the evidence of accomplices is made use of when a gang or association of criminals is sought to be destroyed. Such evidence, if corroborated, is always regarded as legal evidence; and hundreds of criminals have been convicted and punished on similar evidence. But the prejudice is so strong, and the often repeated 'charges' of torture, and 'moral pressure' are so easily credited, that it is very difficulty for a Police Officer, however anxious he may be to perform his duty, steadily to pursue the object he has in view; he is assailed on every side, and any judicial Officer has it in his power to record unpleasant remarks, which, however untrue and unsupported by evidence are, to say the least, exceedingly injurious. Again, Poisoning cases generally do not come to light until after the lapse of a considerable period of time—the victims are generally travellers from *different* Districts, and often from distant Provinces, who not only neglected at the time of occurrence to give any information to the Police, but are exceedingly unwilling to come forward, and subject themselves to the harrassment of a *double* prosecution before a Magistrate, and ultimately before the Court of Sessions. There is, again, the unwillingness of the authorities to credit statements of recognition after such a lapse of time."

"Lakha stated that in the month of Chyte last, Dharee Sahoo told him that Teluk Sing was waiting for him; on his going, he found Teluk Sing seated by a well—which is in a garden at Parthoo—and a traveller was sitting by him. On seeing Lakha, Teluk Sing got up and met him, and whispered to him that the traveller had 117 Rupees with him; and that Lakha should go on the road with Gowree, Dahoo, and Roocha, and that he would follow with the traveller. Lakha did as he was told. After Teluk had joined them, Dharee Sahoo prepared two *lotahs* of sherbut; in one Poison was put; this was given to the traveller, when he was tired and thirsty. They went a little further, when the traveller said he felt giddy and strange, and wished to go into a village which was close by. Teluk Sing then remarked 'if he goes to the village, we shall find it difficult to rob him; we must put an end to his life.' Teluk Sing and the rest murdered him by squeezing his private parts, while Lakha watched that no person approached; after he was dead, the gang helped themselves to the 117 Rupees he had, and threw the body into the river Punpun."

"The Special Inspector learnt that his case had been investigated by the Police last year, when Boroo Gwala was committed to the Sessions on a charge of having murdered the traveller, but was released. On examining the record of the case, the Special Inspector found that three men, named Heramun Brahmin, Bijlee Dosad, and Bodie Dosad had testified at the investigation, that they had seen Teluk and others throw a body into the river. The Chowkeedar of the village Syebur had also stated, that Teluk had shewn him the body, and had prevented his giving information at the Thanah. The Special Inspector also ascertained, on enquiry, that there was no doubt whatever, that Teluk Sing had made away with the body of the traveller. The corroborative evidence being good, the Special Inspector sent up Teluk Sing for trial, naming the witnesses Heramun, Bijlee and Bodie Dosad, and the Chowkeedar of Syebur, as corroborative evidence. The Magistrate at the time had credited this evidence, and had summoned Teluk for concealing evidence by making away with the body."

"In this case it was necessary to take the evidence of Lakha. The Joint Magistrate of Patna did so on the 1st of April, but subsequently declared he had done so under a mistake; and wrote a long explanation why Lakha should not be made a Queen's Witness under Section 209. He re-examined the witnesses who had deposed in the first investigation; declared their evidence untrustworthy, because the Deputy Magistrate had discharged Teluk after Baroo Gwalla had been released by the Court of Sessions; and also urged that the evidence of the witnesses named by 'the Special Inspector was apparently rejected as untrustworthy, or even concocted evidence.' The Joint Magistrate also speculated on the motives which may have induced Lakah to confess."

"It is not material to the case what were Lakah's motives in confessing. The real question was, whether the case was true or false? The corroborative evidence had been acted upon by the Magistrate in the first investigation, when on that evidence he had summoned Teluk. At that time no one suspected that Teluk was privy to the Murder: the impression then was, that Borroo was the murderer; and it is not surprising that the evidence of the Chowkeedar and the three witnesses were then regarded as unconnected, and therefore suspicious and inconsistent. The confession of Lakha threw a light on that evidence, which now was perfectly consistent and truthful. It appeared to the Police, that there was *primâ facie* evidence against Teluk, and that the charge was sufficiently established to warrant a commitment. The Joint Magistrate, however, thought otherwise, and released the prisoner, without making any fresh investigation into the case."

"In another case, Lakha stated that he, and his gang, last year, had drugged a Rajpoot at Panapore, when on his way from Midnapore to Chuprah. The Special Inspector, after some delay, ascertained that one Tokun Roy was returning home from Midnapore with property belonging to his son Rowshun Roy, who had been employed in the Police of that District as a constable, but who had died there, and whose effects had been made over to him by the District Superintendent of Midnapore. Lakha stated that he had made the articles over to the same Teluk Sing who belonged to the gang. The Special Inspector, finding that Teluk Sing was implicated in the case of murder, and that there was evidence to show he had disposed of the body, proceeded to search Teluk Sing's house, and found a quantity of suspicious property. Tokun Roy claimed certain of these articles. Application had been made to the District Superintendent of Midnapore to know if Rowshun had been a Constable in the Midnapore Police, and if his effects had been made over to his father Tokun Roy. The District Superintendent in his letter, dated 7th May 1866, sent a list of the property which had been made over to Tokun Roy. In that list two brass *thalas* are mentioned, which were found on Teluk Sing. There is a great deal said about the impossibility of recognizing *brass plates*; but a plate which a native uses every day of his life, he can identify quite as well as any gentleman will tell his hat, or his gloves. In this instance, however, the *thalas* are peculiar to the Midnapore District, and cannot be easily procured in Behar; and the Sub-Inspector and two constables of Midnapore, who had lived with Rowshun, and had *daily* used the plates, clearly identified them. There is the direct evidence of Lakha corroborated in this satisfactory manner, and there is the fact that this very Teluk Sing was connected with the mysterious murder of Heramun: the Joint Magistrate, however, discharged the prisoner."

"Lakha further stated that eighteen months ago, Gowree, Dahoo, Roocha, and Purtab Gwala followed a man connected with the Post Office. On their reaching Pursa, they offered to drink with the traveller. He purchased some liquor, and they all drank. Lakha then bought some more liquor, and in the cup which he gave the traveller, managed to drop *dhatoora* powder, which took effect before they had proceeded far, and the traveller became giddy and fell. The gang took from him a gold *kordhanee*, a rupee, and a *dhootee*."

"On enquiry, the Special Inspector ascertained that a peon in the post Office, employed at Baktearpore, had been drugged and robbed. With the assistance of the Post Master of Bankipore, the peon, named Ramobotar, was sent for: his story corroborated Lakha's statement. He stated that in the month of Kartic or Assin, he was returning from his father Umritlall with a goat; on the road he fell in with four or five men, who gave him something to drink with liquor, and on his becoming insensible, robbed him of a waist chain."

"The case had excited attention amongst the people connected with the Post Office at the time of its occurrence; and the Special Inspector learnt that Bolaki Hurkura had seen Ramobotar, while suffering from the effects of the drugged spirits. In this case, the Special Inspector succeeded in arresting one of the gang, Pertab Gwala, and sent him up for trial, on the evidence of Lakha and of Ramobotar, who positively identified him as one of the men who had drugged him. There was evidence also adduced to shew that Lakha and Pertab Gwala were associates, and usually seen in company with each other."

"The Magistrate in this case discharged Pertab Gwala, and committed Lakha for trial to the Sessions, on his 'own confessions, having refused to make him Queen's witness against Pertab Gwala. The case was brought to the notice of Gevernment. Lakha was acquitted by the Court of Sessions, and was sent back to the Department to be employed for detective purposes."

"Lakha in his confession further stated that he and Metoo Doshad and others of his gang had drugged a washerman at Digah, and had robbed him of a pair of gold earrings and some sweetmeats, and other eatables. On enquiring amongst the washermen at Digah, the Special Inspector ascertained that one of them, named Bola Dhoba, had been drugged. The washerman, on being traced, stated that about two years ago, when going to his father-in-law's house, he purchased some liquor at a grog-shop, near Digah, and journeyed in company with four or five men. That, leaving the liquor on the road, he went a short distance, to answer a call of nature. He returned and drank the liquor, and went back to the shop, and asked for a *chelum* of tobacco. Two men sitting at the shop gave him a *chelum* to smoke. Soon after he felt giddy, and the shop-keeper turned him out of the shop. He recollects leaving the shop, and the two travellers following him, and that he fell down senseless when he came near a garden. The washerman recognized Lakha and Metoo Doshad, and declared, he had been drugged by means of the tobacco which the two men had given him to smoke. It was also evident from the statement of Inspector Hurdutt Sing, that the washerman had lodged a complaint at the Thannah at the time he was drugged; but unfortunately no records relating to the case could be discovered. In this case, the Joint Magistrate committed Metoo Doshad to the Sessions, without examining Lakha as a witness on whose confession the case had been brought to the notice of the Police; but, while doing so, he stated in his remarks, 'that he did so with much hesitation.' The Jury acquitted the prisoner, because the Judge did not consider the identification of the prisoner by his victim sufficient; and because he had not given a descriptive roll at the time. If the evidence of the traveller who has been drugged, corroborates the confession of one of the gang, such evidence has been considered sufficient for conviction in a number of cases confirmed by the High Court. It is also possible for a man, belonging to the class of Bola Dhoba to recognise a fellow traveller after the lapse of two years, though he may fail to give a descriptive roll of the man, according to rule and compass."

"There are a great number of other cases in which Lakha's confessions have been corroborated by enquiries made on his statements; these cases are pending further enquiry. Another member of the same gang, named Dahoo, (who has since been arrested) has confessed before the Magistrate of Chuprah, to a number of cases, which were also mentioned by Lakha.

The information furnished by Lakha and Dahoo, will enable the Police to detect the members of this mischievous gang of poisoners."

"Two cases of drugging travellers had been made over to the Detective Department, at the requisition of the Officiating Deputy Inspector General of the 3rd Circle.".

"In one of these cases, the Police of Patna made Uzgur Alli prosecutor with three others, while one Baboo Khan was made the defendant. The Special Inspector Nobokisto Ghose, after examining the men who had been drugged, reported that it was evident to him that Uzgur Alli was the principal defendant, and that Baboo Khan belonged to his gang; and the former had deceived the Police by feigning to have been drugged. The reasons which induced the Special Inspector to come to this conclusion, were the repeated attempts which Uzgur Alli made to obtain possession of money, which Kalay khan, one of the travellers, had in his possession. Kalay khan, after selling some horses, was returning home with the money; at Buktearpore he met Uzgur Alli, who suddenly professed great friendship for him, accompanied him to Patna, and secured him lodgings in the City. He then attempted to sell to Kalay khan some *gilt brass* ornaments as gold. Uzgur Alli then induced his friend to advance Rs. 8 to two *Debeewallahs*, and also to start with him for Benares. They were to leave by the train; and his pretended servant, Baboo khan, was sent on ahead to prepare dinner at Uzmut khan's *Serai*. Uzgur Alli, Kalay khan, and the two *Debeewallahs* reached the *Serai* about 8 o'clock at night; Baboo khan had there cooked dall and rice. The two friends ate out of one plate, but Kalay khan remarked that Uzgur Alli did not eat the dall. The two *Debeewallahs* and a beggar, who lived at the *Serai*, named Bechoo, also partook of the dall and rice. After eating the food Kalay Khan complained of feeling giddy, and went to the house of a friend who lived near the *Serai*, named Chowdry Sha, where he soon became insensible. The two *Debeewallas* and Bechoo also became insensible at the *Serai*. Baboo Khan decamped, and his pretended master found it was his only plan to feign to be himself drugged. He acted his part so well, that he succeeded in deceiving the Police, who sent him to the Hospital. It will be remarked, that Kalay Khan, by proceeding to the house of his friend, unconsciously foiled Uzgur Alli in this his second attempt to obtain possession of his money. Uzgur Alli informed the Police, that his servant Baboo Khan was the delinquent,—that he was an inhabitant of Ghazeepore,—and that Baboo Khan had robbed him of a Hoondee for 200 Rupeés. Had the Police enquired where he had obtained the Hoondee, there is no doubt the trick would have been discovered. Uzgur Alli succeeded better in his third attempt to defraud his victim. He induced Kalay Khan to trust him with 10 Rupees, under the pretence that he would secure Railway Tickets. Kalay khan believing that Baboo khan had drugged the party, and that Uzgur Alli was a fellow sufferer, gave him the 10 Rupees; with these ten rupees Uzgur Alli decamped. Then Kalay khan's eyes were opened, and he discovered the character of his pretended friend. On learning the above particulars, an experienced Police Officer at once came to the conclusion, that Uzgur Alli was the real defendant in the case, and that Baboo khan most likely belonged to the gang."

"In the second case made over to the Department, which occurred at Pursah, one of the travellers who had been drugged, and who lived at Nobutpore, in the Patna District, arrived. On examining her, she stated that a man had joined her party, (consisting of four other travellers) at Jahana, on the Gya road, while they were returning from Calcutta. On reaching Pursa, this man very officiously collected pice from the party of travellers, and offered to purchase food and cooking materials. He did so, and after they had eaten, he persuaded them to hurry on to Metapore, on pretence of meeting the train, but, in truth, to get them out of the public *serai* at Pursa. On the road, the drug began to affect the travellers, and they lay down near Metapore, where they were found by the Police, robbed of all the ready money they had. The description the woman gave of the man, agreed exactly with that of Uzgur Ali; she was accordingly taken to Burh where Uzgur Alli had been sent. The Deputy Magistrate placed Uzgur Alli with seven or eight others, taken from the crowd, and the woman, when brought in, at once recognized him as the man who had met her at Jahana, who had purchased dall and rice for the party at Pursa, and who had disappeared when the travellers fell down near Metapore, where they lost their money and clothes. The Deputy Magistrate took down the woman's statement on oath."

" The Magistrate committed Uzgur Alli to the Sessions on these two charges, but the Jury acquitted the prisoner. The best commentary that can be offered on the verdict of the Jury in these two cases, is the fact that a few days after Uzgur Alli was convicted by another Jury, of having caused the death of a traveller, by drugging him; and has been sentenced to capital punishment, thus proving that he belonged to a gang of poisoners."

Printed at the Genl. Supdt.'s Office Press.

E.J. Gunthorpe

***Notes on the Criminal Tribes Residing In, or Frequenting the Bombay Presidency, Berar, and the Central Provinces*. Bombay: Times of India Steam Press, 1882.**

NOTES ON CRIMINAL TRIBES.

CHAPTER I.

BOWRIE* (Budhuck).

BOWRIES, who are Hindoos, are known by different names, according to the part of the country in which they have settled, *i.e.*, Bagoris, Bagris, or Wagris, Budhucks, Moghyas, Delhiwal Bowries, Malpooras, Marwarras, &c., &c. All make use of the same language, which was originally Guzeratee, and observe

* In Khandeish, Berar, parts of the Central Provinces and Deccan generally, there are six tribes who are of the true Bowrie family, who immigrated south into these parts many generations ago, and still retain their caste names, though they are known in the provinces by assumed ones. They are—

1. Wagris or Moghyas known as Takenkars.
2. Bowries known as Lungotee Pardhis.
3. Bowries known as Cheetawalla Pardhis.
4. Bowries known as Seelajeet Pardhis.
5. Maywarrees known as Phansi Pardhis.
6. Bowries known as Kalbailias, disguised as Kanipou Naths.

All these use a language similar to that of the Bowries or Budhucks of the north.

the same customs and rites. When away from their homes on a thieving expedition, in the presence of strangers Budhucks always talk Hindustani to one another. Those who come periodically down to the Deccan in search of plunder are chiefly the "Malpoora" Bowries from Bhopal, "Marwarras" from Marwar, and "Delhiwals" from the districts of Delhi. They penetrate as far south as the southern parts of the Madras Presidency, but do not cross over to Ceylon. Moghyas rarely come further south than Indore. All assume various disguises when visiting the Deccan. The Malpooras and Marwarras adopt those of Byragees and Gosseins; occasionally, but very rarely, as ordinary Purdesees in search of work, and also as Marwari Brahmin mendicants; Delhiwals at one time invariably as Byragees, but very often now as Aghorees and Gosseins; and Moghyas only as Byragees.

Their disguises are extremely well got up, and they learn so well the prayers, sayings, and doings of the religious mendicants whose guise they assume, that it is next to impossible, save for a real Gossein or Byragee, to see through the artifice. A few suggestions as to how to detect them are offered further on. All Bowries have been from ages past and are still by profession inveterate and irreclaimable robbers. In former days they were most daring dacoits, but the Thuggee and Dacoity Department has much broken up violent crime amongst them, and their great *forte* now is burglary, at which, and at cutting into tents and robbing camps, they are most expert and daring. It is only the Delhiwal Bowries, however, and not the others, who practise the latter styles of crime. Moghyas still commit dacoity. Bowries were originally Rajpoots, and still retain the same "ghotes" or sub-divisions, &c. They are very fond of liquor, always live well, and are fond of mutton and buffalo flesh, but not beef. After a successful exploit the gang have a feast, at which much liquor is drunk. When disguised as Byragees or Gosseins, Bowries always put up at a temple (a halting-place is called "Asen" by them), and when otherwise they do as do the people whose guise they have assumed.

Women never accompany them. They move about in gangs of from three to eight or even more, sometimes thirty or forty. The headman of a gang is styled "Kadoo;" it is his duty to make the breach and to enter a house, and to be the leader in all exploits. The house-breaking implement is called a "Gyan." If talking about it in the presence of strangers a "Dass" is added to it, making it "Gyandass," as if it were a comrade being alluded to. It is from $11\frac{1}{2}$ to 12 inches long in all, of iron and tipped with steel. The steel part is about three inches long, is made square tapering off to the point; the rest of the instrument is round, with a ball for the handle. The "Gyan" is carried by one of the party about half a mile either in advance or rear of the main gang when travelling, and is generally put into the folds of a cloth which is thrown over the shoulder, so that should any Government servant appear it is handy to cast away, which is always done, and picked up again when the supposed danger is passed. When halted the "Gyan" is buried a long way off from their resting-place. Some Bowries have been known to carry the instrument under the pommel of the saddle on the march when ponies have been used by the gang. Every "Kadoo" carries a short strong-bladed knife ("Natree") with him when entering a house, and which he will use if attempt is made to catch him and he finds no chance of escape, otherwise the knife is only used as a last resource; his companions outside will rescue their "Kadoo" at any hazard, and if necessary even by taking life. By day Bowries are not to be feared and will never resist arrest, but will do their best to escape from custody; the favourite time for so attempting is when under escort out of a lock-up. They break away suddenly and throw stones at their pursuers.

When disguised as Gosseins or Byragees a "Ghir" or a "Dass" is added to their real names; thus, "Girwur*ghir*," "Gooman*dass*." They worship "Devi," the principal one being at Kerolee, about 100 miles from Jeypoor. Pilgrimages are made to this place by all the Bowrie tribe from great distances. Oaths are taken in the name of this deity; they worship none other. Before proceeding on an exploit the spirits of deceased relatives (known for their expertness and bravery) are invoked for good or bad omens. The "Kadoo" of each gang is the one who generally consults. For this ceremony grains of unboiled wheat are used; if this is not procurable "jowari" is substituted. But recourse is rarely had to the latter grain, as the "Kadoo" usually carries some of the prepared wheat about his person. It is prepared by being soaked in ghee and the husk rubbed off between the palms of the hands. The ceremony of consulting the spirits is performed as follows:— The "Kadoo," having washed and cleaned himself, sits on the ground facing the west; a handful of wheat is put down on the corner of a sheet or blanket. Two grains are taken and placed on the right or propitious, and one grain on the left or unlucky side. A few grains are then taken up haphazard with the tip of the fingers and thumb of the right hand, and thrown down and counted out by fours. If the number be odd, the odd grain is put in a line under the grain to the left hand; if the number be even, the last two grains counted out are put in a line under the two grains placed to the right hand. A few more grains are again taken as before and counted out and disposed of as above. If the first essay produces an *odd* number, and the next an *even*, all the grains are collected and the business begun afresh till either three odd grains are obtained consecutively to the *left* or three even pairs consecutively on the *right* or lucky side. The former signifies the undertaking will not prosper, and the latter that it will. No burglary is committed during moonlight nights. The days when the moon enters her first quarter till the end of the third quarter are used for exploring houses, which is very easy in the guise of the religious mendicants usually assumed. They never trust to others for information; the "Kadoo" obtains it himself. During this period the gang does not shift its resting-place, but directly dark nights commence all are on the move again. Burglary is never committed anywhere near where they may be putting up at the time, but they go long distances for the purpose. They have been known to break into a house and to put 30 miles between it and their halting-place the same night. Bowries have two modes of entering a house. Their favourite one is by the "Buglee," as they call it. A hole large enough for the arm to be introduced is made in the wall at the side of a door frame, in a line with the latch, the fastening is undone by the hand and the door opened; if nothing is found in that room the same plan is adopted to enter another. A "Kadoo" told the writer he could break into as many as eleven houses in one night by the "Buglee," and that he had done so on several occasions. If certain of the position of the treasure or jewellery, and it cannot be reached by the "Buglee" entrance, the second mode is adopted of making a breach in the wall at the exact spot or as near as possible to where the valuables lie. The hole is made just large enough to admit the "Kadoo," who always enters a breach head foremost, and retreats feet foremost, usually with the knife between his teeth ready for defence should an inmate of the house attempt capture. They are very expert at wrenching jewellery off the persons of sleeping women (this operation is termed "Oojânto"), and is invariably resorted to if a jewel-bedecked slumbering female is seen in a house entered by them. Whilst a "Kadoo" is making a breach in a wall, one man (called a "Pootwariâ") stations himself a few paces behind him to keep watch and warn him of danger. It is the duty also of the "Pootwariâ" to receive the plunder from inside and hand it to his comrades, two or three of whom are always close at hand armed with short stout sticks. On entering a room either a match is struck to explore, or mustard seed or bajree grains are gently thrown forward. This is to learn the position of any brass or copper pots or any boxes in the apartment, the noise of the seed hitting against them indicating the exact spot, and thus showing in which direction all is clear and no obstacle to be expected for a further advance. One or two members of a gang are always left at the resting-place ; whilst the remainder are away house-breaking, the absent members are represented by stones covered with long dhoturs, to make it appear they are present and asleep. Should any stranger come to the place those present get up, and say the others, being very tired, are sound asleep.

Bowries never administer poison. With the exception of a rich shawl which is taken now and then, not to be retained by themselves, but for presentation to the zemindar, or other chief, of the part of the country they come from, they never steal anything but cash and jewellery. Stolen property is secreted by Malpooras, Marwarras, and Moghyas, by burying a good distance away from where they may be putting up at the time. Delhiwals bury it just below the fire-places made for cooking purposes. Stolen property is never carried by a gang when on the move. It is left at the last " Asen," or halting-place, and ne of the gang is sent back under cover of night to fetch t to the new "Asen," where it is reburied, and moved n next day in the same manner, and so on. All jewelery is at once broken up, and, if possible, melted, and when sufficient amount of plunder is collected, a member or wo of the gang are sent off with it by rail or by road to heir homes; having safely delivered it, they return and ejoin the gang. Bowries leave their homes on thieving xpeditions (which expeditions are called by them "Raméth") about the end of October or beginning of November, and freely utilize the railway. The Malpooras and Marwarras take the train generally at Itarsee, Shohagpoor and Badee. The Delhiwals at stations near Delhi. They return to their villages at the commencement of the rains. Some few, who are "wanted" in their own country and are well known, remain behind and spend the rainy seasons in the Deccan, joining gangs when they return in the cold weather.

As stated above, Bowries generally come to the Deccan disguised as Byragees or Gosseins, and the only means of discovering them is to get a sharp Hindoo to watch a suspected gang of religious mendicants at their morning devotions. Bowries do not go through it in the orthodox manner, which can be detected at once by a man knowing the different ceremonies which should be performed.

When food is being prepared by the cook of the party, and a member of the gang joins him in his cooking-place, and is allowed to take away any food and eat it, the conclusion is that the gang are Bowries. Should the party be drinking liquor, any man who understands the Guzeratee language, who may be near the gang, would be sure if they are Bowries to hear them at times converse in their own language. A true Byragee or Gossein catechising them in their prayers and rites, and watching them at their different ceremonies, will often detect them as not being the right sort.

An entrance made into a house at the side of the door-frame is a good sign of Bowries' work, as also the presence of mustard seed or bajree grains on the floor of the room broken into.

CHAPTER III.

LUNGOTEE PARDHI, TRUE CASTE NAME "BOWRIE."

LONG subsequently to the moving southward of the Wagris (Takenkars) another branch of the great Bowrie family followed them, and settled in parts of Khandeish and the northern portion of Berar, and carried on their professional pursuits of dacoity and highway robbery and burglary with impunity, till they, with the Wagris, became the terror of the simple agriculturists of these parts. To save their villages from the depredations of these two new classes of robbers, patels entered into written agreements that their villages might be spared on payment of black-mail, and they enlisted numbers of both tribes as village watchmen. In those days British rule had not extended to Berar, and old agreements drawn up between villagers and these robbers are now preserved as curiosities in some towns. The new immigrants were fond of snaring game, and of shooting, so were called Pardhis, from the Mahratta word "paradh," "chase," but many others were also termed thus, and from the fact that these men wore, and do still, a lungotee,* were named Lungotee Pardhis in contradistinction to all other Pardhis.

As a rule they are a fine race of men with a physiognomy peculiar to themselves and very similar to the Meywarees or Phansee Pardhis (who are also Bowries), the professional game-snarers, a wandering race, who are to be met with in almost every district and weekly village market. The Lungotee Pardhi is simple in his clothing, a dhotur round his loins, a white sheet over his shoulders, and a similar-coloured turban on his head completes his toilet. The hair of the head is cut once when quite young and never again touched by scissor or razor. When first the tribe reached these parts the women wore laingas or petticoats, a tight jacket (cholee) fastened behind like Rajpoot women, and a cloth over the head ; but time and intercourse with Mahratta-speaking people caused a gradual change in costume, and now the saree and ordinary cholee have usurped their original dress.

* Strip of cloth between the legs and fastened both before and behind to a cord round the waist.

Perhaps in no race except the Meywarees, who are very similar in their ideas, is so much reverence paid to their principal deity, "Devi," as by these people. Every house has its Devi in silver. Women may not wear silver anklets, because the household goddess is of that metal; they may not wear anything red about them, because Devi is placed on a ground of that coloured cloth. Cots may not be slept on, because Devi is supposed to always rest on one: a shoe is not allowed inside a hut for fear of offending the goddess. Sacrifices of rams and young buffaloes are offered at regular periods each year, on which occasions a great feast is held. Unlike the Takenkars, polygamy is allowed. On the death of a brother the surviving eldest brother must marry and support the widow. Lungotee Pardhis are not a wandering race, but live in substantially built huts in the outskirts of villages, so that their movements may not be watched by inquisitive neighbours. They readily enlist as village watchmen, but will not take any service which involves leaving their homes in their adopted villages. British rule, with her stern determination to put down crime, has much calmed the predatory habits of this tribe, and violent crime is not practised so much as a profession by them now as in days gone by. The love of plunder, though, has not yet died out in the breasts of these sons of a race of inveterate robbers. Dacoity is still committed by some of the older men, but the new generation have taken to burglary in its stead. At this they are very expert and successful. The breach in the wall is very similar in appearance to that made by Takenkars, though not so neat in finish. So afraid are they now of trusting one another, that it is rare for more than two or three to undertake a burglary together, very often it is done single-handed. In dacoities men of other castes are allowed to join the gang and share in the plunder. As a rule, they go fully armed, and are very reckless in the use of weapons. Faces are invariably muffled. Stolen property is never brought home at first, but is buried at once in some secluded spot, and there it remains for months, till the hue and cry of its loss has calmed down, when it is unearthed and shared.

Should one of the gang be killed, his widow and children, if he has any, get full share due to the deceased, and the latter are supported by the rest of the tribe till able to provide for themselves. Unlike the Wagris (Takenkars), these people are not taking so much to agricultural pursuits, they prefer hunting and snaring game and taking service as village watchmen. Great numbers are to be found in this latter capacity in many parts of northern Khandeish and Berar. It is curious the race has not spread more southward, but they seem to hold tenaciously to the parts of the country their ancestors originally settled in. Amongst themselves, like the Wagris, they still use the Guzeratee language. The slang of these two tribes is similar, and many of the words are those employed by the Budhucks of the north, thus showing without doubt their Bowrie origin.

CHAPTER XIV.

DECCANEE KUNJUR.

THESE people, now residents of the Deccan, have the ordinary Deccanee cast of countenance, are of dark complexion, and have regular features. The men wear their hair long in the Marwaree style. The women wear long laingas which reach down to the ankles, like the Rajput women of the Deccan. These laingas are made of either dark blue or red material, out of sarees cut up for the purpose. Cholees are worn fastened at the back by two knots, one at the top near the neck and another at the bottom of the cholee. Over this cholee a sleeveless jacket or "koorta" is worn; it has a border of a different coloured material round the bottom. Their hair is worn tied up in a knot or plaited at the back. A nose ornament in the shape of a flower, always of gold, is worn on the left side of the nose. Nose-rings (nuths) and anklets are never worn. Both sexes, like all the criminal tribes, are addicted to liquor. They speak Urdu and

Mahrathee very fluently, but with a slight foreign accent. The language common to themselves is Guzerattee much mixed with Marwaree. Bowries from up-country and these people can understand one another, though their language is is not quite the same.

Deccanee Kunjurs pass themselves off as "Kolhatees," "Beldars," "Bhats," also as "Topeewalla Bhats," as they have recently taken to making caps and knitting gloves and socks as an ostensible means of livelihood. Being a true wandering tribe, pals are used. Numbers of donkeys are always to be found about their encampments, by which fact and by the costume of the females this tribe can be easily recognized. The outskirts of a town or village are favourite camping grounds. Dacoity, highway robbery, robbing travellers whilst asleep, donkey and pony stealing are practised by these Kunjurs as a profession. Burglary is not committed by themselves; but others, chiefly *Budhucks* and Mangs, are hired for the purpose, and the spoils are shared. This tribe has also taken now-a-days to stealing bags of grain, bales of cloth, &c., off railway trains, when the engine stops to water at out-of-the-way stations. They are great hands at stealing donkeys, and make away with large numbers of these animals out of every district they may pass through. One mode is to drive their own donkeys to graze with those of a village, and in the afternoon all are driven to the encampment openly, as if all were theirs. Should an owner recognize his property among those being driven away, he claims it, and the Kunjurs plead ignorance of the fact that any other than their own are present, and with many apologies tell him to take his animal or animals away ; but should they happen to reach the encampment unnoticed by their owner, they are sent off that same night miles and miles away in charge of one of the men, the whole gang following the next morning. Another mode is to catch donkeys unobserved, drive them to a lonely nullah, and there throw them and tie up their legs and leave them. At night the spot is visited, and should the animals be still there, undiscovered by their owner, they are released and driven off as stated above. Ponies are stolen at night from the pegs to which they may be tied, and even out of stalls, and taken off great distances at once. A case has been known of a Kunjur lad who stole a pony in a town one night : he rode him straight off to Bhooranpoor, a distance of 76 miles, where he sold him next day, and returned by rail at once to the place he started from. Deccanee Kunjurs are also much addicted to cutting away bales of cloth off carts on the road to fairs. They are adept sheep and goat stealers, which crime is committed at night. Poultry are also stolen.

Having discovered the fowlhouse, it is approached under cover of darkness, the door is broken upon, and a wet cloth thrown over the roosting birds. The damp cloth induces them all to squat and keep quiet, when one by one their necks are dexterously wrung. The women of this tribe enter towns and villages in parties, sing and dance, and thus gather information, which is imparted to the males. For the purpose of disposing of stolen property these Kunjurs always manage to get very friendly with some patel or villager (the former is always preferred). All plunder is at once handed to the safe keeping of this friend, who sells it for them; none is retained, as a rule, should they be encamped anywhere within twenty or thirty miles from the scene of the crime whence the property was taken. Beyond this distance a few cloths are generally brought in to be cut up and made into clothing for themselves. If unable to hand over the property at once to the friend, it is buried some distance away from their camp, and made over to him on the first opportunity occurring. Whenever any patel or villager seems to be on intimate terms of friendship with Deccanee Kunjurs, it is almost always a certain sign that he is the receiver of their ill-gotten gains.

ABOUT THE EDITOR

Pramod K. Nayar teaches at the Department of English, University of Hyderabad, India. His most recent books include *Alzheimer's Disease Memoirs* (2021), *The Human Rights Graphic Novel* (2021), *Ecoprecarity: Vulnerable Lives in Literature and Culture* (2019), *Brand Postcolonial: 'Third World' Texts and the Global* (2018), *Bhopal's Ecological Gothic: Disaster, Precarity and the Biopolitical Uncanny* (2017), *Human Rights and Literature: Writing Right* (2016) and the edited collection *Indian Travel Writing 1830–1947* (2016). His essays have appeared in *Modern Fiction Studies, South Asian Review, South Asia, Narrative, Celebrity Studies, Asiatic, Journal of Postcolonial Writing, Prose Studies, a/b: Auto/ Biography Studies, Biography, Image and Text* and *Postcolonial Text*, among others.

Nayar also holds the UNESCO Chair in Vulnerability Studies at the University of Hyderabad.